INCO

LOUIS MACNEICE was born in 1907. The son of a clergyman, he grew up in Carrickfergus on Belfast Lough. He was educated in England at Marlborough College and Oxford University. After some years as a lecturer in classics, he became a producer and scriptwriter for BBC radio. He also wrote radio plays, of which the most celebrated is *The Dark Tower* (1947). During the 1930s, MacNeice's poetry was usually, if not always accurately, linked by critics with that of W.H. Auden, Stephen Spender, and Cecil Day Lewis. His long poem *Autumn Journal* (1939), written during the Munich crisis and its aftermath, is a masterpiece which draws together many threads of his personal life and of public events. Today MacNeice is less often labelled a 'thirties poet', partly because his Irish dimension has been more fully recognised. On the one hand, he can be seen as Yeats's most immediately significant Irish successor. On the other, he greatly influenced the emergent Northern Irish poetry of the 1960s. Before his premature death from pneumonia in 1963, MacNeice was writing powerful new lyrics, collected in *Solstices* (1961) and *The Burning Perch* (1963). MacNeice's centenary year was marked by widespread recognition of his centrality to modern poetry in these islands.

FRAN BREARTON is Reader in English at Queen's University Belfast. She is the author of *The Great War in Irish Poetry* (Oxford University Press, 2000) and *Reading Michael Longley* (Bloodaxe, 2006).

EDNA LONGLEY is Professor Emerita at Queen's University Belfast. Her books include *Poetry and Posterity* (Bloodaxe, 2000) and, as editor, *Edward Thomas: The Annotated Collected Poems* (Bloodaxe, 2008).

A selection of Irish writing from Carcanet Press

Jody Allen Randolph (ed.)
Close to the Next Moment: Interviews from a Changing Ireland

Eavan Boland
A Journey with Two Maps: Becoming a Woman Poet

Moya Cannon
Carrying the Songs

Austin Clarke
Collected Poems

John F. Deane
Eye of the Hare

Greg Delanty
Collected Poems 1986–2006

Padraic Fallon
'The Vision of MacConglinne' and Other Plays

Thomas Kinsella
Collected Poems

Edward Larrissy (ed.)
The First Yeats: Poems by W.B. Yeats, 1889–1899

Peter McDonald
Pastorals

Paula Meehan
Painting Rain

Sinéad Morrissey
Through the Square Window

Mary O'Malley
A Perfect V

Frank Ormsby
Fireflies

Incorrigibly Plural

Louis MacNeice and his Legacy

Edited by

Fran Brearton and Edna Longley

First published in Great Britain in 2012 by
Carcanet Press Limited
Alliance House
Cross Street
Manchester M2 7AQ

A CIP catalogue record for this book is available from the British Library
ISBN 978 1 84777 113 1

The publisher acknowledges financial assistance from Arts Council England

The editors acknowledge support from the American Ireland Fund

THE AMERICAN IRELAND FUND

Typeset by XL Publishing Services, Tiverton
Printed and bound in England by SRP Ltd, Exeter

CONTENTS

ACKNOWLEDGEMENTS

The cover image is one of several watercolours painted by MacNeice during his years at Marlborough. He did not title his paintings, and the title 'Noah's Ark' for the cover image was given by his daughter, Corinna MacNeice, to whom we are grateful for permission to reproduce the image. We are grateful to the following for permission to quote copyright material: David Higham Associates, for poems by Louis MacNeice; Carcanet Press Ltd, for poems by Robert Graves; Faber and Faber Ltd, for poems by Philip Larkin; David Higham Associates, for poems by Dylan Thomas; Random House Group Ltd for poems by Robert Frost. Every effort has been made to trace and contact copyright holders before publication, and any omissions will be rectified at the earliest opportunity. The editors also gratefully acknowledge the support of the American Ireland Fund.

ABBREVIATIONS

Works by Louis MacNeice

Collected Poems, ed. Peter McDonald (London: Faber, 2007) – *CP*
Letters of Louis MacNeice, ed. Jonathan Allison (London: Faber, 2010) – *L*
Modern Poetry: A Personal Essay (1938; Oxford: Clarendon Press, 1968) – *MP*
The Poetry of W.B. Yeats (1941; London: Faber, 1967) – *PY*
Selected Literary Criticism, ed. Alan Heuser (Oxford: Clarendon Press, 1987) – *SLC*
Selected Plays, ed. Alan Heuser and Peter McDonald (Oxford: Oxford University Press, 1993) – *SP*
The Strings are False (London: Faber, 1965; repr. 2007) – *SF*
Varieties of Parable (Cambridge: Cambridge University Press, 1965) – *VP*

Other works

Robert Frost, *Collected Poems, Prose and Plays* (New York: Library of America, 1995) – *FCP*
Robert Graves, *The Complete Poems*, ed. Beryl Graves and Dunstan Ward (Harmondsworth: Penguin, 2003) – *GCP*
Philip Larkin, *Collected Poems*, ed. Anthony Thwaite (London: Faber, 1988) – *LCP*
Jon Stallworthy, *Louis MacNeice* (London: Faber, 1995) – *JS*
Dylan Thomas, *Collected Poems 1934–1953*, ed. Walford Davies and Ralph Maud (London: Dent, 1988) – *TCP*

PREFACE

In Louis MacNeice's poem 'Snow', the mind tries to keep pace with a flood of images and sensations: 'World is suddener than we fancy it. // World is crazier and more of it than we think, / Incorrigibly plural …' (*CP* 24). At one level, 'incorrigibly plural' characterises the world of MacNeice's poetry. It now also applies to his posterity.

Louis MacNeice was born on 12 September 1907. He died on 3 September 1963. The circumstances of MacNeice's death uncannily echo his own dark myth-making. He developed pneumonia after going down Yorkshire potholes with BBC engineers to record sound effects for his allegorical radio play *Persons from Porlock*. Underworlds had always fascinated MacNeice: the salt-mines near his childhood home in Carrickfergus; Jules Verne's *Journey to the Centre of the Earth*; the classical Hades. His poem 'Charon' moves towards Acheron and Styx: 'And there was the ferryman / Just as Virgil and Dante had seen him' (*CP* 593). *Persons from Porlock* concerns a painter distracted from his work by various interruptions. The last of these is Death, encountered in a deep cave system. MacNeice's own premature death interrupted the fresh creative direction his poetry had taken in the late 1950s, and delayed full recognition of his poetic achievement.

Yet by 2007, his centenary year, it was becoming clear that Louis MacNeice is central to modern poetry in the English language. A centenary gathering in Belfast drew poets, critics, and 'common readers' from all parts of these islands and beyond. Some contributions to this book derive from that occasion, and reflect its excitement. In 2007, too, BBC Northern Ireland inaugurated an annual Louis MacNeice Memorial Lecture, the first being Peter McDonald's 'The Pity of It All'. Further memorial lectures, also included here, were given by Paul Farley and Glyn Maxwell. As regards criticism, scholarship, and the currency of MacNeice's work, his centenary marked not only a culmination but a beginning. The new *Collected Poems*, meticulously edited by McDonald, provided a foundation stone for the future. There were reprints: the *Selected Poems*, MacNeice's wartime autobiography *The Strings are False*, his idiosyncratic Scottish travelogue *I Crossed the Minch*. More recently, Jonathan Allison's edition of MacNeice's *Letters* (2010) has increased our biographical and literary understanding.

MacNeice's lyric transforms biography into psychodrama. Here he resembles Yeats, and there are strong cultural, as well as artistic, affinities between the poets. In his important critical book, *The Poetry of W.B. Yeats* (1941), MacNeice says: 'Like Yeats, I was brought up in an Irish middle-class Protestant family. I allow for the difference that he spent his childhood in the primitive west, whereas I spent mine in the industrial north' (*PY* 50). MacNeice's sense of this 'difference' – which actually replicates Yeats's tension between London and 'Innisfree' – goes deep. His father, Rector of St Nicholas's parish Carrickfergus (later a bishop in Belfast), had grown up in Connemara, as had MacNeice's mother. Thus 'the west', somehow imbued with the early loss of his mother, became an imaginative source for MacNeice too. In 'Landscapes of Childhood and Youth' he recalls: 'for many years I lived on a nostalgia for somewhere I had never been' (*SF* 217). MacNeice's actual landscapes, whether urban or rural, span many points of the Irish and British compass. He eventually made up his western deficit. He went to school and university in England (Sherborne, Marlborough, Oxford). He crossed the Minch. He taught classics at Birmingham University, and so 'lived in Birmingham through the slump' (*CP* 118). He then moved to London, where he soon ceased to be an academic and joined the BBC as a producer. All these locales have left poetic traces, and several intersect in *Autumn Journal* (1939), MacNeice's great poem of Europe on the brink of war.

Even so, MacNeice's first world underlies the rest. Carrickfergus, a town on Belfast Lough with a Norman castle and sectarian history, enters his poetry as a vivid microcosm, an underworld or unconscious, stained by his mother's death and other unhappiness. In 'Experiences with Images' MacNeice stresses the 'early stratum of experiences which persists in one's work just as it persists in one's dreams'. He lists his own persistent images as: 'Sea (i.e. the grey Lough fringed with scum and old cans), fields (i.e. the very small, very green hedged fields of Northern Ireland), factories (i.e. those small factories dotted through the agricultural patchwork), and gardens (i.e. my father's medium-sized lush garden with a cemetery beyond the hawthorn hedge)' (*SLC* 159). While some of these images figure stasis or death, the Lough also launched MacNeice's poetic odysseys, his attraction to everything that flows. He makes this opposition explicit in 'Carrick Revisited': 'Out of the sea / We land on the Particular and lose / All other possible bird's-eye views' (*CP* 262). If his poetry became notable for 'dialectic, oxymoron, irony' (his own words), the Carrickfergus 'stratum' had a lot to do with it (*SLC* 248). Yet, how poets' lives condition their work is an intricate matter – a point often made by MacNeice himself; and 'condition', rather than 'determine', is his preferred verb. Contributors to this book add to the intricacies traced by Jon Stallworthy's biography (1995). Jonathan Allison, for instance, discusses the relation between the voice(s) of MacNeice's letters and poems. David Fitzpatrick tests MacNeice's portraits of the Rector/Bishop against historical archives. And, in writing his own powerful autobiography, MacNeice's son, the late Dan MacNeice, has illuminated his father's life.

In a book of this kind, it is inevitable that critics should sometimes converge on the same poems ('Star-gazer' seems to be climbing the charts): yet their different readings are themselves further proof of MacNeicean 'plurality'. MacNeice hated the categories that critics use to fix poets and leave them there forever. He always stresses poetry's dramatic and generic shifts:

> 'So I am to speak only as myself,' the poet might say, 'my whole self and nothing but myself? If you know what my whole self and my only self is, you know a lot more than I do. As far as I can make out, I not only have many different selves, but I am often, as they say, not myself at all. Maybe it is just when I am not myself – when I am thrown out of gear by circumstances and emotion – that I feel like writing poetry.' (*PY* 146)

MacNeice's plurality has been circumscribed by national canons as well as by aesthetic blinkers. That is, he has been classified as a poet of the English or British 1930s; (less often) as an 'Irish' poet of the generation or so after Yeats; and, since the collective success of poetry from Northern Ireland, as a proto 'northern Irish' poet. The essays here expose the limits and blur the borders of these categories. They suggest how MacNeice's diverse cultural and literary contexts play into the archipelagic currency of his poetry, and into its significance for modern poetics. They also imply the obvious: his poetry could never have had either its immediate or precursory effect, were it not such a rich and broad conduit; had MacNeice not created his own synthesis from the various 'legacies' that he himself inherited. Although he wears traditions lightly, MacNeice is among the most tradition-conscious modern poets. His criticism regularly ranges from Homer to the contemporary, taking in the Elizabethans and Romantics en route. Of course, as Valentine Cunningham shows, it was still common for his poetic generation to be steeped in the classics – also in Christianity. But, at once the Rector's son and an academic classicist, MacNeice takes these cultural resources further and deeper.

MacNeice shared his centenary year with W.H. Auden. They shared other things too: a famous trip to Iceland; a decade during which poets were hyper-conscious of history and war; views about how poetry might negotiate all that. In his criticism, MacNeice often evangelises for the poetic values of 'my generation'. That phrase is a mask which allows MacNeice both to advocate Auden's poetry; and, under cover of Stephen Spender and Cecil Day Lewis (neither of whom he really rates), to hint how his own aesthetic connects with, and differs from, Auden's. Auden sounds rather like MacNeice when MacNeice writes: 'Auden's great asset is curiosity. Unlike Eliot, he is not (as a poet) tired ... He reads the *newspapers* and samples ordnance maps. He has gusto, not literary gusto like Ezra Pound, but the gusto which comes from an unaffected (almost ingenuous) interest in people, politics, careers, science, psychology, landscape and mere sensations' (*SLC* 37). Where MacNeice registers his difference from Auden is usually where Auden patterns his poems too rigidly (or 'ingenuously'), whether in terms of ideas or opinions or syntactical telegraphese or simplified ballad rhythms. And in his 1937 public 'Letter to W.H. Auden', MacNeice writes: 'Your poems are strongly physical but not fastidiously physical. This is what I would expect from someone who does not like flowers in his room' (*L* 305). In other words, Auden could not have written 'Snow'. Glyn Maxwell's discussion of *Autumn Journal* uses the adjectives 'creaturely' and 'corporeal' to underline his own sense of the 'planetary distance' between MacNeice's poetry and Auden's. But perhaps that suggests the extent to which their separate and linked contributions to modern poetry remain to be explored. They are certainly allied in their attitude to form. MacNeice writes of 'my generation': 'Most of the younger generation have returned to more regular forms, while trying to be their masters not their slaves ... believers in meaning (though not a wholly rational meaning) they try, in the European tradition, to convey it by all the means at their command' (*SLC* 141).

MacNeice deploys all the structural devices at his command to offer his own take on 1930s motifs, such as traffic and travel, and to elicit meaning from the flood of history. Several essays here show how he can internalise the material and social fabric of the modern world; make this fabric metaphorical or symbolic; and transmit historical dynamics as felt (and thought) experience. These powers, if fostered by the 1930s, did not end with them. For example, starting from 'Cradle Song for Eleanor', written during the Second World War, Peter McDonald works towards the ethical core of MacNeice's imagination: 'a form of courage'.

MacNeice involves Ireland in his approach to European crisis. As David Fitzpatrick demonstrates, his family history is closely meshed with political and religious conflicts. MacNeice's legacy to contemporary Irish poetry is manifold. But his critique of Irish politics, sharpened by his sense of wider disaster, has been a key point of reference, as when section XVI of *Autumn Journal* ironically 'envies the intransigence of my own / Countrymen who shoot to kill and never / See the victim's face become their own' (*CP* 137). If MacNeice's literary moment has come, perhaps – with the Northern Ireland peace process – his political moment has also come. Not that all conflict has been resolved. Clair Wills, who writes here on MacNeice's postwar *Autumn Sequel*, took the title of her book *That Neutral Island* (2007) from MacNeice's still-controversial wartime poem 'Neutrality', which attacks Irish isolationism: 'Look into your heart, you will find a County Sligo / A Knocknarea with for navel a cairn of stones //... ducats of dream and great doubloons of ceremony' (*CP* 224). MacNeice makes his point by subverting Yeatsian touchstones like 'dream' and 'ceremony'. Yet it is his absorption of Yeats that enables him to do so. Unlike other poets of his Irish generation, MacNeice did not follow Yeats in banning direct allusions to technological modernity from his work. But it was only he who grasped the epoch-making significance of *The Tower* (1928), and truly assimilated the forms, structures, and genres of the later Yeats. As *Autumn Journal* (like 'Neutrality') proves, MacNeice learned from Yeats's public voice, as well as from his psychodrama, and also learned how to combine them. Thus, like Yeats too, he channels history's nightmares, its 'not wholly rational' meanings, through myth and symbol. 'Night Club' (1939) succinctly updates Yeats's 'Nineteen Hundred and Nineteen': 'Salome comes in, bearing / The head of God knows whom' (*CP* 202).

The contents of this book reflect the fact that MacNeice's reputation mainly rests on his poetry. As regards other writings, his criticism
may ultimately matter more than his radio work. Besides *The Poetry
of W.B. Yeats*, it includes *Modern Poetry* (1938); the essays and reviews
reprinted in *Selected Literary Criticism* (1987); and his Clark Lectures
collected as *Varieties of Parable* (1965). In addition, MacNeice was
always occupied by the intersection between aesthetics and metaphysics, and this shapes his poetry's subtle self-awareness. His
criticism, including its coded presence in poems, plays out crucial
arguments about poetry that mark the last century. This is sometimes
insufficiently recognised because, unlike Auden, he never lived in the
USA. But his links to the Irish Revival on the one hand, and to the
1930s British new wave on the other, uniquely fitted MacNeice to
weigh Yeats and Eliot as exemplars of 'modern poetry': to stake out
the post-*Waste Land* ground. He wrote in 1935: 'All the experimenting poets turned their backs on mummified or theorised
tradition, but the more intelligent realised that living tradition is
essential to all art; is one of the poles. A poem, to be recognisable,
must be traditional; but to be worth recognising, it must be something new' (*SLC* 12).

For MacNeice, as for Yeats, Pound's *Cantos* take experiment too
far – beyond the reach of form: 'Mr Pound does not know when to
stop; he is a born strummer' (*SLC* 17). During MacNeice's lifetime,
the term 'modernism' was not applied to poetry as narrowly as
academic critics began to apply it in the late 1960s: that is, to denote
free verse along with other kinds of disjunctive structure (e.g. the
Cantos). But poetry becomes modern by more means than one.
MacNeice's philosophical sophistication must be reckoned with. And
his friendship with Anthony Blunt at Marlborough made him preco-
ciously aware of avant-garde art. Witness his schoolboy watercolour
on the cover of this book. Witness his poetry's painterly self-images,
its stress on perception and reflection, how it translates colour and
light into sound effects. As for 'experimenting' novelists: Joyce,
Lawrence, and Woolf attracted the young MacNeice as 'acolytes of
Flux' (*SF* 118–19). Perhaps because he later attacked 'The Leaning
Tower', Woolf's critique of the 1930s generation, her influence on
his poetic streams of consciousness has been under-noted. In a letter
of 1927 MacNeice wrote: 'I am very eager to read "Mrs Dalloway"
by Virginia Woolf. I have read some wonderful extracts from it,
strange rhythms and an exquisite correlation of sensations. She must

be a good Modern, I think' (*L* 147). He later adapted *The Waves* for radio.

MacNeice's own 'strange rhythms' remake traditional forms. As regards line and stanza, his forms are less regular than Yeats's. But this is partly because he gives new twists to other elements of Yeatsian structure: especially to refrain, syntax, and their interrelation. Neil Corcoran's essay 'MacNeice's Repetitions' shows that, in the later poetry, refrain becomes 'destabilised, self-deconstructing, and alto-gether anxiety-inducing'. So, too, with syntax, MacNeice writes: 'I have often been surprised that reviewers of verse pay so little atten-tion to syntax. A sentence in prose is struck forward like a golf ball; a sentence in verse can be treated like a ball in a squash court' (*SLC* 245). Informed by his knowledge of Greek and Latin, MacNeice's poetic syntax increasingly plays every angle. He dramatises disjunc-tion, not by collapsing syntax, but by stretching its capacities to the limit. In his last two collections, *Solstices* (1961) and *The Burning Perch* (1963), syntax and refrain interact with new intensity, as MacNeice probes existential mysteries in what he called 'parable' poems. For instance, 'All Over Again' might be an extreme rewriting of 'Snow'. This poem is an inconclusive multi-refrained sentence which tries to hold it 'all' together; which depends, like poetry itself, on an 'as if':

> As if I had known you for years drink to me only if
> Those frontiers had never changed on the mad map of the years
> And all our tears were earned and this were the first cliff
> From which we embraced the sea and these were the first words
> We spread to lure the birds that nested in our day
> As if it were always morning their dawnsong theirs and ours …
>   (*CP* 572)

Writing on 'Louis MacNeice's Posterity', Peter McDonald concludes: 'MacNeice's work is not merely one among a number of available influences for contemporary British and Irish poets, but has become more clearly one of the indispensable conditions for their poetry's existence.'[1] Hence the poets who contribute to this book. We asked some to write brief pieces on what MacNeice means to them. Among poets' more extended contributions, Paul Muldoon and Paul Farley bring not only themselves but also two possibly surprising poets into the MacNeicean orbit: Robert Frost, John Clare. Other contributors add T.S. Eliot, Robert Graves, Dylan

Thomas, and Philip Larkin to this magnetic field. The distinctive findings of each 'MacNeice and X' essay enrich our sense of his artistic plurality, and of his presence in contemporary poetry. But if MacNeice is a poets' poet, he is not so in any narrow or technical sense, although technique is intrinsic to what makes him a poetic hub, to the different things that different poets take from his work. MacNeice's poetry resembles its own cities (cities that have influenced later poetry of Hull, Belfast, Dublin, Glasgow, London, and Liverpool) in that all human life and language, 'this whole delightful world of cliché and refrain' (*CP* 68), seems to jostle there. To quote a recent tribute by the poet Alan Gillis: 'I really responded to his freshness, to his city poems, to his wit and verve. There was something about the energy of his lines and sense of detail. And this still stands ... he claimed a broad reality of day-to-day living for the lyric which was quite new: others had approached this "as a subject", presuming themselves apart from it.'[2]

Seventy years ago, for the young Philip Larkin, MacNeice's impact was equally fresh: 'his poetry was the poetry of our everyday life, of shop-windows, traffic policemen, ice-cream soda, lawn-mowers, and an uneasy awareness of what the newsboys were shouting'. For Larkin, MacNeice was also somehow unofficial: less established by academy or nation than Eliot, and even Auden, had become. Hence the 'secret taste' that Larkin formed for his poems.[3] That secret may now be out. But we should still heed MacNeice's warning in 'Variation on Heraclitus': 'Nor need you be troubled to pin me down in my room / For the room and I will escape ...'

FRAN BREARTON
EDNA LONGLEY
Belfast, 2010

THE PITY OF IT ALL

Peter McDonald

At the end of his 1941 collection *Plant and Phantom*, Louis MacNeice
printed a poem entitled 'Cradle Song':

Sleep, my darling, sleep;
   The pity of it all
Is all we compass if
   We watch disaster fall.
Put off your twenty-odd
   Encumbered years and creep
Into the only heaven,
   The robbers' cave of sleep.

The wild grass will whisper,
   Lights of passing cars
Will streak across your dreams
   And fumble at the stars;
Life will tap the window
   Only too soon again,
Life will have her answer –
   Do not ask her when.

When the winsome bubble
   Shivers, when the bough
Breaks, will be the moment
   But not here or now.
Sleep and, asleep, forget
   The watchers on the wall
Awake all night who know
   The pity of it all. (*CP* 209)

The poem had already appeared between hard covers, in *Poems
1925–1940*, published in the USA at the beginning of 1941. There,
too, it was the final poem in the book; there, too, it was assigned by

the author a date of composition ('*October, 1940*'); and there it bore
as a subtitle the dedication '*For Eleanor*', which in *Plant and Phantom*
is carried by the whole book, dedicated 'To Eleanor Clark'. As a love
poem, 'Cradle Song' brings both of its volumes to a close on a seemingly personal (rather, that is, than a seemingly public) note. At the
same time, both these poles of concern, personal and public, are in
some ways ill-fitted to the poem's actual intent and effect; for 'Cradle
Song' concentrates its autobiographical meaning in a repeated phrase
– 'The pity of it all' – that fuses the attentiveness of a lover with a
broader and more melancholy kind of watchfulness.

That lover's attentiveness, however, is itself far from uncompli-
cated. Although 'Cradle Song' operates with a deliberate simplicity
of means, 'The pity of it all' brings into play matter not at home in
the registers of straightforward love. The immediately obvious echo
(which may or may not be an allusion) is of *Othello*: 'but yet the pity
of it, Iago; O Iago, the pity of it, Iago!' (*Othello* 4.1.189–90). If this
is an allusion, it could hardly, on the face of things, be more out of
place: for what is the wounded rage of sexual jealousy doing in a
lullaby? True, MacNeice takes away the staccato edge from Othello's
words, smoothing and calming a repeated 'the pity of it' into 'The
pity of it all', but this act of transformation cannot, all the same,
completely erase the presence of the Shakespearean text. Moreover,
the voice in MacNeice's poem is that of a lover addressing a young
woman asleep – asleep on a bed, quite possibly – whose innocence
shades into a kind of ignorance; like Desdemona, discovered on her
bed asleep at the beginning of the last scene of *Othello*, she seems
unaware of the 'cause' which will keep the speaker (and those
'watchers on the wall') so busy.

But here another (and arguably an incompatible) allusion becomes
an equally persuasive possibility. For any poet of MacNeice's generation, 'pity' was a word charged with potent literary (and
literary-political) content. This comes, of course, from Wilfred
Owen's draft 'Preface': 'Above all I am not concerned with Poetry.
/ My subject is War, and the pity of War. / The Poetry is in the pity.'[1]
In October 1940, more than a year into the British war with Nazi
Germany from which he had so far absented himself, MacNeice
could not keep Owen's 'pity' from impinging on 'the pity of it all'
through which Eleanor Clark is sleeping. In 1936, MacNeice had
written of how with the Great War 'Pity reappeared in English
poetry', and claimed that 'The pity of Owen, the Whitmanesque lust

for life of Lawrence, and the dogmas of Lenin are now combining to make possible the most vital poetry seen in English for a long time' (*SLC* 63–4). Four years later, the poet might not have felt quite so fulsome about these positive effects, and especially about the benefits of Lenin; though the young Eleanor Clark was all for dogmas, albeit those of Trotsky in succession to those of Lenin, in relation to the artist. In 1940, MacNeice would still include Owen as one of the four finest modern poets in England (along with T.S. Eliot, Lawrence, 'and, within narrower limits, Robert Graves') in his book on W.B. Yeats – the same Yeats who had scandalously rejected Owen's appeal to 'pity' in excluding him from his 1936 *Oxford Book of Modern Verse* (*PY* 178). 'The pity of it all' builds Owen, and the arguments about Owen, into MacNeice's love poem, with an awareness both of the potency of 'pity' and (with Yeats casting his customary shadow) a sense of its inadequateness as a poetic principle. 'Passive suffering,' Yeats had pronounced, 'is not a theme for poetry'.[2] Here perhaps there is a point of contact with the *Othello* allusion: 'Cradle Song' might summon the image of a Desdemona, and thus potentially of one kind of 'passive suffering'; but it opts instead to spare its Desdemona her suffering, and leave her her passivity. If it is a poem that uses *Othello*, its voice makes a point of not being Othello's; if it brings to bear Owen's 'pity', it has also absorbed a knowledge of 'pity''s limitations: 'The pity of it all / Is all we compass if / We watch disaster fall'. The pity, then, is not *all*, and it is not all there is to say, or do, in this situation: there is more, perhaps, that can be compassed here, and must be.

It is useful to explore the degree to which MacNeice blurs the boundaries of love poetry, and some of the ways in which, as a poet, he imaginatively absorbs and puts to use the power and the liabilities of 'pity'. MacNeice started the critical commonplace of an 'impure poetry' in the light of which so much of his own work has subsequently been read (*MP* xxxi); but readers and commentators have applied this largely to poems which have, one way or another, obvious public bearings, whether in the 1930s or afterwards. Yet MacNeice's love poetry, too, is 'impure'. The personal elements here have soaked up all kinds of difficult and recalcitrant material: not as things to be transfigured, as though poetry could effect some alchemical change in them, and they are not to be transcended, by assimilating them to the self-awareness of a transcendent poetic personality; instead, MacNeice lets (and makes) them do their worst to the poetry, and their worst in the poetry. In 'Cradle Song', 'pity' brings both private pain and public anxiety to the show, Othello's stricken cry and Owen's deliberate moral imperative finding a distinctly unhappy marriage in the repeated phrase.

To read a poem closely is sometimes to bring to bear all kinds of perspectives which may appear, to some, to be themselves 'impure'. Biographical elements are amongst these, but they are introduced inevitably in a poem like 'Cradle Song' where, after all, names are named, and dates are given. On a wider scale, MacNeice's writing is often autobiographical in part – if by 'autobiographical' we understand a kind of writing that uses particular life experiences, and returns to them with changing purposes and emphases, as parts of an essentially creative rather than a documentary effort. Both with and without a definite article, life is central to MacNeice's art: the life – like life – is written into this work. We need to be careful as readers, just as MacNeice himself was careful as an artist, to respect the differences between the absence and presence of those definite articles.

The Eleanor Clark 'Cradle Song' addresses was a young left-wing American writer with whom MacNeice was in love (and in whose company he felt, as he told E.R. Dodds, 'timelessly happy') from late 1938 (L 356). The poet's decision to go and work in the USA at the end of 1939, which seemed to have so many political meanings and ramifications, was probably attributable more than anything else to the need to see Eleanor again. In the autumn of 1940, having spent much of the year with her, MacNeice was recuperating from a serious case of peritonitis at Eleanor's parents' home in Connecticut. Here, several important poems – most notably, the poem 'Autobiography' – got themselves written. By this time, too, the love-affair itself was, if not cooling, then coming to terms with the insuperability of obstacles in its way. Some of these were decidedly public things: the war in Europe, above all, and Louis's adult responsibilities towards his infant son, whom he had left behind in 1939. Others were more private, and specific to the lovers: two, however, have something to do with 'Cradle Song'. Louis and Eleanor quarrelled, partly about politics. In a long letter sent to Eleanor in May, 1940, Louis rebukes her for her accusation that he has 'an awful lack of curiosity about the world'. The tone as well as the content of this rebuke is important:

> I was curious about the world & suffering for my curiosity about it before you were born. And if you think you can judge my

curiosity about the world by the fact that I don't look at newspapers when you're around, you show an appalling lack of feminine imagination. Apart from which, newspapers aren't the world anyway [...] And if you think the only way 'the world' impinges on me is through my nerves, you are – I am sorry to say, darling – a fool. When for the last week I have been feeling steam-rollers go over me all the time, that wasn't just nerves; it was imagining (with my brain & also – if I may be hackneyed for want of a better word – with my heart) what this war is going to do to England and Ireland as I know them & to particular people whom I know there ... (*L* 393)

MacNeice writes as Clark's elder here, and puts her right about his own relationship to the world events whose significance is clearly something at issue between the two. He lets her know, in these terms, that he is both capable of and pained by the process of watching 'disaster fall'.

There was a second issue lurking in this quarrel, though, and it was to prove finally too formidable a stumbling-block for the pair: although Louis and Eleanor were in some ways lovers, there was one sense in which they were not, since their relationship seems never to have reached a sexual consummation. In the May letter, which is full of recriminations about levels of 'curiosity' and the need (or otherwise) for a 'world view', it is Eleanor's nature as 'sexually inhibited & to some extent self-deceiving' which draws out Louis's harshest remarks:

As to your sexual inhibitedness I don't say this on the strength of you & me because for all I know I am not at all your type but it comes out in a lot that you do & say & I think it is a great pity because, even if the novelist is more concerned with the environment than instinct, I can't see how he can present the world at all adequately if he hasn't got *inside* knowledge of what is about the most important of the instincts. If he hasn't got that, his *internal* reality remains in a sense in the nursery. (*L* 397–8)

This is interesting – though not exactly disinterested – advice to give to a budding novelist. Although Louis and Eleanor did in fact share a bed in the summer of 1940, it appears from Louis's farewell letter when he embarked for Britain at the end of the year that his practical

advice for Eleanor's writing career was not (at least with him) fully
taken up. These particular circumstances impinge upon the poetic
circumstances which 'Cradle Song' makes for itself: 'Sleep, my
darling, sleep' – and *just* sleeping is, in this light, what Eleanor seems
determined to do. But the cost of this, in the serene poem as in the
fraught letter, is that Eleanor's '*internal* reality remains in a sense in
the nursery', just as the poem sets itself formally at an angle to the
nursery rhyme to which it alludes – 'Rockabye baby, on the tree top'.
'When the bough / Breaks, will be the moment,' MacNeice writes,
with the emphatic acknowledgement that the moment will be 'not
here or now'. But what will this be the moment *for*? One kind of
answer is known to this poem's speaking voice: it will be the moment
for sexual love; another kind of answer, of equal importance in the
poem, is known as well to 'The watchers on the wall', who can see
things beyond the sleeping Eleanor's horizons in 'The pity of it all',
such as 'what this war is going to do to England and Ireland as I know
them & to particular people whom I know there'.

This 'pity' is clearly something apart from the feeling that Eleanor's
refusal to become Louis's lover 'is a great pity'. The distinction here
is performed very naturally, of course, by the definite and indefinite
articles: consider, for example, the difference between's Owen's 'the
pity of war' and a statement that 'war is a pity'. An early poem of
Yeats, 'The Pity of Love', replaces the definite article of its own title
in the first line:

A pity beyond all telling
Is hid in the heart of love:
The folk who are buying and selling,
The clouds on their journey above,
The cold wet winds ever blowing,
And the shadowy hazel grove
Where mouse-grey waters are flowing,
Threaten the head that I love.[3]

'A pity' here leaves something in the voice exposed and vulnerable,
open to the misconstruction of the weak 'it's a pity that…', where
the voice of the poem's title (so to speak) elevates itself into general
significance. Yet the poem itself is perfectly specific when it comes
to what it at stake, for things threaten a particular loved head, 'the
head that I love'. If this short poem stands somewhere in the back-

ground of 'Cradle Song', it is more directly in view in W.H. Auden's 'Lullaby' (composed in 1937), with its prayer for protection of 'your sleeping head' and invocation of 'the winds of dawn that blow / Softly round your dreaming head'.[4] It is likely that MacNeice's poem shadows Auden's; but of course both poems' generic situations, as lullabies, involve the theme of protectiveness, of an adult wishing to shield his child, or an older lover wanting to keep safe a younger partner.

'Cradle Song' is a revealing MacNeice poem, since it builds into its workings so many of the elements that make others amongst his love poems (and more than just his love poems) so distinctive. The autobiographical elements which are, on one level, so specific are on other levels complicated, shadowed and overlaid by other parts of the life, and other parts of life, from which MacNeice habitually drew poetic resource. To revert, for a moment, to the situation of 'Cradle Song': the poem's voice is awake while the object of its address is asleep. To that extent, generic convention is firmly in control. But wakefulness is important to MacNeice, and sleep is figured in his work either as something that does not come or, when it comes, as something which can contain nightmares and dreams: and the nightmares outnumber the dreams. The early poetry contains many vivid traces of the sleep anxieties which MacNeice's mature writing revisits and puts to work. In his juvenilia, these things are more stark, and the bed is routinely regarded as a grave. In *Blind Fireworks* (1929), the child's consciousness is wholly unprotected from night terrors that abound:

> The candle in his white grave-clothes, always turning his cowled
> head,
> Stood in his own shadow at the foot of my grave-bed,
> Ho, said the candle with his rich dark beard,
> How they howl like the dead!
> And wagging his cowled head,
> Ho, said the candle, they would make a body afeard.
>   ('Candle Poems', *CP* 638)

> I fell in a nightmare down suddenly
> Into a hole without a bottom. Music
> Died above my head, died in silence.
>   ('Child's Terror', *CP* 616)

Yet all the time on the window-pane
Shadow fingers of the trees
Grope, grope, grope again
After unseen fatalities.
('Impermanent Creativeness', *CP* 646)

The candle lights MacNeice to bed, but not to sleep; the nightmare is that of literally dropping off, into a limitless void; and the world outside the haunted bedroom enters only to 'grope, grope, grope again'. In a way, the voice of 'Cradle Song' tries to render these fears positively, as things that can now (in the person of the unsleeping lover) be guarded against:

The wild grass will whisper,
   Lights of passing cars
Will streak across your dreams
   And fumble at the stars ... (*CP* 209)

Now, it is not 'shadow fingers of the trees' but 'Life' that 'will tap the window'; but this will come 'Only too soon'. Instead of MacNeice's outlandish teenage Gothic, it is just 'Life' that waits to interrupt the slumber; but like the earlier grisly figures, this 'Life' is going to bring something to an end – something, potentially but nonetheless specifically, like love.

The unsleeping, or sleep-troubled, persona in MacNeice is of course something with strong connections to the particular life of the author. Much of what we know about this is present in MacNeice's autobiographical writings, published after his death as *The Strings are False*. It is here that bad nights in the Rectory at Carrickfergus are written up, and here that some fairly traumatic memories are tried out in prose. The date of this enterprise is important, for MacNeice seems to have set himself to write his autobiography while preparing to move to America, and much of the composition was probably done there, with some on the dangerous voyage back at the end of 1940, and some more in the first half of 1941. E.R. Dodds, the book's posthumous editor, reported that the manuscript was given to him for safe-keeping while MacNeice was living in London, during the nightly attacks of mid-1941; the author, it appears, never retrieved his work, whether because he forgot about it or (far more likely) because he had no wish to claim it back. It is here, though, that a childhood unprotected from nightmares is set down, to disturbing effect. When he did go to sleep, MacNeice remembers, the dreams 'got worse and worse':

'Oh God, I do not want to have any dreams. If I am going to go to sleep, do not let me have any dreams. And if I am going to have dreams, do not let me go to sleep, God, please I will do anything if only You keep me awake.' But I always went to sleep all the same. One night I woke up and yelled, my father came up from downstairs, there was light and his voice, he told me nothing would hurt me. I felt quite safe when he had gone but next morning Miss Craig was very angry; my father had forgotten to go down again to the study and had left the lamp burning there all night. I was a very wicked boy and might have burnt the house down. (SF 46)

In MacNeice's recollection here, the falling asleep is dangerous – not just in the sense that it ushers in the dreams that the child prays not to have, but because it occasions danger in the real world, a kind of dereliction of duty which might have catastrophic consequences.

The Strings are False is partly an autobiography, but it is also partly (and perhaps primarily) a love story. Giving fictive life to his own life in 1940 and 1941, MacNeice cast it as a series of women lost, to be concluded with the story of a woman found and kept, 'someone whom according to fairy story logic I was bound to meet but according to common sense never', 'A woman who was not a destroyer' (SF 204). The lost women are Louis's mother, whose going away from home and subsequent death early in his childhood contributed largely to that childhood's nightmares, and his first wife, Mary Beazley, with whom his own married life had ended cata-strophically, when in 1935 she too left without warning. The third woman, with whom the book tries to find its happy ending, is Eleanor Clark. It was life that refused to give the raw materials for the kind of ending MacNeice hoped this narrative might have, when Eleanor and he parted at the end of 1940, and this might provide one reason why the MacNeice of mid-1941 and after had no wish to return to his unfinished book. What he did complete, however, was the working through of losses, both of his mother in childhood and, as an adult, of his wife Mary.

It is noteworthy that MacNeice presents his early married life (and indeed his whole relationship with Mary) in terms of a kind of shared innocence. The young lovers brave family disapproval on both sides, and inhabit their own romantic vignettes in places like Achill Island and Provence, before settling in a deeply domestic nest, surrounded by, but essentially impervious to, the Birmingham of the early 1930s. Increasingly, the couple's comfortable retreat is figured as a hothouse, or an aquarium; all comes to an abrupt end with a domestic catastrophe, the outbreak of a fire in the house – 'Soon there was a large hole in the floor and the bucketfuls of water and fragments of cement were falling on the head of our landlady's lodger' (*SF* 151). And with this, the next morning Mary leaves in the company of her lover, the young American student Charles Katzman.

Is there a connection between the fire in the Rectory that did not start, and the fire in Birmingham that did? The literal disruption of a domestic environment, in the latter case, mirrors metaphorically the end of a marriage – in which it is Mary who walks away – while the imagined conflagration in the Rectory is the consequence (as MacNeice arranges his memories of childhood to suggest) of the absence of another woman, his mother. The biographical facts here are naturally tangled, obscure, and equivocal; but the creative connections made in MacNeice's artistic transformations of them are both simpler and more direct. If the figure of MacNeice's mother is that of someone who disappears mysteriously, not to come back early for her child, and then never to come back at all, that of his first wife is of someone who also leaves abruptly, abandoning not just her husband but also her infant son. In this repetition, as it were, of a pattern of loss, it is not illness and death that enforce the parting but personal unfulfilment and sexual infidelity. For the 33-year-old author of *The Strings are False*, this parallel only makes creative sense in so far as it prepares the way for the arrival of 'a woman who was not a destroyer', who will be neither mother nor domestic partner, but will call forth from MacNeice his own powers of protectiveness and collaboration; not someone to rock his cradle, but whose cradle, so to speak, he can rock; and not someone in whose company he can retreat from life but with whom he can work to meet life on real terms.

Perhaps the acknowledgement of 'fairy story logic' already contained the seeds of eventual disappointment in actuality. At any event, life did not allow MacNeice's autobiographical narrative to be finished according to that logic, and the book was put aside for good in 1941. The two self-absenting women, then, Louis's mother and his wife, were not to be reduced to figures in allegory: they remained to trouble and provoke an imagination often stretched and tested by their loss. In his ambitious stage play of 1958–9, the posthumously published morality *One for the Grave*, MacNeice faces his hero Everyman with a wife and mother in quick succession. The wife is called Mary, who '*comes downstage in a straw hat and a summer frock c.1930*'; she and Everyman sit by a riverbank, and replay the scenario of MacNeice's early love poem 'Mayfly' ('Look at all those mayflies. To think they live for one day only!') The idyll dissolves suddenly, as the Director's Voice calls out 'Cue Forgetfulness' – '*a female figure, wearing dark glasses*':

> (*Forgetfulness taps first Everyman, then Mary, on their shoulders*)
> FORGETFULNESS (*sadly*) Break it up, children; break it up.
> (*They draw apart and stand up with their backs to each other*)
> MARY (*as if doped*) Where was I?
> FORGETFULNESS You were dreaming.
> (*She points to an Exit. Mary walks out as if sleep-walking*)
> EVERYMAN I've been asleep. Was anyone here?
> FORGETFULNESS No one. (*SP* 225)

Almost as soon as the scene is done, Everyman is a child again in the company of his mother, '*wearing Edwardian dress*': 'Here's Mummy, back from her rest cure.' She is not back early ('It's been ages,' says Everyman, 'It's been awful!') but she is back with gifts of Hans Andersen and a box of chocolates. The fairy tales scare the child, and the box contains only empty wrappers. Then this:

> DIRECTOR'S VOICE Hold that blackout. Let her get off.
> FLOOR MANAGER (*in darkness*) This way, Madam. Come with me.
> (*In the darkness, off, a child's voice is heard singing a hymn as far as the lines:*
> '*Teach me to live that I may dread*
> *The grave as little as my bed…*'
> *The voice is cut as the lights come up. Everyman is still sitting on the kiddy stool as if in a trance*)
> EVERYMAN The grave … as little … as my bed? (*SP* 227)

The box of chocolates is there in *The Strings are False*,[5] but it is now part of a fast-moving and deliberately problematic conjunction of images and ideas, as MacNeice tries to expose private anguish to the ironic light of a staged environment. Wife and mother are lost, but now as figures ushered off the stage, while Everyman is left without the ability to resolve the personal dilemmas of their loss. The hymn becomes a riddle.

In fact the hymn in question, Thomas Ken's 'All praise to Thee, My God, this night' (1695) offers a good example of the night-time certainties denied to MacNeice's writing:

When in the Night I sleepless lye,
My Soul with Heavenly Thoughts supply;
Let no ill dreams disturb my Rest,
No Powers of Darkness me molest.

Dull Sleep of Sense me to deprive,
I am but half my time alive;
Thy faithful Lovers, Lord, are griev'd,
To lye so long of Thee bereav'd.[6]

It may not be fanciful to catch here the accents of MacNeice's 'Prayer before Birth'. The religious intent in the hymn is to give God the role of comforting parent; at the same time, sleep itself is being depicted as a kind of waste time, threatened by the 'ill dreams' and 'powers of darkness' which do haunt MacNeice's religiously uncomforted imagination. Increasingly, MacNeice went to the level of 'dream' in search of poetic logic; and this development is most marked in his last three volumes, where he wrote some of his greatest poetry. Often, however, the 'dream-logic' is really the logic of nightmare, as though the perils of unprotected, unwatched-over sleep were the price of admission to the creation of this strange, haunted writing.

In America in 1940, MacNeice could still identify the potential for good dreams in a love-affair, and see the possibility of nightmare as coming from somewhere outside the purely personal sphere. 'Cradle Song' makes its poetic voice the mediator between the loved one and the 'watchers on the wall / Awake all night', but another poem, written very shortly before, inverts the lullaby genre, and is not comforting, but comfortless. This is 'Autobiography', where the wakeful child makes a song out of his own abandonment in the night;

the refrain, '*Come back early or never come*', is not one of reassurance, but of wounded ultimatum. MacNeice's poem is a lullaby thrown into reverse, or turned inside-out, but like a lullaby it has to run the risk of a certain sentimentality: in presenting a lonely and frightened child isolated from comfort, its pathos has to be carefully contained to prevent it dropping into bathos. The steeliness of the refrain is important for this; so too is the laconic directness of the voice MacNeice employs:

> When I woke they did not care;
> Nobody, nobody was there.
>
> *Come back early or never come.*
>
> When my silent terror cried
> Nobody, nobody replied.
>
> *Come back early or never come.* (CP 200–1)

Although both father and mother are mentioned, it is the mother who dominates this poem, or who is, rather, most powerfully not there. The poem seems to bite back its own remembered pain – so much so, that its last image, of 'the chilly sun', might stand for a chill at its own heart. The figure of the poet constructed here is not – as it would be in a poem given to the easy option of sentimentality – a candidate for mothering, but someone fitted to join the 'watchers on the wall / Awake all night'. In the context of Louis's courtship of Eleanor, this is important; in the longer context of the way his poetry was in fact to develop, it also marks a significant rejection of comfort in the way it frames and imagines the self. This voice does not solicit pity, and one way this is shown is in its utter rejection of self-pity.

MacNeice's poetry tends, in any case, to inflect the word 'pity' negatively, and often towards 'self-pity'. In 'Valediction' the visitor is instructed to 'leave ten per cent of pity / Under your plate for the emigrant'; in 'Letter to Graham and Anne Shepard' 'we ... feed our brains on backchat and self-pity', while in 'Eclogue from Iceland' a voice tempts the listeners to 'let your self-pity swell with the music' (*CP* 9, 49, 78). In *Autumn Journal*, there is a need to 'abjure the luxury of self-pity', along with a reminder that 'the delights of self-pity must pall' (*CP* 106, 160). In the wartime poem 'Babel' 'We cut each

other's throats out of our great self-pity', and in 'To the Public', from
Visitations, 'We do not need your indulgence, much less your pity'
(*CP* 228, 495). Another, more literary, use of 'pity' comes in Canto
XI of *Autumn Sequel* (1954), which concerns itself with romantic
attachment and loss. Here, the voice of the Parrot coldly 'Repeats "I
told you so, I told you so, I am Pretty / Polly who knows that one
peck makes a kiss"', to be answered by the lines 'But what does one
lost handkerchief make? The pity / Of it, Poll Parrot, the pity!', and
then the idea of how 'the wronged lover does himself more wrong
/ Waking in Circe's room'. This unequivocal calling upon *Othello*
ushers in the anxieties of sexual jealousy and betrayal, but these are
being brought to bear on a kind of sexual nightmare, for which
Circe's menagerie of lovers is the requisite myth:

> And as the young man shrinks away, the white
> Body beside him vanishes and leaves
> The bed to him and the beasts, while the bitter bright
>
> Day creeps under the door and under the eaves
> Outside the sparrows yield to a louder bird:
> 'I told you so, I told you so,' it grieves ... (*CP* 422)

From 'the wronged lover' to the young man in Circe's crowded
room, MacNeice's images for the sexual life (which, like every other
aspect of life, *Autumn Sequel* relentlessly makes into myth) are shadowed by 'the pity of it'. But this 'pity' is not enough – it is, indeed,
a part of the problem.

There is a point to looking again at MacNeice and *Othello* – or,
rather, MacNeice and Othello, and the ways in which his relation to
that character plays across the 'pity' of, the 'pity' in, and even the 'pity'
about his life and work. When he puts 'The pity of it' in the mouth
of *Autumn Sequel*'s Parrot, a character in that poem who embodies all
that is facile, self-serving, and reductive in life, MacNeice indicates
something of how he understands Shakespeare's play and its protagonist. Both theatrical and critical traditions have always been divided
about the nature of Othello – as 'noble' or 'dull Moor', as the
romantic artist of transcendent love arias, or as a lethal fantasist whose
best poetry is, in T.S. Eliot's phrase, 'cheering himself up'.[7] For
MacNeice, true to the modern readings of his time, there is a dreadful
inadequacy in Othello's appeal to Iago about 'The pity of it'; and that

inadequacy is certainly there in the play, for 'pity' is the one thing which the deluded hero is not going to show. And appealing thus to Iago, for whom love is 'merely a lust of the blood and a permission of the will' (*Othello* 1.3.333), is to expose the word 'pity' to the most sceptical and ironic of audiences. Not being Othello necessitates a resistance to the appeals of 'pity', a detachment from the word which is also a measure of self-detachment, residually present even in 'Cradle Song'. But then 'Cradle Song' is also a poem in which the 'lust of the blood' in one lover has not been met by 'a permission of the will' in the other, and its sexual content is therefore something postponed at best. The lover's voice in the poem, however, makes a point of its experience of 'Life', and while a world war is one part of that 'Life', a sexual history is another. In this respect, it is interesting to read *The Strings are False* as part of the evidence Louis offers to Eleanor, for it builds in both sexual betrayal and promiscuity to its account of a personal life in which she is to offer the happy resolution. An American (or at least would-be American) MacNeice writes of how 'In respect of sex I see England in the thirties as a chaos of unhappy or dreary marriages, banal or agonised affairs,' adding satirically graphic details of 'The pattern of every night shot through with the pounding and jingling of bedsteads'. But MacNeice is being true to another aspect of his personality when he makes this into a (Freud-inflected) text for a sermon of his own: 'If it was a pathetic mistake to think that chastity in itself has spiritual value, it is also a pathetic mistake to think that acts of fornication piled up indiscriminately will somehow give value to life' (*SF* 172). 'Life' tempts us towards the 'pathetic' in our sexual mistakes, then; and 'pathetic' here carries a slightly scornful spin, for to fall for the 'pathetic' is to succumb to the merely pitiful – as did Desdemona, when she listened to Othello's courting stories and 'swore in faith 'twas strange, 'twas passing strange; / 'Twas pitiful, 'twas wondrous pitiful' (*Othello* 1.3.160–1). As MacNeice warms to his theme, which is that of how in fact 'to give value to life', he conjoins sex and economics:

> Sexual promiscuity in our England was a legacy from nineteenth-century Enlightenment. The Emancipation of Women, Every Girl her own Harlot. The resulting paradox is like the paradox of Free Trade – there is nothing free about it. Those whose ship comes home have probably bankrupted others, if not by breaking up a marriage or making the future uncertain, at least – less directly –

by encouraging others to gamble in a field where the majority must lose. (*SF* 172)

It is not clear just how far this would be likely to move the heart of the average American Trotskyite girl in 1940, but sex and the broken marriage would certainly speak to something in MacNeice's history which, by this stage, he needed to make into a positive. 'Life' and its 'value' are at stake, but in a remarkable paragraph MacNeice finds his would-be panoptic view interrupted by the very thing it is attempting to rise above, for Othello, as well as Marx and Freud, is still at the party:

The modern Don Juan is the counterpart of the nineteenth-century self-made Captain of Industry. Winning through against odds he assumes that the world is his oyster, and always will be for those who have the requisite courage, technique, imagination. Which of course is a black lie. Man cannot live by courage, technique, imagination – alone. He has to have a sanction from outside himself. Otherwise his technical achievements, his empires of stocks and shares, his exploitation of power, his sexual conquests, all his apparent inroads on the world outside, are merely the self-assertion, the self-indulgence, of a limited self that whimpers behind the curtains, a spiritual masturbation. (*SF* 173)

'Self-' does not come out of this well; and Othello, 'cheering himself up', is of course at one point reduced to being (or, it may be fairer to say, is exposed as) a whimperer behind curtains, when he voyeuristically spectates on the false evidence of his own cuckolding. MacNeice's condemnation of the 'limited self' includes the limitation of sexual obsession; and in looking at his own past life (which had, after all, included at least the occasion for rage at sexual betrayal), MacNeice identifies the kinds of 'self-indulgence' to which it is his business (implicitly, his business as a writer) not to succumb.

Taking refuge in the self – which, in a sense, is exactly what Othello does in his verbose and self-commentating form of revenge – is the thing MacNeice sets out to exclude. This is something much more easily set out as a programme, of course, than followed through in a writing life; and MacNeice was well aware that his work could accommodate superbly the life of the senses, and the whole range of pleasures, aesthetic and otherwise, which are pleasing, first and fore-

most, to the self by whom they are experienced. A self-indulgent
isolation, whether hedonistic or self-pityingly miserable, is the danger
attendant on some of MacNeice's greatest artistic strengths. The realisation of this is, in fact, fairly constant in MacNeice's career, but it
becomes acute when personally difficult subject-matter is broached.
The persona of 'Autobiography', whom 'The chilly sun / Saw ...
walk away alone' walks away both from self-pity and any presump-
tion of pity for him on the part of the reader; while in a poem from
Springboard (1944), a very different figure isolates himself from human
involvement through sex. 'The Libertine', who 'ran through women
like a child through growing hay / Looking for a lost toy' is imaginatively self-crippled:

> He never found the toy and has forgotten the faces,
> Only remembers the props ... a scent-spray
> Beside the bed or a milk-white telephone
> Or through the triple ninon the acrid trickle of day:
> O leave me easy, leave me alone.
>
> Long fingers over the gunwale, hair in a hair-net,
> Furs in January, cartwheel hats in May,
> And after the event the wish to be alone –
> Angels, goddesses, bitches, all have edged away:
> O leave me easy, leave me alone. (*CP* 230–1)

The refrain here is '*Come back early or never come*' in a different register:
for MacNeice's 'Libertine', it is not a question of loneliness, but of
chosen isolation. In his way, this figure has also chosen a kind of sentimentality, the sentimentality of serving the self; and it is this which
has driven him beyond the wish for human contact – has driven him,
in effect, away from life.

The avoidance of histrionics is part of an artistic determination not
to prove 'a limited self that whimpers behind the curtains'; in the case
of the Othello predicament, this means a rejection of jealousy on the
grounds that it is finally self-serving and self-diminishing. 'The pity
of it' is not enough, and the experiences incorporated into 'Cradle
Song' therefore include the experience of not being a jealous
cuckold. In a poem which he included among a number of short
narratives he called 'Novelettes', 'The Old Story', MacNeice wrote
out of the situation of seeing his former wife, now in the United

States, for the first time since her elopement with Katzman ten years before. The trip is included in *The Strings are False* too, but MacNeice's poem takes the more decisive route away from self-regard. 'Here she stands,' MacNeice writes in his third-person account, 'who was twenty and is thirty':

> The same but different and he found the difference
> A surgeon's knife without an anaesthetic;
> He had known of course that this happens
> But had not guessed the pain of it or the panic,
>
> And could not say 'My love', could hardly
> Say anything at all, no longer knowing
> Whom he was talking to but watched the water
> Massing for action on the cold horizon. (*CP* 186–7)

In the cadence of 'the pain of it or the panic' MacNeice allows the ghost of Othello's staccato rhythm 'The pity of it, O the pity of it ...' to pass across the line – not inappositely, but still not as a moment of identification; rather the reverse. The poem's central figure is left alone, and without the means of expressing his pain because 'no longer knowing / Whom he was talking to'. The action here is all outside the self, and it is 'the water / Massing for action', chiming with the wartime of the poem's composition, which holds all the destructive potential.

'The Old Story', which can be read as obliquely autobiographical, helps to explain how MacNeice saw himself in 1940; but it also gives an example of the distancing from sentimentality which was to continue to be important for his work. This is not to say that the crisis of five years before was easily overcome in terms of MacNeice's emotional life, and it is likely that the traces of those traumatic events remain in much later writing also. In MacNeice's last major project, the Cambridge lectures later published as *Varieties of Parable* (1965), the Elizabethan poet Edmund Spenser is much mentioned – quite properly, given the overall subject. What is more odd is the incident in Spenser's *The Faerie Queene* on which MacNeice chooses to dwell: this is the story of the jealous Malbecco (*The Faerie Queene* 3.10), whose wife Hellenore is stolen by the knight Paridell from under his nose (*VP* 40–1). To make their escape, the lovers set Malbecco's house on fire:

This second *Hellene*, faire Dame *Hellenore*,
  The whiles her husband ranne with sory haste,
  To quench the flames, which she had tyn'd before,
  Laught at his foolish labour spent in waste;
  And ranne into her louers armes right fast...[8]

The parallel with his own life, which MacNeice's audience had no means of knowing, makes this choice of incident an interesting one. Malbecco's increasingly desperate and unfortunate pursuit of his erring wife ends with him becoming a literal monster of jealousy, so that 'His madness', as MacNeice puts it, 'now becomes a sort of apotheosis.' The story in Spenser is a satirical one, making cruel and bawdy fun of possessive old husbands (who had always been fair literary game), but its depiction of uncontrolled jealousy is also, in MacNeice's reading, a way of mastering such lack of control. The ranting maniac into which Malbecco is transformed is an ancestor of Othello (and might, incidentally, offer in this way evidence for Shakespeare's implicit criticism of the 'dull Moor'). Othello, bent on revenge, compares himself to 'the Pontic Sea, / Whose icy current and compulsive course, / Ne'er feels retiring ebb, but keeps due on / To the Propontic and the Hellespont' (3.3.453–6), while Spenser's Malbecco 'Out of the flames, which he had quencht whylere / Into huge waues of griefe and gealosye / Full deepe emplonged was, and drowned nye'. In the end, this creature lives on a cliff over the sea, 'Ne euer rests he in tranquillity, / The roaring billowes beat his bowre so boystrously'. MacNeice's waves, 'massing for action', carry a less melodramatic and altogether more chilly significance, one which has personal ramifications perhaps, but which remains indifferent to the self it threatens.

By the end, in *Varieties of Parable*, MacNeice knew the kind of writer he hoped he was, or hoped to become. He had learned to prize a plainness of style which was not an instinctive gift in much of his early writing. Praising Bunyan, he writes of how 'The plainness is like a truth drug or, putting it very differently, the knife that almost killed the writer will cut the reader to the bone' (*VP* 23). Certain religious and cultural cards are now on the table, but the insistence on a relation between style and honesty had in fact been long ago intuited by MacNeice, and is an important undercurrent in works like *Autumn Journal* (1939) and that poem's literary-critical companion, *Modern Poetry* (1938). Plainness like 'a truth drug' or a surgeon's knife does not suggest much comfort in the matter it conveys, but it also brings into focus the unsentimental awareness which MacNeice's best poetry had always cultivated. MacNeice's great love poems (and 'Cradle Song' is amongst these) work partly because of their internal resistance to the kinds of comfort for which (on a human level) they wish. 'Insincerity', MacNeice writes elsewhere in *Varieties of Parable*, 'is one of the commonest causes of sentimentality but lack of head can cause it as well as lack of heart' (*VP* 73). The thought is a complex one, but in its light MacNeice's own love poetry, which insists on 'head' as well as 'heart', and avoids the easy options of sentimentalism, self-pity or appeals for pity, is all the more impressive. 'Life will have her answer', and if poetry is to be answerable to life (as MacNeice thought it was), then head and heart need both to be involved, with such honesty as a poet can muster.

But 'Life' also takes its toll, on poets if not on poetry. Success tends to come and go, and in the literary world, smart young men become the targets of smarter, younger men. This, at least, is what happened to MacNeice in his middle age. And poets' personal lives, like any others, are subject to cruel and wasteful vicissitude: love does not last, or, if it lasts, it lasts by changing, and living with change. As a reflective and self-aware human being in 1940, MacNeice would not have known this exactly, not at least in anything but abstract terms, and might reasonably have hoped for the best in his own case, at any rate; yet his poetry knew it at some level, and 'Cradle Song' folds this kind of knowledge into 'The pity of it all'. By the time of 'The Truisms' in *Solstices* (1961) the knowledge is particular and plainly named:

> Then he left home, left the truisms behind him
> Still on the mantelpiece, met love, met war,
> Sordor, disappointment, defeat, betrayal,
> Till through disbeliefs he arrived at a house
> He could not remember seeing before... (*CP* 565)

Many poets are happy to incorporate love and (if it is painlessly possible) war into a curriculum vitae; fewer see the point of dwelling on 'Sordor, disappointment, defeat, betrayal', even if they are capable of acknowledging these things in their lives. None but MacNeice, surely, would find the word 'Sordor' – 'Physical or moral sordidness', according to the *OED* – to describe this aspect of life that must be answered to. As MacNeice uses it here, 'Sordor' is another thing to be met with, akin to the allegorical monsters which Spenser's knights might meet on their quests. Now, however, the monsters are life-sized. One of the extraordinary achievements of MacNeice's last three volumes of poetry is their ability to admit 'Sordor, disappoint-ment, defeat, betrayal' as fully matters of the head and the heart – real things, and not mere appearances of them due to be dispelled somehow, by force of personality or intensity of self-reference. Utterly unsentimental, these poems give Life a true answer.

Yet 'Sordor' remains strange, a word very difficult to assimilate to the plainness of the poem in which it occurs. It happens that MacNeice had used the word long before, in a love poem for his fiancée Mary in 1929, another 'Cradle Song', this time 'For Miriam', where:

> The world like a cradle rises and falls
> On a wave of confetti and funerals
> And sordor and stinks and stupid faces
> And the deity making bored grimaces... (*CP* 660)

For the young man who writes this, 'sordor' is an aspect of the world which lovers can rise above, and will not have to encounter; and the cradle, to which the world itself is likened, is something that rises and falls to the rhythm of marriage and death. 'We all lie alone,' MacNeice writes, 'having long outgrown our cradles'; but the poem is not, perhaps, quite as grown-up as it supposes itself to be, suffering from a self-indulgence which comes too close to self-pity. With 'The Truisms', 'sordor' remains odd, but it is not included now for oddity's sake, and is as precise as it is exotic – precise, that is, like the unspeci-fied precisions of 'love ... war ... disappointment, defeat, betrayal'. The sentimentality of self-reference has evaporated completely from this; early MacNeice, on the other hand, can luxuriate in the author's own dilemmas and neuroses. In 'Sleep', an uncollected poem from 1932, MacNeice's drowsy speaker has to 'remember to forget that I know / That there are no persons either to know me or love me':

> To whom waiting
> Came with quiet breath, as strained through silk,
> But with a body that was desire made body,
> Without dreams, with a force not known to many,
> Sleep the brother of Death. (*CP* 721–2)

Superficially, this is vivid enough; but poetically it is *just* surface, an attempt to gain profundity merely by sounding deep. The problem is (in common with other experiments in MacNeice's writing) that a personal force in particular images and ideas has pushed the poetry into a certain conventionality, as the passive provider of required special effects. Perhaps because there is not a 'lack' but an excess of 'heart' in the particular images here and their personal associations, the verse responds with a 'lack of head', resulting in something both insincere, in MacNeice's terms, and sentimental.

Poetry, like all good writing, forbids either 'head' or 'heart' to flourish at the other's expense. This means that words (and images), however potent their private associations, are exposed in the writing itself to the full force of the difficult, sometimes hostile, sometimes indifferent or misconstruing life of which they are also parts. 'Cradle Song' is one of the poems in which MacNeice puts this to proof; like all his best work, it is capable of soaking up all the punishment that life can (and will) dish out – punishment to words like 'pity', for example, which cannot be ducked by enshrining that word in a zone of private significance. 'Sleep', too, is a word MacNeice wants to protect, but cannot quite, as a word of personal comfort. The final section of *Autumn Journal* opens with just this wish:

> Sleep, my body, sleep, my ghost,
>   Sleep, my parents and grand-parents,
> And all those I have loved most:
>   One man's coffin is another's cradle.

But it won't work, or not so neatly as this; for one man's cradle is the same man's coffin. The cradle and the coffin's interchangeability – or identity – spoils the innocence of the lullaby, so that the next line, 'Sleep, my past and all my sins' works partly because it knows itself doomed to failure. Much, of course, is wished for, and properly to be wished for:

> Sleep, my fancies and my wishes,
>   Sleep a little and wake strong,
> The same but different and take my blessing –
>   A cradle-song. (*CP* 161–2)

Yet this cradle song, like others by MacNeice, is voiced for one of the unsleeping 'watchers on the wall' who know, amongst other things, the truth about lullabies, and about the relation between the cradle and the grave.

In his 1946 radio play commemorating Graham Shepard (a very close friend who had died at sea during the war), MacNeice topped and tailed the broadcast with his protagonist in the cradle:

(*Fade up Mother singing softly 'Rockabye Baby', then, after one verse, humming and breaking off in the middle*)
MOTHER Ah, he's asleep at last.
TOM Yes, I'm asleep at last. Drowned in muslin flounces, I am only six months old, I cannot crawl, I cannot speak, when I am hungry I feel myself all mouth. (*SP* 76, 109)

Then, at the play's end (when Tom is in fact drowning in mid-Atlantic) his mother repeats 'Ah, he's asleep at last', and the music of 'Rockabye Baby' fades up over Tom's last line, 'Now let me sleep; I'm tired.' In MacNeice's late poems, this cradle mutates into the grave-bed, where a dream- or nightmare-logic mixes everything up: 'The Introduction', with its extraordinary splicing of lovers' tryst and 'a green grave', and its turning upside down of 'too old' and 'too young', 'too late' and 'too early', combines dream and nightmare in the same poem – one of MacNeice's very best (*CP* 593). But there is one late poem in which sleeping and waking have an uncompli-catedly good outcome. In 'Good Dream' (from *Solstices*) the speaker is asleep, but convinced that he must be awake; a hand takes gently from the table his bedside book (a Bible), and a woman's voice begins to read, then gives instructions to the sleeper. He is not in the room he supposed himself to occupy, but in fact on a river, in a boat, and must row in the darkness towards the female voice that calls him. Next:

> The hand
> That stole the book that was left in the dark
> Comes out of the dark, the hand that is hers,
> Hers, none other's, and seizes his
> To help him on to the bank.
>   'And God
> Said let there be light'.
>   His usual room

Has lost its usual walls and found
Four walls of sky, incredible blue
Enclosing incredible green enclosing
Her, none other.
      Completely awake. (*CP* 571)

The poem's narrative undoes a number of previously dominant patterns in MacNeice's treatment of sleeping and dreaming, of women and loss, not least by ending in an awakening to a real world, and to 'Her, none other'. Here, it is the female figure who is watching over the sleeping speaker, keeping him safe to the point at which he wakes. On the personal level, this is another Mary, the poet's last partner, Mary Wimbush; more generally, it is the figure whose possibility haunts (or sometimes torments) so much of MacNeice's love poetry, that of 'a woman who was not a destroyer'.

It must be added that 'Good Dream' is a relatively isolated instance in MacNeice's late poetry, where nightmares of various kinds tend to dominate. Yet MacNeice was aware that fully achieved poetry makes any grimness of its subject or occasion incidental matters; that poetry is not an excuse for feeling sorry for oneself, or looking for others' admiring sympathy, just as reading poetry is not an opportunity for enjoying a finally self-indulgent sense of pity for its author. A good poem takes courage, and is a form of courage; it may give courage too, for courage is the lesson MacNeice most offers to any poet. 'Life will have her answer': and Louis MacNeice's poetry, at its best, is fully answerable not just to the life he lived, but to life – in the hectic midst of which it came to being, and in which it so vigorously continues to exist. In poetry, the grave is also the cradle; ends are beginnings; and for MacNeice's work, the words of his own poem 'Thalassa' apply: 'Our end is Life' (*CP* 783).

MEMOIRS

Dan MacNeice

1. That Was Then, This Is Now[1]

I was born on 15 May 1934 in a suburb of Birmingham, where my father was a 26-year-old Lecturer in Classics at the University. Louis MacNeice (his name, and later I sensed, his 'title', as I became aware that he was a celebrity: I have ever since tended to have a split view of the name) had met my mother, Giovanna Marie Thérèse Babette Ezra, the same age, at Oxford where he had been an undergraduate. Her stepfather, J.D. ('Jackie') Beazley, was the world authority on Attic vases, Professor of Greek Archaeology at Oxford, and a five-minute cracker of German codes for the Admiralty. Her mother, an eccentric virago who has figured in several memoirs, ran the house as a sort of salon. 'The Bible should have been written in French' and the (firmly asexual) observation, 'My husband can make sparks fly from my loins', were among the nonplussing dicta that astounded academics at the dinner table. Troops of young men played tennis and danced with my mother – she was reputed to be the best dancer in Oxford, practising the Charleston in private for hours with a chair until bursting on the scene as though born with the ability – and at a very young age she acquired a sophisticated knowledge of every type of male personality. My father, on the other hand, had hitherto known almost no females at all except his stepmother and older sister, having grown up in the sombre atmosphere of a clerical household in the North of Ireland and later attending boys' boarding schools in England. (At the age of sixteen he saw a Greek statue of a female torso and actually vomited at the shock from the physical differences.)

They were drawn together for perhaps rather minor reasons. He was contemplative and poetic, an excellent tennis player though quite unable to dance, and must have seemed altogether much more worthwhile to my mother than the butterfly types fluttering around the house. She impressed him as an anomaly: a china doll tennis whizz who had actually read James Joyce – at that time almost unheard of. In fact, hers was very much a self-made personality. The product of what was regarded almost as a 'mixed' (even though arranged) marriage, her father's family were Baghdadi Jews who had settled in Calcutta in the early nineteenth century to become rich merchants and philanthropists; whereas her mother's were Eastern European Ashkenazim with a strong intellectual and musical tradition.

She was supposed to be a toy for the grown-ups in the drawing room, but at the age of five she insisted on shedding all her names – she had been called by all of them as though they were one – and refused to answer to anything except 'Mary', by which she remained known. At the same time she called for, and got, a governess to teach her to read, because then she 'would know everything'. Later she demanded to be sent to school, to which her family reluctantly acceded, and she cheerfully endured the austerities of English girls' schools rather than stay at home to be suffocated by her mother. The most liberating event of her childhood was the death of her father, David Ezra, a cavalry officer in the British Army and a violent man who had terrorised his whole household. He was killed in France in 1918 'leading his men over the top'. Her mother's speedy second marriage was a relief to Mary, as it diverted her energies.

As my mother grew up she developed a great love for and empathy with animals, which I think to this day [1987] she regards as more worthwhile than people. But she entered marriage with dedication and serious resolve to be a supportive wife and champion mother. Prudently, my parents suspended my birth until my father had tenure (he had gained his job prior to his graduation in 1930, in competition with over 400 applicants, many of whom had had actual teaching experience. But 1934 was still the Depression, and to have become unemployed with a newborn child would have been disastrous). As a young child learning about the four-year interval between their wedding and my birth, I had the resentful misunderstanding that I wasn't really wanted and that my birth was not only by mistake but contributive to the subsequent break-up of their marriage.

In 1935 my mother's family sent an impoverished American Rhodes scholar to stay with us for the summer vacation. My mother, who later came to feel that he had represented an idealised version of her father, although he was younger than herself, was swiftly attracted to him, and in November of that year they left together, eventually settling in New Jersey where his family lived and she still does. My father was left with an eighteen-month-old infant to care for – and I later came to feel that we had both been abandoned. (Much later I learned that my mother experienced the leaving of us as being somehow involuntary and that had she taken me with her it would have completely destroyed my father. The eventual divorce judgment awarded him my custody.) One of my earliest 'memories' is really a vague sense of being responsible for his emotional well-being, as though I owed him a more than filial love. Whether this obligation was provoked by him or not, I do not know, but I definitely remember perceiving an aura of melancholy about him that I attempted to reduce. His own mother had died when he was five and his whole life was consciously affected by this; possibly the replication in mine, or repetition in his, magnified his sadness.

The house in Birmingham became too ghost-ridden for my father to endure and shortly after my mother's disappearance he took a post at a women's college in London where we lived an almost rural existence in a house with a big garden at the edge of Regent's Park. The household at this time also contained a Borzoi bitch (who, I think, added to the melancholy mystique) and a succession of 'nannies' as caregivers for me. The earliest of these I do not remember clearly, except for a faint sense of fondness for a Scottish one who had to be let go because, as I was later told, she became too domineering and also censorious of my father's neo-bachelor life.

The first real mother-replacement I remember well was a young Hungarian Jewish refugee, Miss Popper, who came with her father to live with us in another house, not far from the first but nearer to the college and the London Zoo, about which my father was now engaged in writing a book. Miss Popper must have had a very clear view of the requirements and limitations of her job because I don't think I was able to convert her into a full-blown mother figure. As an employee she probably felt that my father should be my primal source of parental warmth and the object of my first loyalty. But I *did* acquire a secure relationship with her (which compared favorably with a much later one with my stepmother). During this period, of course, I didn't really know I had 'lost' a mother. It wasn't till much later that I became consciously aware of the normal family structure, at which time I exploited my coming from a 'broken home' (a relative rarity then) as at once a credential and a crutch.

The earliest displeasure with me that I recall on my father's part occurred when I was about three or four when he was working on the manuscript of his *Zoo* book and I was playing nearby. Jumping up impetuously, I tripped over a phone cord, which yanked the phone and all the manuscript pages off the desk, sending them flying all over the room. His exasperation was probably rather mildly expressed but I was astounded that he was capable of anger at all. The point that strikes me now is that I was as old as three or four before doing anything to incur his irritation, but then Miss Popper had the physical maintenance of me and he was never up against the sort of daily annoyance that I might have induced earlier.

At about this age I attended an avant-garde nursery school about which I remember little save its insufferable siestas, but as the Second World War approached it was deemed advisable to evacuate me from London. It was fully expected that England would be invaded and as I was half-Jewish I might have succumbed to Hitler's Final Solution; so I was sent at the age of five to live with my paternal grandparents in Belfast in the North of Ireland. My grandfather was the Church of Ireland (Anglican) bishop of the diocese that included Belfast, then as now a troubled city. Luckily for my development my grandfather was a liberal and ecumenical churchman, almost uniquely in Northern Irish history, and I learned later that he performed many courageous acts that probably would have got him lynched today. An imposing, stockily built man he was the more impressive by virtue of his vestments. A small dressing room off his bedroom was entirely filled by these, and recognising that 'clothes make the man', or at least confer power, I soon enjoyed dressing up, either actually in his robes or with equivalent seaweed at the beach. Although Miss Popper continued to have the mundane caretaking of me, abetted by a whole Downstairs troupe of motherly Irish maids and to a considerable extent my step-grandmother, my grandfather came to fill a more parenting role than my father had before him. With no difficulty that I can remember, he taught me to read in about three weeks.

As air raids later extended from London to Belfast it was thought safer to send me to live with friends and relatives in the hinterland and I began a series of brief visitations with various (usually clerical) families. These all had children, and I was introduced for the first time to the feeling of being a guest, or foster, sibling. Miss Popper continued to accompany and support me on these sojourns – on one occasion indicating proudly to a horrified family where I had 'expressed' myself with crayons all over a freshly wallpapered room. But her influence had become more muted, and by the age of six or seven I recognised my emotional vulnerability and lack of control over my fate. I handled this by retreating inwardly and creating a

fantasy existence where I had power and commanded respect. My
fantasies were elaborate and evolved to suit changing conditions, but
a constant feature of them was a land called 'Vamidia'. Many years
later a friend pointed out the obvious (to his ear, since he was originally German-speaking) evocation of 'family'.

My education during this period was continued briefly at a girls'
day school where I was one of the only two boys attending. Miss
Popper accompanied me to improve her English but increasingly I
felt incompetent at dealing with women. I did not understand that,
for instance, teasing might connote affection and I became readily
lachrymose, bursting into tears at the least provocation. A heavy
disappointment to me early in the war was the collapse of plans to
send me to America where my father was now teaching at Cornell.
Two weeks before I was to leave, several shiploads of children being
evacuated from the British Isles were torpedoed, so it was all called
off and I went instead to live with distant relatives in the Irish Free
State, a neutral country and presumably safe from invasion. Life with
this family probably affected my personality as much as anything hitherto, though I stayed with it for less than two years.

These people were 'Ascendancy', which is to say Protestant,
Anglo-Irish landed gentry who owned the landscape, including
whole villages, to beyond the horizon, but what I didn't perceive at
the time was that their way of life was doomed. A traditional regimen,
unchanged in some respects since the twelfth century, was maintained for the children as though they would automatically inherit
and continue it all for ever. As a result of my shortcomings and my
waif-relation status I swiftly became a target for the mild sadism of
the family nursemaid, Alice. Although our education was in the hands
of a series of governesses of varying degrees of gentility, Alice was
our real monitor and she would punish our lapses by caning us on
our proffered palms. On one occasion my misreading of 'quay' as
though it were pronounced 'kway' provoked her savage ire and I had
to stand with ringing hands, duncelike in the corner for eternity. Our
daily afternoon walks for what seemed interminable distances
through dripping woodlands were rendered brisker than they might
have been by Alice who brought up the rear with a switch in her
hand, cutting at us on the back of the legs like a cattle drover. But
we were fond of her, and I imagine she, in her slightly perverted way,
was of us.

This period introduced me to the possibilities of affection fused with violence, and years later in pubescence I grafted my experience with Alice on my relationship with my stepmother. Physical contact was at least contact, whereas both ladies could reject and wound me more deeply by their utterances. Once while Alice was giving me a bath she announced: 'You were a nice little boy when you first came here and your hair was all curly, but now it's not curly any more and you're no longer nice', and this sort of judgment contributed to my growing sense of a fall from grace. Everything that had gone before was better than what followed, in my view, and I became a Peter Pan, declining to grow up. I think I quite consciously felt disfranchised from the future and dug into non-volition.

During these years my father had changed his career from academe to script writing and producing for the BBC in London. He had also become an established poet whose name was recognised throughout the English-speaking literary world. This purchased for me a certain respect from my otherwise philistine Irish household and we would be allowed to stay up late to listen to his radio plays. Actually by now he had become a confused memory as a father and seemed almost as remote from me as he must have been to my fellow listeners. But in 1942 when I was eight he wrote telling me that he was going to marry 'someone [I] would love very much', and I thought everything was going to turn out all right after all. I would be at the centre of my own family and would shed the restricted life in Ireland for the dimly remembered delights of the big city. He brought her over to Ireland to model her, as it were, to his family in the North and to me in the South and I was enchanted. Firstly, she was youthful and attractive and contrasted vividly with the rather frumpy old people around me; and secondly, she was a singer – an occupation in the prevailing Victorian view not far removed from 'going on the boards' – and thus emancipated. Hedli Anderson was a middle child of three and the daughter of ultra-strict Plymouth Brethren and was very much the result of her origins, but of course that didn't emerge during the honeymoon.

During their visit I accompanied them on a brief trip to Dublin, so that Hedli and I could get to know each other better off my turf. Dublin was a sinister city to a child during the war because it was neutral and hence full of military personnel from opposing sides who apparently intermingled harmoniously. Our hotel room was flanked by German officers with swastika armbands and I was half convinced I would be kidnapped at any moment. My new family was not sufficiently reassuring about this, and I had a twinge of misgiving. Indeed, I remember the occasion as an early instance of my growing tendency to handle bullying by fawning on the bully – though I doubt if the Nazis even noticed me, no matter how presentable I tried to be.

My father decided to reintegrate me into English life by stages. Instead of sending me immediately in the normal way to a rough-and-tumble boys' boarding school, he astutely felt that I would do better in the supposedly gentler environment of a co-ed school, but neglected to edit my first appearance there. I showed up like a Little Lord Fauntleroy, outfitted by my step-grandmother in the clothes she had thought suitable to ship me back to England in. A three-piece herringbone suit with shorts, button down girls' shoes, blouse with elastic around the waist, pocket watch on a chain, and a bulldog-headed walking stick with gold collar were my innocent attire and I never lived it down thereafter. The school would have been a good choice for a child coming from a less sheltered environment than I did but in fact it deepened all my timidities. It had its own farm for wartime self-sufficiency and the children took care of the animals, all of which terrified me indiscriminately whether they were pigs, goats, rabbits or hens. We also did much of the school housework, leaping up in the morning to sign up for the more desirable chores. Peeling great tureens of potatoes under the critical eye of a tyrannic cook was the least popular and fell to whoever was last, invariably myself. But it was safe and undemanding and went on long enough to displace having to work in the farmyard and I felt increasingly justified in aiming low in life; there was plenty of room and anonymity at the bottom.

The family, of course, existed, but very much in the background and disappointingly at that. I chronically longed for the vacations but was invariably betrayed by them. My father was almost always too busy to play with me (genuinely; in addition to script writing he had to do air-raid duty, spotting fires all night from the roof of St Paul's Cathedral) and my stepmother was in constant practice for concerts, so vacations were a letdown.

My stepmother and I clashed almost immediately over the question of housework. What should have been a reasonably harmonious joint endeavour became a rancorous tussle of wills. Hedli (I settled into calling her by her name after some uncomfortable attempts to come up with a mother-type of label) thought that I should pull my weight around the house by sweeping the stairs or nipping out to the store, but her manner of presenting the idea struck me as taunting and I resisted it. Fresh from the privileged life of an aristocrat in Ireland (not to mention needing a reprieve from school chores), I announced 'I'm not your servant!' with all the hauteur I could muster, but inevitably had to back down and do it anyway. Sulkily I brushed the mockingly vivid purple carpet on the stairs while Hedli's contralto scales rippled triumphantly through the house. She was capable of explosive loss of temper, shouting and slapping, while I must have been unbearably goading. Many years later she expressed remorse for having been an inadequate parent, citing complete lack of preparation for an extremely difficult job, and other reasons.

One of these was the war. Away at school in the country I was behind the lines, one might say, but going to London during the 'hols' seemed like an adventurous outing to the Front and I failed to recognise how relentlessly unending it was to the adult world. It was particularly noisy where we lived at this time on a street next to Lord's Cricket Ground, which had been converted into an anti-aircraft battery. During air raids the guns next door were louder than the bombs and showered the house and garden with shrapnel and my family sought convivial solace at the pub. (I don't intend to overstress this point: I doubt that they deliberately abandoned me during air raids so much as they were caught out when one started and were unable to get home, but it did seem that they were never there in the evenings.)

I was much more afraid of the house than the war. My room was three floors up in the attic and going to bed was a torment. I dreaded the dark and procrastinated about entering it. Later, in 1943 when my half-sister Corinna was born and lived in the room below mine, it became my responsibility, if we were alone in the house when the sirens sounded, to get her down to the indoor air-raid shelter in the dining room. The dining room was on the ground floor, dark with wood panelling and made gloomier yet with pictures from Picasso's Blue Period of cadaverous nudes and melancholy clowns, and the shelter was a sort of black iron table with caging round the sides. As the sirens blew I scrunched down in bed pretending I didn't hear them rather than having to face the stairs and dining room with a screeching infant in my arms. But as the bombing got nearer (as an ack-ack battery, with searchlights leading back down to it, Lord's itself was a target), it would become unavoidable. My greater fear was that the family would return to find the house bombed and the shelter empty, when it would become apparent that I had made no effort to reach it.

Despite all the destruction going on around one, my only wartime experience with death occurred a few years earlier when my grand-father died of natural causes. I was extravagantly upset upon hearing of this, jiggling my grief like a bad tooth the better to feel it. Any ecclesiastical music would set me off, and on one occasion when such was being played I embarrassed my father by exploding into tears while we were visiting a family we didn't know very well (John Betjeman's). He was irritated, I think, with my sentimentalising what to him must have been more genuinely moving. Or possibly my behaviour burlesqued his own ambivalent feelings; I do not know. Upon his own death some twenty years later I again felt deficient in deep feeling and twisted the event around and about in my head to bump a nerve. Since his death was also of public interest, I collected all the obituaries from *Time* and the *New York Times*, etc., to try and get a line on how to value it, but never developed a purely private reaction to it.

As I got older I developed a clearer focus on my family. My father, whom I half-consciously modelled myself on, on the one hand, I perceived as being weak and abdicating as a parent, on the other. Perhaps to compensate for his deficiency in standing up for me in combat with my stepmother, I tried not very successfully to make a virtue of her defects – reading inconsistency and anger as warmth and depth of personality. I hungered for her tempestuous handwriting in letters at school, letters which even I could see almost competed with my own lists of football scores and requests for food by being invari-ably accounts of successes on the concert stage and important people met. Above all, I couldn't help but feel that my father didn't really like her, but had slipped into marrying her through laziness. When they separated within a few years of my emigration to America I was quite unsurprised, although now I feel I wasn't altogether entitled to such a glib lack of surprise at the time. Indeed my own first marriage many years later caricatured in some respects the polarisation of the partners as I had perceived it.

In the winter of 1946–7, when I was twelve, my mother had to come over to England in connection with the various and complex Wills her 'rupee' grandfather had left before his death during the war. Her coming caused my family considerable anxiety as to what effect it might have on me. The decision was made to limit our contact to two brief visits in order to perpetuate the somewhat unreal fairy-godmother role she had filled hitherto. Throughout the war she had sent us copious parcels of food containing such exotica as peanut butter and Sun Maid raisins. She was also a prolific letter writer, always signing her name 'Mary' as my father had originally recommended. The agreement on limited contact was discarded almost immediately, as the opportunity to use her as a babysitter, not only for me but for my three-year-old sister who promptly fell in love with her, was too fortunate to ignore. The winter of 1946–7 was grimmer than most and coincided with the depths of postwar austerity: people went about shrouded in blankets and endured constant power shutdowns. My mother's arrival at such a time was sensational. Enormously large (her petite doll's figure had become and remained matronly upon my birth), she appeared huger yet in an opulent fur coat and her American accent broadened the image further. Everything about her seemed to be brand new yet with throw-away value, from luggage to ballpoint pens (barely known in England at that time), and hence unreal. She left as she had come, a fantasy figure from a fantasy world.

I remained at school in England, continuing to find life overly demanding and myself not too well-equipped to deal with it. None of my schools were horror places in any Dickensian respect – indeed as English private schools they bordered on the benign – but they were uncomfortable, physically and socially. I had so little self-confidence in dealing with my peers that for quite a long time I attempted to curry favour with them with sacrificial gifts: a valuable stamp collection of my grandfather's, American food that I had scarcely touched, and other things went in this manner, to short-term avail. Because I was 'different' (the only dark-eyed brunet other than myself was called Blume and he was eventually hounded from the school, leaving me as the sole Jewish hostage, as it were), I felt compelled to over-prove my worth and I became a buffoon and raconteur, keeping a tableful of mealtime listeners respectfully engaged, if hardly spellbound, by serial storytelling. Half-consciously craving the male guidance and authority I didn't get from my father, I sought it in some of my schoolmasters, making great efforts to win the approval of those I deemed worthy. My school assignments were carried out in an almost wooing manner and presented like the stones penguins lay at the feet of their prospective mates.

My final year at public school was somewhat of a disaster. I projected my despondency onto the universe and developed a severe case of what my stepmother called the Cosmic Blues, managing to ridicule and reduce their gravity thereby. 'What's it for? What's the meaning of it?' etc., and if I couldn't discover the purpose of it all, there was little point in bothering about anything. I became indifferent to grades and let everything slide. The only time I can remember my father being seriously dismayed by my school performance was when my reports for Art became as bad as for anything else. He now declared that he had always hoped that I would find my own province in art, beyond everyone's shadow as it were.

The summer of 1952 when I was eighteen years old and about to leave school was a watershed period in my life. My family had now fully wakened to the realisation that I apparently had no particular aim as to what to do next. Indeed the whole question of my future had been barely alluded to up till then by anybody. My father sporadically joked to friends (in my presence) that he would probably 'have to support Dan in a garret!' without appearing to mind the prospect. My stepmother once wondered whether 'Dan should go to Oxford before going in the army?' (England still had conscription and had military contingents in Korea. Some of my school acquaintances had died there.) But on the whole there had been remarkably little concern and I think the assumption was that connections and string-pulling would take care of things. I remember vague talk of picture cleaning at the National Gallery in London.

Shortly before I left school it was decided that my problems must derive from the need to reconnect with my mother and urgent appeals were sent to her to come over 'if only for a weekend' before I drifted into the army. I think there was a conscious fear that I might get myself killed from sheer inertia or at least do something psychologically messy, and nobody wanted to be left holding the bag. My mother at that point was running a chicken farm in New Jersey almost single-handedly and couldn't drop everything to rush over to England even if she had believed she could solve it all in a weekend, which of course she thought was absurd. So plans were reversed and I was plonked on a transatlantic liner and shipped off to New York after being granted two months' deferment from National Service.

Despite the family's anxiety to have me straighten out the mother thing, the incredible attempt was made to run it all like 1946. I was sent off with a notebook of names and addresses from Connecticut to Chicago and urged to visit them and get around generally after a few requisite days on my mother's farm. The greater and well-founded fear was that I might reach the farm and move no farther, which is exactly what happened. It didn't take me long to realise that I could stay there forever and avoid having to deal with the question of my future. My mother's second husband, whom I had never met except during infancy, had divorced her several years previously and in some respects I was able to step into his shoes. After I had sufficiently horrified her with revelations of my 'neglected' childhood, my mother did little to dissuade me from digging in and catching up on the motherless years. What was supposed to be a six weeks' visit became seven months after I obtained further deferment from the British National Service. But in order to convert my visitor's visa to an immigrant's I had to return to England, running the risk of being drafted while there. My English family and friends were appalled to hear of my intentions though hardly surprised.

In March of 1953 I returned to England (ironically while my family was on a lecture/recital tour in the US) and immediately started trying to obtain a visa with all possible speed. I was not so enamoured of my mother that I was prepared to be drafted twice, or so enchanted by America although it was obvious that life could be easier here. Neither was chicken farming unreservedly alluring. I was still afraid of animals and dreaded collecting eggs: the hens would pluck at the back of one's hands while fixing one with a malevolent gaze. But once I got it all started it developed its own momentum and I clung to the requisite ambition.

I almost pulled it off. The visa was about to be granted, only a few weeks after I had applied, when the American Embassy in London noticed that I was a minor (nineteen) and insisted on having my father's written consent for me to emigrate. He refused to give it, not because of my going to America *per se*, but he couldn't sanction my retreat to the womb. I broke from him absolutely and went into hiding while my mother's London lawyers attempted to circumvent the consent requirement. For nine months I was subsidised by my mother and lived in suburban hotels, moving from one to another whenever I bumped into acquaintances who might reveal my where-abouts. During this period I nurtured my hostility to the family, although as time went on I began to have second thoughts about leaving England, which I now began to see through adult eyes. I also started meeting bright girls, who were doing interesting things like anthropology or sociology (subjects I had barely heard of) at

Cambridge or the University of London, and who urged me to chuck the mission and go to a university like everyone else.

By the greatest fortune I was rejected by the British Army on account of my nearsightedness. (They were sensitive to eyes at that moment having just caused a scandal by conscripting somebody who was totally blind. Three years later the US Army had no such squeamishness and I was summarily drafted, notwithstanding my claims of the hardship imposed thereby on my mother.) Finally in December the lawyers produced a Queen's Counsel's Opinion that persuaded the American Embassy that it could grant me the visa without any liability on its part despite my father's objection.

On the day I sailed I was urged by mutual friends to say goodbye to my father in person as I would probably regret it one day if I did not. I had won my case and my anger at his earlier obstruction had cooled so I agreed without much demur and we met for a couple of poignant hours before I caught the boat train to Southampton. Our discussion was light; he asked what I thought of the documentary movie then playing about the ascent of Mount Everest for which he had written the narrative, and was curious whether I had noticed some technical lapses in the footage. One of these, although I had not noticed, was the naked hand of Hillary or Tensing when they were at, or close to, the summit. An ungloved hand would not survive at that altitude (this part of the film was obviously made elsewhere) and I later wondered whether his pointing this out had symbolic significance, even though we discussed it with amusement. I think we both realised at this moment of parting that in some ways we had never really known each other and that each had failed the other in our relationship, probably from the fear of closeness. Then he gave me a scarf which I put away carefully like a religious relic and wore for the first time when I visited his grave almost thirty years later. The train pulled away and we never met again.

2. A Grandson's Memories of Bishop's House

When I was little I noticed that all the really admirable grown-ups around me had occupations that required the wearing of some sort of uniform. All my step-grandmother's male cousins or in-laws were military officers with tabs and braid, moustaches and hearty voices. My grandfather, while softer spoken, had a roomful of garments and gaiters and I knew that the quantity of buttons on the latter denoted the highest rank of all. He had surplices of various hues and although I didn't know what their differences signified I was impressed by their number: you could tell the man deserved them, as he did the tumbling amount of his dioceses, 'Down, Connor, and Dromore', possibly much more.

But at the same time they were cloaks of invisibility, almost like a waiter's or doorman's. I seem to remember the fact of him more than I do the person and when I look at photographs showing the both of us, the occasion may be clearly revived and my little sailor-suit familiar, but my grandfather's presence in the deck chair beside mine is just that, an unexpected image. Perhaps because we were so constantly together I never developed a three-dimensional view of him, or if I did, it faded sooner than the image of more minor players who outlived him.

Looking back on it, I can recognise that he was skilled in his civilian role of grandfather and could perform the minor magic that goes with the part. When I blew on his gold watch the lid flew open and I suspended any suspicion that it might be done by his thumb – as I would to this day. We spent much time together in the Bishop's House study, deep in studded, creaky leather that was hard to arise from. It was the studdiest room in the house, hence its name, and the darkest and it was conducive to our jointly separate occupations. Memorable among these in my own case were long hours spent messing about with sealing wax, which I stamped extravagantly with his episcopal ring on large sheets of paper provided for the purpose. I can't imagine my father being allowed to do anything so incendiary at the same age or, come to think of it, to profane the insignia of office with such trivial use. Meanwhile, I must have put more mileage on the ring than ever the rightful owner did and am thus the rightful heir to it. It rests with the gold watch and the other mementos in purple velvet-lined cases in a safety deposit box, but all their lids fly open when my back is turned.

Both my grandparents indulged my running rings around them but somehow I knew when to stop. I beat the gong for meals in moderation and would scratch the microphone of my grandmother's hearing aid with no more vigour than would amuse her. Above all I respected the solemnity of religion in the house and would sit next to my grandmother in church or at dining room prayers without fidgeting. They both read to me from the Old and New Testaments or 'Little Lamb, Who Made Thee?' and I knew to keep any misgivings to myself. I was badly spooked by the story of Nicodemus, who 'came by night', and listening to it in a subdued pool of light in the darkened study I was convinced that anyone with the name Nicodemus would inevitably come skulking round in the small hours. In fact, I had recurring nightmares about him for years but I never insulted my grandparents' sympathy for him by letting on about them.

Perhaps stronger than my memory of Nicodemus is the one I have of motoring with the family early in the Second War. We were constantly on the road, either within Belfast or on stately progresses to far-flung churches or Big Houses in the hinterland. The big maroon car would crunch up the gravel to the front steps and my grandfather would get in the front with his 'doctor's' type of bag and sit next to John, the chauffeur. My grandmother and I and anyone else would sit in the back – she with her hearing aid suddenly squealing on her knee like a black cereal box awakening. These trips were at once enjoyable – most children approve of movement – and harrowing: there were occasional barricaded checkpoints where one could be stopped for identity card inspection. I had a crushing fear that we would be caught at one of these, having forgotten to bring our cards, and would wind up in prison or worse. I think this anxiety was contributed to by the appearance of the police: with their squarish caps and black uniforms, truncheons and revolvers, they were a distinct species and certainly not to be trifled with.

I don't think we were ever actually stopped at a barricade – with or without our identity cards – and were usually waved through, snaking slowly around the obstacles, but I never noticed a pattern and was convinced that disaster awaited us. In retrospect I am now impressed that my grandparents refrained from any reassurance based on social position. They could perhaps have said, 'You don't have to worry; we'll never be stopped and even if we were it wouldn't matter if we didn't have our identity cards: the law isn't aimed at the likes of us', but they didn't. They merely tried to assure me that we always had our cards at the ready, showing them to me if I became too persistent, but I was never really satisfied that that was sufficient.

My father had noticed that my grandfather 'seemed to know half the population by name' (though he was referring to the West), and it's pretty obvious to me now that the other half must have known who *he* was. Certainly our presentation must have gained us safe passage even when they didn't: his 'square black figure' next to his chauffeur's lanky one – the latter, indeed, costumed very much like the police of the barricades – would hardly suggest that we might be illegal aliens or German agents.

German bombs in the garden eventually compelled my evacuation to the neutral side of the Border, but before they did I accompanied my grandmother around the house as she taped the windows against blast. She did this very precisely, crisscrossing the panes with exact rectangles of brown tape and I could understand why she took on the job herself rather than delegating it to the domestic staff. Among the latter, though, was the equally responsible Rebecca Shaw, my grandparents' long-term housekeeper, whom I revered and would follow about the house like a little equerry. She and I worked as a team preparing the dining room for periodic Ordination Dinners. I cranked the expandable table to its greatest length, almost that of the room itself, and together we inserted the extra leaves. My grandfather was not present, of course, during these preparations which swirled about him as they might the tranquil eye of a hurricane. The centre of the household, his presence at these times was as invisible as God's.

Towards the end of my sojourn in his house I went with him on the occasion of his 'christening' a recently built aircraft carrier which was about to depart on its maiden mission, but I'm sorry to say I don't remember its short-lived name. I was excused from attendance at the ceremony before the massed crew while a sailor was appointed to escort me on a tour of the ship. Our progress was slow as I clambered through the many bulkhead doors which had thresholds at least a foot high above the deck, although I was delighted by this feature of naval architecture. Our tour culminated in the captain's empty cabin, a remarkably small room for such an officer but filled with intriguing artifacts. Among these I remember a pair of spectacles that folded in the middle of the bridge piece like a collapsing bicycle and a broad-based decanter that broke into music when lifted. Then we repaired to the flight deck to watch crates of ammunition being loaded aboard, each shell vividly tipped in varying colours according to calibre.

A month or so later we heard that the ship had been sunk by enemy action, and I began to realise that the world must be less reliable than I had supposed. How could wickedness have triumphed after the insurance of my grandfather's blessing? All those carefully painted shells and the folding glasses and the friendly crew, all vanished away for what? And when my grandfather declined the offer of the Church of Ireland Primateship shortly afterwards on grounds of declining health, and retired from the bishopric soon after that, I became yet more dismayed. When the word 'retirement' was explained to me I felt it was quite out of character for him to do such a thing. His death, following almost immediately, devastated me although I was hardly surprised. Perhaps I knew him better than I now remember after all.

PURE FORM, IMPURE POETRY, AND LOUIS MACNEICE'S LETTERS

Jonathan Allison

However much is known about the poet, the poem remains a thing distinct from him. But poetry being firstly communication, a certain knowledge of the poet's personal background will help us to understand him, for his language is to some extent personal. It may be true that any contemporary poet is a mouthpiece of the Zeitgeist, but, as mouthpieces alter what you put into them, it is helpful to consider the shape of the mouthpiece itself. (*MP* 89)

1

In response to Pope's disavowal of any wish for 'Epistolary Fame', Bolingbroke added that his pleasure in reading others' letters arose partly from the fact 'we pry into a Secret which was intended to be kept from us'.[1] MacNeice was not immune to the appeal of literary letters, and admired the letters of Keats, but was disappointed by Joyce's. It may not always be entirely clear whether a poet's letters will help us or distract us from an understanding of the work, but MacNeice himself made claims in *Modern Poetry* for the value of 'a certain knowledge of the poet's personal background' (*MP* 89). Such contingent knowledge was part of the process of finding things out about a work which was necessarily 'impure' and highly mediated to begin with. The MacNeice letters – by turns urgent, philosophical, and polemical; charming, vivacious, or very occasionally dull – are crucial for an understanding of the accident and incoherence out of which the poetry emerged and found form. He was an inveterate letter writer, from his schooldays at Sherborne Prep to his final days at home, when he wrote to his daughter Corinna of a 'mystery temperature' acquired while potholing in Yorkshire to obtain recordings of sound effects, for his radio play, *Persons from Porlock*. Letters from school were at first a mandatory Sunday scrawl but he came to think of writing letters as an essential task, and for the adult poet the letter was sometimes a necessary release and a lifeline. At the same time, he was conscious that letters have an appeal precisely because they contain 'a Secret' which was intended to be kept from all but one reader and accordingly did not relish the idea of his private correspondence having a wide circulation. To his literary executor E.R. Dodds he wrote in November 1940, on the eve of a dangerous Atlantic crossing:

> In case any mug wants to publish any of my letters (my solicitor in London kept mentioning that possibility), I do not want any letters to my father or stepmother to be published as they nearly always contain some falsity. I also regret most of my undergraduate letters (esp. to Anthony Blunt) which are nearly always v. affected & forced but I suppose they might be amusing to social historians. (*L* 415)

It might be claimed that few boarders have written a letter home entirely free from some falsity, and part of the pleasure of his letters to Anthony Blunt and John Hilton is that very affectation – sometimes reaching to a high camp – which was an aspect of his burgeoning sense of personality as a writer and artist, what Peter McDonald has called his 'artist's pose... a deliberate, almost aggressive decision to be "difficult"'.[2]

MacNeice is known as author of *Autumn Journal* and as co-author of a volume with the epistolary title, *Letters from Iceland*, where the intimacy between the speaking voice of the poet and that of the diarist and the correspondent respectively is implicitly acknowledged. He would brood upon the image of the letter elsewhere, as in the poem 'Day of Renewal', in which discarded and useless letters have piled up like garbage, signs of a decaying past that must be immolated by the poet's imagination: 'old letters and dead leaves; / My odd job conscience lights a bonfire / Which gasps and crackles, exults and grieves' (*CP* 353). In the later poem 'October in Bloomsbury' (1962), the Royal Mail postbox and its contents comprise a scene of nostalgia and death, where 'Edwardian pillar boxes wait for Edwardian letters; the Museum / Spreads its dead hands wide' (*CP* 591). And in 'Letter from India', dedicated to his second wife Hedli (he wrote the poem in 1947, on his first expedition to India), he describes letters crossing in the post ('each answer coming late and little') as a metaphor for missed connections and self-division:

Our letters cross ...
[...]
The air-mail being no avatar,
And whence I think I know you are
I feel divided as for ever. (*CP* 295)

In some ways therefore, the epistolary scene in MacNeice's imagination is haunted by silences and unfulfilled expectations, and the
letter is unsatisfactory not least because of the distances between the
written and the spoken word, and between literature and life itself.
Writing to his American lover Eleanor Clark in 1940, he expressed
frustration with the limits of his own writing but also perhaps with
the limits of writing in general:

> Darling, ink is a God-damned frigid medium, isn't it? There are
> so many things I feel like saying to you but as, even when I am
> with you, it sometimes seems like playing out of turn, I guess it is
> even more out of turn on paper.[3]

Communicating by letter is like a card game in which timing is everything and one cannot play (or write) out of turn, but the conditions
in which letters are derived and delivered make perfect timing and
clear communication difficult or impossible. It is appropriate that for
a poet whose ear was pitch-perfect, timing, like cadence and nuance,
should be so important. The word 'frigid' suggests the distance he
feels between the life of language and the life of the body and the
emotions; it is a common enough complaint about the aridity of the
written letter in comparison with the physical presence of the
beloved; it is an instance of the lover's plea for the insufficiency of
letters. Yet despite these laments, MacNeice's letters in all their
warmth, vitality, and precision, in fact prove something close to the
opposite. If his poems might suggest that letters are dead leaves, in
the deadly grip of inertia, his own letters are richly expressive of a life
lived fully, and ultimately the letter for MacNeice was a figure vari-
ously of community and friendship, of intimacy and desire.

I suppose one of the pleasures to be found in an author's letters is
hearing the poet's voice in a different register from the registers he
or she uses in the poems. Or hearing a trusted poetic voice, with its
trusted authority, in the informal cadences of a scribbled note. W.B.
Yeats attempted to delineate the relationship between these kinds of

voices, or between poetry itself and the quotidian, in a famous passage from 'A General Introduction for My Work' written for the Scribner edition in 1937:

> A poet writes always of his personal life, in his finest work out of its tragedy, whatever it be, remorse, lost love or mere loneliness; he never speaks directly as to someone at the breakfast table, there is always a phantasmagoria. Dante and Milton had mythologies, Shakespeare the characters of English history, of traditional romance; even when the poet seems most himself, when he is Raleigh and gives the potentates the lie, or Shelley 'a nerve o'er which do creep the else unfelt oppressions of mankind', or Byron when 'the heart wears out the breast as the sword wears out the sheath', he is never the bundle of accident and incoherence that sits down to breakfast; he has been re-born as an idea, something intended, complete.[4]

Yeats insists that poetry is rooted in the personal but that the voice of the poem is always in a different category from the voice of the biographical subject, which is heard in this conceit over breakfast. This too was MacNeice's point when he wrote 'However much is known about the poet, the poem remains a thing distinct from him' (*MP* 89). Yeats's 'phantasmagoria' may be understood as the shaping power of the imagination, the force which transforms the personal into the formal order of poetry, bringing the personal life into the impersonal mask of the poem. And Yeats's poetry, while rooted in the personal, strives for the authority of a public persona which is almost the opposite of the personal but which has an intimate relationship with the self, as its 'anti-self'. In Yeats's work, the notion of remaking the self would be central, whether in the case of revising his early poetry for the 1895 *Poems* – or in the case of proclaiming, in his later poem 'An Acre of Grass': 'Myself must I remake,/Till I am Timon and Lear / Or that William Blake / Who beat upon the wall'.[5] If the personal is changed by the 'phantasmagoria' in the poetic process, the letter presents itself as a mode of writing much closer to that 'bundle of accident and incoherence' that sits down to breakfast. The relationship between the voice in the letter and the persona of the poem can tell us much about the tension between the incoherence of the life and the order and shape of the artwork. The letter is closer to modes of life-writing like diaries and journals (which are themselves at one remove from the more polished and sculpted forms of memoir and autobiography), but at times the letter can be close to the work of the journalist, as for instance MacNeice's letters home from India at the time of the handover of power in 1947, or from the Gold Coast in 1956, on the eve of Ghanaian independence, where letters to his wife Hedli included detailed observations of people and events, self-conscious records of what occurred. All of which was part and parcel of what MacNeice considered the work of and the persona of the poet. After all, one of his central claims in *Modern Poetry* (1938) is that the poet should be 'a reader of the news-papers, capable of pity and laughter, informed in economics, appreciative of women, involved in personal relationships, actively interested in politics, susceptible to physical impressions' (*MP* 198). As such, the work of the journalist, the correspondent, and the polit-ical commentator was fundamentally tied to the imaginative and intellectual life of the practising poet.

2

MacNeice went to Marlborough in 1921 at the age of fourteen, remaining there until 1926, when he left for Oxford. In his last year at Marlborough, he shared a room with Anthony Blunt, whose views on the visual arts, and much else, proved very influential. MacNeice read Joyce, Lawrence, and Woolf, participated in debating societies, and contributed to literary magazines, including *The Marlburian*. As E.R. Dodds writes, the young MacNeice was an aesthete and purist and believed (or affected to believe) in what he called Significant (or Pure) Form: 'From his school days onwards Louis had been influ-enced by the aestheticism that was fashionable in the nineteen-twenties: things (he had been taught to believe) were more interesting than people; art was more interesting than life; and in art all that mattered was Significant Form – its content was quite unim-portant.'[6] He took this notion from Clive Bell's 1914 study *Art*, which had an enormous impact on MacNeice's circle at the time: 'Even before leaving Marlborough we had swallowed Significant Form' (*SF* 234). Blunt, who was the leading proponent of Bell's theories at Marlborough, argued that objects should be examined in isolation from their immediate surroundings, the better to examine their fundamental structure and shape, their 'most essential and intrinsic quality'.[7] By the time MacNeice had left Marlborough in the summer of 1926, he was already distancing himself from all this. As he later explained, he took it upon himself when he went to Oxford to dispense with his schoolboy beliefs: 'I felt hampered by this lack of belief or system and in my first term there (1926) I wrote a paper which was a puritanical recantation of the doctrines expressed in my school papers' (*MP* 63). Disowning Pure Form (and 'pure anything') was the first heave. And he claimed that an alternative to Pure Form was 'Self-Expression', i.e. 'the expression of certain Egotistical Moods – for example nostalgia for childhood, Wanderlust, terror' (*MP* 60). He became very good at expressing himself in his letters moodily, petulantly, exorbitantly, and portentously. It helped to know that it was called 'Self-Expression'. He wrote to Anthony Blunt from Carrickfergus on 25 September 1926, shortly before going to Oxford:

> I don't believe in pure form. I don't believe in pure anything. Anything pure is an abstraction. All concretes are adulterated. Sorry to rave. I wish you dreams of Edward's eyes. I am afraid they're not pure anything either. Only space is pure and won't it dull, except from the edge. The shore of the sea is far jollier than the middle. (*L* 122)

He would not have used the term 'liminal' but it seems clear that the shore is more attractive precisely because it is in-between the land and sea; it offers a zone of encounter where two elements meet. Dialogue is more interesting than monologue, and how one object stands in relation to another is more important than the essential structure of an object in isolation. Implicit here is the contrast between the purity of the Platonic Form and the particularity and 'impurity' of the concrete. The idea of purity therefore (apart from any puritanical sexual notions which may adhere to it) MacNeice associates with abstraction, and in the same letter this budding student of Oxford philosophy rails against philosophical theory:

> I'm tired of theories. It will be some time before I read another 'aesthetic'. Theories are the combination of abstractions & an abstraction is the rough & ready term that covers a lot of individual concretes. It saves time but it doesn't lead anywhere. To talk about the man-in-the-street is easy but doesn't give you any information about the men in the street.

A year later (27 June 1927) he would tell his stepmother, Georgina, whom he came to think of as rather Victorian, to go in fear of abstractions:

> The point is that the Victorians fed on abstractions and were sick. We have returned to the concrete and so laid ourselves open to the charge of triviality. But we can build art out of those tangible odds and ends. The day of the chameleon who feeds on air is over. Ordinary man is more like an ostrich. He thrives on broken glass and rusty nails. I have just read a brilliant novel – 'To the Lighthouse', by Virginia Woolf – illustrating this. (*L* 169)

The semi-conspiratorial 'we' is intended to implicate him with modernist authors such as Joyce and Woolf, and suggests a manifesto-like gesture towards what he aspires to in his own work, based on concrete image and the fragment. If this seems to echo Pound's strictures on literary abstractions, it foreshadows the kind of declaration he himself would make in *Modern Poetry* and other essays almost a decade later. Similarly, in a public letter to W.H. Auden in *New Verse* in October 1937, he praised his fellow poet for introducing to modern poetry the language of politics, economics, and psychoanalysis (which is 'one in the eye for Bloomsbury'):

> Other philosophies have described the world; our business is to change it. Add that if we are not interested in changing it, there is really very little to describe. There is just an assortment of heterogeneous objects to make Pure Form out of. (*L* 305)

By this stage, MacNeice is as close as he will come to espousing a poetics of political engagement, although the heady notion of changing the world remains without any root in a specific political practice, and is perhaps equally assimilable to a vaguely Yeatsian romanticism as it is to a more focused, or limited, or Audenesque political commitment. One can certainly sense his satisfaction at joining with Auden in a group dismissal of the anachronistic Pure Form, without sensing anything much more specific than that.

3

Soon after the *Queen Mary* sailed from New York harbour on 21 April 1939, MacNeice started writing to Eleanor Clark, whom he had recently met at a *Partisan Review* party in New York ('It was simply horrifying not being able to see you on the pier', *L* 314). So began a correspondence that lasted until July 1942, when he married the singer Hedli Anderson. It may be said that Atlantic crossing is an apt term for their correspondence more generally. His first extended letter to Clark from the *Queen Mary* contains much that is stylistically typical of his letters in general and his love letters in particular: the division of the letter into parts, over several days; the use of the ubiquitous ampersand to conjoin sentences breathlessly; lots of underlining and capitalisation for emphasis; the combination of imploring amorous demands and personal narrative; recounted anec-dote (often comic) with detailed listing of descriptive imagery; the account of reading and writing recently completed – with glancing judgments on that; the use of dashes (and parentheses) to frame asides and express self-interruption or self-qualification, following the flow of thoughts and feelings and second-thoughts. The frequent admis-sion of agitation and emotional dependency; the frustration with his work and his admission of incomplete and fragmented projects (the failed Greek translation): all of these are typical. One is made aware of a degree of accident and incoherence in the life witnessed by letters like these, and at the same time one senses the struggle – often through tabulated argumentation, persuasive rhetoric, cataloguing of reasons or facts – to establish coherence, whether amatory, affective, artistic, and even political.

During the latter part of 1939 much of their discussion concerns the imminent war and its outbreak, and whether or not to join the war effort, (MacNeice remained divided on this issue until 1940, at which point, when teaching at Cornell University, he realised that if he did not return to Britain he would be, in his own words, 'missing History'). A recurring subject, too, is the Left and in particular the Trotskyite position on the war, since Clark had been a fellow-traveller and had been married to Trotsky's Czech secretary, Jan Frankl, although was by now disillusioned both with her husband, from whom she was separated, and to a greater or lesser extent with his Russian master and his followers. At the same time, her views on Britain and the outbreak of war were firmly shaped by her political

education. MacNeice frequently entertained the idea that a choice
between Chamberlain and Hitler was a choice between two evils,
before firmly coming down against Hitler.

Few sequences in the extant correspondence of MacNeice are
more passionate than the letters to Clark, and the full range of his
intelligence and personality is on constant alert, and on full show. He
had published *Autumn Journal* in spring 1939 and his influential essay
Modern Poetry the year before, and several of the arguments rehearsed
in that book surface refashioned in the course of his arguments with
Clark. His quarrel with Significant Form and his rejection of Pure
Form led to the notion of a poetry of 'impurity' and to his dismissal
of the so-called 'pure poetry' associated with Mallarmé and Valéry.
By contrast, the poets of his own generation (Auden, Spender) have
'a Greek preference for information or statement'. They 'have something to say' (*MP* 22). His own attempts to develop 'a world view'
were influenced early on by his notion of flux. He started using the
concept of flux in relation to the modernists whom he admired,
Joyce, Lawrence, and Woolf – 'who give you the flux but serve it on
golden platters … they were the acolytes of Flux' (*SF* 118–19). 'I am
in a sad state over art and am all for flux as opposed to hard lines' he
explained to Blunt in 1926 (*L* 120), but it is not a notion he had much
recourse to thereafter, except for a moment of comical self-dramatic
dithering in a letter to Clark in June 1939:

> It's awful to be so fluxy as me, you know. The only things I feel
> definite about are concretish things & what I like to eat or to wear
> or other people to wear or the sound of a line of verse or how to
> sleep with people or whether X is nicer company than Y or Z a
> nicer place than Q. [B]ut when it comes to these awfully compli-
> cated international problems where one's never seen X or Y or Q
> or Z, I feel terribly uncertain. (*L* 343)

By the spring of 1940, he was of a mind to put away childish things
like flux, and to steer a course between Heraclitean flow and the
Marxian dialectic. He was formulating a new attitude, he explained
to Mrs Dodds, that freedom was not getting out of things but getting
into them. Maybe the war might be a good thing after all? 'Because
it seems high time neither to be passive to flux nor to substitute for
it, Marxist-like, a mere algebra of captions' (*L* 381). Being passive to
the flux was like being passive to the war itself, indeed the war was

itself one enormous chaos, against which one might create private spheres of order and grace, the grace of friendship. He noted to Clark in April 1941 that he was becoming more friendly on the whole, 'getting pallier & pallier with the World in General – rather on a taproom plane, I suppose, & perhaps it's a substitute for sex. But – in this great flux – it's comparatively a solid' (*L* 429).

In *Modern Poetry*, MacNeice regrets that a world view is something the Georgians lacked, but he admired Yeats's, even though it was obscure, and Eliot's, even though it was 'defeatist'. Ought he not to have one then? Yes, eventually, but not if it attached one to some philosophy that did not fit. Having been angered by Clark's accusation that he was 'aloof' and aesthetic (particularly irksome after he had pointed out he had become more pally with the world), he replied that 'world view', like *weltanschauung*, seemed very 'Teutonic' and that his scepticism about the American Left was not merely a matter of British 'hand-to-mouthness'. Here, as elsewhere, readers may feel grateful that MacNeice's letters to Clark provided so many opportunities for him to stage the debates which clarify his position with such vigour, even if the 'position' does not always stay the same. In May 1940 he wrote to Clark:

> I suppose you think the reason I haven't got a lovely comprehensive world-view is that I amn't interested in world-views. When I was married I <u>did</u> try to do without a world-view but it was a failure & I have known for years that I must develop one & I am trying to develop one but I am damned if I am going to swallow Marx or Trotsky or anyone else lock stock & barrel unless it squares with my experience or, perhaps I should say, my feelings of internal reality. (*L* 396)

If MacNeice's 'impure poetry' entailed the rejection of viewing objects and discourses in isolation, his rejection of Marxist and Trotskyite readings of politics and society (and in particular the state of Britain in 1939) entailed opposing what he saw as all kinds of reductive, 'purist' thinking. His attacks on Trotskyism in his letters to Clark in 1939 frequently resort to the notion of purism – 'a nice pure revolution' – as a signal intellectual failure in relation to politics and society. Clark seems at times to be arguing for a strategically pacifist response to Nazi aggression in order to prepare for proletarian revolution in Britain, but MacNeice finds the idea childish, impractical and preposterous. His inclusion here of the word 'pure' in a letter of April 1939 suggests the depth of his disgust:

> It's no good telling the ordinary people throughout Europe to keep their hands clean of power politics & sit down & let Hitler win until they have the chance of a nice pure revolution of their own – a <u>holy</u> war. Because if Hitler wins Europe, they won't have the chance. (*L* 318)

He points out that Lenin himself did not recommend 'this pure no-compromise attitude' but recommended working with 'reactionary' Parliamentary reform and the trade unions (*L* 336). Childishly and impractically, the English Trotskyites wish to keep 'their hands pure of degrading contacts' (*L* 337). One must choose the better of two evils and that means supporting Chamberlain. Anything else is uncompromisingly purist, based on stubborn adherence to 'theory' and 'abstract' dogma. Survival depends upon making the pragmatic compromise:

> If you are dying of thirst & you have to choose between filthy water & poison, you choose the filthy water; you don't say 'I only drink pure water.' Your position, darling, wouldn't be realistic over here.[8]

It is likely that his rhetorical dependence at this time on the notion of purity had to do not only with his platform for a poetry of impurity but also with a mostly conscious preoccupation with the state of his romantic and eventual sexual relationship with Clark; he baulks at the possibility the friendship might become platonic:

> I'm not by nature in the least pure & I don't want to be but now, if you were to suddenly tell me to go impure, I feel I should be like someone who had forgotten the language.[9]

And occasionally MacNeice was capable of using the word 'pure' as a defence when it suited, as for instance when he insists to Dodds that sleeping with Margaret Gardiner 'happened as a pure accident'. Surely she should have known that any relationship with him would have to be 'purely ephemeral' (*L* 363). If this was an inconsistency he might have said that was an aspect of being human, and one cannot expect pure consistency except in the gods. Perhaps that would have been hedging his bets, of course. It was perhaps part of being Irish he might have said and he was not above resorting to using national stereotypes in order to borrow an empowering Irishness as the occasion demanded. The light always changes in Ireland, he remarked in the course of inviting Eleanor Clark for a walking holiday in the West: 'Ireland is just a prism, you know, which is why you can't depend on the Irish – except one').[10] In February 1940 he shows he is not entirely immune to the charms of the pure, transcendent forms: snow is an absolute until it turns to slush (because it makes compromises). But it somehow remains snow, and the slush is something else entirely:

> [I]t is fun for the snow to have its moments because the Universal always longs to be concrete. Now I am beginning to sound Germanic so I must lay off because the Celtically minded don't talk about universals, they just sense them. (L 377)

If MacNeice found ink to be a 'frigid medium' it was through that other frigid medium, snow, that he found a way of bringing together some of the various strands of his preoccupations during this time: the universal might long for the concrete, and the pure might long for its opposite. In the frigid, written word he would figure the living, spoken word, and in the lineaments of the letter he might discern the lineaments of his lover. Snow seemed to him an absolute but so too did the roses in his poem 'Snow' in which he had intuited 'the drunkenness of things being various' (CP 24). He tells Clark in April 1939: 'The roses I wrote that poem about – in a window against the snow – always seem to be permanent, so perhaps Friday's could be too?' (L 321).

Back in June 1927, MacNeice was planning a trip to Paris with John Hilton (and, he hoped, Anthony Blunt), and wrote to his mother from Hilton's home in Northwood. He knew his parents had initially been reluctant to let him go, but 'one needs this reorientation'. Was Paris not today 'the vortex of art'? He would need his mother's written permission to apply for his passport. The passport was British, but on the eve of war in September 1939 he obtained an Irish passport. And it is perhaps appropriate that in the conclusion of a letter calculated to obtain a document which would guarantee the singular, stable national identity of the subject, MacNeice focused whimsically on the 'impure' variety of ethnic identities and selves which had been attributed to him, in a comic catalogue which owes something to the comic lineage he drew for himself three months earlier, establishing his descent from Conchubar MacNessa and Clytemnestra, and from Hamlet and Katherine of Aragon. From our vantage point, his claims to be 'polyglot' seem inadvertently to mock the kinds of essentialism which have informed discussions of Irish, British, and Anglo-Irish identities over the last century, and suggest the sense of plurality which has often been attributed to this poet's work:

I must really be very polyglot; John and I were counting up yesterday the racial qualities which people claim to have found in me: -

American	Indian
French	Japanese
Spanish	Negro
Italian	(Russian?)
Jewish	German.

This heterogeneity is very painful. I expect to fall to pieces like a jigsaw. (*L* 171–2)

'I WILL ACQUIRE AN ATTITUDE NOT YOURS': WAS FREDERICK MACNEICE A HOME RULER, AND WHY DOES THIS MATTER?

David Fitzpatrick

'Just another bourgeois liberal, I would have said. Although he was a great Home Ruler, in his day.' Nick laughed. 'Not a popular position for a Protestant clergyman, surely?' 'Carson hated him. Tried to stop him being made bishop.' 'There you are: a fighter.'

This exchange appears in John Banville's melodrama *The Untouchable* (1997), where Victor Maskell (Anthony Blunt's world-weary double-agent, incongruously grafted onto Louis MacNeice's Irish roots) discusses his father with Nick, another hybrid figure who turns out to be the Fifth or Sixth Man. Banville's account, though a travesty of what scholars have written about Frederick MacNeice,[1] demonstrates the pervasiveness of his posthumous reputation as a heroic outsider within the 'Black North'. Critics and biographers concur that Louis MacNeice's attitudes towards religion, morality, politics, and above all Ireland, were profoundly influenced by those of his clergyman father. Louis was both attracted and repelled by the unity and humanity of his father's world view, sustained by his serene faith in Christ as peace-maker and reconciler. The Rector (later Bishop) is almost universally portrayed as a tolerant if puritanical southerner, courageously opposing all forms of sectarianism and violence, abhorring both revolutionary Republicanism and Ulster Unionism, and supporting Home Rule.[2] Admittedly, Frederick MacNeice's early association with the Society for Irish Church Missions to the Roman Catholics, notorious for its 'aggressive' campaign of proselytism in both Connemara and Dublin, casts some doubt upon his liberal and non-sectarian credentials. However, it has been surmised that his parents' bruising experience of sectarian conflict while missionary teachers on Omey Island, culminating in the family's fabled flight in 1879,[3] left Frederick (then thirteen years old) with a lifelong detestation of sectarian confrontation and intolerance. His mental world as an adult was that of a liberal Protestant nationalist, fundamentally at odds with the political outlook of his congregations and neighbours in Belfast and Carrickfergus.

Louis MacNeice's supposed childhood experience of alienation within Protestant Ulster is often cited in explaining his youthful repudiation of its values and symbols, his romantic identification with the West of Ireland, and his sympathy with non-violent nationalist and anti-imperialist movements. By this account, while rejecting his father's religion and morality, Louis paradoxically embraced much of his outlook on Ireland and Irish politics. The Rector's presumed support for Home Rule is crucial to this widely held analysis of the poet's Irishness and political vision. Yet the supporting evidence is remarkably threadbare, being restricted to assertions by Louis himself, ambiguous utterances by his father in later life, and academic inferences based on possibly misleading extracts from published sermons and addresses. This essay will assess the credibility of such interpretations, present fresh evidence indicating a very different political viewpoint, suggest reasons for the subsequent disregard of such evidence, and assess the consequences for our understanding of the poet's Irishness and for our reading of some of his most celebrated works.

The most authoritative testimony to Frederick's nationalism is that of his son, whose imaginative and finely embroidered autobiographical writings have been so widely accepted at face value as a reliable factual source: 'My father was one of the very few Church of Ireland clergymen to be a Home Ruler. This was another reason for despising Co. Antrim and regarding myself as a displaced person. Sometimes this feeling caused an inner conflict in me' (*SF* 223). Another passage implies that Frederick's reputation as a Home Ruler was established before 1917, when his second wife was thought 'very daring' for having gone 'so far afield as my father – especially as he was a Home Ruler' (*SF* 62). These recollections were written in 1940, two decades after Home Rule had ceased to be a practical option (except for six counties of Ulster), and they reflect the 33-year-old poet's renewed respect for his father and for many aspects of both Southern Ireland and Ulster. Slightly earlier testimony may be found in *Zoo* (1938), where Frederick (as a 'pacifist' and a 'Home Ruler') is set apart from Ulster's 'patronising and snobbish' gentry, that 'inferior species';[4] and also in 'Auden and MacNeice: Their Last Will and Testament' (1936):

I leave my father half my pride of blood

And also my admiration who has fixed
His pulpit out of the reach of party slogans
And all the sordid challenges and the mixed

Motives of those who bring their drums and dragons
To silence moderation and free speech
Bawling from armoured cars and carnival wagons. (*CP* 732)

It is notable that Louis's numerous evocations of his boyhood give no particular illustrations of his father's nationalism, and that (in Jon Stallworthy's words) 'neither his letters home [from preparatory school] nor his parents' letters to him mention the worsening situation in Ireland' (*JS* 65). When at home, he appears to have paid little attention to political conversations, for his sister Elizabeth recalled that 'there was so much talk in the house about Carson and the [Ulster] covenant that he must have heard it though he never in later years seemed to have memory of doing so. Of course, he heard the history of it later on.'[5] It is difficult to avoid the conclusion that Louis MacNeice's account of his father's supposed nationalism was based on adult rather than childhood observations.

It is a curious fact that Frederick MacNeice himself never advocated or endorsed Home Rule in his many published booklets and sermons. As Christopher Fauske has guardedly averred: 'MacNeice had gone to Carrickfergus with a reputation as a Home Ruler, a reputation bolstered by his stance against the Covenant, but of his politics he actually said nothing in public throughout his life.'[6] Though not strictly accurate, as we shall show, this assessment highlights the difficulty of defining the political stance of one whose politics were avowedly non-partisan. The only text that has been cited as a direct affirmation of nationalism, as distinct from a disavowal of (Unionist) party politics, is Frederick's engaging historical sketch of Carrickfergus (1928):

The extension of the franchise in 1884 made inevitable some form of Home Rule for Ireland ... Election after election gave similar results. That surely was a writing on the wall. It was thought, however, that such warnings and verdicts could be disregarded. Arguments were reiterated for more than a generation which were a denial of the assumed meaning of democratic government. The true entity, it was urged, is Great Britain and Ireland. It is the majority in that unit that should count ... Ireland in so far as it was educated and rich was against Home Rule! Such arguments, and they had a very Prussian ring about them, did duty for a time.

MacNeice goes on to dismiss Carson's initial confidence that resistance in Ulster 'could defeat, and not simply delay, the whole Home Rule policy', and to deplore the growing acceptance of partition as the Ulster leaders themselves 'began to think along Nationalist lines'.[7] On the face of it, this analysis demonstrates that Frederick was not merely an opponent of partition, but a pragmatist who accepted, however reluctantly, the necessity for Home Rule. We shall return to the question of whether as a younger man he had indeed, like the prophet Daniel, accurately divined the ominous writing on the wall of Belshazzar's palace, *'mene, mene, tekel, upharsin'*: 'God hath numbered thy kingdom, and finished it. Thou art weighed in the balances, and found wanting. Thy kingdom is divided, and given to the Medes and the Persians.'

The practical proof of Frederick's nationalism, liberalism, and non-sectarianism, as expounded by a distinguished procession of MacNeiceans, relates mainly to four episodes: his public refusal to sign the Ulster Covenant in September 1912; his espousal of an ecumenical League of Prayer for Ireland between 1920 and 1924; his initiation of a similar campaign in 1935–6 in response to renewed sectarian conflict in Belfast; and his successful resistance in the same period to the Government's proposal that the Union Flag should officiate perpetually over Carson's grave in St Anne's Cathedral.[8] In each case, scholars have drawn inferences from Frederick's words and actions which are by no means self-evident. Opposition to the Ulster Covenant implied rejection of the threat of violence as a political tool, but not approval of any particular political programme. Collaboration with other Protestant clergymen, in two ecumenical and non-partisan campaigns for reconciliation, was likewise consistent with Unionism as well as nationalism. Finally, Frederick's refusal to sanctify Carson's legacy in the form of a flag raises the issue of which aspect of Carson's political career gave offence to his fellow-southerner. In order to test the implications of these episodes for our understanding of Frederick MacNeice's politics, we must first re-examine the historical record.

As Rector, Frederick joined several other local ministers on a committee to make 'arrangements for the celebration of Ulster Day in Carrickfergus' in 1912; although, 'in the absence of the text of the Covenant', he insisted that attendance at the various church services should not entail automatic endorsement of that document.[9] When addressing his congregation in St Nicholas's church, he undoubtedly caused a sensation by declaring that he personally (like others who approached the issue 'primarily from the Church's standpoint') would not sign the Covenant, feeling that 'Ireland's greatest interest is peace, and they shrink from a policy which, as is avowed, in the last resort, means war – and worse still, civil war'. Such a course would tend to 'intensify the bitterness that many of them hoped was fast dying away'.[10] This final passage from the sermon was extracted by Frederick himself in *Carrickfergus*, with a comment which conceals as much as it reveals: 'The ministers of religion in Carrickfergus, in permanent charges, did not sign the Covenant. They represented a minority, negligible indeed in numbers, whose conscientious scruples exposed them at the time to some adverse criticism.'[11] In a celebrated response, a butcher on the Select Vestry remarked: 'That was a grand sermon the Rector gave us. But he spoiled it all at the end by telling us he wasn't going to sign the covenant.'[12]

Oddly, no scholar appears to have scrutinised the omitted elements of that 'grand sermon', which reveal its author to have been an orthodox and unrepentant Unionist. The Rector declared that the opposition to Home Rule was 'democratic', working men being united by 'a common conviction that Home Rule would be a death blow to the industrial life of Ireland. In this opposition they are joined by the farmers of Ulster, and I may add of Ireland.' Even non-conformists in Ireland (unlike Britain) opposed Home Rule, because 'they know this country, its history, its circumstances'. MacNeice eloquently endorsed the widespread fear that a predominantly Roman Catholic parliament 'could not be trusted to do justice to a Protestant minority', citing the examples of Québec, Italy, France, and Spain: 'Is it any wonder that the Irish Roman Catholic has been described as a rebel whose feet are in British fetters and whose head is in a Roman halter? ... Are not the Bishops the patrons of the Party? Are not the Priests, almost as a rule, the chairmen of the local branches of the United Irish League?' Citing the absence of lay protests against enforcement of the infamous *Ne Temere* decree regulating 'mixed' marriages, he asked: 'Isn't the fear of the Irish Protestants a reasonable fear?', rejected all previous Irish parliaments as 'ghastly failures', and asserted that 'Ireland has self-government just as England and Scotland have'. MacNeice predicted that 'as the masses advance in prosperity and in education the desire for Home Rule and the interest in agitation will die away'. Meanwhile,

> let no word be spoken, let nothing be done to wound the feelings of our Roman Catholic neighbours. ... One of the chief reasons we oppose Home Rule is because we believe it would lessen individual liberty. ... And because such are our ideals, therefore, we recognise the rights of others, whether majorities or minorities, to think their own thoughts and be true to their own convictions.[13]

MacNeice's exposition of the case for the Union is utterly conventional in its terminology and assumptions, blaming nationalist disaffection on lack of education and on clerical domination, detecting signs of opposition to Home Rule among respectable Catholics, deploring all policies tending to undermine the gradual process of Anglo-Irish reconciliation, and echoing the ideals of liberty and toleration embedded in the 'Qualifications of an Orangeman'. Far from discerning 'a writing on the wall', MacNeice in 1912 still adhered to those very arguments with their 'very Prussian ring' which he was to formulate and dismiss so scathingly in 1928. By using the passive voice to express the failed Unionist position that he had once espoused, Frederick managed to mislead credulous posterity without actually lying. Like his son, he was an accomplished rhetorician who knew when and how to be economical with the truth. As Elizabeth observes so acutely: 'Both Louis and his father were very complex people, I think, and it was often hard to understand what was in their minds (though their minds were in many ways so different).'[14] Contemporaries, of course, were not so easily misled. When praising his 'brave act' in declining to sign the Covenant, a liberal weekly pointed out that 'Mr. MacNeice's Unionism is of too staunch a character and has been too often manifested in his parish for him to risk being dubbed a Home Ruler because he is commended in a Home Rule organ'.[15]

Frederick's sleight of hand was not an exercise in casuistry, but an understandable attempt to antedate the process by which he had gradually moved from optimism about the future of the Union to the conviction that it was doomed. On the first anniversary of Ulster Day, he reaffirmed his Unionist ideals:

> Why may not we claim, and rejoice to claim, that we are Irish, no matter what our remote ancestors called themselves, and that while remaining Irish we also can be members of a wider unity, sharers in the strength and glory of the Empire for which our fellow-countrymen have made such splendid sacrifices?

By then, however, he felt that 'a great wrong has been done on our side' through appeals 'to race hatred, and to religious, or rather irreligious bigotry'.[16] Seven months later, he warned a parade of Ulster Volunteers that they must submit, *in extremis*, to the mandate of the electorate:

> And speaking as a Unionist to Unionists I say – 'We must make it plain, abundantly plain, that while we are opposed to the change of Government now proposed, and with which we are now threatened, we are no less opposed to the thought of a war which would range us against the soldiers of the King, or against our fellow-countrymen.'

In the absence of an agreement, 'then there's no alternative but to demand that the question be submitted to the people of the United Kingdom. In making such appeal we know there are risks.'[17] The Rector's public commitment to the Union was expressed in his annual election as a Vice-President of the East Antrim Unionist Association between 1912 and 1918. But the threads of his Unionism were beginning to unravel as Carson's Ulster campaign shifted inexorably from all-Ireland rejection of Home Rule towards provincialism and acceptance of partition.

By December 1918, when 'the people' of Ireland returned a Republican majority while Lloyd George's coalition parties swept the polls in Britain with a bipartisan commitment to Home Rule, the existing Union had clearly lost its popular mandate. Four years later, with partition fait accompli and the Union 'gone', the Rector reminded the Orangemen of Carrickfergus that 'the old order whether for good or evil has passed away'. Ireland remained 'a unity geographically' and to some degree commercially, but 'political unity' could never be secured through military force. It could come only through the consent of the people themselves, North and South. ... If it became clear, as it might, that what was desired was a political unity, within the British Commonwealth ... then it should be possible, with goodwill on both sides ... to find a way to a final settlement of what has been known as the Irish question.[18]

Far from being a repudiation of his earlier beliefs, this cautious contemplation of unity by consent, within the Commonwealth, in the indefinite future, echoes the sentiments of a procession of liberal Unionists in Northern Ireland stretching from Sir James Craig to Sir Kenneth Bloomfield.

In July 1920, when Frederick MacNeice inaugurated his first ecumenical crusade for peace and reconciliation among all religious groups throughout Ireland, no practical possibility remained of keeping 'Southern Ireland' within the Union. Rather than campaigning against partition, also a lost cause, the Rector attempted to mobilise Christians of all denominations, 'Roman Catholic and Protestant alike', in a succession of enterprises designed to create 'a new outlook in Ireland' and to curtail the accelerating cycle of reprisals and counter-reprisals. The campaigns of 1920–24 and 1935–6 were exceptional only for their non-sectarian rhetoric, which carefully avoided both selective ascription of blame and expressions of selective empathy. Otherwise, the Christian message broadcast by MacNeice and his fellow-ministers was indistinguishable from that of countless sermons addressed to all denominations. The appeals for priestly collaboration in these crusades brought no response, though in late 1920 the Parish Priest of Carrickfergus commended his Protestant fellow-clergymen for helping to keep the town 'free from the evils that have arisen out of the recent labour troubles', by 'assiduously preaching peace and a Christian tolerance of the rights of their neighbours'.[19] MacNeice's Catholic counterpart as Bishop of Down and Connor (Dr Daniel Mageean) continued to portray his flock as guiltless victims of Protestant persecution while uttering his own separate appeal for peace in July 1935.[20] Though MacNeice's campaigns drew rapturous responses from the Catholic press and indignation from some diehard Ulster loyalists, his private assessment of Catholic leaders such as Bishop Mageean was far from laudatory. As 'Daddie' wrote to Louis and his then wife in September 1936: 'Yes, I fear the R.C. bishop & I were a bit mixed up in the English

papers. He was given credit for some of my appeals for fairminded-
ness &c, & I suffered occasionally because of some of his criticisms &
attacks!'[21] Though an eloquent advocate of ecumenical cooperation
and eventual reunion among the Protestant churches, Frederick was
less sanguine about the prospects for rapprochement with the Church
of Rome.[22] His only known public collaboration with a priest
involved the game which was later to obsess his son: in September
1909, both the Rector and the Parish Priest of Carrickfergus were
enrolled as 'Vice-Presidents or Patrons' of the town's Rugby Football Club.[23] Otherwise, Frederick's non-sectarian partnerships were
restricted to other Protestant denominations, several of his clerical
collaborators being prominent Orangemen.

MacNeice's reputation as a liberal dissentient from Ulster orthodoxy was enhanced by the decision of the Belfast Cathedral Board,
which he chaired, to withhold permission for the permanent display
of a Union Flag above Carson's tomb. The ostensible justification for
resisting Lord Craigavon's proposal was the lack of precedent in other
cathedrals for setting such emblems over civilian tombs or monuments, and the Board eventually mollified its detractors by agreeing
to place a flag over the memorial rolls of honour at the west end of
the cathedral.[24] Remarking on this compromise in a letter to Louis,
'Daddie' found 'much to rejoice over: the Clergy, in the main, and
the respectable people, including the working men, are with us'.[25] It
is far from clear that the Bishop had been primarily responsible for
the Board's unexpected declaration of independence. MacNeice was
nevertheless criticised by a Catholic correspondent for allowing
Carson's burial in the cathedral in the first place, so allowing St
Anne's to 'become a fashionable graveyard for "sham statesmen"'.[26]
'Sincere Churchmen' of his own persuasion also deplored the
conversion of a place of worship into a 'Mausoleum' for 'political
pilgrims', while pointing out that 'Ulster pilgrims from Monaghan,
Cavan and Donegal' would inevitably be reminded of 'a broken
covenant'.[27]

MacNeice was careful to avoid any public slight upon Carson's
memory, expressing 'deep regret' at the death of 'one of the
outstanding figures of his day, and one whose great gifts of head and
heart gave him a place of his own in the hearts of multitudes'.[28] The
Bishop played an admittedly minor part in the funeral service,
uttering the final words of prayer after the lowering of the coffin, over
which a Methodist minister had emptied the contents of a 'silver bowl

presented by the Northern Ireland Cabinet and containing soil from each of the Six Counties'.[29] This narrative was characteristically improved by Louis in a letter to Anthony Blunt, alleging that his 'father, a passionate Home Ruler, "had to sprinkle earth from the 6 Northern Counties on the coffin of … his lifelong bête noire out of a large gold chalice"' (L 258). Despite the Bishop's measured responses to these rituals of veneration in his cathedral, there is no reason to doubt the sincerity of his remark (in a letter to his daughter) that Carson would 'be remembered as the man who broke the unity of Ireland'.[30] This statement is generally assumed to refer to the unity promised for Ireland under Home Rule. In reality, it surely arose from the sense of betrayal felt by former 'Southern Unionists' with respect to those who opted for Home Rule in Northern Ireland, while ditching their southern brethren and antagonising nationalists throughout Ireland. This betrayal was aptly symbolised by the selection of soil from six counties (rather than nine or thirty-two) in tribute to the arch-partitionist. Carson's offence was to shatter Frederick MacNeice's dream of winning over Catholic minds and hearts to the ideals of the Union.

If Frederick MacNeice was never a Home Ruler, neither was he unreservedly liberal in matters of faith. Not only was he reared among the 'soupers' (proselytisers) and 'jumpers' (converts) of Connemara, but he followed the example of his parents and three elder siblings by taking paid employment with the Irish Church Missions. After two years' training and teaching with the Missions in Dublin, he went on to teach at a Protestant boys' orphanage in Ballyconree, near Clifden, near the Mission school where his future wife worked for over a decade before their marriage in 1902.[31] Frederick's father remained as a Scripture Reader with the Missions in Dublin until his retirement in 1905; and his widowed father-in-law, a zealous convert from Connemara, lived with Frederick and Lily in Belfast until his death in the following year. Far from severing his connection with the Missions and their aggressive sectarianism after the mythic flight from Omey, Frederick maintained an active connection with the Society throughout his career. His congregations in Belfast and Carrickfergus raised subscriptions for its work on at least seven occasions between 1903 and 1928; he served as an executive member of the Belfast Auxiliary for several years after 1907; and, like most Irish bishops, he became a Vice-President of the Society, upon his election in 1931.

On several occasions, he invited T.C. Hammond, an incorrigible proselytiser and Orangeman who became superintendent of the Dublin Missions, to address his congregation in Carrickfergus. Hammond was among the preachers at a festival in aid of the Missions staged in thirty-one churches in the Belfast region on 10 February 1935, the Sunday after Frederick's enthronement in St Anne's Cathedral. Though unable to attend the annual meeting of the Belfast Auxiliary on the following day, the Bishop wrote 'that the work of the Missions was primarily a work of witness for the faith in its primative [sic], uncorrupted form. ... He knew well that all who supported the Missions in Belfast and elsewhere had as their aim the uplifting of Christ, the King of Love.'[32]

In his campaigns for peace and reconciliation, Frederick applied the techniques perfected by Alexander Dallas, founder of the organisation, whose marketing strategies included massive mailshots and distribution of a multitude of handbills to supplement incessant exhortations from the pulpit and through the press. Though MacNeice's parishes in Belfast and Carrickfergus presented limited opportunities for the conversion of Roman Catholics, the rapid growth of secularism among nominal Protestants presented a more urgent challenge to ministers struggling to save souls through more efficient dissemination of the gospel of Jesus Christ as expounded in the 'open Bible'. He came to see secularism rather than popery as the principal threat to salvation, just as partition supplanted Home Rule as the principal threat to liberty in Ireland. Though modifying his strategies as external conditions changed, Frederick MacNeice remained profoundly true to his youthful ideals in both faith and politics.

The quintessential embodiment of both all-Ireland Unionism and evangelical Protestantism was, of course, the Loyal Orange Institution. It is, therefore, scarcely surprising that the Rector belonged to three Orange Lodges in Belfast between 1903 and 1909, acting as a chaplain for no less than four of the city's ten District Lodges.[33] Within a year of his controversial appointment as Rector, 'Bro. Rev. F. J. McNeice' was welcomed by the brethren of Carrickfergus Total Abstinence L.O.L. 1537, whereupon 'he assured the lodge of his sympathy and assistance whenever called on'.[34] Though an infrequent attender who appears never to have paid dues, he presided over the unfurling of a new banner on Easter Monday, 1911, served as Lodge chaplain for the years 1912 and 1913, and last appeared on the roll in 1915.[35] After a rare outburst of violence against Catholic windows in

July 1912, he exhorted a meeting of local Orangemen and Unionists to 'assist the local [Constabulary] force in the event of assistance being required'. The meeting obediently resolved to enrol the brethren and club members as special constables, who were to help preserve the peace 'by placing themselves each evening in different parts of the town'.[36] His wife Lily had recently presided over an Orange Bazaar, after which both MacNeices were effusively thanked for their services. In response, Frederick reminded the brethren that

> the society was not a political, but a religious society. They opposed Home Rule because they believed it meant Rome Rule. … Convince them that Home Rule was not Rome Rule and that it would benefit the country and they would be Home Rulers. And to prove that Home Rule really was Rome Rule, he spoke about the *Ne Temere* decree as an example.[37]

In January 1915, L.O.L. 1537 was one of the few local organisations to publish a resolution of condolence after Lily's death, in remembrance of 'the valuable services rendered to the lodge by her, and of the esteem and respect in which she was held by the brethren'.[38] As late as March 1920, though evidently no longer an active Orangeman, the Rector revisited the Orange Hall to witness his second wife's sister-in-law, Dorinda MacGregor Greer, unveiling a roll of honour for local brethren who had served in the Great War.[39]

Frederick took little interest in the ostentatious celebrations each Twelfth of July, and was only once reported among the chaplains seen 'on or near the platform', at the Castlereagh field in 1902. He therefore witnessed the epic confrontation between Colonel Edward Saunderson and Thomas Sloan which eventually led to the creation of the Independent Orange order and a serious rift in Belfast Unionism.[40] The Rector seems never to have had a public part in the East Antrim demonstrations, apart from apologising for his absence in 1920.[41] Though addressing at least three July 'anniversary services' for Orangemen in Carrickfergus in 1909, 1917, and 1922, he used these occasions to preach the virtues of temperance, tolerance, internationalism, reconciliation, and respect for law and order, paying scant attention to the customary commemorative themes. Already, in 1909, he wished 'to God we had the strength and wisdom not only to remember but to forget. Surely there is no true wisdom in recalling year after year the story of wrongs inflicted on Protestants in 1641, or any other rebellion.'[42] For MacNeice, Orangeism was a potentially useful tool in promoting godliness, sobriety, and respectability among workers of all Protestant denominations, offering access to a far broader range of souls than that reachable from the pulpit of St Nicholas. Like so many Orange chaplains, he regarded the order as a 'religious' rather than a 'political' institution, concentrating on the cultivation of morality within the Lodge rather than the assertion of supremacy outside it.

So long as Orangeism did not stand in the way of Irish unity within the Union, MacNeice remained involved. As the institution followed Carson's lead towards acceptance of partition, he dissociated himself from its inner counsels and transferred his fraternal enthusiasm to Freemasonry. By 1935, he was regarded as an antagonist by many leading Orangemen, especially when he applauded clerical 'aloofness from party politics' and warned that 'the influence that is gained by a clergyman in the political sphere lessens his influence in the spiritual sphere'.[43] In response to widespread protests, some by his own clergy, he declared:

> I was not thinking of the Orange Order, and I was not insinuating anything whatsoever. ... The Orange society is not a political society. ... I know well that many most excellent men have used the opportunity, which membership of the society has given them, in advocating the basic principles of Christian revelation.[44]

The Bishop himself was, of course, among those 'most excellent men'. When pursuing his campaign for peace in the shipyards a few weeks later, he made a 'very special appeal' to Orangemen, offering a remarkably positive account of the order:

> I witnessed the great procession on the Twelfth of July. It was magnificent. I was deeply impressed by its orderliness, one might say, the solemnity of it. I feel sure that the thousands of splendid men whom I saw at close quarters were and are lovers of order and justice and peace. I believe that those men, worthily led, could more than any other men now find a way, an honourable way, out of a vicious circle. I implore the leaders of the Orange Society not to let such an opportunity go by.[45]

At the very apogee of his liberal reputation, it is clear that the moral ideals of Orangeism had not lost their allure for the Lord Bishop of Down and Connor and Dromore.

The father that Louis MacNeice put behind him as a rebellious adolescent, and re-embraced as a tormented adult, was not in my view the liberal, non-sectarian nationalist with whom MacNeiceans have become so familiar. During Louis's early childhood, Frederick remained a conventional all-Ireland Unionist and Orangeman. As Louis matured, his father's political and religious priorities were changing in response to the catastrophic effects of war and revolution, all other objectives being subordinated to the necessity for peaceful reconciliation of both international and local antagonists. Frederick's postwar sermons and addresses were remarkable in the Irish context not for their content but for their irenic tone, from which all elements of rancour and partisanship were excised. Indeed, a neglected aspect of Louis's early rejection of his father is his adoption of a bitterly censorious style, whereas in later life he emulated his father's preference for measured words and balanced judgments. Yet, tolerant and broad-minded though he was, Frederick remained to the end a son of the Irish Church Missions, a loyal subject of the monarch, a celebrant of the moral and political mission embodied in the British Empire, and an upholder of many of the tenets of Orangeism. In rejecting his father, Louis was also rejecting the Loyal Orange Institution. This provides a vital subtext for that curious passage in *The Strings are False* where Louis (aged thirteen) panders to his headmaster at Sherborne by agreeing that the Twelfth was 'all mumbo-jumbo', thus offending a teacher from darkest Portadown: 'Oh this division of allegiance! That the Twelfth of July was mumbo-jumbo was true, and my father thought so too, but the moment Mr. Cameron [*recte* Lindsay] appeared I felt rather guilty and cheap' (*SF* 78–9). In truth, he was surely betraying not only his teacher but also his father, the former Orange chaplain. This could not be made explicit, since by 1940, when the account was composed, Louis was in effect collaborating with his father in the attempt to redraft Frederick's biography and to obscure the less palatable elements of his earlier career.

The poet's own view of Orangeism was becoming more benign, and closer to his father's attitude in later life. The Twelfth was no longer a nightmarish 'banging of Orange drums' or 'voodoo of the Orange bands / Drawing an iron net through darkest Ulster' (*CP* 25, 138), but 'an emotional safety-valve' or 'catharsis' for men who were privately 'quiet and unemotional'. The Orangeman's ideal, so Louis declared in the mid-1940s, was to be 'a decent wee man' – 'unostentatious, sober, industrious, scrupulously honest, and genuinely charitable'.[46] Echoes of Orangeism and the Irish Church Missions suffuse Louis's poetry and prose throughout his career, as in the affectionate tributes to Archie White, rectory gardener and Orangeman;[47] and those Dallas-like references to 'the garish Virgin', 'your dolled-up Virgins', 'the garish altar', and 'cormorants / Waiting to pounce like priests' (*CP* 25, 10, 138, 779).[48] These elements belonged to the MacNeice heritage just as much as the virtues of sobriety, tolerance, breadth of vision, and hatred of violence with which they coexisted in Frederick's mental world. There was more in the celebrated 'box of truisms' than one might have supposed:

> His father gave him a box of truisms
> Shaped like a coffin, then his father died;
> The truisms remained on the mantelpiece
> As wooden as the playbox they had been packed in
> Or that other his father skulked inside. (*CP* 565)

When the prodigal son returned to bless his parental home, it was surely the Orange verities of civil and religious liberty, symbolised by the open Bible, which 'flew and perched on his shoulders' and nourished the tree that 'sprouted from his father's grave'.

ON MACNEICE ON TRAINS

Leontia Flynn

My first encounter with Louis MacNeice was reading 'The Sunlight on the Garden' and 'Meeting Point' in anthologies of Irish poetry – beautiful, prismatic lyrics which I came to think were not entirely characteristic of the poet. Later, MacNeice became the Godfather of a Northern Irish poetry I had been only dimly aware existed. Through Derek Mahon and Michael Longley's close identification with the poet, I read back to 'Valediction' and *Autumn Journal* XVI, astonished by MacNeice's passionate, angry, and *unpoetic* encounters with place. More recently, however, I have come to think of Louis MacNeice as a poet of trains. So pervasive is the image of the train journey in his work, and so appropriate a context for reading MacNeice is the train ride, that I think his collected poems should be issued in railway stations.

The obsession seems to have begun early ('Trains came threading quietly through my dozing childhood', he writes in 'Reminiscences of Infancy') and to have endured to the end. This is because, as MacNeice ironically observes in 'Train to Dublin', much of our existence is spent in transit: 'the trains carry us about. But not consistently so, / For during a tiny portion of our lives we are not in trains …' I think I understand how conducive these journeys are to poetry. Both an interregnum in the day and an event in themselves, they have the right quality of active passivity (or passive activity) for inspiration. In these poetic interludes MacNeice is the observer at the window. 'I give you the incidental things which pass / Outward through space exactly as each was' he writes – and so much of MacNeice's poetry satisfies because of the accumulation of detail, true and specific, whether of urban landscapes like Belfast and Birmingham, or of, sooner or later, the sea. Much of his poetry, as anticipated by 'Train to Dublin', also has the quality of a mind allowed to wander in rhythm – a mind as complex, various, and divided as the things he observes:

Our half-thought thoughts divide in sifted wisps

Against the basic facts repatterned without pause,
I can no more gather my mind up in my fist
Than the shadow of the smoke of this train upon the grass –
This is the way that animals' lives pass. (*CP* 17)

The journey, then, is *the* metaphor for MacNeice's poetic – attentive
to what is inside and outside the window, passing through, but also
part of history.

Windows between you and the world
Keep out the cold, keep out the fright;
Then why does your reflection seem
So lonely in the moving night? (*CP* 255)

When it isn't trains, it might equally be buses, boats, or cars. There
is a vehicle for every stage of MacNeice's career, from his masterpiece
Autumn Journal (which I eventually got round to reading), where the
speaker boards a train in the first section, to later poems such as 'Hold-
up', 'Charon', and 'The Taxis', which explicitly figure life as a weird
ride in the back of a cab or bus. Thrillingly dark and odd as these last
poems are, I also love MacNeice's broader, sillier stuff, specifically
'Bagpipe Music', in which, of course, the vehicular image recurs
again: 'It's no go the Yogi-man, it's no go Blavatsky, / All we want
is a bank balance and a bit of skirt in a taxi' (*CP* 95). If MacNeice's
restlessness and refusal to find much consolation in roots (as well as
his often palpable neurosis) make him feel oddly contemporary, so
too does his curiosity about everything. Travel, politics, high and low
culture are all allowed to fuel his poetry, which is unafraid to be funny
as well as very, very clever. The work is also, finally, an object lesson
in discursiveness. Whatever the times, it seems to say, there is a way
of writing about them; it's all part of the journey.

'WHAT AM I DOING HERE?' TRAVEL AND MACNEICE

Terence Brown

1

In 1929, the year in which Louis MacNeice published *Blind Fireworks*, his first collection of poetry, the American poet Hart Crane contributed an essay entitled 'Modern Poetry' to a symposium on 'Revolt in the Arts'. Crane, in this short essay, ponders the role of poetry in 'a Machine Age'. He accepts that the machine's 'firm entrenchment in our lives has already produced a series of challenging new responsibilities for the poet'. 'For unless', he continues, 'poetry can absorb the machine, i.e. *acclimatize* it as naturally and casually as trees, cattle, galleons, castles and all other human associations of the past, then poetry has failed of its full contemporary function.' Then, in a compelling passage, he anticipates how poetry could absorb this new reality:

> Machinery will tend to lose its sensational glamour and appear in its true subsidiary order in human life as use and continual poetic allusion subdue its novelty. For, contrary to general prejudice, the wonderment experienced in watching nose dives is of less imme-diate creative promise to poetry than the familiar gesture of a motorist in the modest act of shifting gears. I mean to say that mere romantic speculation on the power and beauty of machinery keeps it at a continual remove; it cannot act creatively in our lives until, like the unconscious nervous responses of our bodies, its conno-tations emanate from within – forming as spontaneous a terminology of poetic reference as the bucolic world of pasture, plow and barn.[1]

Hart Crane's attempt to absorb the machine age in his poetry scarcely suggests that he has read his own lesson. For in his epic poem *The Bridge* (1930), a salute to Brooklyn Bridge, the world of machinery and the opportunities of travel and movement it provides are celebrated with romantic afflatus. Here is his take on air travel:

> Wheeled swiftly, wings emerge from larval-silver hangars.
> Taut motors surge, space-gnawing into flight;
> Through sparkling visibility, outspread, unsleeping,
> Wings clip the last peripheries of light ...

The new age is greeted ecstatically as 'Years of the Modern! Propulsions towards what capes?' Rhapsodically, Crane imagines aircraft 'launched in abysmal cupolas of space / Towards endless terminals' in a blend of the Italian Futurists' exhilarated exuberance and a Whitmanesque romanticism of the open road. Nothing, in fact, could be further from the naturalisation by poetry of the machine age that Crane's essay calls for; nothing further from that familiar gesture of a motorist changing gears in a car.[2]

Intriguingly, that is an act that recurs in MacNeice's poetry at the level of metaphor, suggesting that it is MacNeice, by contrast with Crane, who so interiorised the machine age that it became for him a spontaneous 'terminology of poetic reference'. For in 'Ode', a prayer for his son, the poet hopes:

> Let him have five good senses
> The feeling for symmetry
> And the sense of the magnet,
> His mind deft and unflustered
> To change gear easily
> And let not the blasphemy
> Of dusty words deceive him. (*CP* 33–4)

In 'Bluebells' 'all green Nature has gone out of gear' (*CP* 257), and in *Autumn Sequel* MacNeice represents shifts in conversation as: 'one quick change of gear / And we were in reverse' (*CP* 409).

It is not only the natural, almost unconscious way in which MacNeice uses such imagery that suggests he is instinctively a poet of the machine age. This fact becomes even more obvious when we consider how he seems entirely at ease, early in his career, in deploying traffic as a key metaphor. In 'The Glacier', collected in *Poems* (1935), to demonstrate that 'A paradox unfolds on any who can tamper with time' (*CP* 28), he chose the following extended metaphor of city life and its traffic:

Where bus encumbers upon bus and fills its slot
Speed up the traffic in a quick motion film of thought
Till bus succeeds bus so identically sliding through
That you cannot catch the fraction of a chink between the two;
But they all go so fast, bus after bus, day after day,
Year after year, that you cannot mark any headway,
But the whole stream of traffic seems to crawl
Carrying its dead boulders down a glacier wall. (*CP* 28)

The poem might easily have been entitled 'Two at Once' so familiar
is it, in its conversational tone, with the daily grind of urban life and
its gridlock.

Blind Fireworks gave little enough hint that MacNeice would
become a poet of the machine age: one who would not only register
the experience of travel by car, train, bus, and boat (though, oddly
enough, not plane) in many poems; but who would also frequently
employ, as a mode of composition, the kind of travel the machine
age made possible. *Blind Fireworks*, however, does include 'Reminiscences of Infancy' which tells us how 'Trains came threading quietly
through' the poet's 'dozing childhood' (*CP* 615). This poem aligns
the iron horse with an image of train-smoke as 'full-rigged galleons'
in a way which Crane might have approved. It concludes with
'menace from the sea, / The steel-bosomed siren calling bitterly' (*CP*
615). A poem later in the volume, 'Impermanent Creativeness',
makes man and machine one as the poet imagines:

Over asphalt, tar and gravel
My racing model happily purrs,
Each charted road I yet unravel
Out of my mind's six cylinders. (*CP* 645)

The quiet sound of the trains, the siren calling from the sea, the
purring of a well-tuned motor car, alert us to how MacNeice's poetry
is a poetry of sounds. We are so sensitised to the visual, tactile, and
olfactory in the poet of 'Snow' that we sometimes fail to note how
aural a poet he is,[3] and that 'Snow', ending with that mysterious silence
in a visual perception, is also where we hear the 'bubbling sound' of
the fire (*CP* 24). In MacNeice's echo chamber of poetic sound effects
the noises of the machine and travel age are ubiquitous. In 'Morning
Sun' we hear 'Horns of cars, touché, touché, rapiers' retort' (*CP* 15),

while in 'Spring Voices' the 'hoots of cars' excite 'the small house-
holder' (*CP* 29). In 'Letter to Graham and Anna' the poet has gaily
run away 'From the grinding gears, the change from day to day' (*CP*
51). In 'Street Scene' we hear 'instead of silence racket, / Brakes gears
and sparrows' (*CP* 276). In 'The Window' the daily traffic of
consciousness with external reality includes the 'neurotic screaming
of brakes' (*CP* 310). And elsewhere we hear the droning of planes,
the sound of trains, the sounds of railway station ('Perdita', 'Departure Platform') and harbour ('Convoy') as journeys begin. For this is
a poet who can compose a love poem such as 'Trilogy for X', where
he makes the 'power of trains advancing / Further, advancing further'
serve as metaphor for sexual intercourse; and where he can incorporate into an aubade after a night of love, the line: 'The first train passes
and the windows groan' (*CP* 176). It is entirely appropriate, therefore, that in 'The Ear' – which addresses the phenomenon of human
audition, the purely sonar, the many noises 'which are neither music
nor voice' – MacNeice includes the sound of a train passing: 'The
thin and audible end of a dark wedge' (*CP* 200–1). In the earlier
poem 'A Contact' he had imagined the whistle of a night express as
'Sharp and straight on the ear like stigmata' (*CP* 26).

MacNeice's poetry not only instinctively employs an imagery
drawn from a world of cars, buses, trains, not only assumes that the
machine age offers ready tropes for poems as in 'The Glacier', not
only registers the noises of a world of mass transit; but also often registers the immediate experience of travel in cars, trains, buses, and ships.
In 'Sunday Morning' the speaker encourages a drive beyond 'Hind-
head' and urges: 'Take corners on two wheels until you go so fast /
That you can clutch a fringe or two of the windy past' (*CP* 21). 'June
Thunder' has the poet in high summer driving through an almost
Keatsian flood of sensation rather than thought:

> the mudguards brushing the cowparsley,
> Through fields of mustard and under boldly embattled
> Mays and chestnuts
>
> Or between beeches verdurous and voluptuous
> Or where broom and gorse beflagged the chalkland ... (*CP* 56)

In 'Now that the Shapes of Mist' it is night-time that makes the
driving experience headily sensuous:

... the lamps draw trails of milk in ponds of lustrous lead
[...]
... wet roads at night reflect the clutching
Importunate fingers of trees and windy shadows
Lunge and flounce on the windscreen as I drive ... (*CP* 92)

'The Dowser' notes, in a vivid perception, 'effulgence / Of headlights beyond the rise in the road' (*CP* 207). The night drive in Canto
XIV of *Autumn Journal*, when the poet takes the road for Oxford, is
an extended evocation of a car journey which, in its helter-skelter
imagism, manages to suggest the perceptual onrush which is an effect
of speed:

The wheels whished in the wet, the flashy strings
    Of neon lights unravelled
[...]
And coming over the Chilterns the dead leaves leap
    Charging the windscreen like a barrage of angry
Birds as I take the steep
    Plunge to Henley or Hades.
And at the curves of the road the telephone wires
    Shine like strands of silk ... (*CP* 133)

Travel by train is also a recurrent subject, if without quite the
impression of headlong rush that Auden catches so compulsively in
his documentary poem for the Post Office, 'Night Mail'. In
MacNeice's 'Train to Dublin', although the 'train's rhythm never
relents, the telephone posts / Go striding backwards like the legs of
time', the poet also has the leisure to 'count the buttons on the seat',
to think of moments when 'we are not in trains', and to salute 'the
incidental things which pass / Outward through space exactly as each
was' (*CP* 17). The train carriage can also offer the epiphanic, as in the
'andante' dreaminess of 'Slow Movement', where the poet awakes in
an early train as the world slows down: 'Great white nebulae lurch
against the window', 'The movement ends', the train 'come[s] to a
stop / In buttercup fields' (*CP* 280). But it can also involve the sensations of dislocation, alienation, and isolation, as in 'The Drunkard',
whose underground (underworld?) 'last train home is Purgatory in
reverse':

Clutching a quizzical strap where wraiths of faces
Contract, expand, revolve, impinge; disperse
On a sickly wind which drives all wraiths pell-mell
Through tunnels to their appointed, separate places. (*CP* 277*)*

'Corner Seat' has the poet nonplussed by his image in the carriage
window: 'why does your reflection seem / So lonely in the moving
night?' (*CP* 255).

2

Valentine Cunningham in his *British Writers of the Thirties*, in a chapter
entitled 'Seedy Margins', tellingly explores how the 1930s was a
decade of literary travel. The new age of easy transport for the upper-
middle classes, for the *deraciné* intelligentsia and the bohemian,
brought most of Europe and other parts of the world within the ambit
of the literary imagination. The travel book was a sure-fire pitch to
your publisher (MacNeice's Hebridean jaunt, recorded in *I Crossed
the Minch*, 1938, was one of many such potboiling exploitations of
the vogue for travel writing).[4] And, as Cunningham notes, thinking
of MacNeice's 'The Hebrides' and 'Leaving Barra', as well as the
many poems written by MacNeice and others about Spain: 'Such
texts announce a literature living greedily off its authors' experience
of foreign places.'[5] Travel could offer income by way of travel
journalism and travel writing, and could also fertilise the
imagination of the novelist or poet. The problem was that much such
travel was merely tourism, with the attendant risks of superficiality
and incomprehension. MacNeice himself, in the voice of a character
in his play *Out of the Picture*, mildly satirises how wealth has made the
world your oyster in the decade, promising 'miles and miles of
distance for your money'.[6] Despite this he was not averse to writing
self-consciously touristic poems, in which amused, curious, liberally
concerned reportage of local colour, as in 'Postscript to Iceland',
makes for poetic copy. 'But a fancy turn you know / Sandwiched in
a graver show', he admits of his Icelandic sojourn with Auden (*CP*
96); and in 'Letter to Graham and Anna' he dispatches breezy
commentary:

There are no trees or trains or architecture,
Fruits and greens are insufficient for health,

Culture is limited by lack of wealth,
The tourist sights have nothing like Stonehenge,
The literature is all about revenge. (*CP* 48)

However Canto VI of *Autumn Journal* – when Spain is 'ripe as an egg
for revolt and ruin / Though for the tripper the rain / Was worse
than the surly or the worried or the haunted faces' (*CP* 112) – blends
touristic sightseeing with the travel writer's notes of curious encounters and instances: all retrospectively understood as an obtuse failure
to grasp how 'Spain would soon denote / Our grief, our aspirations'
(*CP* 114). Tourism is effectively indicted as the poet and his
companion 'take the boat' uncaringly for home.[7]

If travel as tourism is sometimes suspect in MacNeice's poetry, this
does not preclude him from using the trope of tourism and holiday
travels as compositional supports in poems of real substance. 'Valediction', for example, a poem of renunciation of the natal place
written in 1934 (*CP* 7–10), assesses Ireland from the car-driving eye
of a man who represents himself as a tourist in his own country: 'Park
your car in the city of Dublin, see Sackville Street'; 'See Belfast,
devout and profane and hard'; 'Park your car in Killarney, buy a
souvenir'; 'But take the Holyhead boat before you pay the bill'. The
speaker seemingly accepts that he must become one of Ireland's
'holiday visitors': 'I must go east and stay, not looking behind'. Yet
this poem that runs through the 'accepted names' in the expected
places (Dublin, Belfast, Galway, the romantic West), that knowingly
shuffles a deck of stereotypical images, has also a bass-note of pained
ambivalence, making it a work of bitter resignation which belies its
organising principle as merely a travel guide.

MacNeice was one of Ireland's 'holiday visitors' in the early
autumn of 1939, when the Second World War began. The poem
that responds to that epochal event is, in fact, a travel poem,
describing a tour by car of the Irish West that MacNeice took with
his friend, Ernst Stahl (a South African academic, whose subject was
German, whom MacNeice met at Birmingham University). It was
first collected as 'The Coming of War' in the Dublin-published *The
Last Ditch* (1940), and subsequently appeared in edited form as 'The
Closing Album'. The latter title captures, of course, the touristic
aspect of the poem's occasion (showing a foreign friend the sights),
and its method as a series of poems of place, with the resultant snap-
shots pasted in an album. As such, the work is packed with the kind

of detail that a travelogue might be expected to contain. Dublin in the first poem is a site of historic and social contradictions resolved by the city's capacity to absorb 'all / The alien brought' (*CP* 180). In the next two poems, Cushendun and Sligo and Mayo have the sensuous immediacy that holiday travel gives as one of its principal pleasures. Ireland is experienced as its sights, sounds, and smells, as its effects of light and dark, of shadows, twilight, and night coming down 'With all-enveloping wings' (*CP* 181). Ireland is its flora and fauna and topography too, and its aesthetic impressions of contrasting colours and tones. Above all, it is a place in which to forget: a place that offers the tourist a world set apart. Indeed, the first three poems evoke Ireland as possessed of almost magical powers that can tempt the unsuspecting traveller to accede to its lotus-land appeal. In 'Dublin' the poet acknowledges: 'You give me time for thought / And by a juggler's trick / You poise the toppling hour' (*CP* 180). In 'Cushendun' is found

> Forgetfulness: brass lamps and copper jugs
> And home-made bread and the smell of turf or flax
> And the air a glove and the water lathering easy
> And convolvulus in the hedge. (*CP* 180)

In 'Sligo and Mayo' as 'the twilight filtered on the heather / Water-music filled the air'.

In fact, what makes this sequence so much more than a travelogue, although it employs the method of such, is the ongoing contrast between war's encroachment and the narcotic, trance-inducing appeal of country that is no 'place to talk of War' (*CP* 180). In each of the first three poems war is alluded to, but does not really impinge on the idyllic escapism Ireland tantalisingly offers. 'Dublin' is 'historic with guns and vermin' (*CP* 179); and in Cushendun, 'With the curtains drawn against the winds and waves' that seem more than mere setting (*CP* 180), a voice from the wireless reminds of the European crisis. In 'Sligo and Mayo' the settling of night on bogland offers a symbolism of chiliastic portent: 'The coal-black turfstacks rose against the darkness / Like the tombs of nameless kings' (*CP* 181). This anticipates the doom-laden final, tellingly untitled, poem that questions 'why, now it has happened, / Should the atlas still be full of the maps of countries / We never shall see again?' (*CP* 182). The lack of a place-name here, in a sequence that emphasises places and place-names (even more pronouncedly so in the extended version published in *The Last Ditch*, though not all the poems are titled there), suggests the places that will vanish in the coming cataclysm: the places that will be closed, indeed, to any, let alone holiday, travel. The fourth poem 'Galway', while it still allows for Irish enchantment, with its salmon 'Gently swaying' and its 'hundred swans / Dreaming on the harbour', also has a 'dredger grumbling / All night' and Mars 'angry / On the hills of Clare' (*CP* 181–2). It is here that the war 'came down' on our travellers. So the sequence sets up an intensifying conflict between the mesmerising attractions of Ireland as experienced by the holiday traveller and the more powerful sense of encroaching doom that overtakes it. It therefore takes forward MacNeice's own dialogue with himself about his native land. In 'Valediction' the country had been eschewed because of a 'drug-dull fatalism' (*CP* 9). In *Autumn Journal* it had been a site of 'self-deception' (*CP* 139). And later, during the war, Irish neutrality would be indicted in a similar imagery to that deployed in 'The Closing Album', to suggest (in 'Neutrality') a tempting yet corrupting anachronism associated with County Sligo, which had figured on the eve-of-war itinerary.

'Valediction' and 'The Closing Album' suggest how MacNeice could exploit the vogue for travel-based literature in the 1930s as the basis of serious poetry. It was a mode of writing he would continue to deploy for most of his subsequent career, when travel writing would become much more a matter of specifically generic literary production than in had been in the 1930s. The journeyings registered in MacNeice's poetry take him to Iceland, the Hebrides, the Irish West, Wales, Spain, the United States, India, Ceylon, Greece, France, Italy, South Africa, Egypt. His last posthumously published volume *The Burning Perch* (1963) contains, among its bleak perspectives on the world, 'Ravenna', with its recollections of Ravenna's complex past and deflated present, its query: 'What do I remember of my visit to Ravenna?' (*CP* 589). And this poem is followed in the volume by 'Constant', which wearily evokes a city with 'too much history / Tilting, canting, crawling, rotting away' (*CP* 590); while 'This is the Life' is the ultimate, jaundiced take on tourism, with 'Elderly ladies in slacks' descending into 'the tombs of kings' in Egypt, assured, whatever may befall them, of 'a Pharaoh's portion of turkey and pumpkin pie' (*CP* 601).

For MacNeice, the travel or tourist poem serves various poetic purposes. In many poems the trope of travel, by train especially, enables the poet to situate himself in a landscape or topography that bespeaks significant social realities. The opening canto of *Autumn Journal* is a case in point, as the speaker takes a train from Hampshire to London at the end of a summer holiday. The landscape travelled away from is made to represent a fossilised *ancien regime* that gives way to 'London's packed and stale and pregnant air' (*CP* 102). The effect is to suggest not just a social awareness but a historical one too, for the journey from summer to autumn reads like a journey from a defunct past to the demanding present. Similar journeys are undertaken in *Autumn Sequel*, though without the sense of historical crisis that gave the earlier poem its special edge. In Canto III, for example, a train journey through London's suburbia treats that setting as a blandly unheroic backdrop to musings about the nature of contemporary heroism, epitomised by the conquest of Everest.

In other poems travel and associated tourism provide occasions for encounters with the exotic and the strange that stimulate cultural and philosophic self-reflection, even religious questionings. Such poems reinforce our sense that MacNeice understood how travel writing could serve complex aesthetic purposes; and remind us that, in 1957, he had contracted to write an autobiographical book in prose that would 'explore in the light and shade of my own experience, the corroborations and refutals of my myths, the frustrations and illuminations I have found in various travels' (*SF* 14). His poem 'Mahabalipuram' (1948) supplies a powerful example of an encounter with otherness that provokes a troubling awareness of the limitations of occidental thought.

In 1947 MacNeice visited the ancient temple at Mahabalipuram, near Madras, when he took a break from the traumatic horrors he had witnessed after India's independence and partition, to do a little sightseeing with friends. The result is a complex meditation that never forgets its touristic occasion. Indeed, what tourism can involve for the unwary is part of the poem's import. 'Mahabalipuram' (*CP* 305–7) opens with travelogue scene-setting, as the stanzaic form, in lines of elaborately varying length, seeks to suggest the temple's monumentality and iconic extravagance. Descriptive overload, as the sightseer is almost defeated by the temple's exoticism, gives way to a sense that what confronts the westerner at Mahabalipuram is not so foreign after all, but an avatar from some profound mode of consciousness that our scientific materialism, 'science and chance', has inadequately sought to supersede. For it slowly dawns on the observer at the temple that the carvings of an ancient sculptor 'are the dreams we have needed / Since we forgot how to dance'. The reliefs on the temple walls 'at once annul the lust and envy of tourists / Taking them out of themselves and to find themselves in a world / That has neither rift nor rim'. Face to face with intimations of 'The creator who is destroyer' who 'stands at the last point of land / Featureless', the 'visitor' of the poem is relieved that he 'must move on', carrying with him the knowledge of 'what an avatar is'; and appropriately chastened before ultimate mysteries of creation and negation.

Travel, even a tourist's day trip, can, it seems, truly unsettle the traveller, prompt metaphysical reveries. Increasingly, however, in MacNeice's poetry as the years went on, travel became less a generic mode that permitted various forms of poetic reflection than the subject of poetry itself. The *oeuvre* begins to suggest that, for MacNeice, life is experienced as if by a traveller who suffers the wearying ennui of belonging nowhere. Despite his being 'Dumb-founded', as he puts it in 'Carrick Revisited' when evoking a return to his childhood hometown, to find himself 'in a topographical frame' (*CP* 261), later poems of travel report on a variety of such frames until journeying itself becomes an alienating condition of being. In 'Half Truth from Cape Town', 'through the swinging doors of the decades', the poet must 'Confront a waste of tarmac, a roaring sky' (*CP* 556). In 'Solitary Travel' 'The hotels are all the same', and the poet must take 'coffee alone in the indistinguishable airports' and 'feel the futility of moving on / To what, though not a conclusion, stays foregone' (*CP* 557). Concurrently, as travel becomes for MacNeice a metonymy of a restless, *deraciné* modernity (mobile but futile), his frequent poems about riding in trains, cars, buses, lose their sensuous pleasure in the immediate impression of movement and speed in a world of sensations, take on the stark outlines of allegory, and offer the implied abstraction of grim parables. In 'Restaurant Car', for example, the train travellers avoid their 'neighbours' eyes and wonder what // Mad country moves beyond the steamed-up window', as the poem concentrates on an inner world where the journey, 'still in the nature of a surprise', has only one possible conclusion: an allegorical terminal 'where all must change' (*CP* 562).

Some of MacNeice's best and best-known later poems are of this type: 'Figure of Eight', 'Hold-Up', 'The Taxis', and the incomparable 'Charon'. A poem that gets less attention is 'The Wiper' (*CP* 562–3), in which the experience of night driving in rain is made an extended trope of living itself. The exhilarated drives in some of MacNeice's earliest poems (remember 'Impermanent Creativeness') have now become a single-minded attention to a 'tiny segment / Cleared and blurred by the wiper' in a car windscreen as the vehicle shudders on and we 'hardly hold the road'. Like other late poems of vehicular travel, this one inhabits a curiously mechanised world of dials, glass, 'the wiper backward and forward'. But, rather than naturalising these things, as many poems have naturalised gear-shifting and other details of the machine age, this poem defamiliarises them, so that the experience it evokes seems to demarcate some limbo-like zone of being, where we are afflicted by an existential vertigo. 'After the Crash' in *The Burning Perch*, with its motorcyclist waking after an accident to 'asphalt ... high with hemlock' and a transmogrified 'crash / Helmet' (*CP* 585), is the most daring of such poems, but 'The Wiper', too, has its moments of unnerving disorientation. For there is

... never a gauge nor needle
To tell us where we are going
Or when day will come, supposing
  This road exists in daytime.

For now we cannot remember
Where we were when it was not
Night, when it was not raining ... (*CP* 563)

So, in MacNeice's late poetry, travel, which had helped to form the basis of an extraordinarily variegated poetic, tends towards a metaphoric uniformity – the journey, as the overall mood of the poetry darkens, is the journey towards death. There is no doubt, as 'Figure of Eight' has it, 'Who will be there to meet him at the station' (*CP* 517). However, there remain moments when the gloom lifts and the journey seems worth the price of the ticket. In 'Charon' in *The Burning Perch*, the volume MacNeice himself on his deathbed noted as containing a 'high proportion of sombre pieces' (*CP* 795), a bus jogging through the streets of London may deliver us to the banks of the Styx; but in 'Round the Corner' there is the hope that 'Round the corner', on whatever journey we take, 'is – sooner or later – the sea' (*CP* 578). And there is too 'Star-gazer', which recalls a boyhood journey in a 'westward train' on 'a brilliant starry night' (*CP* 607). The poem manages simultaneously to be a dizzying expression of metaphysical awe and an excited celebration of the ultimate voyage: humankind's mysterious, individually perilous, journey through the universe.

MACNEICE AND THIRTIES (CLASSICAL) PASTORALISM

Valentine Cunningham

The imagining and writing of the 1930s are extraordinarily pastoral-minded: on both political wings, extreme right and far left, and at all points in-between, including the critical, self-doubting left, where Louis MacNeice stands. *The Earth Compels*, as MacNeice's title of 1938 has it – on all sides. 'What you want is some good earthy contacts', the character Moll advises the poet Portright in MacNeice's play *Out of the Picture* (1937), accusing him of being too 'Romanticist' for wanting to be always in some foreign place. 'Earthy contacts': down to earth, and down on the earth: good for the self and for art and for writing as an ethical and politically instrumental means. *Ventre à terre*: it is where George Orwell wanted his art and his society to be:[1] in the country; preoccupied with country matters. Country matters in every sense – mere rurality, but also Hamlet's punning sense of uninhibited bucolic sexuality: cunt in the country.[2] 'I lived on country matters', says Cecil Day Lewis in the 'Dedicatory Stanzas' of his translation of Virgil's *Georgics* (1940), addressed to Stephen Spender. And Day Lewis, country-dwelling poet, of course relishes Hamlet's double entendre. In the country: in what Edmund Blunden called *Cricket Country* (1940) – in the village cricket-team, on the village green, it might be, with Cecil Day Lewis and Rex Warner, both keen village cricketers; or with Louis MacNeice, avid cricket-fan from his schooldays on, down for the day, persuaded to make up the numbers. Village Cricket: what Orwell rhapsodises about in his April 1944 review of Blunden's *Cricket Country* – a good thing, in a good place, an English idyll, a haven of peace in times of modern war; not snobbish, beyond class considerations, in fact; an ethical and social utopia: 'where everyone plays in braces, where the blacksmith is liable to be called away in mid-innings on an urgent job, and sometimes, about the time when the light begins to fail, a ball driven for four kills a rabbit on the boundary'.[3] In other words: *pastoral,* for humans if not for rabbits; pastoral in every sense – actual idyllic place

and occasion of rural existence and pastime; metaphorically a place
and condition of being which generates, which *is*, human content-
ment, which works for, as it is the sign of, the good ordering of a
person's body and spirit and soul in a well-ordered society and
culture.

And what is striking about the craving for pastoral in this period is
that it is – as my deliberate invoking of Orwell, Day Lewis, and Rex
Warner, as well as of MacNeice, indicates – a rather dominant vision
and issue on the left. Conventionally, of course, we are encouraged
to think of ruralism (then, as now) as a right-wing thing, the world
of squire and landowner and foxhunter, of right-wingers like
Edmund Blunden, indeed of Fascists such as Henry (*Tarka the Otter*)
Williamson, and to think of 1930s socialism as all urban, technological, Futurist, devoted to a *Brave New World* of Fordised
modernismus and *mechanismus*, involving the mechanising of agricul-
ture, the eradication of the peasant, the Kulak, the country-person;
that is, Audenesque in the sense of Auden's preferring the industrial
landscapes of the Midlands, the North of England to Richard Jefferies
and the Wiltshire Downs (as he puts it in his *Letter to Lord Byron*).
And there is, of course, some truth in this opposition – crudely epitomised in the sustained jeers of the Marxist-baiting ruralist T.H.
White. John Marx, Communist anti-hero of White's pro-hunting
novel *Earth Stopped: or, Mr Marx's Sporting Tour* (1934), is offered as
a representative leftist townee who is hopeless in a village pub. He
begins 'to be human' as he gets acclimatised to the country and its
ways – 'beginning to discover people, as apart from the proletariat'.[4]
(*Stopping* was plugging foxes' holes or *earths* as part of the business of
hunting them to death: White's punning title offers the thought that
the earth itself is being destroyed, stopped in its tracks, hampered, in
the course of left-modernism's destructive progress.) 'How safe
would Karl Marx have been, I wonder, walking in a line of guns?'
White gibes in his polemicising *England Have My Bones* (1936).
Communists, he suggests, will be 'weaned from their cross' by
learning how to fish and hunt and get on in country pubs.[5] But as
binaries go this one is much too simple. T.H. White's sneers don't
lay a finger on those eager Communist ruralists C. Day Lewis and
Rex Warner (bird-watching Warner, to boot), nor even the reluctant Communist country-cottage owner Randall Swingler.[6] They fail
utterly to take in the way socialism's political pastoralism, its utopi-
anism, its desire to find and create the Great Good Socialist Place, is

not only cast metaphorically as a country-quest, the quest for a metaphorical *New Country* (as that famous 1933 poetry anthology put it), but seems to have rather often involved quite literally some form of country living, of ruralism: literal pastoral, where the good life could be lived for real, not least by poets and artists. The bourgeois poet must, according to the common leftist cry, 'go over' to the side of the working class, taking along his/her artistic practices in an act of personal and aesthetic conversion. Going into the country, moving out of town, living rurally, was a practical expression of that political-aesthetic imperative.

Britain and the Beast (1937), that classic 1930s attack on the ruination of Britain's rural life by *town-rash* (suburban brick and concrete, ribbon roads, factories, aerodromes), was deeply approved of on the Right (Baden-Powell said its message was very timely: England needed rescuing from litter-louts – which did not exist in Hitler's Germany). It was in fact not only a chorus of assorted political voices, left, liberal, centrist, as well as right (Maynard Keynes, Joad, S.P.B. Mais, E.M. Forster, and so on), but was edited by the Soviet-sympathising architect Clough Williams-Ellis. Communist Cecil Day Lewis embraced its anti-urban concerns with great Marxised enthusiasm in the Communist cultural-front paper *Left Review* (August 1937) – by then edited by that fraught urbanist-countryman poet, Randall Swingler. Socialism alone, said Day Lewis, could rescue Britain from the Beast. 'We Marxists declare that the English tradition has passed into our hands.' 'Can your revolution do something about' urbanisation, Day Lewis had asked in this 'Letter to A Young Revolutionary' in the *New Country* anthology. Can it 'break up the superficial vision of the motorist and restore the slow instinctive, absorbent vision of the countryman'; make 'the land a land of milk and honey'? It must, he said, and it can.

So left-wing literature could not only be pastoral in the sense of being socialist-utopian, but also literally so. As indeed much of it was. Notably in regional, working-class, 'proletarian' fiction – in the novels of Ralph Bates, it might be, or of Lewis Grassic Gibbon, or in H.E. Bates's stories. Certainly in the art of the documentary movement, especially the films of John Grierson's GPO Film Unit (in which Auden and Benjamin Britten worked): as William Empson's momentous little 1935 book *Some Versions of Pastoral* had it. Empson had witnessed literally pastoral scenes – European peasants treading grapes. And for him good proletarian art was usually covert pastoral:

'Proletarian literature usually has a suggestion of pastoral.'[7] Most of
that literature is not, he thinks, pastoral enough. The greatest case of
proletarian art as pastoral, for him, is *Drifters*, John Grierson's documentary film about North Sea herring fishermen – and *Drifters* was,
of course, the quintessential model for all the 1930s documentarists
and would-be documentarists.

Much to my point about the period's left-wing pastoralism, and
much to my take on MacNeice's part in it, is that a striking number
of the pastoral leftist writers were also classicists, men brought up on
the classics, schooled in the classics, and not least in the classical-
pastoral tradition. So they approached the great 1930s question of
pastoral – metaphorical and literal – through their reading in and their
sense of the great classical-pastoral tradition, Theocritus, Virgil,
Horace, Pindar: in particular, the idylls and odes and eclogues of these
great predecessors who precoccupied them in boyhood at Prep
School, throughout their Public School years and on into university
classical studies. Of course these leftist classicists are interested in classical literature and in recycling classical texts and genres at large –
MacNeice translates the *Agamemnon* and is arrested by Thucydides;
Rex Warner becomes a specialising translator of Greek tragedy and
Greek and Roman history; Day Lewis does the *Aeneid*. But they do
seem especially drawn to pastoral modes. Jack Lindsay, the Australian
Marxist classicist poet, translated Theocritus's *Idylls* (1930), those
progenitors of Virgil's pastorals – translations featured in the Maurice
Bowra/T.F. Higham wartime anthology *From the Greek* (Clarendon
Press, 1943). Bowra's pupil, the Communist Day Lewis, did Virgil's
Georgics, dedicating the volume to quondam Communist Stephen
Spender with words about Virgil as pastoralist model for a left-wing
poet in time of war: Virgil the pastoral poet in every sense, cultivating
his own garden and cultivating gardens in his verse, his *Eclogues* and
his *Georgics*:

> But chiefly dear for his gift to understand
> Earth's intricate, ordered heart, and for a vision
> That saw beyond an imperial day the hand
> Of man no longer armed against his fellow
> But all for vine and cattle, fruit and fallow,
> Subduing with love's positive force the land.[8]

And MacNeice, one more left-leaning Oxford classic, is of course besotted by this particular tradition – cutting his teeth on Theocritean/Virgilian-type eclogues, and the eclogues of their great imitator Edmund Spenser; translating Virgil's friend Horace; thinking of himself, his career, his writing right to the end as a mirror-image of what pastoral, agriculturalist Horace was and did. Horace as he appears in MacNeice's 'Memoranda to Horace' (in *The Burning Perch*, 1963), the ancient version of a poet of 'the 1930s', with his own over-bearing Leninist authority, namely Augustus, to cope with, and a similar struggle between the political and the personal to the one which MacNeice and his contemporaries all went through. MacNeice's ideal of the poetic, of the aesthetic, seems to have been utterly classical, and indeed pastoral. Certainly, it was ancient pastoral that he found most *splendid*, most *glamorous*, most *glittering* of all the old poems he was set to read. Poetry must *glitter*, and at school he had found that crucial *glitter* in Horace, and in particular in the celebra-tion of the fabled Bandusian spring in *Odes* 3.13, *O fons Bandusiae splendidior vitro* (O spring of Bandusia brighter and clearer than crystal). He quotes it in *Modern Poetry: A Personal Essay* (1938). As for Virgil, his glamour was in the *Georgics*. MacNeice liked the attraction expressed in Virgil's lines about bears fearful of getting wet in the sea; pursued hares getting wet; the hum of bees. Translators, he said, find the Virgilian pastoral 'glamour' elusive. A line like *tantus amor florum et generandi gloria mellis* (*Georgics* 4.205), about bees loving flowers and being proud of their power to generate honey, is very hard for a trans-lator to render; but is 'always there to be chased'. Day Lewis's version, 'Such is their love for flowers, their pride in consuming honey', does not, MacNeice thought, capture the glamour, though Day Lewis generally gets closer to it than R.C. Trevelyan.[9] Just so, the prose of Apuleius's *Golden Ass* has 'a verbal glamour that English cannot emulate' (this is in MacNeice's Introduction to William Adlington's famous sixteenth-century translation of *The Golden Ass*). The Eliza-bethan John Lyly got close to it with his euphuistic flash; but not that close. What is at issue is the glamorous Apuleian pastoral moment in lines – which could be set as verse, says MacNeice, who did just that – about tilling the earth of Sicily, and the slow advent of night.[10] What MacNeice gets from Pindar – Pindar who, as *Autumn Journal* IX has it, 'sang the garland of wild olive' – is, of course, 'unforgettable phrases'; but, more than that, Pindar's *Odes* have a symbolic unity according to Gilbert Norwood's *Pindar* (1945), which MacNeice reviewed and approved of – again in the left-wing *New Statesman*

(*SLC* 132–5). Those unforgettable phrases trade in 'natural symbols' – rose, bee, pebble. Which are just what MacNeice relishes: the bees of Virgil's Georgian concerns; the flowers whose fashionable absence from Auden's poetry MacNeice keeps adverting to by contrast with his own verses; the pebbles which are examples of the *local object*, the *small particular* that MacNeice thinks poetry should be concerned with.

Classical pastoral, then, fertilising the pastoral interests and approvings of the several leftist classicists. And, even more arrestingly, of the Irish, and Irish Protestant, and, even, Ulster Protestant classicists. For there is an utterly striking presence in this particular critical-historical, classical-pastoral story of Northern Irish Protestants. Of Ulstermen, what is more, who have gone over to the un-natural (for them) Nationalist side; like Cecil Day Lewis, born in Ballintubbert in 1904 in what was then the Queen's County (now County Laois), son of a Church of Ireland minister. And like MacNeice himself, Ulsterman, son of yet one more Church of Ireland minister, who was singled out for his professional career as a classicist at Birmingham University by Classics Professor E.R. Dodds, a radical Protestant Nationalist Ulsterman.[11] Dodds's successor in the Birmingham Chair was the Greekist George Thomson, English-born son of a Protestant Nationalist Ulsterman (born, Dulwich, 1903); member of the Executive Committee of the British Communist Party; popular lecturer on literature and politics to Communist Party branches in Birmingham factories and such like (and in later life a Maoist). Thomson's politics and politicised aesthetics were – in complete keeping with his time – utterly pastoral in every sense. As a schoolboy in London he took Irish lessons run by the Gaelic League; and from 1923 onwards started visiting the Blasket Islands off the tip of West Kerry, where he embraced as ideal the pre-capitalist culture of that small illiterate peasant-fishing people – who, he quickly perceived, practised the oldest kind of folk song and oral poetry. The translation from Irish of the autobiography of Thomson's Blasket Islands friend Muiris O'Sullivan, *Twenty Years A-Growing* (1933), which Thomson did with Moya Llewellyn Davies (Irish Republican: veteran of the IRA and Independence struggles), became a classic of 1930s left-pastoralism. (It was introduced by liberal-leftist E.M. Forster – Irish Protestant grandfather; quondam Cambridge classics student – and was brought out in the Oxford University Press's World's Classics series in 1953: a world classic already.) Thomson's experience of the

Blasket Islanders' singing, storytelling, poeticising culture influenced all of his studies of ancient Greek culture and literature: his first big book *Greek Lyric Metre* (1929), and his two big tomes on Greek culture and society and art, *Aeschylus and Athens: A Study in the Social Origins of Drama* (1941), and *Studies in Ancient Greek Society: The Prehistoric Aegean* (1949) – both of them published by the Communist Party's own publisher Lawrence and Wishart.

Down there in west-coast Ireland was, for Thomson, the real thing of leftist-pastoral desire – folk culture, the authentic singing folk, people doing poetry (epic and tragedy and, of course, pastoral) in a simple pastoral place – a people modelling, though they did not know it, Homer, Aeschylus, Pindar. Thomson had spotted the repetitions in the Homeric texts, but only in the Blasket Islands did that poetic practice make sense. He had 'put them all down as "primitive", but without understanding what that meant':

> Then I went to Ireland. The conversation of those ragged peas-ants, as soon as I learnt to follow it, electrified me. It was as though Homer had come alive. Its vitality was inexhaustible, yet it was rhythmical, alliterative, formal, artificial, always on the point of bursting into poetry. There is no need to describe it further, because it had all the qualities noted by Radlov in the conversa-tion of the Kirghiz …[12] Returning to Homer, I read him in a new light. He was a people's poet – aristocratic, no doubt, but living in an age in which class inequalities had not yet created a cultural cleavage between hut and castle. His language was artificial, yet, strange to say, this artificiality was natural. It was the language of the people raised to a higher power. No wonder they were enrap-tured.[13]

Thomson's rhapsodic is a nearly verbatim repeat of the passage in his 1945 Lawrence and Wishart pamphlet, *Marxism and Poetry*, where he reports how he came to see that Aeschylus and Pindar, as well as Homer, composed like the oral poets of the Blasket Islands. Here, then, repeatedly set out, is a vision of the classics historicised but also politicised – for this sort of poetry and narrative is still going on, says Thomson, in the Soviet Union's eastern provinces. This is a Marxist model of popular poetry, harking back to the radicalism of Shelley and William Morris, and pointing the way dramatically to the literary future. An aesthetic future epitomised in Ireland – western, pastoral

Ireland; Romantic Ireland no less; an emblematic place and mode (adumbrated, of course, by Protestant Irish Yeats, whom Thomson keeps quoting in the matter of the dance and song of the future); a prophetic home, in fact, to which the wise leftist writer must, and will, go over. And go over, not least, in MacNeice's Birmingham, whose Classics Department was, in MacNeice's time and after, a kind of little Ulster – and a Protestant Nationalist Ulster. Birmingham where, of course, MacNeice hooked up with Auden, and met the local left-wing pastoralists, the flourishing 'proletarian' writers of the so-called Birmingham School, including Walter Allen, the working-class novelist and critic, who became a close friend.

Professor Thomson is distinctive not least in that his 1930s leftist pastoralism never flagged: it survived all the shaking events and traumas which undermined the faith of most of the western European aesthetic comrades and fellow-travellers – Spain, the Moscow Trials, the Hitler–Stalin Pact, Soviet postwar expansion, the Soviet invasion of Hungary, and so on. When Stalin failed him, Thomson turned to China, and he died a Maoist – a Yeatsian, Blasket Islander Maoist – in 1987. He was a period rarity, standing out from the conventional 1930s leftist narrative, of disillusionment and loss of faith in utopian futures. The conventional story is that of so many of the key cultural operators I have been naming – the likes of Orwell and Auden, Spender, Day Lewis, and Rex Warner. 'Spain was a death to us', as Day Lewis puts it in stanza 2 of those 'Dedicatory Stanzas' to Spender – a death in every sense, but especially of the political and poetic pastoralism the Spanish Revolution at first stood for. A failure for which, in strong ways, MacNeice's *Autumn Journal* stands as one of the clearest pronouncements: 'Sing us no more idylls, no more pastorals, / No more epics of the English earth' (*CP* 144).

But it would be wrong to take MacNeice as merely a spokesman for the disillusioned majority of the leftist pastoralists, the believers and hopers in pastoral who took flight, the heretics of the George Thomson church as we might call them, for whom, as MacNeice puts it in his poem 'Prologue' (intended for a collection of essays *The Character of Ireland*, which never appeared), the Blaskets had become 'empty' – of force and meaning, as well as of people (*CP* 780, 782). For what is special about MacNeice is his difference from Auden and Orwell & Co., even from fellow-Irishman Day Lewis, in the matter of country matters. His take on the period's country matters is shaped by his most personal of reactions to the matter of Ulster.

'I have no intention of recanting my past', he can assure Virginia Woolf in 1941, not so much because he intends to stick by 'thirties' positions, but because he has not got precisely the same positions to recant as the others.[14] For MacNeice, Pindar, or what Pindar might stand for, had died some time before 1938–9, the time of *Autumn Journal*. 'Pindar is dead', says the radio announcer in MacNeice's *Out of the Picture*, reading out a poem 'in praise of the great Greek athlete Pindar, a statue of whom stands, as we all know, in our own Piccadilly Circus'. There are sports and races galore, and 'flowers in all the markets', but no one to make victors' wreaths, and no one to sing celebratory songs:[15] the kind of poetry that linked Pindar to the Blasket Islanders, according to Thomson – odes to prizewinners, hymns, encomia, paeans, dithyrambs, *partheneia* (processional verses sung by choirs of girls).

The disillusionment with Greece and Greekism and classical dons that MacNeice expresses in *Autumn Journal* could not be clearer. It began at Marlborough, continued at Oxford, and was transported to Birmingham, where 'the prison-like lecture room' resounds 'To Homer in a Dudley accent' (*CP* 117) – not for MacNeice anything like Thomson's crusading efforts to make learning classical languages from scratch easier. 'The Glory that was Greece' is over; if it ever existed (*CP* 121). Classical literature and philosophy do not connect with 'the man in the street', as Thomson supposed; they shut you off from 'life in the particular always' which the humanist in his Oxford panelled room thinks of as 'Barbarian' (*CP*, 121; 131–2). And these later 1930s concernings about what one of his very earliest published poems (in *Blind Fireworks*, 1929), described as 'A Classical Education' and its effects – 'Why, then, do I loiter round these chartered sanctuaries[?]' (*CP* 641) – poke painedly through all over the earlier poetry: in the deprecated 'Bits of broken knowledge brittle and dead' in 'Spring Sunshine' (April 1929; *CP* 30); in the irony of the 'delight' in 'a dead language' that 'never shocks us by [its] banal revelations'; in 'A Contact' (April 1933; *CP* 26); in the 'minnow-twistings' of the Latinist in 'The Glacier' (July 1933; *CP* 28). According to 'Eclogue from Iceland' (originally in the Auden/MacNeice *Letters from Iceland*, 1937), the great Irish Greekist Stephen MacKenna – a great friend of E.R. Dodds – has wasted his life in spending twenty years 'translating' the Greek philosopher Plotinus. (This was a not-so-covert slap in the face for MacNeice's mentor Dodds, who had staunchly brought out MacKenna's *Journal and Letters* the year before, and who was also greatly interested in Plotinus.[16]) 'Postscript to Iceland', in *The Earth Compels* (1938), has MacNeice feeling fenced in by the 'forest of dead words' in the 'Rows of books' on the classicist's shelf (*CP* 197).

MacNeice is, of course, drawn to pastoral, in all its senses, from start to finish of his career. And from start to finish his various versions of pastoral are deeply troubled. His public writing career began in pastoral: a replay of his life, which started off in the unfallen vicarage garden, the green Eden of an innocent childhood, where the trees were all 'green', as the poem 'Autobiography' has it (in *Plant and Phantom*, 1941). But the pastoralia would not stay, well, pastoral. Would-be idylls did not ever stay idyllic. The idyllic kept on resisting the repeated summons of the pastoral mode and intention. Winter always breaks in on summer. The natural is flawed. The earth soon offends. The countryside won't do. 'It's no go the country cot with a pot of pink geraniums' ('Bagpipe Music', *CP* 96). For MacNeice country matters are upsetting, never lasting. 'The garden is going to rack' (in 'Eclogue Between the Motherless', *CP* 82). 'An April Manifesto', from April 1934, insists (three times) that 'Our April must replenish'; Spring's promise of play and sex and sun is like giving doors a new 'coat of varnish', but soon the 'leaves grow heavy and the good days vanish' (*CP* 25). The varnish in these melancholic poems inevitably vanishes. The mayfly's season is soon over, 'its gay-rags gone', and this small creature's transitoriness is a 'Barometer of my moods' (*CP* 31–2). The *winsome bubble* will always *shiver*; the *bough* always *break* ('Cradle Song for Eleanor', *CP* 209). There may be *huge roses* as well as snow pressing against 'the great bay-window' from outside the fire-lit room where the lyrical-I of 'Snow' shelters, peeling and eating a tangerine and spitting out the pips; but it is still affliction of some sort which presses in on tongue, eyes, ears, the palms of the hands (*CP* 24). The 'great bay-window' recalls the great Yeatsian windows of the Gore-Booths' Lissadel (in 'In Memory of Eva Gore-Booth and Con Marciewicz'), 'open to the south', but these MacNeicean windows only access the cold north, not the pastoral Keatsian/Yeatsian south – the sunny south registered in that tangerine, held for only an instant in the hand before being 'portioned' and reduced to its pips; a tangerine, a sort of orange, ironic reminder of the orange of Ulster and Ulster's Orange Order that would keep Ireland portioned, divided (a fruit oddly proleptic of the woman known as 'Tangerine' in the hit song of 1941 by Johnny Mercer, who is 'all I need', and in MacNeice's case is going to spit him out soon). In these spoiled pastorals all you are soon left with is the pips.

Death's cynical presence is insistent in the MacNeice eclogue (as in 'Eclogue by a Five-Barred Gate'). The great good place of love, of society, of art, is terribly shortlived, even should you locate it. The buses in 'Eclogue for Christmas' are indeed all lit up, 'With an oscu-lation of yellow light, with a glory like chrysanthemums' (CP 5). Glory as in gloriousness, and also as in haloes. But these metaphoric haloes exist only by courtesy of the city's smog. In reality, there are no chrysanthemums, only buses. The early sun of 'Morning Sun' is gay and makes the street-fountain and the butcher's and fishmonger's stalls and the cars all bright and shiny and singing; but it soon departs, leaving only dead meat, fried fish, dead-faced people, and a dusty fountain whose dryness engulfs the brightness, as (in a quite wonderful image) the ash forming on a woman's cigarette gradually 'covers the red' of her lipstick's traces (CP 15).

And the winter-garden sunlight always 'Hardens and grows cold' because it is an Ulster sun in an Ulster garden. MacNeice has learned early on that there is no Irish island of pastoral delight because of how this bit of the island of Ireland works. It is the terrible earth of Ulster which compels in 'The Sunlight on the Garden' (in The Earth Compels). The Ulster sky has been 'good for flying'. And this sky does offer a defiance to 'the church bells', and 'every evil iron / Siren' – to the religious noise of Ulster and the sounds of the Belfast shipyards (those utter opposites of the Yeatsian/George Thomson/Blasket Islands/West of Ireland Pindaric). But still the poem, and Louis MacNeice (and we the reader) cannot help but hear this bad music. The going earthly compulsion is, after all, deadly, turning young MacNeice, and indeed all of us, into Shakespeare's ageing Antony: 'The earth compels, / We are dying, Egypt, dying' (CP 57–8).[17]

This is the despondent mode and mood of the most personal early work: of 'Carrickfergus' (CP 55), the opening poem of The Earth Compels (where the Tennysonian brook, big sister of Horace's Bandusian spring, is a stinking, malodorous yellow); and 'Belfast', where the Lough is 'melancholy' and the shops are full of manmade materials (rubber gloves, celluloid), and 'the sun goes down with a banging of orange drums' (the invasive 'stupid beating' of the 'drums of Summer' in the prose-poem 'Summer Remembered', CP 658). These despondent Belfast poems remind one of that terrible passage in MacNeice's memoir The Strings are False about the two Lambeg drummers practising: one of them flailing the great drum with his canes until his wrists bleed, proof of being a good Orangeman; the pair of them marching slowly, 'faces set like Crusaders and the whole country rocking with the noise' (*SF* 57).

The notable 'Valediction' of *Poems* (1935), where it is sandwiched between 'An Eclogue for Christmas', and 'Eclogue by a Five-Barred Gate' (a positioning which hints at, but at the same time occludes, the pastoral allegiances of its original title in *Life and Letters* [June 1934], 'Valediction: An Eclogue'), is a farewell to Ireland cast in terms of challenged pastoral: the resistible *glamour* of the land of saint and hero – land of Yeats (and St Kevin and St Brandan) as well as 'Wolfe Tone and Grattan and Michael Collins' – now turned over to 'sterile want'. It is the country of heroic, patriotic Dublin, but above all of Belfast where the fife bands play and the moan of the ships' sirens sounds out over the 'sodden haycocks' and the 'water-shafted air', and the (wonderful) 'horses' feet like bells of hair / shambling beneath the orange cart'. The orange cart. A shambling horse. Pastoral Ulster has been sold in the Orange shambles. And so MacNeice must leave his mother's paps, curse his mother, go east, putting behind him pastoral memories of Achill Sound and his father's (and Thomson's) glamorous West of Ireland (*CP* 7–10). It comes as no surprise to find that the collapse of leftist-pastoral desire in Spain is figured in *Autumn Journal* XVI in terms of such Irish, and Protestant Irish, pastoral failures: 'Drums on the haycocks'; northern city Belfast, grimy as Glasgow; Yeatsian dreams shattered – the round tower 'aloof / In a world of bursting mortar!'; schoolchildren 'fumbl[ing] their sums / In a half-dead language' (*CP* 139).

And, of course, excellent classic that he is, MacNeice knows that this is what indeed happens, traditionally, with pastoral as such. His own persistently flawed pastorals are only drawing on the rooted anti-idyllicism of the pastoral tradition: the way Theocritean idylls keep being non-idyllic, and Horatian Odes and Virgilian Georgics keep being mightily troubled affairs. Winter in the tradition is as seasonal as spring and summer – as MacNeice's admired Edmund Spenser, that Protestant confronter of resistant wild traditional Ireland, and Milton, that Spenser admirer, both well knew. 'Weep no more, woeful shepherds, weep no more', urges Milton's 'Lycidas', for Lycidas is not dead: but he is dead, and the shepherds are weeping. The Garden – it is, of course, Milton's strongest note – is where the Fall always takes place. MacNeice's discomfited eclogues are in good traditional company. So that he can say with a kind of rightness in the passage from *Autumn Journal* XVIII about pastoral music in the early days – the songs for *corn* and *barn*, reaping and spinning – that 'only the shepherd ... was silent beside the tarn' (*CP* 144). Silent then; and silent now: 'Then as now': silenced now, as of old, by the failure of 'idylls' and 'pastorals' (and 'epics of the English earth').

It is a realisation MacNeice loudly declares in *The Earth Compels* in his 'Solvitur Acris Hiems (Horace, *Odes*, 1.4)'. Mind the Horatian tradition, he is exhorting the would-be pastoralist, in this close-up version of the Horace (*CP* 61). Spring does indeed arrive. 'Solvitur acris hiems' ('the harsh winter is dissolved'): 'Winter to Spring', as MacNeice renders it. The time comes for 'the thirsty hull' to be hauled to the sea by a pastoral-serving 'windlass' (Horace's *machinae*: machines); time for the animals to go out into the unfrozen fields; for dancing and art and celebration and religion. But – without MacNeice or Horace missing a beat – death and night also arrive: life is short; it does not sustain hope; you are about to enter 'the narrow house of nothing' (MacNeice's adaptation of Horace's *domus exilis Plutonia*: the *meagre abode* of Pluto, God of the Underworld). Anti-pastoral is the authentic note of the pastoral tradition, and all contemporary pastoralists had better know that.

Which is not to say that MacNeiece's craving for pastoral – in all of its senses – ever abated, did not keep on being striven for. He will do, or try to do, pastoral 'All Over Again', as his 1959 poem of that title (last item in *Solstices*, 1961) has it – and find it fail all over again – and again. In poem after poem: in 'Visitations' and 'Solstice', in 'Donegal Triptych', 'Country Week-End', 'Nature Notes', the 'park' poems, 'Spring Cleaning', 'October in Bloomsbury', 'Goodbye to London'. On and on. He will try to write as if lost pastoral, like lost love, were nonetheless possible. As if (in 'Apple Blossom', opening poem of *Solstices*) the apple could be eaten again; as if the first, lost, pastoral ensemble of garden, tree, ocean, sun, blue sky might be recovered; as if the morning after the Fall could possibly recreate the 'first day' of creation. All over again: in the perpetual *As if* of the renewed, retrying of the pastoral poem, forever (re)investing in the necessary *As if* of the poetic, of the metaphoric as such ('That's my last duchess painted on the wall / Looking as if she were alive', Robert Browning).

A constant return, a repetivity signalled, of course, from very early on. Momentously, no less, in the endlessly captivating 'The Sunlight on the Garden'. Sunlight – pastoral, pastoral desire – it returns to be thwarted, hardened, cold, yet once more. Returning, because unforgettable (like the pastoral tradition). An unforgettability signalled, as ever, in MacNeice's intense verbal anaphorics – his rhymes, those verbal returnings. His particular rhymings. Not, I think, as Robin Skelton thinks, a matter of Gaelic rhymes, of a Thomsonian Irish Pindaric[18] – MacNeice never goes West, or that far West, for his formal proceedings. But, rather, a case of Gerard Hopkins's Psalmaic and Welsh rhymings: the intense repetivity of that Protestant convert to Catholicism who suffered so much in Catholic Ireland. Returning, like all rhymes (all echoes), with a difference – emblem of the difference in the samenesses of all MacNeice's pastoralia. The *varnish:vanish* effect of 'An April Sunshine': the *varnish* reappearing with distinct loss as *vanish*: shine gone, an awful unvarnishing. The differential returning that is the greatest feature of 'The Sunlight on the Garden' – MacNeice's play with *epanastrophe* (the figure by which the end word of one sentence becomes the first word of the next): *garden/Hardens*; *lances/Advances*; *upon it/Sonnet*; *flying/Defying*; *iron/Siren*; *under/Thunder* (*CP* 57–8). A returning, near the poem's end (the beginning of the final stanza) of the most pronounced (semantic) difference of all: *pardon, / Hardened* (the only one of these returns that makes you pause in the reading, the voicing, with that comma after *pardon* – gives you pause, no less – before hurrying you on to that utterly rebarbative opposite of pardoning, that hardening).

And yet, for all these losses, the poem's pastoral note persists – in the returning final word, *garden*. On which the sun still shines, gratifyingly. But this is not, as is sometimes suggested, a matter of a simple relieving reliving, a simple consoling return of the garden that the poem's opening line starts us in. No simple recursive this. Rather, here is a complex return in a chiasmus: the rhyming *garden: pardon* of the first and last lines of stanza 1, chiasmically reversed as *pardon: garden*, in the first and last lines of stanza 4. So that the *garden* of verse 1, place of necessary but impossible *pardon*, returns, as the poem's last word, to have the last word, arising as if now forgiven, pardoned indeed, out of the old unpardonability (transgression in and of the garden, pastoral loss); but for all this 'grateful' and 'glad' conclusion, a return still not able to discard or shed the burden of its forever reminding chiasmic doubles partner: the pardon which is still impossible to *beg for* (as stanza 1 has it), which is for ever tauntingly present, but only as what is now no longer really for 'expecting'.

In the poem's end, then, is its beginning; the pastoral note at the last *as if* at the first: the final note one of (schooled, knowing, life-weary) longing still for the pastoralia, the old idyll dream, the recovery of the lost, the fallen garden. In which breaking-dream mood, MacNeice addresses his former, now broken-hearted comrades, in 'Thalassa', that (aptly) final-sounding replay of the urgings of Tennyson's old-man traveller from the classical tradition, namely his Ulysses, urging his men to set sail (once more) for the Happy Isles, the pastoral destination, where 'some work of nobler note may yet be done':

Run out the boat, my broken comrades;
Let the old seaweed crack, the surge
Burgeon oblivious of the last
Embarkation of feckless men,
Let every adverse force converge –
Here we must needs embark again.

Run up the sail, my heartsick comrades;
Let each horizon tilt and lurch –
You know the worst: your wills are fickle,
Your values blurred, your hearts impure
And your past life a ruined church –
But let your poison be your cure.

Put out to sea, ignoble comrades,
Whose record shall be noble yet;
Butting through scarps of moving marble
The narwhal dares us to be free;
By a high star our course is set,
Our end is Life. Put out to sea. (*CP* 783)

As with Tennyson's older crew, the comrades in this poem do not put out to sea. The sense of endedness, of everything being actually all over despite the hortatory possibility that it is not really, which the poem holds out, fits the mood of end-of-thirties downheartedness when the poem was apparently first mooted, in the early 1940s perhaps, even more than the last months of MacNeice's life when it was apparently completed. And you have to admire the desire for the thirties dream not to be over, even if you know that the poem is clamantly about how its rather ragged wishes must be for ever after taken for the deeds that the comrades – *broken, heartsick, ignoble* – will never manage for real.

ECLOGUES BETWEEN THE TRUCULENT

Derek Mahon

I met Louis MacNeice twice if you can call it that, and both times he was in rugby mode. Calling one afternoon at the flat in Regent's Park he shared with the actress Mary Wimbush, we found him watching rugby on TV and saying little. Constrained by his rugby-watching silence, I said little myself. What did I expect, poetry talk? (A big fan, I had recently read his latest collection *Solstices*, which I thought was disappointing; this must have been 1962.) We watched some rugby and then it was time to go. I got the impression that, even without the rugby, he would have been uncommunicative. The curtains were closed and I saw only a grave grey head and a sombre equine face; though literally long in the tooth, he had 'presence'. I was virtually ignored but didn't mind, aware that, while to me he was the great poet, to him I was nobody in particular.

Grand houses in Regent's Park were not my usual ambience. I was much struck by this one, by the elegant Mary Wimbush, and by the voices. Louis was nasal Oxford, a sonorous growl, Mary pure BBC circa 1960; those there of my own age had already adopted 'Mockney' and a shared idiom of branché, cool, and ciao.

Some months later I was sitting with other students in a well-known Dublin pub and noticed two older men at a nearby table, one talkative, one taciturn. The taciturn one was MacNeice. With the bumptiousness of youth we went over and introduced ourselves; he didn't remember me of course. He wore some kind of an anorak, looked unkempt, and acknowledged us with a polite snarl and a side-long flash of the horsy teeth. The talkative one, Bill Webb, books editor of the *Manchester Guardian*, as it then was, chuckled at our intrusion. He was a lively man in tweeds, with a short pepper-and-salt beard, who had put himself in charge of the truculent Louis.

Both were on the whiskey, the effect being to make Webb witty and MacNeice morose. We spoke to Webb and I tried in vain to get a response out of MacNeice, preferably some poetry talk. Perhaps, frustrated by his reluctance, I got a bit truculent too. (What a pain in the neck I must have been.) They had been to a rugby international at Lansdowne Road, and MacNeice's report appeared the next week in the *New Statesman*, its circulation higher then than now. He mentioned Dublin pubs and remarked on their 'aggressive' (bad mannered) students. We had been put in our place. He died the following year.

Not exactly Keats and Coleridge, is it? But it's seldom a good idea to meet your admired authors; you will often be disappointed. (Not always: Keats wasn't, for one.) Not meaning any harm, they may take no notice of you; or, meaning a little harm, they may put you down. Besides, they are generally older, wearier, and less forthcoming than you might wish, and words of wisdom will be few. Such was my experience of MacNeice. I was just some Belfast whippersnapper of course. He was in rugby mode; though once a nifty scrum-half, I'd lost interest in rugby. He didn't want to be bothered (why should he?) and he was tired of words, of which he had written a great many. Tired too, perhaps, of life itself: it's there in the last poems. But you knew that, even if you got on the wrong side of him, he wouldn't clobber you like some. His eyes were kind, and it was his eyes that spoke. The mouth might snarl, the gnashers flash, but that was just his manner: the gaze was a speculative and not unfriendly one. He seemed like his later work, grim and sardonic, scored by long experience, though there was a wistful nobility too. If the world he loved so much had let him down, the long head rose above it – as his best work now rises above that of his contemporaries.[1]

MACNEICE'S VEHICLES

Hugh Haughton

1

MacNeice is not only a moving poet, but a poet with an interest in movement. This is particularly evident in his fascination with vehicles. 'Trains came threading quietly through my dozing childhood', he says in 'Trains in the Distance', and trains and other vehicles thread through the *Collected Poems*, bringing MacNeice's interest in modern technology (clocks, gantries, mirrors, spinning-wheels, newsreels, and the like) to bear on the sense of movement that propels his verse. 'Riding in cars / On tilting roads', he says early on, 'We have left behind / Our household gods' (*CP* 41). Having left the household gods behind, such vehicles and roads move through his poems, and his poems through them.

In his 1924 essay 'The Poet and his Age', Richard Aldington praised the 'instinct which has prevented most English poets of this age from running after Marinetti, to praise motor-cars, or to grow hysterical over aeroplanes'.[1] There are other attitudes than propagandist 'praise' or Futurist euphoria, however, and MacNeice was interested in modern vehicles for different reasons. He had no aesthetic or cultural axe (or axle) to grind, but was following his instinctive appetite for mobility, his dependence on travel in his daily life, and his need to reflect the world through the new angles of vision offered by modern transport. As a poet he was acutely aware of things in motion as well as the lost 'household gods'.

MacNeice wrote an essay on 'Subject in Modern Poetry' (1937), and, at one level, vehicles are just typical modern subjects, as when he announces 'Pindar is dead − / The petrol pumps are doing a roaring business, / Motors are tuning for the Easter races' (*CP* 43). In this respect cars and petrol-pumps are like telephones, cinemas, and pylons, stuff that any latter-day Pindar has to take on board. In 'Poetry Today', however, MacNeice observes that 'to be merely topical, by mentioning carburettors or complexes, is not truly modern' (*SLC* 34). Indeed he criticises Day Lewis for being 'sometimes too facile in introducing his culverts, gasometers, cylinders and other modern properties'. MacNeice's vehicles may sometimes be facile, but they fuel some of his best poems. In this respect he is like his near contemporary the Irish novelist Elizabeth Bowen, who spoke of wanting to capture people 'in fluidity, in (apparent) motion', and of her tendency to 'impart' to her characters 'unconsciously, an enthusiastic naivety with regard to transport which in my own case time has not dimmed. Zestfully they take ship or board planes: few of them are *blasés* about railways. Motor-cars magnetise them particularly.'[2] MacNeice was equally magnetised, and since metaphors and transport are etymologically twinned, liked to turn them into poetical vehicles in their own right.

'Carrickfergus' begins with memories of childhood amid 'the hooting of lost sirens and the clang of trams' (*CP* 55), and his earliest published poems are full of vehicles and traffic noise. As early as eleven, he wrote a squib beginning, 'It was in a quite modern year, / That, in an aeroplane / An enterprising pioneer / Set out to study Spain', and later the pioneering poet commandeered many other vehicles (*L* 32). 'Happy Families' includes a family entirely defined in terms of public transport: 'John caught the bus, Joshua caught the train / And I took a taxi, so we all got somewhere' (*CP* 626–7). In 'Impermanent Creativeness', the creatively mobile poet announces 'Over asphalt, tar, and gravel / My racing model happily purrs', and 'Each charted road I yet unravel / Out of my mind's six cylinders' (*CP* 645). The would-be Marinetti from Carrickfergus (one cylinder for each of the six counties) is at home behind the wheel, as vehicle, route, and 'mind' purr (and power) together. 'Transportation is civilisation', Ezra Pound announced in 1917, but neither he nor Eliot purred along a Blakean 'charted road' with a 'six-cylinder' mind.[3]

Other early poems show MacNeice registering transport as an observer. 'Birmingham' begins with 'Smoke from the train-gulf hid by hoardings', and registers 'the brakes of cars', a 'queue of fidgety machines', and 'eyes staring through traffic' (*CP* 22). In 'Museums', the poet is 'running from among the buses' (*CP* 29), while in 'Sunday Morning' he observes the way 'Man's heart expands to tinker with his car' (*CP* 21). 'Morning Sun' begins with an evocation of 'Shuttles of trains going north, going south, drawing threads of blue, / The shining of the lines of trams like swords'. It goes on to record sun 'bouncing on traffic that never stops' and 'horns of cars', representing the city as a 'moving cage, / A turning page of shine and sound, the day's maze' (*CP* 15). This poetry of traffic takes programmatic form in 'Train to Dublin', which speaks of the 'train's rhythm', comments on the 'tiny portion of our lives we are not in trains', and appropriates the passenger viewpoint on 'the incidental things which pass' (*CP* 17). Though MacNeice is not always on trains, the Irish Heraclitus spends a lot of his *oeuvre* looking from or at motorised vehicles of one kind or another, and very often trains, as we shall see.

In 'Eclogue Between the Motherless' the poet wakes 'with the window / Jittering in its frame from the train passing the garden', and remembers a woman 'mostly in the car, stopping by the white / Moons of the petrol pumps' (*CP* 82–7). There are poems called 'Passage Steamer' and 'Riding in Cars' as well as 'The Taxis', and his major sequence *Autumn Journal* opens on a railway: 'And I am in the train too now and summer is going / South as I go north' towards 'London's packed and stale and pregnant air' (*CP* 101). Social change is registered by 'cars that pass the gate-lodge', and 'the rebels and the young' who take 'the train to town or the two-seater / Unravelling rails or road' (*CP* 101). Later in the opening section, 'the train's rhythm becomes the *ad nauseam* repetition / Of every tired aubade and maudlin madrigal' (*CP* 102), setting up an opportunistic analogy between poetry and the vehicle, and insisting on the need to move on from pure repetition of earlier poetic forms, as in his own new-minted jazzy song 'I love my love with a platform ticket' (*CP* 102). His consciousness of new poetic rhythms is caught later in the sequence with his easy counterpointing of the natural and cultural, old and new, in lines beautifully attuned to modern transport:

> And now the woodpigeon starts again denying
>   The values of the town
> And a car having crossed the hill accelerates, changes
>   Up, having just changed down.
> And a train begins to chug and I wonder what the morning
>   Paper will say,
> And decide to go quickly to sleep for the morning already
>   Is with us, the day is to-day. (*CP* 111)

The pigeon song, train 'chug', and newspapers compete equally for attention as the poet drifts towards sleep in London, while the verse flexes to register the car's gear-change across the line-break with a weird flurry of changing tenses. 'Changes / Up, having just changed down' subtly registers the ways in which our experience of the world is changed utterly with new forms of transport.

In *Letters from Iceland*, co-written with Auden, MacNeice was a pioneer of the poetic travel book; and he wrote numerous poems such as 'Leaving Barra', 'Wessex Guidebook', and 'The Solitary Traveller', which are about travel. What is more striking is the way travelling vehicles shaped his poems. In 'Poetry Today', he says 'when the poet tries to explain his work, he is much less helpful than the mechanic explaining an engine', and his explanatory analogy between poem and engine suggests we could even look at his poems as dynamic machines offering moving images of the contemporary world (*SLC* 10). The contemporary sociologist John Urry has made mobility, and the transport revolution, the key to his studies of modernity, and I would argue that MacNeice's poems anticipate such a view. He is one of the first poets to be interested in transport of all kinds, and to see the world through the eyes of a driver, a passenger, and an observer of traffic, as attentive to roads and railways as the landscape they take him through.[4]

2

In what follows I hope to document something of the scale of MacNeice's investment in what Urry calls 'mobilities', dwelling in particular on the early poems where this first comes into focus and then a run of late poems where his sense of modern transport systems contributes to some of his finest lyrics.

To begin, I want to consider the special case of taxis, a form of transport with which MacNeice was associated, first and last. In the first poem in the new *Collected Poems*, 'An Eclogue for Christmas' (from *Poems*, 1935), the city dweller tells the countryman 'Go back where your instincts call / And listen to the crying of the town-cats and the taxis again' (*CP* 3). This associates taxis with a place where 'instincts call', the world of primal drives. In 'The Taxis' (from his last book, *The Burning Perch* of 1963), the taxi driver becomes an incongruous version of the infernal ferryman, to be joined in the companion poem 'Charon' by a London bus conductor, transporting the poet to the border between the modern city and classical under-world: 'And there was the ferryman just as Virgil / And Dante had seen him' (*CP* 593). In the much earlier 'The Preacher' MacNeice conjures up a life-denying fundamentalist for whom 'Every train or boat he took was Charon's ferry' (*CP* 191), and in these late poems, MacNeice frequently finds himself in the same boat (or train). Between these early and late taxis, 'Bagpipe Music' cynically conjures a 'bit of skirt in a taxi', while the closing lullaby of *Autumn Journal* envisages an individual 'endowed / With the split vision of a juggler and the quick lock of a taxi' (*CP* 163). The 'quick vision of a juggler' is instantly intelligible, but that 'quick lock of the taxi' is a measure of the strange persistence of the cab in this juggler's repertoire.

Reflection on the word 'taxi' throws some light on MacNeice's taxi fixation. The *OED* confirms it as a recent coinage, quoting the *Daily News* of 1908 saying 'Within the past few months the "taxi" has been the name given to the motor-cab' (less than twenty years before 'An Eclogue'). The dictionary derives it from the French *'taximètre'*, a compound of *'taxe* meaning "tariff" and *mètre* meaning "meter"', a word referring to 'An automatic contrivance fitted on a cab or other vehicle to indicate to the passenger ... the distance traversed and the fare due'. In a nice case of a metaphorical synecdoche, the term was transferred from an internal measuring gadget to the vehicle itself. This makes the taxi a particularly suitable vehicle for poetry, since it is the only one to have a built-in meter. This helps explain its role in 'The Taxis', and the taxi that draws up to the desk in 'Reflections', invading and mobilising the scene of writing itself.

3

MacNeice's *Collected Poems* offer a field day to the train-spotter – or car-spotter. There are lots of poems about the poet as motorist, which offer views from speeding cars or celebrate windscreens, wipers, headlights, accelerators, and brakes, making MacNeice the first laureate of the era of the private motor car. There are many others about public transport, with scores of poems about travelling in trains, specialising in moving views from train windows, as in 'Train to Dublin' or *Autumn Sequel*. Though there is a poem called 'The Cyclist' from *Holes in the Sky* (1948) which focuses on memories of schooldays, bikes do not generally count for much in MacNeice's world. Nor, with the solitary exception of 'Solitary Travel' (*CP* 557–8), do boats or planes, though he gives a fine account of a transatlantic liner and air trip over the USA in *The Strings are False* (25–6).

A vivid early instance of MacNeice's poetic trafficking in traffic is to be found in 'Eclogue for Christmas'. In it the speaker talks as a

motorist driving through the city ('my right leg creating speed'),
arrested by the sight of an attractive woman on the kerb: 'Making me
catch and stamp, the brakes shrieking, pull up dead' (*CP* 4). Body,
psyche, and poem, blur into each other in this account of city driving.
The poet as driver goes on to report that 'On all the traffic-islands
stand white globes like moons': 'The city's haze is clouded amber that
purrs and croons, / And tilting by the noble curve of bus after tall bus
comes / With an osculation of yellow light, with a glory like chrysanthemums' (*CP* 5). Traffic islands were a comparatively new invention
in the 1930s, but immediately absorbed into MacNeice's motoring
currency. Yeats was horrified by the bright lights on O'Connell
Bridge, but MacNeice's buses pass a 'noble curve', inspiring 'a glory
like chrysanthemums'. *OED* defines 'glory' as 'Resplendent beauty
or magnificence', or 'An effulgence of light such as is associated with
our conceptions of heaven; *fig*. An unearthly beauty attributed by
imagination.' It recalls the aureoles and halos in paintings, and their
transferred sense of 'Any circle or ring of light; a halo, corona'.
Optics, theology, and poetic transcendence overlap in the light of the
traffic lights and mechanical 'moons' in MacNeice's urban vision. His
word 'osculation' (from Latin) refers to both 'kissing' and, in geometry, the 'contact of curves or surfaces which share a common tangent
at the point of contact'. It captures something of the erotic aura of
the twentieth-century city, with its cubist geometry of traffic systems
that might have been 'Posed by Picasso' (*CP* 3).

MacNeice's rarer boats are also mechanically powered. Naval ships
figure in 'Convoy' and 'Casualty' as well as the related World War
Two play *He Had a Date*, which opens on-board ship with 'Track in
the water approaching. Tin fish' (*SP* 76), and of course in his 1942
radio play *Christopher Columbus*, with its cry of 'Westward! Westward!
Legendary isles / Call our ships to sea and who knows where / We
shall come to port!' (*SP* 7). *Christopher Columbus* was written soon
after MacNeice's return from his trip to the States, and it is significant that it was on shipboard that he began *The Strings are False*, which
opens with an account of himself as a transatlantic passenger returning
to wartime Britain: 'Thus here I am now on a boat going back to a
war and my feelings are too mixt to disentangle. The passengers' faces
are settled in gloom and I have plenty of reason to be gloomy too,
being a mere nomad who has lost his tent' (*SF* 17). The sense of being
a 'nomad who has lost his tent' has to do with being a passenger, and
it is the state out of which the autobiography builds. He goes on to

describe his previous journey to the USA, the chapter ending with an account of his arrival and 'second night ashore', when he describes himself 'riding to my doom in a steamer that was running amok', 'the machines at last taking over, the skippers and pilots and engineers ignored – in a boiling yellow incredible sea' (*SF* 21–2). It is with this tangled dream voyage, a replay of the real journey to the States, that the first chapter ends; and these two transatlantic journeys, actual and dreamed, frame the self-exploratory autobiographical journey that follows (*SF* 35).

MacNeice mentions the presence of refugees from Europe on the liner and his poem 'Refugees' uses the movement of the boat to capture their arrival in New York: 'These, disinterred from Europe, throng the deck / To watch their hope heave up in steel and concrete' (*CP* 197). The poem shows Manhattan through their displaced eyes, as their glances 'feel / Around the sliding limber towers of Wall Street / And count the numbered docks and gingerly steal / Into the hinterland of their own future'. The poem's cinematic eye-view is mobile as ever, as the refugees see Wall Street as 'sliding limber towers' and 'The liner moves like a magnet'. New York, with its 'trains like prayers / Radiating from stations haughty as cathedrals', is all motion ('barrows of cement are rumbling / Up airy planks'), and when they finally descend the 'Gangways' and reach 'the hand-clasp of land', the refugees 'still feel / The movement of the ship while through their imagination / The known and the unheard-of constel-lations wheel'. The wheeling of those 'known and unheard-of constellations' suggests the heavens, of course, but also the ship's engines and the revolutions undergone by the refugees in flight from Europe. It is that carefully registered and 'magnetic' 'movement of the ship' which focuses the exiles' view of New York as it looms into focus.

If ships mainly figure in these scenes from wartime, trains not only threaded through MacNeice's childhood but through his entire *oeuvre*, as represented by those stations 'haughty as cathedrals'. MacNeice described his Dublin play *Station Bell* as a 'tragic farce in a railway station', and wanted a musician to devise 'an orchestral Irish PotPourri super-imposed … on the noises of trains coming & going in a station' (*L* 240, 253). Like ships, trains acquired a different force during the war. 'Carrickfergus', looking back to World War One, remembers the camouflaged 'steamer that took me to England' and immediately afterwards 'Sweat and khaki in the Carlisle train', while in the World War Two poem 'Trilogy for X', we hear 'The power of trains advancing', how 'The first train passes and the windows groan', and the poet sings 'O my love, the / Southward trains are puffing'. This generates one of MacNeice's most explicit trains of thought about trains, as he contemplates the last months of peace: 'From the moving train of time the / Fields move backward' (*CP* 175–8). Though this is an almost too glibly allegorical account of the passing of the pre-war world, 'Poised on the edge of absence', those 'southward' trains are presumably carrying soldiers, and suggest troop movements towards the continent of Europe (as references to the 'goal / Unknown we march to' and the soldier who 'tightens his belt and outlook' confirm). If the train is an image of 'the moving train of time', it is also an image of time galvanised by the specific historical moment.

'Corner Seat' opens with another clip of wartime train travel:

> Suspended in a moving night
> The face in the reflected train
> Looks at first sight as self-assured
> As your own face – But look again. (*CP* 255)

Despite the 'windows between you and the world', the poet asks 'Then why does your reflection seem / So lonely in the moving night?' MacNeice is always expertly aware of reflections, mirrors, and windows, and here 'the face in the reflected train' superimposes face and train in a compound mirage, while what is 'moving' is the 'night' (its effect of movement generated by the train's). 'Slow Movement', from the same volume, also begins with a train journey: 'Waking, he found himself in a train, andante, / With wafers of early sunlight blessing the unknown fields' (*CP* 279–80). Train ride, musical movement, and dream dissolve into each other, each becoming a metaphor for the others:

> The movement ends, the train has come to a stop
> In buttercup fields, the fiddles are silent, the whole
> Shoal of silver tessellates the aquarium
>   Floor, not a bubble rises...

'The movement' here refers to a piece of music, like Honegger's 'Pacific 231' (which was subtitled 'Un mouvement symphonique'), and to the motion of the train, both of which are marked by rhythm and momentum, like the poem. Honegger, who had 'a passionate love of locomotives', said 'Pacific 231' was a 'translation into music of the visual impressions' of train travel, and the same could be said of MacNeice's poem. The equation of the two senses of 'movement' confirms the aesthetic importance of 'transport' for the much travelled poet.

4

Nevertheless vehicles seemed to fall out of the picture in the 'middle years' after the war, when MacNeice's imagination also seemed less mobilised in every sense. An exception is 'Our Sister Water', where he interrupts a hymn to water with a satirical ballad on steam:

> Back in the Seventeen-Seventies to Birmingham he came,
> The Scot, John Watt, of combustion engine fame,
> Having lived overlong in a hobside dream,
> Murdering his sister Water, turning her to steam … (*CP* 339–40)

Though noting his 'great Soho foundry is there to this day', MacNeice's rant against the combustion engine lacks any concrete sense of transport, machinery or contemporary life, suggesting the poet may have run out of steam himself.

With *Autumn Sequel* (1954), a return upon his earlier *Autumn Journal*, the challenge of returning to the journal form stiffened now by Dantean *terza rima*, brings with it a return to MacNeice's earlier preoccupations. The third Canto, for example, echoing the opening of 'an autumn journal – or journey' (*CP* 373), conjures a trip to work by 'suburban train' past 'the antennae of Wembley Hill / And Sudbury Hill, drab realms of television' (*CP* 383). The laboured *terza rima* verse, however, lacks the self-adjusting mobility of *Autumn Journal* and risks capitulating to the 'drab realms' it records. Nevertheless, train and car journeys thread their way through the sequence, as when the speaker presents himself as paradoxically immobilised by speed, 'Glued to my seat, whirled down a ruthless track' (*CP* 462). This renewed interest in what Urry calls modern 'mobilities paradigms' was a prelude to the memorable and memory-haunted vehicular lyrics of MacNeice's last books, *Solstices* (1961) and *The Burning Perch* (1963).

Two intermediary poems are 'Figure of Eight and 'Death of an Old Lady'. The first sets two different vehicles against each other in paired symmetrical six-line rhymed stanzas. The opening stanza features a would-be motorist on a double-decker bus:

> In the top and front of a bus, eager to meet his fate,
> He pressed his foot and mind to gather speed,
> Then, when the lights were changing, jumped and hurried,
> Though dead on time, to the meeting place agreed,
> But there was no one there. He chose to wait.
> No one came. He need not perhaps have worried. (*CP* 516)

The initial image captures the fantasy agency of the bus passenger who imagines himself a driver, pressing 'his foot and mind to gather speed'. MacNeice plays on the metaphorical possibilities lurking in everyday idiom like 'eager to meet his fate' and 'when the lights were changing' (which refers to 'traffic lights' but suggests other kinds of changing light). The poet of 'Meeting Point' gives that phrase a new twist with 'dead on time, to the meeting place agreed'; where once 'Time was away and somewhere else', this time the term 'dead' signals the real subject, the time of death. The stanza is about changing speed, and a sense of anti-climax on arrival, with the variations of line and punctuation capturing the passenger's changing experience of pace. The 'foot' reminds us of the poetic foot, while the rhymed line-endings suggest intermediate destinations (or meeting places) and the metrical ambiguities suggest the quiet drama of expectations raised and thwarted. Though many of the lines can be read as pentameters, they can also be read other ways. The first line, with its opening anapaest ('In the top') reads as a symmetrical hexameter, with a central chiasmus, while the second, uninterrupted by punctuation, rushes forward with regular iambic momentum. The third, however, with its three strong verbs, offers a contrast with both. Its opening abrupt single stress ('Then') is followed by a comma, another anapaest ('when the lights'), and a huddle of active verbs contorted by commas. Like the first line, it can be read as having either five or six stresses. There is no hint of rhyme in the opening lines, and it is only at the end of the fourth, where 'agreed' agrees with 'speed', that we realise we are in a rhymed stanza. Immediately afterwards the poem changes gear with 'But there was no one there'. The 'But' follows the 'Though' and 'Then' opening the previous lines, but confuses our grammatical sense of direction, so that, after we get to the 'agreed' stop, we are propelled into a rhythmically different world of stops rather than commas. The three negatives ('there was no one there', 'no one came' and 'he need not perhaps have worried') sound less a note of positive relief than of a fate deferred.

The second stanza changes vehicle, tense, and mood:

> Whereas today in the rear and gloom of a train,
> Loath, loath to meet his fate, he cowers and prays
> For some last-minute hitch, some unheard-of abdication,
> But, winding up the black thread of his days,
> The wheels roll on and make it all too plain
> Who will be there to meet him at the station.

Rolling wheels are the hub of MacNeice's vehicular imagination, and this last stanza, with its sense of ineluctable forward motion, has the form of a single rolling sentence, with a built-in sense of an ending. After the un-enjambed first stanza, this has two over-spilling lines, emphasising the lack of obstacles to the dreaded encounter. The 'black thread' suggests railway lines in the first instance, but recast as 'the black thread of his days', returning us, via the reference to the Greek Fates, to the opening image of 'his fate'. This time the final line offers a sense of destination and destiny. The full rhyme of 'station' and 'abdication' gains force by the para-rhymes with 'plain' and 'train', consummating all MacNeice has set in train.

'Death of an Old Lady' is another poem about impending death, taking a vehicle as its vehicle. Its opening takes us back to a flash of childhood memory in Carrickfergus:

> At five in the morning there were grey voices
> Calling three times through the dank fields;
> The ground fell away beyond the voices
> Forty long years to the wrinkled lough
> That had given a child a shining glimpse
> Of a boat so big it was named Titanic. (*CP* 517)

Dwelling briefly on the ship's name, the poem converts the liner's voyage into an image of the old lady's death. Like the ship, she 'sails / Toward her own iceberg calm and slow', 'We hardly hear the screws', and 'At eight in the evening the ship went down'. In contrast to Hardy's 'The Convergence of the Twain', MacNeice hijacks the liner for a domestic and private elegy, as the fate of the anonymous and unnamed lady (his stepmother) is absorbed into that of the famous ship. Though the six-line stanzas are generally unrhymed, the final stanza generates a sense of closure with its self-rhymed repetitions:

> They called and ceased. Later the night nurse
> Handed the day over, the day went down
> To the sea in a ship, it was grey April,
> The daffodils in her garden waited
> To make her a wreath, the iceberg waited;
> At eight in the evening the ship went down.

The last 'down' recalls that in the second line, as 'waited' in the penultimate line repeats 'waited' in the line before, bringing the literal world of the woman's day into line with the overriding metaphor of the sinking Titanic. The reference to 'going down to the sea in ships' wittily aligns the great twentieth-century ship with the biblical world, and the poem's modern vehicle with archaic ships of death.

The vehicular vision of mortality embodied in these poems is developed in MacNeice's last two books, looming large in 'The Atlantic Tunnel' (*CP* 535), another view of wartime America from a transatlantic liner, and 'Homage to Wren' (*CP* 536), a dream-like view of wartime London as a storm-tossed ship, 'on deck with the spray / Of bombs in our ears'. 'Solitary Travel' (*CP* 557–8), a study of airports, is his only poem about air travel, while 'Variation on Heraclitus', with its vision of 'the chairoplane of a chair' (*CP* 560), compounds the sedentary and the mobile, capturing the twentieth century's technological variant on Heraclitean flux. 'The chairo-plane' reflects a sense of transport in the home, as does 'Reflections', his most fluid mirror-poem. It starts from the proposition that 'The mirror above my fireplace reflects the reflected / Room in my window', and then turns his room into a hall of mirrors in which 'Lamp comes thrice in my mirror, twice in my window, / The fire in the mirror lies two rooms away through the window' and the 'actual room stands sandwiched between confections / Of night and lights and glass' (*CP* 561). The poem begins as a relatively straight-forward empirical report, with its first four lines rhymed ABBA, and one 'window' rhyming with another at the end of lines 7 and 8 (in the lines quoted above). Thereafter, however, the rhyme scheme goes increasingly haywire, and the poem morphs into a Surrealist maze of reflections that climaxes with the hypothetical arrival of MacNeice's signature vehicle in his room:

> I can see beyond and through the reflections the street lamps
> At home outdoors where my indoors rooms lies stranded,
> Where a taxi perhaps will drive in through the bookcase
> Whose books are not for reading and past the fire
> Which gives no warmth and pull up by my desk
> At which I cannot write since I am not lefthanded.

This virtuosic poem ends with a vision of the poet unable to write, that final 'lefthanded' rhymed with 'stranded', and giving the sixteen-line poem the effect of a painfully stretched sonnet. The vision of a taxi driving in through the bookcase and pulling up by his desk is like something out of Magritte or *Through the Looking Glass*. It also, however, bizarrely confirms the recurrent connection in MacNeice's poetry between modern transport and the scene of writing.

'Restaurant Car' represents a comparable vision of ominous fluidity, with the world of ordinary everyday objects and actions transformed by the surreal motility produced by modern technology. According to the poet, the diners on the train

> … roughride over the sleepers, finger the menu,
> Avoid our neighbours' eyes and wonder what

> Mad country moves beyond the steamed-up window
> So fast into the past we could not keep
> Our feet on it one instant. (*CP* 562)

Again, the train is an image of things passing, with the 'steamed-up window', 'single tickets only' and 'sleepers' all giving this vision concrete embodiment. The fact that 'the water in the carafe / Shakes its hips' and the 'waiters totter / Along the invisible tightrope' is a confirmation of speed, a speed that 'the past' suggests is temporal as well as spatial, and the 'tightrope' suggests is precarious as well as following a 'line'. The reference to 'feet', shaking hips and 'tomtom' all suggest poetic rhythm, and the stanza is converted into a mirror of the restaurant car, or vice versa. Since the word *stanza* derives from the Italian for 'room', a 'Restaurant Car' seems an appropriate modern 'variant'.

'The Wiper' returns us to cars, and to the view through the wind-screen rather than 'steamed-up window':

> Through purblind night the wiper
> Reaps a swathe of water
> On the screen; we shudder on
>   And hardly hold the road,
> All we can see is a segment
> Of blackly shining asphalt
> With the wiper moving across it
>   Clearing, blurring, clearing. (*CP* 562–3)

Screens and windows are crucial to MacNeice, particularly in his poems about vehicles, as in this lyric with its cinematic sense of move-ment and intermittence. The opening image ('the wiper / Reaps') turns the wiper into a reaper, giving the claustrophobic view through the window a sense of precariousness. There are no rhymes, but there is a humming sonic and rhythmic pattern, as 'wiper' is taken up by 'water' at the end of the next line and 'shudder' in the third, while the 't' in 'night' and 'water' is repeated at the close of 'segment', 'asphalt', and 'it', only to be supplanted by the repetitively dominant present participle in the final lines ('shining', 'moving', and then in the last line 'Clearing, blurring, clearing').

Presenting night as broken by 'lights that pass or meet us / From others in moving boxes', MacNeice comments on the 'camber' of the road, the 'dials / Professing to tell the distance / We have gone, the speed we are going', turning the journey into a bleaker, more desperately enclosed version of 'Train to Dublin'. The view from the moving box is again vertiginous and unsettling, and it leads, in a sustained final sentence that stretches across two eight-line stanzas, to a comparable sense of perceptual confusion, with the mesmeric forward/backward motion of the wipers 'blurring' the difference between what is moving forwards and what backwards, past and present, what is in front and what is behind:

> Before this car moved forward
> Lighting so little before us
> Of a road that, crouching forward,
>   We watch move always towards us,

Which through the tiny segment
Cleared and blurred by the wiper
Is sucked in under the axle
    To be spewed behind us and lost
While we, dazzled by darkness,
Haul the black future towards us
Peeling the skin from our hands;
    And yet we hold the road.

'Cleared', 'blurred', 'sucked', 'spewed', 'dazzled': the verbs situate the singularly plural motorist within desperately turbulent forces (offering a single driver's view from a single vehicle, but from the perspective of the first person plural). At the opening the wiper 'Reaps a swathe', and by the end of the complex unfolding sentence, like fishermen, 'we' are hauling the 'black future towards us'. Though designed for transport through space, the car has become a terrible time machine. The phrase 'Peeling the skin from our hands' is ambiguous, leaving it unclear whether the darkness, the future, or the driver is responsible for peeling the skin. It suggests horrible mutilation as well as aging, but it also underlines the manual element in the poem's final assertion: 'And yet we hold the road.' *OED* defines this as 'to continue to occupy the road' or 'keep to the road without skidding', giving as its first instance a T.E. Lawrence letter of 1938 ('The S.S. 100 holds the road extraordinarily'). Again MacNeice is absorbing modern experience and idiom, to renew the metaphor of life as journey. The poem holds to the psychological reality of the motorist's experience, and in doing so shapes a compelling modern equivalent of a 'dark age gloss' on Bede's passing swallow. It also brilliantly embodies John Urry's account of how sights and sounds 'get reduced to the two-dimensional view through the car windscreen and through the rear mirror, the sensing of the world through the screen being the dominant mode of dwelling in the contemporary world'.[5]

'The Taxis' is another poem about time passing, with its 'clock' referring both to the 'taximeter' after which the vehicle is named, and time more generally:

In the first taxi he was alone tra-la,
No extras on the clock. He tipped ninepence
But the cabby, while he thanked him, looked askance
As though to suggest someone had bummed a ride. (*CP* 583–4)

The 'clock' here counts the cost of the journey rather than time. *OED* has 'no results' for 'tra-la', but the free online dictionary (Farlex) defines it as 'a set of nonsense syllables used when humming a refrain', defining a refrain as 'the part of a song where the soloist is joined by a group of singers'. The poem is also about a soloist being joined by others, first one secret sharer (the 'someone' who had 'bummed a ride'), then increasing numbers of invisible fellow-passengers until the last stanza:

> As for the fourth taxi, he was alone
> Tra-la when he hailed it but the cabby looked
> Through him and said: 'I can't tra-la well take
> So many people, not to speak of the dog.'

Here the 'dog' is just one more item to be transported, but has the effect of turning the jauntily anonymous ballad into a shaggy-dog parable. It also suggests how many people the lyric might inadvertently include, recording the pressure on the metre of the number of things being transported in the poet's metaphorical vehicle. In its jaunty way, the poem manages to combine the oracular with the vernacular, making that final apparitional 'dog', the cabby's last straw, into something like Charon's hound (Cerberus). When the cabby 'looked / Through him', it is as if he had acquired the ghostly status of the earlier (to him) invisible passengers. In this poem about numbers (in many senses), the nonsense refrain 'tra-la' occurs six times in the four quatrains, but never where you would expect a refrain to be (at the end of the stanza). Instead it occurs at the close of the first line of the first two stanzas, four times occurring after 'alone' in the quasi-composite choric phrase 'alone tra-la', once in the middle of a line ('You have left nothing behind tra-la between you'), and once at the start of a line, in the second line of the fourth stanza ('he was alone / Tra-la when he hailed it'). So, the nonsense phrase about being alone itself suggests company, iteration, and mobility, giving the reader a sense that, however jauntily solitary the passenger seems, he is always part of a larger group, with an accompaniment and in company.

'Déjà Vu' is also about travel and repetition. It begins and ends with the phrase 'It does not come round in hundreds of thousands of years', offering a personal locomotive counterpart to Yeats's 'The Second Coming': 'It does not come round, it does not come round, and compactly / The wheels will mark time on the rails' (*CP* 577–8). 'After the Crash' (*CP* 585), with its 'crash / Helmet', describes someone coming to after an accident, while 'October in Bloomsbury' gives us a London vignette of modern parking systems: 'Now the parking meters picket and pick the Georgian locks and invisible / Meters tall as the yellowing trees docket and dock our history' (*CP* 591). *OED* gives the first use of 'parking meter' as 1936, and MacNeice's spacious lines conjure a more traditional metre to 'dock' the post-Georgian traffic.

However, it is in the very late poems 'Charon' and 'Star-gazer' that MacNeice most eloquently conjoins the physical and the meta-physical, bringing a cosmic dimension to modern transport. 'Charon' begins in the world of London buses, with the remark that 'The conductor's hands were black with money'. The passenger is initially exhorted to 'hold on to / That dissolving map' as they 'moved through London', but the poem shifts into dream gear, as the poet reports they could see 'pigeons through the glass but failed / To hear rumours of wars', and suddenly evokes the ultimate liminal journey to the classical underworld (*CP* 592). Somewhere behind it is Eliot's 'So many, I had not thought death had undone so many', but the conductor's hands, the 'vacant faces' at 'request stops', and the 'revolving lights' all also insist on the realities of bus transport, until with the Thames, the poem lurches into a fully fledged Dantean encounter with the infernal ferryman:

> The bridges were all down, the further shore
> Was lost in fog, so we asked the conductor
> What we should do. He said: Take the ferry
> Faute de mieux. We flicked the flashlight
> And there was the ferryman just as Virgil
> And Dante had seen him. (*CP* 593)

The term 'conductor' initially refers to 'the official who has charge of the passengers, collects fares, and … directs the proceedings' on a bus, but with the flick of his flashlight, the poet turns him into the classical 'ferryman', whose hands 'Were black with obols and vari-cose veins' and who says 'If you want to die you will have to pay for it'. The primary meaning of 'conductor' according to *OED*, is 'One who leads, guides, or escorts; a leader, guide (*lit.* and *fig.*)', as in Bunyan's *Pilgrim's Progress* 'Pray do you go along with us, I will be your conductor'. In Bunyan, it is a 'Conductor' who takes Pilgrim and others to 'a place where was cast up a pit, the whole breadth of the way', and shows them the 'Valley of the Shadow of Death'. It is just this valley the London bus conductor opens to the poet, where in the flicker of the flashlight, they see 'the ferryman just as Virgil / And Dante had seen him'. The move from bus to ferry, from conductor to Charon, is accomplished with dream-like abruptness, and we realise a conductor might himself be an equivalent to 'the ferryman just as Virgil had seen him'. MacNeice's uncanny translation of London transport as a 'dissolving map' of the underworld builds on *The Waste Land*, but gives it a new twist.

'Star-gazer' returns to a schoolboy experience in a train recounted earlier in *The Strings are False*:

> In January 1921 I found myself wonderfully alone in an empty carriage in a rocking train in the night between Waterloo and Sherborne. Stars on each side of me; I ran from side to side of the carriage checking the constellations as the train changed its direction. (*SF* 78)

The poem is set in the same train, and its opening makes it plain that, like so many of his vehicular poems, it is about time as much as space:

> Forty-two years ago (to me if no one else
> The number is of some interest) it was a brilliant starry night
> And the westward train was empty and had no corridors
> So darting from side to side I could catch the unwonted sight
> Of those almost intolerably bright
> Holes, punched in the sky, which excited me partly because
> Of their Latin names and partly because I had read in the textbooks
> How very far off they were, it seemed their light
> Had left them (some at least) long years before I was. (*CP* 607)

The long, straggling, scarcely punctuated sentence, combined with the sprawling, giddily enjambed lines (complete with two sets of parentheses), give the distant memory a hurtling, improvisatory but also fraught sense of the 'rocking train'. Though the effect is irregular, the paragraph is also rhymed in a curiously syncopated way, being built up around two rhyming sounds. One is a set of clearly sounded *Eine Kleine Nachtmusik* rhymes triggered by 'night', which

include 'sight', 'bright', and 'light', but these are interspersed with a
group of rackety 'off' rhymes ('far off' rhymes, perhaps), which are
triggered by that first flat 'else' (they include 'corridors', 'because',
and 'was'). The poem was written in 1963, so that initial 'Forty-two
years ago' is a number 'of some interest', confirming the date
recounted in *The Strings are False* twenty years previously. 'Ago', orig-
inating with the past participle of 'go', 'agone', is classified as an
adjective, though it is a very strange one, and everything in the poem
is about things going and going on, past and passing, depending on
perpetual movement and transient perceptions. The abrupt end of
the first paragraph ('long before I was') sounds at first as if interrupted
– 'long before I was … born? Thought of?' – before one realises that
it is simply the past tense of the verb 'to be'. Part of the fullness of
the experience of this 'brilliant starry night' derives from the sense of
the train's movement, and the child 'darting from side to side' within
it; part of it also comes from the sense of the westward train being
'empty' and without 'corridors', of the poet in his solitary compart-
ment, travelling alone.

The second stanza returns us to the present ('remembering now')
and has a completely different shape and speed:

> And this remembering now I mark that what
> Light was leaving some of them at least then,
> Forty-two years ago, will never arrive
> In time for me to catch it, which light when
> It does get here may find that there is not
> Anyone left alive
> To run from side to side in a late night train
> Admiring it and adding noughts in vain. (*CP* 608)

The first two lines of this second straggling sentence set up an
unpunctuated grammatical and semantic tangle: 'And this remembering now I mark that what / Light as leaving some of them at least
then'. We could disentangle this more easily if we added punctuation: 'And this, remembering now, I mark: that what light was
leaving some of them at least then, forty-two years ago, will never
arrive …' It could, however, be read in other ways, with other stops
and starts, and the uncertainty as to where and how the different parts
of the sentence fit together, is crucial for the poem's unsettling effect
(like the earlier 'darting from side to side'). If it is hard to gauge where

the stresses fall in this poem about counting, it is also very hard to
'count' the metre. Almost all the lines are shorter than those in the
first paragraph, and they run in strangely fluid ways, leaving the join
words 'what', 'then', and 'not' sticking out at the ends of lines, jarring
the weave of otherwise quite binding rhymes ('what' and 'not', 'then'
and 'when', 'arrive' and 'alive'), which are consummated with the
final couplet of 'train' and 'vain'.

The end of this poem about deferred repetition comes round full
circle, back to the opening scene in the train, repeating the scene and
sentences with variations, returning to the moment 'forty-two years
ago', of the poet running 'from side to side in a late night train /
Admiring it and adding noughts in vain'. The negatives, 'Never', 'not
anyone', and 'noughts' loom large, as the stars become 'intolerably
bright / Holes punched in the sky' (another kind of negative, like the
'noughts'). By the close, the prose reminiscence about a schoolday
epiphany has become a Pascalian gloss on the universe of modern
astronomy. The train is a perfect and moving setting for these reflections, since the ideas of light that 'left' the stars years earlier, and of
light that will 'never arrive', gain resonance from the 'westward'
movement of the engine through the night, and a boy or man arriving
where he is going 'in time'. The notion of light arriving 'in time'
plays on the two senses of that pregnant phrase, suggesting both punc-
tuality and that the vehicle travelling through space represents the
expanding universe of modern space-time with its endlessly 'adding
noughts'.

In *The Strings are False* the poet talks of the 'haunting matter-of-
factness' he found in the paintings of Zurbarán (159), and the trains,
cars, buses, ships, and taxis that weave their way through his poems
are marked by just such 'haunting matter-of-factness'. They are part
of the currency of his daily life, but they also represent MacNeice's
personal take on the axiom that 'transport is civilisation', and a
complex understanding of how we are defined by modern 'mobilities'. In searching metaphysical lyrics like 'The Taxis', 'The Wiper',
'Reflections', and 'Star-gazer', MacNeice reflects on the way new
forms of travel have re-shaped our fundamental perceptions of time
and space, and, in doing so, the peculiar space-time of the modern
lyric.

'WHO WOULD BE LOVED BY A GODDESS?' MACNEICE, GRAVES, AND THE LYRIC OF CLASSICAL MYTH

Edna Longley

Louis MacNeice's 'Charon' and Robert Graves's 'Instructions to the Orphic Adept' are constructed as journeys to the underworld. Both poems depend on the mythic map of Hades; both involve the voice of an instructor or conductor; and both invoke the classical roots of European poetry. To quote the climax of 'Charon': 'And there was the ferryman just as Virgil / And Dante had seen him'. 'Instructions' is spoken by the ur-poet Orpheus: the poem first appeared in Graves's novel *The Golden Fleece* (1944), in a proto *White Goddess* chapter where the Argonauts attend Rhea's mysteries. The 'you', the 'mazed spirit', addressed by Orpheus, undergoes a soul-making ritual, which implicitly doubles as initiation into the 'mystery' of poetry itself, its origins and sources. Thus adepts must drink from 'the pool of memory', Helicon's infernal counterpart. The poem ends:

> You shall drink deep of that refreshing draught,
> To become lords of the uninitiated
> Twittering ghosts, Hell's countless populace –
> To become heroes, knights upon swift horses
> Pronouncing oracles from tall white tombs
> By the nymphs tended. They with honey water
> Shall pour libations to your serpent shapes,
> That you may drink. (*GCP* 403)

MacNeice's 'we', who 'move through London', end up in a different place. Insofar as the speaker here is a poet (his journey spookily reprises *Autumn Journal* and he alludes to other MacNeice poems), he lacks the redemptive resources implied by 'Dante' and by an ironical allusion to Henry Vaughan's 'I saw eternity the other night', which becomes: 'eternity / Gave itself airs in revolving lights'. Rather than attaining 'oracular' powers, this speaker is finally spoken for:

And his eyes were dead and his hands on the oar
Were black with obols and varicose veins
Marbled his calves and he said to us coldly:
If you want to die, you will have to pay for it. (*CP* 593)

I should not labour the contrasts between these generically distinct
poems. MacNeice's poetry is not always an attempt to 'hold on to /
That dissolving map'; nor are Graves's underworlds always so positive, although 'serpent shapes' implies the dark side of poetic vocation
('Ophion, / Primaeval serpent ... / Darts out his tongue' above the
'holy pool'). Moreover, 'Instructions', 'in part translated ... from
Orphic tablets', is untypical in its aspect as translation and in its freeish
form. As it happens, the structural role of refrain is another common
factor. Yet the refrains in 'Charon' punctuate an inexorable loss of
control: 'we just jogged on'; whereas, in 'Instructions', refrain powers
the poem's own ritualistic drive towards an apotheosis of control:
'Run to this pool', 'Give me to drink'. And, overall, despite the
conceptual and formal variables, certain differences in how these
poems approach mythic material seem fairly constant across the poets'
work. To take an obvious example: there is some two-way traffic
between Graves's classical scenarios and his Mediterranean environment, but he would never merge Acheron with Thames. Similarly,
both poems are psychic journeys, dream or nightmare, in which myth
and the unconscious interpenetrate. But while 'Instructions' suspends
mythic disbelief, 'Charon' admits history as well as London.

Difference is not antithesis. For Graves and MacNeice, the ancient
world is shared ground in more senses than one: the ground of poetry.
To compare their lyrics of classical myth is to open up perspectives,
not just on their own poetry, but also on modern poetics. Here there
may be strength in numbers. These poets are rarely discussed
together, despite good reasons, including their classical credentials
and Irish contexts, for doing so. Critics often group or segregate poets
according to over-determined categories that ignore deeper currents
and wider dialectics. It is, of course, a Gravesian tactic to represent
himself as a loner, while retaining the collectivity of tradition, and
hailing select precursors, if few contemporaries, as 'friends and equals
in a timeless society, acknowledging the severe but benignant sover-
eignty of the Muse'.[1] There is usually an excluded middle between
his Deya disciples and what Fran Brearton calls his 'collaborations
with the dead'.[2] Thus Graves barely mentions MacNeice, although

he grumbles about Auden's iconic status. In fact, he seems to have liked MacNeice rather better, but *The Long Weekend* suggests that he was scarcely paying attention:

> It was thought incumbent on poets to 'get into touch with reality' … Auden, Spender, and Day Lewis were said to be achieving this by cultivating Left sympathies. With them was associated the cultural [*sic*] and donnish Louis MacNeice, who was realistic because he had written acidly descriptive poems on bourgeois subjects, such as lawn-mowing in Hampstead gardens.[3]

In contrast, MacNeice was always alert to Graves. In January 1927, during his second term at Oxford, he planned a 'pilgrimage' to Graves's Islip house (*L* 147). He had already absorbed his critical book *Poetic Unreason* (1925), which he read in the Marlborough sixth form (*MP* 55, 63). Later, he drew on Graves's and Laura Riding's *A Survey of Modernist Poetry* (1927) for his own *Modern Poetry* and other 1930s critical writings. This shows, for instance, in MacNeice's treatment of the Imagists and in the prominence he gives to E.E. Cummings. As for Graves's poetry: MacNeice, too, registers a generation gap or aesthetic gap, but in more attentive terms, as when he compares Graves with Yeats:

> Yeats began in the Celtic Twilight, then moved on to a period of occasional and disillusioned poetry, and finally took to expressing an esoteric philosophy in verse that is symbolic but hard. Graves began with the romanticism of the nursery, moved on to a period of occasional and disillusioned poetry, and is now writing poetry that is bleakly metaphysical. The chief difference is that, whereas Yeats's poetry became increasingly human, Graves's poetry has moved further and further from humanity. (*PY* 191)

That, passage, with its implied Anglo-Irish triangulation of Yeats, Graves, and MacNeice himself, harks back to MacNeice's perceptive review of Graves's 1938 *Collected Poems*:

> [His] later poems are curiously (but attractively) bleak and puri-tanical. He distrusts science and has grown out of colour; he rebukes 'the foolish senses'. He writes like a metaphysician who considers even metaphysics impure; every poem is to be a case of

parthenogenesis. But in spite of himself the earth comes filtering back into his poetry – love, nostalgia, courage, humour and things like that ... [In contrast, Laura Riding's] poems are almost completely unphysical – on the astral plane, but the stars have already been cashiered ... Austerity ... in Mr Graves' case is [not only tonic but] also palatable, thanks to his remarkable feeling for words and technical dexterity ... Today Graves is no longer an advocate of Poetic Unreason but of something that might be called Poetic Super-reason. His poems in the early 'twenties, he says, were written in spite of his theories. I suspect he will always have theories and will always write poems in spite of them.[4]

Graves may be the subtextual 'other' when, in the Preface to *Modern Poetry*, MacNeice calls his book 'a plea for *impure* poetry ... for poetry conditioned by the poet's life and the world around him'.

Perhaps MacNeice noted Graves's human turn in the early 1940s, or realised that he and Graves were essentially on the same side. In any case, he wrote later: 'What distinguishes the "Movement" ... from a poet like ... Graves is that the latter's neatness is always a means to an end' (*SLC* 209); and again:

Poets are always being required – by the critics and by themselves – to 'develop'. Most critics, however, to perceive such development, need something deeper than a well and wider than a church-door. In certain poets of our time the changes are conspicuous enough; in others, such as Robert Graves, a careless reader might complain that the menu is never altered. (*SLC* 224)

To sum up: MacNeice valued Gravesian form; identified with Graves's subtle mix of self-consistency and self-reinvention; and set Graves's poetry firmly in the modern mainstream. MacNeice's death in 1963 prevented him from editing the *Oxford Book of Twentieth-Century English Verse* eventually edited by Philip Larkin. Graves was one of the half-dozen poets after Yeats to whom he meant to give 'solid prominence' (*JS* 470).

This was no canonical accident. MacNeice and Graves broadly agree on 'modern' or 'modernist' poetry. Graves and Riding were probably first to call poetry 'modernist': the term did not attain wide currency in the literary academy until the 1960s. However (like MacNeice), they never apply 'modernist' in the narrow sense, which that currency has propagated: that is, to denote *vers libre*, experiment, textual disjunction. Graves and Riding write, for example: 'The Imagists *believed* in free verse; and to believe in one way of writing poetry as against another is ... to be in a position of selling one's ideas rather than of constantly submitting them to new tests ... they wanted to be *new* rather than to be poets.'[5] Similarly, MacNeice's essay 'Poetry Today' (1935) warns against the 'extremes of psittacism and aphasia'. His 'aphasics' are 'the enthusiasts (mostly Americans in Paris) who set out to scrap tradition from A to Z' (*SLC* 13–14).

Unsurprisingly, Ezra Pound, the Pound of the *Cantos*, focuses both poets' objections to certain modes of making it new. And their objections implicate the classics. In 'Poetry Today' MacNeice charges the *Cantos* with offences against 'Aristotelian truth': 'Quantity must always affect quality. A metre of green, as Gaugin said, is more green than a centimetre, but a bucket of Benedictine is hardly Benedictine. Mr Pound does not know when to stop; he is a born strummer' (*SLC* 17). Graves's view of Pound's classicising meshes with his consistent dislike for the notion that the past has now become a multicultural 'imaginary museum' open to arbitrary literary raids:

It is an extraordinary paradox that Pound's sprawling, ignorant ... unmelodious, seldom metrical *Cantos*, embellished with esoteric Chinese ideographs – for all I know, they may have been traced from the nearest tea-chest – and with illiterate Greek, Latin, Spanish and Provencal snippets ... are now compulsory reading in many ancient centres of learning.

Graves's essay on howlers in 'Homage to Sextus Propertius' ('Dr Syntax and Mr Pound') is good fun too.[6] MacNeice more mildly deprecates Pound's 'scrap-albums of ornament torn eclectically from history' (*L* 306). For Graves, Pound has also promoted a pumped-up idea of the 'major' poem, which violates the primacy of lyric form.[7] Here he sings from the same formal hymn sheet as MacNeice, although he would hardly name-check Aristotle, whom he considered an Apollonian gatekeeper. And MacNeice upholds the principle of proportion, rather than swears purist loyalty to the lyric.

If Graves and MacNeice query 'modernist' synchronicity, this is no plea for psittacism, neo-classicism or rigid timelines. Rather, it is concern for the poetic resonances released either by internalising and re-imagining aspects of the ancient world, such as its myth; or by

accepting the challenge that MacNeice spells out in 'Poetry Today':
'How are we to do justice, not to the segregated Past or Present, but
to their concrete antinomy?' (*SLC* 14). There is a difference between
eclectically raiding the 'imaginary museum' and bringing past and
present together in the specificity of their otherness – a history of the
world in diachronic precisions. Witness MacNeice's youthful poem
'A Classical Education', which conjures up the 'well-oiled heckling
Greeks' in the same gesture that acknowledges their departure, and
asks: 'Why ... do I loiter round these chartered sanctuaries?' The
answer is: to catch the pulse of poetry ('frivolous phalaecians or stern
hexameters') and perhaps what its beat conveys: 'a heart mark[ing]
time', 'A poet like a pale candle guttering / On a worn window-sill
in the wind' (*CP* 641). MacNeice admired A.E. Housman, another
poet-classicist; but saw Housman's decision to abandon poetry for the
classics, rather than hold them in creative tension, as an act of apos-
tasy that cut a vital connection: 'Housman ... turned his back on a
medium which involved so much contact with humanity and took
to living on his brain in the arid Abyssinia of textual commentary'
(*MP* 83–4).

A decade earlier, Graves had reacted similarly to the 'chartered
sanctuaries' of Charterhouse. Graves and MacNeice think alike on
their 'classical education': on Christian or humanistic appropriations
of the classics, on mushy poetic Hellenisers, on translations of 'the Gk
choruses & Gk lyric poetry ... into pat English metres & slick English
rhythms'.[8] Such translations are the converse of writing poems in
English with an ear also attuned to 'frivolous phalaecians or stern
hexameters' or Horatian alcaics; although academic critics of Graves's
The Greek Myths have a case for querying poetic license. In *Autumn
Journal* IX, speaking as an unorthodox academic 'impresario of the
Ancient Greeks', MacNeice more fully exposes the ideology that
sustains 'A Classical Education', and its complicity with other murky
ideologies in 1938:

> And when I should remember the paragons of Hellas
>   I think instead
> Of the crooks, the adventurers, the opportunists ...
> And the trimmers at Delphi and the dummies at Sparta and lastly
>   I think of the slaves ... (*CP* 121–2)

As this poetic 'remembering', 'thinking', and impresarioship suggest, engagement with the ancient world need not be the same thing as 'a classical education'. For Graves, admittedly, classical education began in the ancient world itself: he blames Virgil, 'the Apollonian anti-poet', for introducing the suspect 'Virgil–Dante–Milton tradition' into English poetry. This is an instance of his being more liable than MacNeice to read the present (or his present obsessions) into the past, instead of respecting their 'concrete antinomy'. Even Homer, seen as helping to institutionalise the goddess-denying 'Olympian system', can merge into Charterhouse.[9] But both Graves and MacNeice absorbed Homer in ways that seem crucial to their aesthetic horizons. Sounding rather like Graves at the outset, but then diverging from him, MacNeice recalls:

> During my first year at Marlborough I began reading Homer, whom I at once recognised as richer than Virgil or Spenser, more congenial than Milton ... Homer gave me an example of verse-writing which was homogeneous but yet elastic enough to represent much of life's variety. I have noticed since that many modern theories of poetry could not make room for Homer. Many people generalise about poetry when they only mean lyric poetry. (*MP* 48)

For my purposes here, the 'lyric of classical myth' includes poems based on Homer. Graves might not approve. In *The Greek Myths* the element of 'heroic saga' in the *Iliad* and of 'realistic fiction' in the *Odyssey* are among the cultural forms that he excludes from 'true myth'.[10] Yet the junctures where gods and humanity meet in Homeric epic provide an obvious template for the Graves lyric, the Graves myth.

Graves's 'Judgement of Paris' and MacNeice's 'Day of Returning' visit such junctures. These poems are also interrogative *ars poeticas*. 'Judgement of Paris', a poetic counterpart to 'what if' history, consti-tutes a reflexive parable of the intersection between myth, history, and poetry: 'What if Prince Paris, after taking thought, / Had not adjudged the apple to Aphrodite ...' The speaker speculates as to whether, without the coalescence of legend and history into literary myth, later history would have been different, as would later litera-ture, later aesthetic 'judgments', the poem itself: 'Could we still have found the courage, you and I, / To embark together for Cranae / And consummate our no less fateful love?' (*GCP* 536). 'Day of

Returning' derives from Book 5 of the *Odyssey*. Its third section moves in the opposite direction to 'Judgment of Paris': away from goddess-led mythic fatefulness, towards 'humanity' perhaps. Here Odysseus asks of Calypso:

> Who would be loved by a goddess for long? Hours which are
>   golden
> But unreal hours, flowers which forget to fall,
> And wine too smooth, no wrinkles to match my own –
> Who would be loved by a goddess who cannot appreciate
> The joy of solving a problem, who never wept
> For friends that she used to laugh with? (*CP* 357)

This scenario invokes a more earthbound Muse than Graves's. The imagery, and the weighty hexametric median of the lines, render Ithaca's status as 'home' symbolic rather than archaic or timeless: 'rights of grazing or wood-cutting', 'the bleat of my goats ... the dung of my cattle' (*CP* 358). Yet both poems are versions of 'concrete antinomy'; both return to Homeric base for aesthetic validation. That is, they do not visit an 'imaginary museum', but make imaginative leaps that depend on close reading or internalisation of Homer.

MacNeice wrote 'Day of Returning' around 1950. Perhaps Graves's *The White Goddess*, published in 1948, sparked off a contrary manifesto, a different poetic take on ancient sources: '*Who* would be loved by a goddess?' We all know who would. As it happens, this is the section where 'Day of Returning' comes alive. There is certainly a significant smack at Graves in MacNeice's 'Memoranda to Horace' written ten years later. The fourth section begins:

> Though elderly poets profess to be inveterate
> Dionysians, despising Apollonians,
>   I find it, Flaccus, more modest
> To attempt, like you, an appetitive decorum. (*CP* 605)

This quatrain opens up two further comparative perspectives: the lyric of classical myth in its psychological aspect (marked in 'Charon' and 'Instructions'); modern conceptions of Greek conceptions of myth.

On the first count: MacNeice's lines psychoanalyse Graves's 'Dionysian' self-mythologising. Much is implied by 'profess', 'modest', and the oxymoronic-ironic 'appetitive decorum'. In effect, MacNeice reads Graves as an Apollonian poet in denial. Similarly, Graves can be seen as denying the psychological dimension both of his own poetry and ancient myth. As regards rival exponents of the Greek myths, he is especially hostile to those who construe them as 'blind uprushes of the Jungian collective unconscious'.[11] If that is a pre-emptive strike against reading 'Instructions to the Orphic Adept' as a Jungian uprush, it hardly succeeds. Or perhaps, in line with what MacNeice says of his metaphysics, Graves now writes like a psychologist too deep for psychology or an advocate of Poetic Super-sublimation. For Graves, in theory, the poetic 'trance' came to override rather than subsume other modes of cognition. This is what MacNeice means by 'parthenogenesis'. Yet the post-Freudian entanglement of psychoanalysis with classical mythology was an inescapable matrix for the modern lyric, although MacNeice astutely observes that the Oedipus complex 'won't explain everything nor even the *Oedipus*' (*SLC* 146). In fact, Graves's denials recoil from his intensive exposure to psychoanalysis after the Great War; and from his resultant zeal, under W.H.R. Rivers's influence, to theorise poetry as an arena of conflicting 'sub-personalities'. Hence *Poetic Unreason*, which also draws the reader into this arena: 'the reading of poetry ... acts for him as a physician of his mental disorders'.[12] Of course, Graves could not abandon his sub-personalities along with the theory. And Greek mythic figures became crucial masks for such selves – or for self and other – in poetry to which the terms 'psychodrama' or 'psycho-sexual drama' apply.

MacNeice, too, is more than a run-of-the-mill post-Freudian. While (or because) he invariably questions *conscious* resort to the unconscious, he conceives lyric poetry as objectified psychodrama. At Oxford he took issue with the excessively 'psychological' emphasis of *Poetic Unreason* (*MP* 73); but his early criticism follows Graves in incorporating psychoanalytical insights. Further, while Greek myth is less conspicuous in his mature poetry than in Graves's, his juvenilia involve such figures as Narcissus, Adonis, Pandora, Perseus, and Circe in attempts to bring myth and psychoanalysis into the same frame. 'Neurotics' begins:

Fire! Fire in Troy! Let the skies pour out
Their flaming bloody buckets. Where did it start?
In Bluebeard's chamber, the door Helen undid,

The gilded shambles of the house of Atreus. (*CP* 625)

'Circe' (1937) recasts and disturbingly blends MacNeice's previous versions of Circe and Narcissus. This poem explores the nature of 'ego' by linking Circe's 'unfertile beauty' with 'Narcissus' error' (*CP* 30–31): 'Be brave, my ego, look into your glass / And realise that that never-to-be-touched / Vision is your mistress'. 'Thyestes', a wartime poem, ironically fuses the classics with Christianity to denote the psycho-historical workings of 'cannibalism and incest': 'such are we / Who garnish to pollute and breed to kill – / Messmates in the eucharist of crime' (*CP* 233).

Perseus focuses the different psychological dispositions of Graves's and MacNeice's poetry. MacNeice's 'Perseus' (1933), begins with a succinct impression of the Gorgon-effect:

> Borrowed wings on his ankles
> Carrying a stone death,
> The hero entered the hall,
> All in the hall looked up,
> Their breath frozen on them,
> And there was no more shuffle or clatter in the hall at all. (*CP* 19)

The chiming chiasmus 'All in the hall' / 'in the hall at all' underscores the petrifying moment. The second stanza less suggestively labours to link this 'frozen' scene with a depressive state: 'the hooded and arrested hours'. The third stanza does better, attaching the speaker's dissociation to a psychotic vista which is also historical: 'the looking-glass in the end room / ... full of eyes, / The ancient smiles of men cut out with scissors and kept in mirrors'. 'Ancient' sets up Perseus' return, and the perennial recurrence of the dualism or oxymoron he symbolises: 'Ever to meet me comes, in sun or dull, / The gay hero swinging the Gorgon's head' (*CP* 20). Given what MacNeice calls 'the *petrifaction* images which appear pretty often in my poems' (*SLC* 160), the Perseus story – or a Medusa complex – goes deep into the poems' childhood roots: where stone and mirror began to figure trauma, where granite obelisks dominated the 'cemetery beyond the hawthorn hedge' (*SLC* 159; *MP* 174–5).

Graves, of course, interprets the Perseus story from a Gorgon-friendly angle. At the end of *The White Goddess* he introduces 'The Destroyer' as 'a satire on the memory of the man who first tilted

European civilisation off balance, by enthroning the restless and arbitrary male will under the name of Zeus and dethroning the female
sense of orderliness'.[13] This is not a poem that fits Perseus-Medusa to
a specific psychic occasion, but a *j'accuse* that fixes Perseus' role in
ancient or, rather, Gravesian myth: ·

> Swordsman of the narrow lips,
> Narrow hips and murderous mind
> Fenced with chariots and ships,
> By your joculators hailed
> The mailed wonder of mankind,
> Far to westward you have sailed. (*GCP* 426)

The monotonously hostile (rather than satirical) diction infects the
rhythm, producing obvious or forced internal rhymes: 'A lame
golden-heeled decoy, / Joy of hens that gape and wince'. To read
psychologically what was not written psychologically: in 'The
Destroyer' a tone of personal hatred or jealousy seems stronger than
that of righteous mythic anger in words like 'lame', 'dunce',
'ignoble', 'ignorant'. Perseus is simply anathema: an incoherent
neurotic projection. On a public level, Graves may seek to encom-
pass recent history by evoking the 'sick fields' of the Great War and
echoing Yeats's 'rough beast' ('While an ignorant pale priest / Rides
the beast with a man's head'). Yet the poem really recalls Yeats's lapses
into violent denunciation that cancels any critique of violence.
Graves dissipates the poetic potential of a clash between Perseus and
the moon-goddess by predetermining its psychic and historical
meaning.

'Ulysses', in contrast, lays down Graves's best mythic practice:

> To the much-tossed Ulysses, never done
> With woman whether gowned as wife or whore
> Penelope and Circe seemed as one:
> She like a whore made his lewd fancies run,
> And wifely she a hero to him bore.
>
> Their counter-changings terrified his way:
> They were the clashing rocks, Symplegades,
> Scylla and Charybdis too were they;
> Now they were storms frosting the sea with spray

And now the lotus island's drunken ease ...

His wiles were witty and his fame far-known,
Every king's daughter sought him for her own,
Yet he was nothing to be won or lost.
All lands to him were Ithaca: love-tossed
He loathed the fraud, yet would not bed alone. (*GCP* 337–8)

On the one hand, the poem is a splendidly sustained conceit, reflexively full of its own witty wiles. The psycho-sexual translation of Ulysses' ordeals and encounters is lightly handled, as are the metaphors of sea, islands, and weather. Yet the poem goes beyond 'witty wiles'. 'Ulysses' carries weight (and personal freight) as a psycho-sexual parable because it channels the *Odyssey's* mythic force. D.N.G. Carter writes: 'The sea is the protagonist's seeming element, and from the outset its restless presence is felt in the rhythms of the verse, the indentations, the answering calls of its rhymes ... there is something appropriately reminiscent of the "surge and thunder of the Odyssey"'. Carter also notes that the hero is not in control but 'tossed' by conflicting impulses.[14] All these structural and formal qualities make 'Ulysses' far more complex than 'The Destroyer' in its approach to gender and power, to mind and body, to desire and guilt, to the zone where myth and psychology interpenetrate. The 'counter-changing' subjective images imply how myth gives shape to 'seemings' – as it does when Graves and MacNeice assume the mask of Ulysses.

These lyrics of classical myth are the tip of an iceberg. Beneath them lurk deep mythic and Homeric structures, not only in their psychological application: underworlds, fateful wars, journeys, monsters, metamorphoses. Among the factors that influence the poets' deployment of such structures, are their different conceptions and hence re-conceptions (see 'Memoranda to Horace') of how the ancients themselves conceived myth.

Unlike Graves, but like Horace and perhaps like the Greeks, MacNeice has no theory or theology. Although Graves insists that his own approach is 'historical and anthropological', his feminised monotheism makes him appear more a believer than most ancient Greeks or Romans: that is, in 'the Great Goddess', 'immortal, changeless, and omnipotent'.[15] What MacNeice says of literary 'dark-godders' may also cover white-goddessers: 'so far as our heritage goes, we are Christians' (*SLC* 143). Besides being more historically self-conscious than Graves, MacNeice is aligned with those classicists who view ancient Greek religion and myth as unsystematic or 'improvisatory'. For John Gould, who uses the latter adjective, the Greeks do not so much 'believe in the gods' as

> acknowledge them, that is, pray to them, sacrifice to them, build them temples, make them the object of cult and ritual. There is never an assumption of divine omnipotence … The same absence of finality is characteristic of Greek myth … a traditional story can be told with new meanings.[16]

So there may never have been 'one story only', as Graves has it in 'To Juan at the Winter Solstice' (*GCP* 405). MacNeice salutes Greek improvisation in *Autumn Journal*:

> Conscious – long before Engels – of necessity
>   And therein free
> They plotted out their life with truism and humour
>   Between the jealous heaven and the callous sea.

Not that, when asked to admire or imitate Greek 'Models of logic and lucidity, dignity, sanity', he forgets Dionysus: 'there were exceptions, of course, but only exceptions – / The bloody Bacchanals on the Thracian hills' (*CP* 120–1). MacNeice's mentor and friend E.R. Dodds, one of Graves's sources for *The Greek Myths*, edited the *Bacchae* and wrote *The Greeks and the Irrational* (1951). But, for MacNeice, 'the bloody Bacchanals' are elements of a larger historical variety, suppressed by contemporary ideology, rather than vestiges of a lost faith, suppressed by ancient censors. If, in *Autumn Journal*, he traces any Greek fall from grace, it is cultural decline from the classical to the Hellenistic, not religious decline from the pre-classical to the classical.

This is, ultimately an aesthetic difference. MacNeice's abundant, oxymoronic, quasi-Homeric cataloguing in *Autumn Journal* (not only in Canto IX) contrasts with Graves's drive to elicit mythic patterns, and to tidy up the 'dreadful mess' of the Greek corpus.[17] So much for Dionysus. Graves's 'collaborations with the dead' include tidying up ancient literature. Thus he prides himself on having translated Apuleius's 'over-ornate Latin [into] a staid but simple English

prose';[18] whereas MacNeice chides another translator of Apuleius for
not relishing 'the chime and glitter' of this 'tessellated' post-classical
prose: 'the Chinese boxes of subordinate clauses, the geometrical
architectonic, have gone; in their place is an arithmetical or cumulative technique, a succession of fairly short phrases, roughly equal in
length and often rhyming, often without conjunctions, just adding
up and adding up' (*SLC* 131).

There is a similar clash over Homer. Introducing *The Anger of
Achilles*, his (mainly prose) translation of the *Iliad*, Graves regrets
Homer's 'wearisome formality of phrase which slows down the
action', although he also says: 'so primitive a setting forbids present-
day colloquialisms, and I have kept the diction a little old-
fashioned'.[19] Reviewing other Homeric translations, MacNeice
criticises the lyrical interludes that alternate with prose in *The Anger
of Achilles,* and he clearly has Graves in his sights when he writes:

> whether one likes it or not, [Homer's] diction is twopence
> coloured … Similarly, repetition, whether of phrases or whole
> lines, is a basic characteristic of Homer as it is of all oral story-tellers
> … Such repetition may be primitive, but it corresponds to what
> George Orwell called 'the florid little squiggles on the edge of the
> page' that create 'the special Dickens atmosphere'. Not but what
> there are people around prepared to rewrite Dickens too. (*SLC*
> 234–5)

The last sentence is a further smack at Graves: author of *The Real
David Copperfield* (1933). Indeed, *The Anger of Achilles* patronises
Homer: the word 'primitive'; Graves's packaging of the *Iliad* as
'mixed entertainment'[20] rather than poetry; the near-doggerel of his
verse passages as if designed to prove the point. Yet perhaps this is
really an extreme 'anxiety of influence' – back to the Oedipus
complex. Graves's need to establish his own mythic framework led
him, as he put it, to 'carry the whole weight of Classical History and
myth about in my mind from sink to coke-house', and Homer was
a huge part of that baggage.[21] MacNeice, too, carried this weight in
his mind, if more lightly, just as he, too, may sometimes remake the
ancient world in his own image.

With its blend of earthiness and otherworld, the lyric of classical
myth highlights the extent to which this mythic field permeates the
psychological and eschatological dimensions of both poets' work.

Among related classical stimuli are some that have more strictly structural repercussions: metre, genre, and – a zone where differences are
marked – syntax, Greek or Roman, plus its rhetorical repertoire.
Graves remained steadily Ciceronian ('geometrical architectonic'),
whereas 'Charon' exemplifies how MacNeice, like Apuleius, came
to bend or stretch syntax to disturbing effect. In his later poetry,
sometimes employing 'an arithmetical or cumulative technique',
MacNeice steps up the quotient of anacoluthon, aporia, asyndeton,
parataxis, and hence of formal and metaphysical untidiness ('we just
jogged on'). Graves persists in making the periods run on time to
coincide with stanza.

To quote again MacNeice's challenge to himself and others in
'Poetry Today': 'How are we to do justice, not to the segregated Past
or Present, but to their concrete antinomy?' He continues: 'The
problem is especially difficult for us because ... we have so many Pasts
and Presents to choose from ... The eclectic is usually impotent'
(*SLC* 14). As regards the Graeco-Roman past, Graves mainly answers
this challenge in one way, at least in theory or imagination: that is,
by collapsing history, by affirming timeless Orphic access to 'variations on a single pre-historic, or post-historic poetic theme'.[22]
Pound's eclectic 'snippets' represent the opposite answer. In
between, MacNeice remains philosophically bothered and creatively
stimulated by the kind of communication 'gap' that 'Memoranda to
Horace' strains to bridge:

> ... And if you never moved in a Christian framework
>
> I never moved in a pagan; for that matter
> I no more found Tír na nÓg than you
>   The Hesperides, yet vice versa
> If you never found Tír na nÓg, then I never
>
> Found the Hesperides. It looks as if both of us
> Met in the uniqueness of history a premise
>   That keeps us apart yet parallel,
> The gap reducible only by language. (*CP* 604)

Not 'only by language': MacNeice calls 'Memoranda to Horace' 'a
conscious attempt to suggest Horatian rhythms (in English of course
one cannot do more than suggest them)' (*SLC* 248). Generalisations

about modern poetry and the classics are often Poundian in their
tendency to favour 'snippets' or 'imitations', rather than the difficult
attempt at 'concrete antinomy'. Even a highly welcome book, *Living
Classics*, edited by S.J. Harrison, over-indulges the 'modern "decon-
secration" of great poetic figures such as Homer and Virgil, in the
sense of removing their cultural centrality as canonical and immutable
texts generally known and read in their original languages'. This
supposedly 'allows contemporary poets ... to create new classic works
using classical material and a sophisticated intertextual approach'.
Harrison instances Derek Walcott's *Omeros*: for me, not a happy
example.[23] Once again, as Graves and MacNeice prove, classical literature has never been the same thing as 'a classical education' –
however 'deconsecrated'. MacNeice's views on translation from
Greek or Latin seem relevant: 'If [the translator] frees himself from
literal accuracy in order to "recreate" the "spirit" of his original, he
most often either creates something quite alien to that original ... or
fails to create anything at all. In English we have had during the last
century many shocking examples' (*SLC* 124). As *Autumn Journal* IX
responds to the Munich crisis in terms of ancient Greece, 'concrete
antinomy' powerfully serves irony:

> And how one can imagine onself among them
>   I do not know;
> It was all so unimaginably different
>   And all so long ago. (*CP* 122)

Without his grasp of the *difference* between the ancient and modern
worlds, MacNeice could not have *imagined* the links whereby 'the
trimmers at Delphi and the dummies at Sparta' at once figure and
prefigure the Munich deal-makers.

How MacNeice and Graves engage with classical literature and the
ancient world should matter to any discussion of myth, tradition, and
aesthetics in modern poetry. To return to 'Charon': 'And there was
the ferryman, just as Virgil / And Dante had seen him.' Of course,
this is not so, any more than Graves saw Orpheus just as Pindar or
Virgil or Monteverdi or Shelley – or Eurydice – had seen him. But
at least MacNeice and Graves kept alive the possibility of 'seeing'
thus.

THE PERNING BIRCH:
YEATS, FROST, MACNEICE

Paul Muldoon

1

In 'The Lake in the Park', a poem from his 1961 collection *Solstices*, Louis MacNeice writes of *l'homme moyen sensuel* of the mid-twentieth century:

> On an empty morning a small clerk
> Who thinks no one will ever love him
> Sculls on the lake in the park while bosomy
> Trees indifferently droop above him. (*CP* 551)

One would need to be indifferent to twentieth-century poetry not to take in immediately the engagement between that 'indifferently' and Yeats's description of the swan's *dis*engagement from Leda:

>   Being so caught up,
> So mastered by the brute blood of the air,
> Did she put on his knowledge with his power
> Before the *indifferent* beak could let her drop?[1]

Yeats's 'drop' is carried over into MacNeice's 'indifferently *droop*', while the 'bosomy' sends us back in a flurry of down to 'her helpless breast upon his breast'.

No one will be taken aback by the discussion of a connection between Yeats and MacNeice, nor even by the connection between Yeats and Frost, though I plan to try to join a few dots that may have hitherto gone unjoined. Much less obvious, I'd say, are the breast to breast, and mind to mind, links between Frost and MacNeice. What I am proposing is that MacNeice learned at least as much from Frost as from Yeats, including the Frost who announced in a 1913 letter to John Bartlett:

There is a kind of success called 'of esteem'; and it butters no parsnips. It means a success with a critical few who are supposed to know. But really to arrive where I can stand on my legs as a poet and nothing else I must get outside that circle to the general reader who buys books in their thousands. I may not be able to do that. I believe in doing it – dont (*sic*) you doubt me there. I want to be a poet for all sorts and kinds.[2]

This position seems rather close to the one espoused by MacNeice in his oft-quoted small ad of 1938: 'I would have a poet able-bodied, fond of talking, a reader of the newspapers, capable of pity and laughter, informed in economics, appreciative of women, involved in personal relationships, actively interested in politics, susceptible to physical impressions' (*MP* 198). This all-inclusiveness and susceptibility to physical impressions is also referred to a year later, in that 1939 BBC discussion between himself and F.R. Higgins, where MacNeice asserts:

Compared with you, I take a rather common-sense view of poetry. I think that the poet is a sensitive instrument designed to record anything which interests his mind or affects his emotions. If a gasometer, for instance, affects his emotions, or if the Marxian dialectic, let us say, interests his mind, then let them come into his poetry.[3]

Subject-matter would be much on MacNeice's mind in 1939, as he embarked on his study of *The Poetry of W.B. Yeats*:

He was orientated towards Ireland, towards a simplified past, towards certain specialised doctrines. He repudiated general knowledge, world ideals, science, and internationalism. That is, he kept his questions comparatively simple and so was less likely to make hopelessly inadequate answers. On the other hand his questions were not, as is sometimes assumed by his detractors, comparatively trivial ones. Unless it is maintained that no one can ask a question of importance if he lives in a backward country and finds the advanced thought of other countries uncongenial. Yeats's limitations may have prevented him writing the greatest kind of poetry but they enabled him to write perhaps the best poetry of his time. Those who take the whole modern world for their canvas are liable to lapse into mere journalism. It is my own opinion, though it was not Yeats's, that the normal poet includes the journalist – but he must not be subservient to him. The normal poet – witness the Elizabethans – should not be afraid of touching pitch. But the pitch is so thick on the world thoroughfares nowadays that a poet needs exceptional strength not to stick in it. Yeats avoided the world thoroughfares. It would be a disaster if all poets were to imitate him. In his own case the great refusal was justified. (*PY* 30–1)

Again, what I shall be proposing here is that, rather than imitate Yeats's 'refusal' of the 'mound of refuse' (though he names it in 'The Circus Animals' Desertion') and the 'pitch' (though he names it, punningly, in 'Crazy Jane Talks with the Bishop', in 'Love has pitched his mansion in / The place of excrement), MacNeice imitated a position we might more commonly associate with Frost, Yeats's 'ladder' down 'where all the ladders start' proving to be less serviceable than Frost's 'long two-pointed ladder'. Frost and MacNeice share a number of common systems of imagery, ranging from a high regard for 'thoroughfares' and the 'trivial' (a term stemming from the medieval university but going back to 'a place where three ways meet' *OED*) and, growing out of that, a fascination with the relationship between the 'journalism' of the day (*journée*) and the eternity of the poem and, growing out of that, a fascination with plurality and singularity, excess and exigency, and, growing out of that, a shared fascination with size and scale and, growing out of that, a shared fascination with systems of energy and entropy and, growing out of that, a shared engagement with the world pictures of Heraclitus and Henri Bergson. I shall be going so far as to suggest that W.H. Auden's description, in *The Dyer's Hand*, of the typical Frost poem will also, *mutatis mutandis*, serve as a description of many MacNeice poems: 'The commonest human situation in his poetry is of one man, or a man and wife, alone in a small isolated house in a snowbound forest after dark.'[4]

The third part of my essay focuses on these affinities between Frost and MacNeice; after the second follows up some connections between Yeats and MacNeice. Let me begin, though, by considering one less obvious side of the to-and-fro between Yeats and Frost and, to that end, let me stay with 'Leda and the Swan'. While it was not collected until *The Tower* (1928), the poem was written in 1923, ten years after Yeats had met Frost in London and, according to Frost himself, 'told my dazzling friend Ezra Pound that my book was the best thing that has come out of America for some time'.[5] 1923 just happens to have been the year Frost published *New Hampshire*, a book in which we come upon at least three poems which I take to inform 'Leda and the Swan' in somewhat unlikely ways. The first is Frost's great paean 'To E.T.': 'I slumbered with your poems on my breast, / Spread open as I dropped them half-read through / Like dove wings on a figure on a tomb ...' (*FCP* 205). In addition to his carrying over of vocabulary from Frost – 'wings', 'breast', 'dropped' and the approximation of 'spread open' in 'loosening thighs' – Yeats echoes Frost's physical positioning of himself under Edward Thomas's 'dove wings' in the positioning of Leda under the swan's 'great wings'. In the chapter of *A Vision* entitled 'Dove or Swan', Yeats himself will link 'the annunciation that founded Greece as made to Leda' with the Annunciation to the Virgin Mary in Christian iconography.[6] Just as significantly, perhaps, as the exchange of dove for swan is the subject-matter of 'To E.T.', which might be described as the shifting relationships between knowledge and power, which turns out to be very close to the question of whether or not 'she put on his knowledge with his power' at the core of 'Leda and the Swan':

> You went to meet the shell's embrace of fire
> On Vimy ridge; and when you fell that day
> The war seemed over more for you than me,
> But now for me than you – the other way.
>
> How over, though, for even me who knew
> The foe thrust back unsafe beyond the Rhine,
> If I was not to speak of it to you
> And see you pleased once more with words of mine? (*FCP* 205)

One of the ways in which I like to try to figure out what is going on in a poem is to contextualise it in the collection in which it first appeared. It turns out that the poem that follows 'To E.T.' in *New Hampshire* is 'Nothing Gold Can Stay':

> Nature's first green is gold,
> Her hardest hue to hold.
> Her early leaf's a flower;

But only so an hour.
Then leaf subsides to leaf.
So Eden sank to grief,
So dawn goes down to day.
Nothing gold can stay. (*FCP* 206)

This poem must have had a peculiar resonance for a former member
of the Order of the Golden Dawn, as well as a fully paid-up Hegelian
with a profound sense of history as having a plot, one driven by thesis
and antithesis, in which he himself had a starring role. A poem proximate to 'Leda and the Swan' in *The Tower* is 'Fragments', a poem
which seems extraordinarily close in content, and form, to 'Nothing
Gold Can Stay':

Locke sank into a swoon;
The Garden died;
God took the spinning-jenny
Out of his side.[7]

The line 'Locke sank into a swoon' picks up on 'so Eden *sank* to grief'
while 'the Garden died' is itself a recapitulation of the meaning of
that very line. We know that Yeats associated Locke with Eve, partly
through his connection with Newton. In a passage from his play
Where There Is Nothing, published as early as 1902, he writes: 'I am
among those who think that sin and death came into the world the
day Newton ate the apple.'[8]

Locke ushers in a mechanical age just as surely as Leda or Mary
usher in their ages, the spinning-jenny plucked like a rib from Locke's
side itself a version of the perning gyre. The mechanical age is also
necessarily the age of entropy, the age in which 'dawn goes down to
day' and 'nothing gold can stay'. 'Fragments' continues:

Where got I that truth?
Out of a medium's mouth?
Out of nothing it came,
Out of the forest loam,
Out of dark night where lay
The crowns of Nineveh.[9]

I want to suggest that the phrase 'Where got I that truth?' is a refer-

ence to the Frost milieu as represented by the third poem that feeds
not only into 'Leda and the Swan' but 'Fragments'. I am thinking of
'For Once, Then, Something':

> Others taunt me with having knelt at well-curbs
> Always wrong to the light, so never seeing
> Deeper down in the well than where the water
> Gives me back in a shining surface picture
> Me myself in the summer heaven, godlike,
> Looking out of a wreath of fern and cloud puffs.

The 'godlike' speaker who is engaged by what might be 'giv[en]
back' is, once again, positioned as the swan-god is positioned over
Leda:

> One drop fell from a fern, and lo, a ripple
> Shook whatever it was lay there at bottom,
> Blurred it, blotted it out. What was that whiteness?
> Truth? A pebble of quartz? For once, then, something. (*FCP* 208)

There is a striking shared vocabulary in Frost's 'whiteness' and Yeats's
'*white* rush', Frost's 'one drop' and, albeit in a slightly different sense,
Yeats's 'could let her *drop*'. More significantly, there is the shared
imagery of 'ripple' and resonance, 'shudder' and aftershock, between
'For Once, Then, Something' and 'Leda and the Swan'. In the case
of 'Fragments', one might re-title it 'For Once, Then, *Nothing*'.
'Where got I that truth?' writes Yeats, remaking 'What was that
whiteness? Truth?' The answer is 'Out of *nothing* it came, / Out of
the forest loam' [emphasis added], that near version of Frost in 'forest'
preparing the way for the even more Frostian poem which immediately follows 'Leda and the Swan': 'Your hooves have stamped at the
black margin of the wood, / Even where horrible green parrots call
and swing.'[10]

Even though 'On a Picture of a Black Centaur by Edmund Dulac'
was written in 1920, it was not collected until *The Tower* of 1928,
and its positioning immediately after 'Leda and the Swan' may serve
as an indirect commentary on Yeats's indebtedness to that 'margin of
the wood' at which Frost had time and time again so strategically
positioned himself from as early as 'Into My Own', the first poem in
1913's *A Boy's Will*:

One of my wishes is that those dark trees,
So old and firm they scarcely show the breeze,
Were not, as 'twere, the merest mask of gloom,
But stretched away unto the edge of doom. (*FCP* 15)

'On a Picture of a Black Centaur by Edmund Dulac' shares some key vocabulary with 'Stopping by Woods on a Snowy Evening', for example, which appears immediately before 'For Once, Then, Something' in *New Hampshire*. This vocabulary includes the words 'wood', 'horse', 'dark' and, as it happens, Frost's same solving rhyme of 'sleep' and 'keep', as if Yeats had so completely absorbed Frost's system of imagery as to anticipate 'Stopping by Woods on a Snowy Evening' by a few short months:

Stretch out your limbs and sleep a long Saturnian sleep;
I have loved you better than my soul for all my words,
And there is none so fit to keep a watch and keep
Unwearied eyes upon those horrible green birds.[11]

2

In this second part of my discussion, I touch *very* briefly on some odd connections between MacNeice and Yeats, whom MacNeice had met on a trip to Dublin in 1934, a year after the publication of *The Winding Stair and Other Poems*. That collection contains 'Words for Music Perhaps', a sequence itself containing the Crazy Jane poems and 'Mad as the Mist and Snow', both likely antecedents of a poem written in January 1935: 'The room was suddenly rich and the great bay-window was / Spawning *snow* and pink roses against it' (*CP* 24). Yeats's frequent positioning in *The Winding Stair* of the speaker seated at a 'window-ledge' ('Coole and Ballylee, 1931') or looking through 'great windows open to the south' ('In Memory of Eva Gore-Booth and Con Markievicz') seems to be picked up by MacNeice in that 'great bay-window'. The 'roses' appear with such frequency in Yeats that I am not going to pluck a single stem by way of example. When MacNeice goes on to describe the world as being 'suddener' than we fancy it, one wonders if he is including the rape of Helen. When he describes the world as 'crazier and more of it than we think', one wonders if he has made allowance for Crazy Jane. Another nod in the direction of Yeats is in the phrase 'I peel and portion / a tangerine', which is reminiscent of both the rhythm and vocabulary of 'The Song of Wandering Aengus': 'I went out to the hazel wood / Because a fire was in my head / And cut and *peeled* a hazel wand …'[12]

Like all stars, the 'moth-like stars' in 'The Song of Wandering Aengus' held a particular fascination for MacNeice. His late poem, 'Star-gazer', collected in his posthumous *The Burning Perch*, recounts a childhood experience of 'darting from side to side' of a 'late night train' to take in the 'holes, punched in the sky' (*CP* 607). But MacNeice and Yeats shared another fascination, for the other posthumous publication by MacNeice was his 350-page monograph not on astronomy but *Astrology*. He explains why Synesius of Cyrene pays more than lip service to astrology:

> One of the reasons he gives for accepting astrology is that history repeats itself because the stars return to their former positions. It is surprising that an early Christian could accept this cyclic view of history; but then the concept has appealed to a certain kind of intellectual (W.B. Yeats for one) down to our own times.[13]

The only other reference to Yeats in all of these 350 pages is a photograph of him on page 11 with a note to the effect that he 'was fascinated by the irrational'. The throwaway manner of these two references to Yeats are pleasingly reminiscent of Yeats's own high-handedness. While *Astrology* is far from being a position paper, like Yeats's *A Vision*, it does nonetheless offer a view into what Ted Hughes, in his 1964 review in *The Listener*, described as a world in which 'the cloud of howlers that it advances on the public is no greater than what we'd see of science, if science hadn't the sense to conceal all but its successes, and if every decade of its history weren't littered with shed fantasts'.[14] Just as Yeats studiously avoids, in *A Vision*, any reference to Viktor Khlebnikov and his theory of cycles of history contained in *The Wheel of Births* (1919), so MacNeice refuses to acknowledge the cyclic nature of his thought on the cyclic nature of thought.

3

In this final part of my discussion of Frost and MacNeice, I shall be trying to tease out some of the 'dark webs' that connect the two poets.

In his famous 1939 exchange with F.R. Higgins, MacNeice counters the way in which Higgins characterises 'the spirit informing
poetry written in English since the European War':

> Higgins: The abundance of such verse is, of course, written in
> England. I suppose you admit that?
> MacNeice: And America.[15]

As we begin to determine which American poets MacNeice might
have had in mind, we do well to remember that, in 1939, the figure
who dominated American poetry, and had done so throughout
MacNeice's writing life, was Robert Frost. Not only did he dominate American poetry but his influence was so widespread as to have
made an impact on MacNeice that has hitherto gone unnoticed, even
in Rachel Buxton's *Robert Frost and Northern Irish Poetry* (2004). Let
me take a quick romp through a few poems which suggest that there
is some 'undesigned / Evidence of design', if I may borrow a phrase
from 'The News-Reel', a poem collected in MacNeice's 1944
volume, *Springboard*, which collected poems written between 1941
and 1944 (in September 1940 he was reading 'a few poems by Frost'
[*L* 404]): 'Since Munich, what? A tangle of black film / Squirming
like bait upon the floor of my mind' (*CP* 240–41).

This image of 'film / Squirming like bait' coupled with the
espoused position that there be 'undesigned evidence of design'
allows us to read 'The News-Reel' as a response to, or an extension
of, Frost's 'Design', a poem collected in *A Further Range* of 1936, in
which 'a dimpled spider' is discovered 'on a white heal-all, holding
up a moth':

> What had that flower to do with being white,
> The wayside blue and innocent heal-all?
> What brought the kindred spider to that height,
> Then steered the white moth thither in the night?
> What but design of darkness to appall? –
> If design govern in a thing so small. (*FCP* 275)

The 'wayside' in 'Design' reminds one of the significance of the
marginal in both Frost and MacNeice, the wayside being one point
at which the thoroughfare and the trivial intersect and where it is
thrown into particular relief that, in Auden's memorable phrase,

'[t]he Frostian man is isolated not only in space but also in time'.[16] It is often at some wayside point, sometimes a wayside house or field, that the great dramatic poems that are such a feature of *North of Boston* (1914) are set – 'The Death of the Hired Man', 'The Mountain', 'A Hundred Collars', 'Home Burial', 'A Servant to Servants', or 'The Code'.

It is precisely out of this circumstance, and in something akin to Frost's dramatic ('eclogue') form, that some of MacNeice's very first poems derive. I am thinking of 'An Eclogue for Christmas' and 'Eclogue by a Five-Barred Gate'. 'Eclogue by a Five-Barred Gate' has one of the most blatant thefts by one poet of another, so that it persuades me, at least, that there are many more larcenies, petty or grand, that go unacknowledged. I am thinking of this exchange between Death and two Shepherds:

> D. I will open this gate that you may see for yourselves.
> 1. You go first.
> 2.   Well, you come too.
> 1.&2. We will go together to these pastures new ... (*CP* 14)

This sends us hurtling back to Frost's introductory poem to *North of Boston* (1914). 'The Pasture' shares with this dialogue from 'Eclogue by a Five-Barred Gate' not only its title but its final invitation to the reader '*You come too*'. The next poem in *North of Boston* is 'Mending Wall', itself an eclogue of sorts, though with nothing of the erotic charge of 'Eclogue by a Five-Barred Gate':

> I found her with my hands lying on the drying hay,
> Wet heat in the deeps of the hay as my hand delved,
> And I possessed her, gross and good like the hay,
> And she went and my eyes regained sight and the sky was full of ladders ... (*CP* 14)

This last phrase might be derived from the poem coming immediately after 'The Code' in *North of Boston*:

> My long two-pointed ladder's sticking through a tree
> Toward heaven still,
> And there's a barrel that I didn't fill
> Beside it, and there may be two or three

Apples I didn't pick upon some bough.
But I am done with apple-picking now. (*FCP* 70)

The speaker of 'After Apple-Picking' may be 'done', may have had
'too much of apple-picking', but it is precisely that sense of 'too
much' that engages the speaker of 'Snow':

World is crazier and more of it than we think,
Incorrigibly plural. I peel and portion
A tangerine and spit the pips and feel
The drunkenness of things being various. (*CP* 24)

This derives directly, I want to suggest, from the very same psychological state as 'After Apple-Picking' in which: 'Magnified apples
appear and disappear, / Stem end and blossom end, / And every fleck
of russet showing clear' (*FCP* 70). The palpability of plurality so
lovingly described by Frost in the lines 'There were ten thousand
thousand fruit to touch / Cherish in hand, lift down, and not let fall'
is picked up by MacNeice in the pun on the Latin word *tangere*, 'to
touch', in the name of those other fruit, the Tangier tangerine, in
'Snow'. Frost's interest in plurality derives largely from his profound
engagement with Henri Bergson, also an influence on MacNeice
along with Bergson's predecessor Heraclitus of Ephesus. Both
thinkers have something to do with the jumble of MacNeice's syntax:

And the fire flames with a bubbling sound for world
Is more spiteful and gay than one supposes –
On the tongue on the eyes on the ears in the palms of one's
                                                    hands –
There is more than glass between the snow and the huge roses.
                                                    (*CP* 24)

I shall come back to the 'glass' in 'Snow' a little later. For the
moment I stay with MacNeice's syntactical mimesis of the rough and
tumble of the world. As early as 'A Cataract Conceived as the March
of Corpses', collected in *Blind Fireworks* (1929), MacNeice was
hanging with Heraclitus:

The river falls and over the walls of cold funerals
Slide deep and sleep there in the close tomb of the pool,

And yellow waters lave the grave and pebbles pave its mortuary
And the river horses vault and plunge with their assault and battery.
(*CP* 623)

That cataract in *Blind Fireworks* is only a little downstream from Frost's
West-Running Brook, published only a year earlier, in 1928, in the
title-poem of which Frost combines an argument for Bergson's
concept of the *élan vital* with an argument against the *pirouette* –
strictly speaking 'a spinning top, child's windmill or whirligig, a
teetotum' – taken from Yeats's side for, as we recall, 1928 was also
the year of *The Tower*.

Some say existence like a Pirouot
And Pirouette, forever in one place
Stands still, and dances, but it runs away;
It seriously, sadly, runs away
To fill the abyss's void with emptiness.
It flows beside us in this water brook,
But it flows over us. It flows between us
To separate us for a panic moment.
It flows between us, over us, and *with* us.
And it is time, strength, tone, light, life, and love –
And even substance lapsing unsubstantial;
The universal cataract of death
That spends to nothingness – and unresisted,
Save by some strange resistance in itself,
Not just a swerving, but a throwing back,
As if regret were in it and were sacred. (*FCP* 237–8)

MacNeice seems to have taken Frost's 'universal cataract of death' as
the theme of his own 'Cataract', taken Frost's isolation of the 'panic
moment' as his cue for the series of isolated 'minutes' at the end of
his poem:

So all they will hear is the fall of hooves and the distant shake of
                                                                    harness,
And the beat of the bells on the horses' heads and the undertaker's
                                                                    laughter,
And the murmur that will lose its strength and blur at length to
                                                                    quietness,

And afterwards the minute heard descending, never ending heard,
And then the minute after and the minute after the minute after.
                                                        (*CP* 623)

It is hard, moreover, not to read MacNeice's 'the distant shake of
harness', particularly when it is followed immediately by 'the beat of
the bells on the horses' heads' as a further echo of Frost, an echo of
his most famous poem:

My little *horse* must think it queer
To stop without a farmhouse near
Between the woods and frozen lake
The darkest evening of the year.

He gives his *harness bells* a *shake*
To ask if there is some mistake. (*FCP* 207)

There is a mysterious aspect to 'Stopping by Woods on a Snowy
Evening' which is reminiscent of the mystery associated with
MacNeice's 'Snow', both poems having to do with a speaker who is
given 'to watch' either the 'woods' or 'a great bay-window'
somehow 'fill up with snow'. We can see, by the way, how Frost's
poem is itself inspired partly by Yeats's 'Song of the Wandering
Aengus', both in his setting 'I went out to the hazel *wood*' and its
iambic tetrameters culminating in a repetition, Yeats's 'The silver
apples of the moon, / The golden apples of the sun' rejigged as Frost's
'And miles to go before I sleep, / And miles to go before I sleep'.
Those apples remind me that I was going to come back to the 'glass'
in 'Snow'. It is of a piece, surely, with the magical 'pane of glass' in
'After Apple-Picking':

I cannot rub the strangeness from my sight
I got from looking through a pane of glass
I skimmed this morning from the drinking trough
And held against the world of hoary grass. (*FCP* 70)

One of the things that is 'more than glass' and comes between the
'snow' and 'the huge roses' is the hoary old pane that is indivisible
from hoary old Frost himself. Another Frost poem on the subject of
indivisibility that seems to intervene is 'Spring Pools', the first piece

in the 1928 volume *West-Running Brook*, in which there is a reflection on reflection which reads more and more like a limbering up for
'Snow':

> These pools that, though in forests, still reflect
> The total sky almost without defect,
> And like the flowers beside them, chill and shiver,
> Will like the flowers beside them soon be gone,
> And yet not out by any brook or river,
> But up by roots to bring dark foliage on. (*FCP* 224)

The themes of time and mutability are picked up in the wonderfully
wicked poem that falls third in *West-Running Book*, two poems
removed from 'Spring Pools', and entitled, of all things, 'The Rose
Family':

> The rose is a rose,
> And was always a rose.
> But the theory now goes
> That the apple's a rose,
> And the pear is, and so's
> The plum, I suppose.
> The dear only knows
> What will next prove a rose.
> You, of course, are a rose –
> But were always a rose. (*FCP* 225)

This 'rose family' is from the same stock as the 'huge roses' in 'Snow'.
While Frost is having some fun at the expense of Gertrude Stein's
poem 'Sacred Emily', published in *Geography and Plays* in 1922, he is
also even more seriously engaged with the relationship between time
and eternity, immanence and permanence, which would be such a
major obsession of MacNeice from such early poems as 'A Cataract
Conceived as the March of Corpses' through 'Snow' itself to a poem
such as 'The Introduction' in *The Burning Perch* in which 'You two
should have met / Long since, he said, or else not now' (*CP* 593).
Along the way there were such pieces as 'The Sunlight on the
Garden' from *The Earth Compels*:

The sunlight on the garden
Hardens and grows cold,
We cannot cage the minute
Within its nets of gold. (*CP* 57)

Again, it is tempting to think of 'The Sunlight on the Garden', collected in 1938, as being influenced partly by Frost's 'Fireflies in the Garden', which comes immediately after 'The Rose Family' in *West-Running Brook* (1928), partly by 'Nothing Gold Can Stay' and its insistence 'So dawn goes down to day. / Nothing gold can stay' from *New Hampshire* (1923). New Hampshire would become an all too physical reality for MacNeice in 1940 when, on a visit there with Eleanor Clark, he found himself undergoing emergency surgery for peritonitis in a hospital in Portsmouth. In 'The Messiah', collected in *Solstices* (1961), he writes:

In Portsmouth, New Hampshire, plugged with morphia,
Cranked up on my hospital bed to see through the window,
I watched in a building one hundred yards away
A light flashing on and off in a window,
Half an hour maybe between the flashes (*CP* 533–4)

Though it transpires, rather drearily, that 'the building that flashed the light was the Maternity Ward', this scene has all the makings of one of MacNeice's 'thumbnail nightmares', of a 'Bad Dream' complete with Frost's 'ice window' from 'After Apple-Picking':

The window was made of ice with bears lumbering across it,
    Bears the size of flies.
The ceiling was one great web with flies cantankering in it,
    Flies the size of men. (*CP* 567–8)

This jaw-dropping shift of scale is a favourite device of Frost's. We have seen it in the '*magnified* apples' in 'After Apple-Picking' and seen it carried over by MacNeice into the '*huge* roses' of 'Snow'. In MacNeice's 'Bad Dream' we have a version of Auden's 'commonest human situation' in Frost's poems, that of 'one man, or a man and wife, alone in a small isolated house'.[17] The wife in this case is a version of the 'glimmering girl' from 'The Song of the Wandering Aengus', who appears as a disembodied arm:

And the arm grew and he wished to bend and clutch the hand
   But found he could no more move,
The arm grew and the fingers groped for help, the voice
   That had grown with the arm, the voice
That was now a woman's about to be saved or lost was calling
   For help. He could not move.

Then everything buzzed and boomed. The chaps outside on the
                                   lamp posts
   Hooted, broke wind, and wept,
Men the size of flies dropped down his neck while the mansized
   Flies gave just three cheers
And he could not move. The darkness under the floor gave just
   One shriek. The arm was gone. (*CP* 568–9)

This image of 'the arm [being] gone' is a direct remake of Frost's
'Out, Out – ' in which a boy loses his hand, then his life, to a buzz
saw. Yet again, the description of Frost by MacNeice as 'one of the
most sinister writers in the language' (*SLC* 246) would have had a
particular resonance for the classicist in that sinister means 'the left
hand'. Another version of the 'small isolated house' as divined by
Auden in 'Bad Dream' may be seen in 'Selva Oscura', perhaps the
most Frostian of MacNeice's poems:

A house can be haunted by those who were never there
If there was where they were missed. Returning to such
Is it worse if you miss the same or another or none?
The haunting anyway is too much.
You have to leave the house to clear the air.

A life can be haunted by what it never was
if that were merely glimpsed. Lost in the maze
That means yourself and never out of the wood
These days, though lost, will be all your days.
Life, if you leave it, must be left for good. (*CP* 571–2)

The phrase 'merely glimpsed' is a nod in the direction of Frost's
epigrammatic lines from 'A Passing Glimpse': 'Heaven gives its
glimpses only to those / Not in position to look too close' (*FCP* 227).
The final stanza of 'Selva Oscura' has the speaker announce 'I strike

a clearing and see / Some unknown house', thereby engaging with
one of Frost's central images – that of clearing as clarification – a
clearing of which the lake, the park, and 'The Lake in the Park' are
versions:

> On an empty morning a small clerk
> Who thinks no one will ever love him
> Sculls on the lake in the park while bosomy
> Trees indifferently droop above him. (*CP* 551)

The phrase 'a small clerk' connects this poem with memories of
Eleanor *Clark* and the visit to America on which MacNeice met
Frost. While the phrase 'the lake in the park' conjures up the all-too-
familiar Yeatsian images of 'The *Lake* Isle of Innisfree' and 'Coole
Park, 1921', the Frostian setting of a 'sinister' natural arena is every
bit as present. Frost's core imagery of being 'in the clearing' (yet never
quite in the clear), is nowhere more to the fore in MacNeice than in
'The Introduction': 'They were introduced in a grave glade / And
she frightened him because she was young / And thus too late' (*CP*
593). The revelation that these lovers are 'introduced in a green
grave' extends preoccupations found in Frost poems from 'The
Housekeeper' in *North of Boston* ('*Too late* now: she wouldn't have
him', *FCP* 82) to 'The Lesson for Today' from *A Witness Tree* in
which he describes his urge to find common cause: 'With poets who
could calmly take the fate / Of being born at once *too early and late*,
/ And for these reasons kept from being great' (*FCP* 318). 'The
Lesson for Today' surely influenced MacNeice's 'Elegy for Minor
Poets' (1946), where the elegist says of those poets 'Who were too
happy or sad, too soon or late': 'I would praise these in company with
the Great' (*CP* 273).

Something of the sense of literary loss as well the lovelorn may
have seeped from Frost into MacNeice's sense of belatedness in 'The
Introduction'. As surely as the phrase 'trees that indifferently droop'
harks back to Yeats's 'indifferent beak' and this 'grave glade' to a
Frostian 'clearing', MacNeice is more and more beginning to find
that kind of success that Frost designated as going beyond merely that
'of esteem'. It is getting harder and harder to find a reason that would
keep him 'from being great'.

'THE LADIES WOULD SAY THAT HE LOOKED LIKE A POET': TOM AND THE SELLING OF LOUIS

Anne Margaret Daniel

On 2 March 1939, T.S. Eliot wrote a quick letter to his old friend Willard Thorp in the English department at Princeton University from his offices at Faber and Faber. Eliot and Thorp, an American literature scholar and leading authority on Herman Melville, knew each other through two women: Margaret Thorp, Willard's wife, was the oldest friend of Eliot's dear friend – and perhaps more – Emily Hale. This friendship between Margaret and Emily is why twelve large brown cardboard boxes of more than a thousand letters from Eliot to Hale ended up under seal in the Princeton University library, ribbed in iron bands and not to be opened until 1 January 2020. What these letters reveal remains a mystery for another decade, but Eliot's letter to Thorp is crystal-clear in its purpose and meaning. In it, Eliot complains that he must write 'in haste to catch the Queen Mary' before it sails, and the letter is accordingly succinct: he wants Louis MacNeice to be invited to come to Princeton for a reading. As poetry editor for Faber, Eliot had finally – after MacNeice had been sending him poems since 1932 – deemed MacNeice worth publishing by the firm, and he was now happy to promote MacNeice in America, even as a world was going to war once more.

Introducing him to Thorp, Eliot left the 'a' out of Mac, but got it right that MacNeice taught Greek at Bedford College. Eliot had already set up the trip to America for MacNeice – 'I have got him engagements at Harvard and Wellesley – I don't seem to know anybody at Yale' – but wanted a few more readings to help MacNeice pay his travel expenses. Of course Thorp was welcome to say no; Eliot reminded him a bit too politely that he was welcome not to 'BOTHER to do anything at all'. But Thorp could not possibly have turned down the request, and indeed he did not, when Eliot concluded his introduction of MacNeice with: 'He has a good deal of charm, and the ladies would say that he looked like a poet.'[1]

Princeton's library, like most research libraries, has a wealth of manuscript material, scattered among many collections. It is not always easy to trace what is to, from, and about Louis MacNeice, but in T.S. Eliot's unpublished correspondence to Thorp and Allen Tate, among others, there are some fascinating moments in the behind-the-scenes building-up of a poet. And in MacNeice's own correspondence with some of the contacts he made through Eliot, and their own still-unpublished memories of him, we can also see the professional, and personal, friendships Eliot fostered for MacNeice. Eliot was not always a help, though. Note that in the letter to Thorp, it is the ladies who say he looks like a poet, and not his editor who says he *is* a poet. The correspondence is rich and full of small surprises about both Eliot and MacNeice, and adds immensely to our knowl-edge of both poets and their sometimes complementary, sometimes complimentary, and sometimes competitive, relationship.

Eliot discovered MacNeice when MacNeice set out to be noticed by him, and contacted him accordingly, in January 1932. When did MacNeice discover Eliot? From his earliest youthful recordings, as compiled by Jon Stallworthy in his excellent biography of the poet, we know that MacNeice had a crush on America – a crush that would turn into a lifelong relationship. And his first surviving poem sounds rather to me as though it could start a volume called *Old Possum's Book of Practical Birds*: MacNeice recalls his youthful rules for poetry thus: 'use "thou" instead of "you" and make the ends of the lines rhyme with each other, no specific emotion or "poetic" content required'. He goes on to quote 'a poem about a live parrot I had seen in a neighbour's house':

O parrot, thou hast grey feathers
Which thou peckest in all weathers.
And thy curled beak
Could make me squeak;
Thy tail I admire
As red as the fire
And as red as a carrot,
Thy tail I admire,
Thou cross old parrot. (*MP* 39–40)

America, rhyme, high diction, and no specific emotion: the little dark-haired boy is already primed for the Eliotic. Being sent away to

school created another, and an unlikely, connection, when
MacNeice arrived in a place just up the road from the Eliots' ancestral village. He was pixilated by Sherborne, and the surrounding
landscape – overwhelmed by the nature he saw and found both in
the fields and hedgerows, and buried in the earth. This part of
Somerset is a gorgeous golden place still; Thomas Wyatt lies buried
in Sherborne Abbey, boys still find fossils in the riverbanks, and along
a heartstoppingly lovely drive south by southeast is the idyllic, almost
theme-park beautiful village of East Coker, where the sheep all stand
out as if freshly washed against the improbable green of the hills, the
Helyar Arms is one of the best pubs in all England, and T.S. Eliot's
grave is in the church.

   Like Eliot, MacNeice had a fine and early sense of the theatrical.
Recall Eliot's youthful interest in dramatics, and his participations at
Harvard. Recall, too, his playing the role of St Sebastian – also a
favourite of MacNeice's – and wearing green makeup at London
parties to manifest the misery of his marriage to Vivienne. MacNeice
also shared Eliot's love of musical theatre and the music hall – that
Shakespeherian rag side of Eliot, the side of Eliot that danced the
Grizzly Bear with Virginia Woolf (a video that we can only be glad,
or immensely sad, will never appear on YouTube).[2] One of
MacNeice's happiest school memories was the moment after games
and a run, with quintessentially English music as a soundtrack: 'when
you got back into the communal bathroom even lukewarm water
would bite you until gradually getting reacclimatised you sunk into
your tub, wonderfully relaxed in an underworld of steam and dim
pink bodies humming Gilbert and Sullivan' (*SF* 86).

   MacNeice was smitten with Malory, Keats, and Yeats before Eliot
got to him: at Marlborough, Louis's early poems for the school paper
sound for all the world like outtakes from 'The Wanderings of Oisin'
and other Yeats works of the late 1880s, particularly 'The Stolen
Child'. An example is 'Death of a Prominent Businessman':

> Death comes for the prominent businessman:
> Come you away to the black peat bog,
> The driving sleet and the drifting rain,
> Where the wee folk weave from the pith of the reed
> And the world is rid of financial greed
> And the gentry dance in a chain. (*CP* 353)

Were there any doubt the young man was a poet, that 'gentry dance in a chain' dispels it. And, more humorously, the fact that in his next published poem Louis rhymes 'unwashed lad' and 'Trinidad' (*JS* 90, 96).

Finally, at Marlborough, the young rhymer encountered the word of Eliot. He tells how he and Anthony Blunt

> went in for eclectic reading; it was either stark and realistic or precious and remote and two-dimensional. We read Tolstoy and Dostoevski and Beckford's *Vathek*, Thomas Hardy and Crébillon *fils*, Blake and Lucretius ... lives of Cézanne and Van Gogh, the three Sitwells, Lord Dunsany's fairy stories, Edward Lear and T.S. Eliot and Aldous Huxley. (*SF* 98)

Huxley, accompanying Eliot and Lear, two masters of the manner in which rhyme and nonsense could carve out a way to make sense in a shattered, illogical, nonsensical brave new world: their modernist lessons MacNeice learned well.

His friend John Hilton saw the impact Eliot had straightaway on MacNeice, when MacNeice recommended some poems '"by a new poet," T.S. Eliot, to a reading organised by the [Marlborough] Literary Society' (*JS* 102). Though impressed by Eliot, MacNeice was not an Eliot fan at first: 'His subject-matter was ugly, I did not like his form, and I found him very obscure' (*MP* 56). Soon, though, MacNeice had studied Eliot's 'principles', and he warmed to his 'technique – the blend of conversation and incantation, the deliberate flatnesses, the quick cutting, the so-called free association' (*MP* 58).

MacNeice arrived in 1926 at an Oxford that was, in his memorable words, 'just at the end of its period of postwar deliberate decadence – the careful matching of would-be putrescent colours'. Oxford was quite over-the-top, or perhaps under-the-bottom, in those days, a riotous and languid *Brideshead Revisited* place where life and literature, fact and fictions, re-created each other, and recreated with each other.

> We used to organise readings of plays such as the *Jew of Malta* or *The White Devil* in a room lit by candles stuck in beer-bottles and a skull on the table with radishes in its eye-sockets. We brought strange fruits such as persimmons and passion-fruit, and I got

myself an ashplant in order to be like Stephen Dedalus. (*SF* 103, 108)

If this is not, Stephen Dedalus perhaps excepted, an Eliotic world, then what is? One cannot read a line of MacNeice's Oxford recollections without recalling Evelyn Waugh's Anthony Blanche, reciting *The Waste Land* from his balcony at the returning rowers; or Auden's crystalline description to Lord Byron of what happened to him, Spender, MacNeice, and their circle of young Oxford poets at that time and place:

> A raw provincial, my good taste was tardy,
>   And Edward Thomas I as yet preferred;
> I was still listening to Thomas Hardy
>   Putting divinity about a bird;
>   But Eliot spoke the still unspoken word;
> For gasworks and dried tubers I forsook
> The clock at Grantchester, the English rook.[3]

Or, as MacNeice would put it later: 'However sheltered our young lives, however rural our normal surroundings, however pre-Industrial Revolution our education, we knew in our bones ... that this which Eliot expressed so succinctly and vividly, this was what we were up against.'[4]

Gollancz published MacNeice's first book of poems, *Blind Fireworks*, in 1929. The collection is full of reminiscences of infancy and schoolboy days not so long past, of human voices and seafilled endings, of clocks and stopping time, and particularly musings on modern modes of transportation: trams, and trains, and taxis throbbing waiting. Of course, Eliot did not have the franchise on all these things and themes, but I think they most certainly were, here, inspired by him.

With this published book under his belt, a novel in progress, and a job in Birmingham University, MacNeice in January 1932 sent his poems to Eliot. No reply. Giving Eliot the benefit of the doubt, in April MacNeice wrote an apologetic, but insistent, letter as a follow-up:

> I think that only a few of them stand on their own merits, but that as a collection and arranged in a certain order they would supple-

ment each other and make an aggregate of some value. Whereas if I chose a dozen individuals, they would remain, perhaps, merely individuals. It seems to me (as far as I can see myself) that I am not sufficiently in a school for my poems to be readily significant; therefore they have to build up their own explanation. This is my apology for what may seem a haphazard mass of indifferent or casual verses. (*L* 228)

That qualifying, self-defending use of 'seem' and 'seems' is worth noting. Along with if and as if, and many thousand woulds, coulds, and shoulds, 'seems' is the one of the commonest words in modernist writing. Eliot refused these seeming-haphazard poems for Faber, but called them interesting, and put a couple, 'The Creditor' and 'Trapeze', in the *Criterion*. He also invited MacNeice to review books for his journal.

Eliot turned down MacNeice's revised poems once more in 1933, terming them 'not quite ripe for publication', but suggesting yet more work. 'I think that my feeling is largely a practical and tactical one. I think that a first volume ought, if possible, to be able to start off with one or two longish poems which will arrest the attention of the reader at once' (*JS* 162–3).

What Eliot asks for are longer poems – like his own – and in a style very suited to MacNeice too. Passing over the fact that this would not be a 'first book' of poems, MacNeice had already started writing his eclogues, and kept them up after Eliot's advice came. In August 1934 he sent a mix of new and revised poems back to Eliot, and finally made it. Eliot liked them at last. 'It seems to me that the new poems are quite the best that you have done, and if you go on in this way, you may have a few more to add to or to substitute for a few of the earlier poems before the book goes to press. In any case I congratulate you on this collection' (*JS* 164). Again, that qualifying, excusing 'seems'. MacNeice has already become a prince of the present-day trend to avoid linguistic commitment and qualify with the conditional, but in any Eliot poem, or prose piece, or letter, we can see who is the king. Faber finally published *Poems* in 1935.

Eliot liked MacNeice's next solo offering (following his collaboration with Auden, *Letters from Iceland*), *The Earth Compels*, saying 'I am very much pleased with it' – but not so much pleased that he did not insist on a few changes. He also wanted particular changes to *Autumn Journal*. Eliot thought *Autumn Journal*

very good indeed. At times I was much moved, and what is still
more unusual in the case of a single long poem, I found that I read
it through without my interest flagging at any point. That is due
partly to the dexterity with which you vary the versification, and,
I think, to the fact that the imagery is all imagery of things lived
through, and not merely chosen for poetic suggestiveness.

Eliot liked its verisimilitude, perhaps, but not its politics. He did not
particularly want to think about the Spanish Civil War, and while
Eliot got the point that bringing in the Oxford by-election 'has a definite symbolic value', he was sorry to see MacNeice 'simplify the issue
so much', without realising MacNeice's irony (*JS* 237).

However, MacNeice's confidence had grown – in the wake of at
least critically successful plays and of his *Modern Poetry* – and he did
not give in to Eliot's grousing about politics and change the poem.
After all, MacNeice did care about politics: 'Bagpipe Music' would
have been a very different poem if he had not, and, as he remembered from his schooldays, 'I was hurt when Anthony [Blunt]
denounced politics as beneath the attention of a civilised person.
Most politics, yes, but not Irish politics. If I had one foot poised over
untrodden asphodel, the other was still clamped to the ankle in the
bogs' (*SF* 231).

In mid-October 1938 MacNeice asked Eliot if he could help to
get a few invitations to some American universities during the Easter
vacation. Eliot did indeed fire off some letters – including the one to
Thorp that he did not send until March – and helped MacNeice set
up a lecture tour that started in New York. One of Auden's friends
remembered MacNeice lecturing on modern trends in English
poetry and prose: 'Calm and handsome in a Donegal tweed suit and
suede shoes, he read without the slightest change of emphasis poems
that were either playfully light and intricate or casually grim and
touched with the forebodings of Neville Chamberlain's England.'
Auden read too, that night. And after the reading a young blond man
in the audience came up to find him and speak to him for the first
time: his name was Chester Kallman (*JS* 243).

Willard Thorp had thoughtfully paved the way for MacNeice's
Princeton lecture with a few of his own. Having received Eliot's
letter, and agreed to help out, Thorp first contacted MacNeice and
invited him. MacNeice's grateful replies survive in Thorp's correspondence files: on 25 March 1939, he wrote from New York to

'Dear Mr Sharp' (MacNeice being no better here with names than his editor) that he wanted to come to Princeton on 14 or 15 April, proposing to 'give a talk on English poetry since the (Great) War'.[5]

In the interim, Thorp presented what the campus paper, *The Daily Princetonian* (the *Prince*) called a 'Popular-demand series on American and English poets' to include 'Eliot, Crane, and Auden'. Why the need for these four extracurricular lectures? Because, as the *Prince* put it in a banner headline, 'University courses ignore subject of modern verse'. 'Not since 1936', when Thorp and another English professor collaborated on 'a series on modern literature, [had] Princeton under-grads been offered a related set of talks on contemporary verse. None of the University's current courses cover the topic.'[6] Thorp's first lecture, on 20 March, was entitled 'Imagism and the War Over Free Verse'; in it, while talking of T.E. Hulme, H.D., Richard Aldington, and Ezra Pound, Thorp said succinctly that 'the real contribution of imagism to literature is the exploration of a special technique used to achieve certain ends, but which cannot be expected to bear the weight of profound thought'.[7]

The next lecture, much anticipated, was on Eliot. Thorp let Eliot rather speak for himself at first, reading aloud 'A Game of Chess' and 'Burial of the Dead' from *The Waste Land*. He then described Eliot 'as a sensitive artist using Restoration wit at unexpected moments to produce desired effects and eventually finding a path out of the despair-filled "wasteland" of the postwar years'. In his last lecture, Thorp spoke on Auden, Spender, Day Lewis, and MacNeice, saving, in his opinion, the best for last. He 'noted that "not all the poets of the new generation have taken the road to Moscow – and the best of them is Louis MacNeice"'. Thorp cited 'To a Communist' as an example of MacNeice's poetry.[8]

'Poetry Since the War' was MacNeice's topic, on the following evening – Friday, 14 April – and he delivered it not on campus but in town, at the Nassau Tavern. The *Prince* gave him a fine advance notice:

> Although not yet 35, MacNeice is considered one of the 20th-century's leading poets. Along with a number of left-wing writers, he has recently been attempting a renaissance in English poetry. The influence of MacNeice's group has made itself felt as far afield as this country … MacNeice's contributions to poetry two years ago were collected under the title *Poems*. Besides this work he was

closely connected with W.H. Auden in the publication of the satirical *Letters From Iceland*. *Modern Poetry*, a volume in a difficult field, was also recently published. In his work MacNeice has played a significant part in the field of literature creating a fresh and muscular idiom for present-day Anglo-American poetry.

Realizing the importance of its guest, the [Poetry] Club is deviating from its usual procedure and opening the meeting to all undergraduates and members of the faculty. The entrance fee for non-members is 50 cents.[9]

MacNeice spoke to a full house that night, and the evening went late and long. Leaning on Walter Pater and select contemporaries, MacNeice also, evidently, bit the hand that fed him – or at least administered to Eliot a swift nip. 'Pointing out that a poet's function should be to resolve this complicated age into something simple and clear cut', MacNeice read from Wilfred Owen, Auden, and Spender as examples. 'In the discussion of the works of T.S. Eliot the young poet questioned the policy of writing obscure and subtle poetry because of our complicated age.' MacNeice also 'stated that poets should not write propaganda but should write art for art's sake alone. Furthermore, he must write what he feels. When questioned as to whether art could be propaganda at the same time, he replied that it could, but that it must be the poet's sincere feeling.' MacNeice concluded his formal talk with a reading from his own work, the unpublished *Autumn Journal*. 'Following the talk there was considerable discussion of modern poetry, its message, and its significance.'[10] The *Prince* doesn't say how late the 'considerable discussion' went, but the Nassau Inn was likely livelier that night than was its already wee-hours wont.

On 9 May 1939 Eliot wrote to thank Thorp 'for taking on Mcneice [*sic*]; I expect to see him soon and hear about it. I gather that he enjoyed his visit thoroughly.' Indeed he must have, and this evidently got Eliot thinking about possibilities not for MacNeice, but for himself: at the letter's close Eliot mentions that a lectureship at Princeton, possibly in conjunction with getting *The Family Reunion* ready for Broadway, 'would suit me almost better than anywhere' depending, he qualifies, on how things in the world are by autumn 1940.[11] The world turned, and he did not come to Princeton until 1948, when, as a fellow at the Institute for Advanced Study, Eliot received the news of his Nobel Prize.

The American contacts that Eliot arranged for MacNeice on this tour and soon thereafter might have been with laconic introduction and touched by Eliot's self-interest to a degree, but Eliot cannot be faulted, as they resulted in lifelong friendships for MacNeice. Another letter of Eliot's went to Allen Tate, in 1940 while MacNeice was at Cornell, and Tate and MacNeice became good friends quickly. Tate had got to know Eliot after Eliot rejected his poems in 1927, as follows: 'I like this stuff very much in some respects but it seems to me, if I may say so, that you are a little tied up in your own tail at present, but I am sure that it will get straightened out in time. Do continue to let me see things from time to time.'[12] Tate did continue, and he and Eliot were soon close, their letters full of an American-ness, and particularly a Southernness, that Eliot clearly revelled in, from colloquial dialect riffs about the Civil War to praise of bourbon, and of course much discussion of poetry and poets. A happy example is this Joycean note Eliot wrote Tate from Harvard in 1933: 'if theres talk of juleps before breakfast I says there wheres theres juleps befire Breakfast theres my squurrettual home in a manner of speaking ... you will always find, hopin you the best, yrs respectfully TSEliot.'[13]

In October 1952, when MacNeice and his wife Hedli came to America on what MacNeice called their 'lecture-cum-singing-cum-reading tour' coordinated by John Malcolm Brinnin at the Poetry Center in New York, he wrote to Tate, 'If you feel like inviting us to Minneapolis – and can pay for us! – would you please contact Brinnin about it? ... In any case, even if you can't afford us, I hope we shall meet somewhere in America while we are over.'[14] Tate came through. Caroline Gordon Tate wrote approvingly to Margaret Thorp, from Minneapolis, 'Louis read some of his poems the other night. Allen says that he is even more impressed by them now that he's heard him read than he was before.'[15]

On 2 August 1963, from his new country home in Aldbury, MacNeice wrote happily to Tate and his new wife Isabella: 'please let us know when you hit this little old vice-ridden capital. Have a new book of poems in proof to show you – said he egocentrically – all thumbnail nightmares. Apart from that, all is fine. You must come & see our new residence – too Olde Rose Cottage to be true' (L 701). The 'thumbnail nightmares' were the posthumously published poems of *The Burning Perch*. On the margin of the letter, in Tate's hand: 'My last letter from Louis.'[16]

Upon MacNeice's unexpected and premature death at fifty-five, a month after he wrote this note to Tate, Eliot was too stunned – and too beset with similar health problems of his own – to say more than the few words he provided to *The Times*. MacNeice died of a sudden lung infection that became pneumonia. Since early 1963, Eliot, a longtime smoker and sufferer from lung troubles, had been in very poor health; only his good friends really knew this. He worked out a cunning plan to stop smoking, as he explained to Tate in 1956: 'The first thing is to have a very thorough fright. The second is to be put into bed for several weeks on top of the fright. People vary in this respect, but I never feel any desire to smoke in bed. My third tip is to take up cigar smoking.'[17] By the year MacNeice died, Eliot was quite ill with both lung and heart trouble. Valerie Eliot had written to Tate on 2 February 1963 about Eliot's health:

> Tom came home about a fortnight ago after five weeks under continuous oxygen in Brompton Hospital. As you may know, he has suffered from emphysema for years and the struggle to breathe has thrown a tremendous strain on his heart. When the four-day smog – easily the worst I've ever experienced – appeared early in December he collapsed … Happily he is making a good recovery, although his heart is not yet stable … He is very serene and helps himself in every way, including the obedient swallowing of 26 tablets a day. Visitors are forbidden.[18]

Eliot, though, elegised MacNeice graciously and movingly in *The Times* (in a clipping that Tate preserved). Said Eliot, MacNeice 'had the Irishman's unfailing ear for the music of verse, and he never published a line that is not good reading'. He felt there was

> little that I can add to the encomiums of Louis MacNeice which have already appeared in the press, except the expression of my own grief and shock. The grief one must feel at the death of a poet of genius, younger than oneself, and the shock of his unexpected death just as my firm had ready for publication a new volume of his verse.[19]

Eliot's use of the third person here shifts from the personal 'I' to the distancing, less painfully proximate 'one' and 'oneself'. Eliot emphasises, too, a combined, and inseparable, sense of his own genuine upset, and the loss to Faber – the company had become his alter ego, in some deep-running way, by then. The loss to him is compelling, and severe.

Allen Tate remembered his friend for the BBC, and saved, in his last file of correspondence with MacNeice, the transcript of his radio broadcast recorded in London on 6 December 1963. In it, Tate conjures a figure of a man whose poetry and personality are, in the end, touched by Eliotic stereotype but firmly individual:

> Some friends described him as 'distant,' hard to get at; I never found him so. He was not reticent; he had something that looked superficially like it but was actually quite different: he was restrained. He never talked about himself − it was always about something over there. This detachment was never cold, and it was not objective; it simply acknowledged the immense reality swirling about us, and about which we can do little but attend to it. And that made him a good listener.[20]

This fellow-poet, whose connection to MacNeice began and thrived through Eliot as everyone's mutual friend, understood the most fundamental difference between Eliot and MacNeice, what set MacNeice most apart from his longtime editor, publisher, mentor, and model. Tate, a modernist himself, needed to gentle his opinion with a well-placed *seems*, but it does not weaken the point he makes about MacNeice's poetic soul: 'He seemed to have been born without illusions; so he could not be disillusioned.'

THE LIVES WE LIVE

Gerald Dawe

Brian Moore, writing in 1992, identified the original edition of Michael Roberts's *Faber Book of Modern Verse* as one of three key books which greatly influenced him – the others were *Ulysses* and *The Sun Also Rises*. The Faber anthology was, he remarked, 'for me, as for many of my generation, our introduction to Eliot, Auden, MacNeice, Wallace Stevens, Hart Crane and others'.[1] The original edition was published in 1936 (when Moore was fifteen); a second edition came out in 1951, and a third in 1965; the later editions both carrying new supplements chosen by (respectively) Anne Ridler and Donald Hall. Subsequent editions have appeared since 1965 with further amendments to the supplements. The *Faber Book* has had a significant literary influence from Brian Moore's teenage years in Belfast in the thirties to a later generation in the sixties who read the anthology as part of their national examination in English literature at A level, myself included. And it was in the *Faber Book* that I first encountered MacNeice. The fine poems with which he is represented, 'An Eclogue for Christmas', 'Perseus', 'Snow', 'Conversation', and 'The Truisms' (the latter two being replacements for 'Sunday Morning' and 'The Creditor') had a zip to them that was instantly recognisable, although it probably passed us by that MacNeice, along with Yeats and Cecil Day Lewis, was one of only three poets who were Irish included in the book.

As I started on my own awkward steps towards writing poems and writing about them, MacNeice's example as poet and critic has never left my mind. (His *Modern Poetry* is a great read, his *Yeats* one of the best introductions, and the literary criticism and travel writing brilliant – a shame that it all has not been collected in standard paperback editions.) Perhaps there is too much in the *Collected Poems* which sounds tried and tested, but who in their right mind would ever do without *Autumn Journal* or the bulk of MacNeice's lyrics? That is, for his unerring perceptiveness about the lives we live, the streetscapes and rites of ordinary people, the individual idiosyncratic mannerisms seen or overheard, the anecdotal evidence of different times and places, the sound of a man talking aloud, the business of getting on, and all framed inside a classically understated intelligence.

More than anything else, when I think of MacNeice, I am struck by a sense of him knowing the vulnerabilities of modern existence, the fragilities of human contact; and by the solitariness at the centre of his own upbringing that matches the bravery and self-belief of what he did with his talent: pushing on and making his decisions on his own – the transition from lecturing to broadcasting, the journeying between countries and cultures, the emotionally volatile man contained within the uptight reticence that one can literally hear in that uncertain accent.

It is sad to think of how he died so young – in his mid-fifties in the early 1960s just as his poetry was returning to a higher voltage with *The Burning Perch* – and of what 'might have' come thereafter: not only further collections of poetry; but also a continuing output of engaged literary essays and autobiographical writing, along with the radio work and drama. Might he have collaborated with Beckett at the BBC? What would he have made of the Northern Irish conflict emerging again by the end of the decade? Had he survived his health problems (and the booze), might there have been a late flowering like Yeats's? Who knows?

MacNeice is now properly recognised as the presiding genius of twentieth-century poetry in Ireland alongside his contemporary Patrick Kavanagh (who survived him by a mere four years) and as poetic equal to the all-powerful Auden. Certainly, to the generations of young readers who came across those few poems in the *Faber Book of Modern Verse*, MacNeice sounded so fresh and alive and of the world, the here and now: a simply wondrous presence without – like the son in 'The Truisms' – our having to know precisely why:

And he walked straight in; it was where he had come from
And something told him the way to behave.
He raised his hand and blessed his home;
The truisms flew and perched on his shoulders
And a tall tree sprouted from his father's grave. (*CP* 565)

A couple of years ago I was looking for a title for a memoir I had written, which was to be reprinted in a new updated version and format. This book about Belfast, along with some autobiographical reflections, quoted a few lines from MacNeice's poem 'Valediction'.

The title jumped out at me: 'This was my mother-city ...' As I read on, an epigraph for the autobiographical section, 'Bit Parts', surfaced within the same poem, perfectly poised, a key to what I was trying to work out in the book about Belfast and myself:

> But I cannot deny my past to which my self is wed,
> The woven figure cannot undo its thread. (*CP* 8)

TURN AND TURN AGAINST:
THE CASE OF *AUTUMN JOURNAL*

Glyn Maxwell

Poems that succeed and survive do so only because they are cased in the right materials. Of course the content matters too: when we break open the casket it matters what remains remain, what grave-goods are sadly and sweetly ranged about it, that all tells us much, but we only know about any of it because the case stayed strong. If one takes advertising to be a perpetual sign of the times, it can be seen that enduring collections of poetry never require content to speak for them, yet collections of prose do, novels and biographies do, collections of letters do most desperately, and the more sensational the content the better. Spiralling down on what is fairly common to us all – love, failed love, lost hope, odd sex, and so on – is the last, very comfortable, resort of the publicist, because without form there is little else that is working to keep those words alive. The right form for a poem, on the other hand, appears – on the meagre evidence of a few thousand years – to render it, regardless of its subject, indestructible.

It may be early to claim indestructibility for *Autumn Journal* – or 'Meeting Point', or 'Snow', or 'House on a Cliff', or any of the poems which, in convivial company, I am happy to do that for – but it has certainly been noted for half a century that MacNeice's long look at everything about him is a magnificent achievement with a puzzlingly inadequate sequel, and perhaps that discrepancy alone is enough to merit a look not at what the *Journal* and the *Sequel* are about, but at what they are made of.

MacNeice was all the things he said a poet ought to be: 'fond of talking', 'a reader of the newspapers', 'appreciative of women', and so on (*MP* 198) – he was neither the first nor the last poet to imagine himself all the things a poet ought to be – but importantly he was a classicist, and the forms of the Greeks were a second nature to him as a working writer. For those of you like me who learned no classics at school or college, for whom it was 'all so unimaginably different / And all so long ago', let us unearth some basics: the *strophe* ('I turn') was the verse spoken by the chorus as it moved from east to west, like the sun, across the *skene*. The *antistrophe* ('I turn against') was the verse spoken by the chorus as it moved back from west to east, like the sun when we cannot see it. Of course the word 'verse' itself has its origins in turning as the plough turns, and one only needs to read a poem by a poet with as formidable an attunement to form as MacNeice's – Edward Thomas – to see the principle working both literally and metaphorically:

> As the team's head-brass flashed out on the turn,
> The lovers disappeared into the wood.
> I sat among the boughs of the fallen elm
> That strewed the angle of the fallow, and
> Watched the plough ...[1]

A line-break after 'and' could only ever work as a serious focusing of sight, as it does here, upon a plough turning, making lines.

I turn, I turn against. We needn't look beyond breath in and out, or day and night, or living and not, to note some possible applications for this ever-changing, ever-constant principle. As a poet, let alone a classicist, MacNeice knew this stuff well enough not to need to access it consciously, so what follows is an observation of how the principle seems to be deployed in a particular poem, not a suggestion that MacNeice built that poem to any formal specifications. One of the things *I* think a poet ought to do is let the form he made in the past bear him into the future, as Anchises is borne by Aeneas: in the short term that is trust, in the long term faith.

Years ago, having absorbed the initial stunning impact of *Autumn Journal* – its humanity, topicality, humour, horror, wit, regret, sexiness, dignity – I was struck by its rhyme-scheme, how perfectly flexible and casual it seemed, how very able to carry the restless currents and eddies of MacNeice's thought. Sometimes it rhymed, sometimes it did not; it appeared to elongate and truncate at will, had its own moods and phases. But the form in this poem needs to be good enough for hurrying through streets, upstanding idealism, sedentary regret, horizontal anguish, all manner of posture. It needs to catch light falling, light making thought, thought itself. It was the earlier 'Snow' that first showed me how matchlessly tuned to physical posture MacNeice is:

World is crazier and more of it than we think,
Incorrigibly plural. I peel and portion
A tangerine and spit the pips and feel
The drunkenness of things being various. (*CP* 24)

The poet throws out some bar-room philosophy (Anglo-Saxon exclamation greying into Latinate abstraction); he hunches cheerily over the fruit (lip-happy alliteration); he lounges back blithely (long vowels and generalisation). Needless to say, this is not a science of any kind: it is more a case of deducing a physical shape from the deployment of vowels, vowel-length, set of mouth, choice of Old, Middle or Modern word-hoard, but, to do that attentively is to detect an extremely subtle range of expression. There is more creaturely shifting of posture here than there is in all of Auden, a poet whose immense stylistic distance from MacNeice – a planetary distance – is not always recognised. This fine, corporeal instinct animates 'Snow' but is the very lifeblood of *Autumn Journal* – or, more helpfully, its DNA. So if the next couple of paragraphs visually resemble a footnote on genetics, all the better.

The chief components of *Autumn Journal* are ABCB and ABAC. As both these forms are well-nigh infinitely resourceful, simple names for them will be as inadequate a description as 'blonde' or 'diabetic' or 'gregarious' is for GCTA-TGTC-AGTT-CTGT-ATGT-GATC-ATGG (and so on *ad extremum*), but simple names might be helpful, so let's call ABCB the Closed Form and ABAC the Open Form.

For the first twelve sections of *Autumn Journal*, that is, the first half of the poem, MacNeice alternates the one with the other – I turn, I turn against – the odd-numbered sections being Closed and the even-numbered sections Open. Section XII breaks the pattern for the first time, because it follows XI in rhyming ABCB; XIII completes a trio of the Closed variant, and towards the end of the poem some new mutations arise, shifting between the two schemes, for example ABCBDEDF (Closed to Open) or ABACDEFE (Open to Closed). Further combinations follow, for example rhymes paired line-to-line for the first time, and one can only be carried on helplessly by the Mendelian metaphor towards the sense that the latter forms of the poem are generated by – are the children of – the former. Now as a poet I know this is no accident, but also as a poet I doubt that it was planned. All I intend to do is watch how, and wonder why, *Autumn Journal* was made that way.

Of course the most conspicuous difference between the Closed and the Open is whether the last line of the four is a rhyme or is not. And it is striking that rhyme in *Autumn Journal* really *means* rhyme, hardly ever half-rhyme, which fact suggests that its deployment is what an actor would call a 'strong choice'. The aural sensation of rhyme/unrhymed is verse's equivalent of major and minor chords: broadly speaking, one appears to complete a thought, or concur, or heal, while the other is more likely to question, to qualify, to lead elsewhere. So as not to appear to be cherry-picking for effect, let's begin at the beginning of both, the first four lines of Section I and of Section II:

> Close and slow, summer is ending in Hampshire,
>> Ebbing away down ramps of shaven lawn where close-clipped
>>> yew
> Insulates the lives of retired generals and admirals
>> And the spyglasses hung in the hall and the prayer-books ready
>>> in the pew ... (*CP* 101)

Though the first twenty lines of *Autumn Journal* are very fluent and enjambed, that second B-rhyme ('pew' in the quoted section) continually tolls a bell that suggests inescapability, as if the manifold options are an illusion, that all the little lanes and avenues lead one way, that the pleasant lives of the populace are the frailest of gestures against something implacable:

> Presents, jewellery, furs, gadgets, solicitations
>> As if to live were not
> Following the curve of a planet or controlled water
>> But a leap in the dark, a tangent, a stray shot.

But we are on a train, and the rhythm is victorious, and the various lives are gathered from chorus into aria, as verse is gently rocked into song:

> I loved my love with a platform ticket,
>> A jazz song,
> A handbag, a pair of stockings of Paris Sand –
>> I loved her long.
> I loved her between the lines and against the clock,

> Not until death
> But till life did us part I loved her with paper money
> And with whisky on the breath ... (*CP* 102–3)

This refrain is as illustrative of *Autumn Journal* as anything: the precious details, the past, the very freedom to expand on a line – all these things hauled back by rhyme and rhythm, standing as ever for the clock, for time, for mortality. 'I loved her' and 'paper money' and 'whisky' may seem to fly out freely, bravely, from the structure, but we know a rhyme is coming and the fragile foolish things strike upon 'breath', which echoes what it has to.

The point is that this singsong Cole Porterish refrain is generated by the lines before, though these happen to be long, gangly, and prosy. The 'Closed' rhyme governs it all, literally and, in any number of ways, metaphorically. The movement, again, is postural, natural, a true progress of thought, ranging from actual observation made at a train window – 'Ebbing away down ramps of shaven lawn' – to generalising pictures, because the eyes of travelling poets do tend to see through walls – 'bacon and eggs on a silver dish for breakfast' – to abstract meditation on culture and country, to satire, self-satire, sorrow. As the details accumulate, MacNeice enacts a kind of misting-over of the eyes, or perhaps the faint appearance of his own face reflected in the window: 'And I am in the train too now and summer is going / South as I go north / Bound for the dead leaves falling', a stretched-out fatigue that encompasses this cute, acute, slightly nutty aside about his dog, 'a symbol of the abandoned order / ... on the carriage floor, / Her eyes inept and glamorous as a film star's ...' The eye drifts from the dog there below, up and out towards the world again: 'Who wants to live, i.e. wants more / Presents, jewellery, furs, gadgets ...' (*CP* 102). This is how attention progresses, it cannot sustain itself in one form, it goes deeper or shallower or sillier or wider, it always does, and in a poet it will often mutate into music: 'I loved my love with a platform ticket, / A jazz song ...'

This strophe, this movement from east to west, concludes in an almost dazed movement downwards, with a strange, elongated look at a single word drawn out – uniquely in the poem – on its single line, then an exhausted, almost defeated tread at evening towards the final rhyme:

And so to London and down the ever-moving
    Stairs
Where a warm wind blows the bodies of men together
    And blows apart their complexes and cares.

II

Spider, spider, twisting tight –
    But the watch is wary beneath the pillow –
I am afraid in the web of night
    When the window is fingered by the shadows of branches …
                                                    (*CP* 103)

Day to night, back across the *skene*, under the earth he travels. The
Open Form is something very different. It is MacNeice's antistrophe,
his turn against. But why is it so different? Centuries of rhymed quatrains may have made our ears what they are – what gifts long histories
give us – but there is something truly unsettling about an unrhymed
'fourth' ('branches' in the section above) when coupled with a full-
rhyming 'first' and 'third'. One cannot help but feel a human,
individuated presence moving free of something, stealing away, out
of tradition, into itself.

    The groups of four lines in *Autumn Journal* are not technically quat-
rains – the poem is necessarily restless and forward-leaning, which
stanza-breaks would compromise because they are the *breathers* the
poet cannot take – but the English ear tends to hold lines to that judgment of 'fourness', and it is this ancient habit of hearing around which
MacNeice operates constantly and deftly. Taking the next quartet of
quartets, we can see that in each case there is a firm justification for the
Open fourth *unrhyme*. Let's determine what they have in common:

When the lions roar beneath the hill
    And the meter clicks and the cistern bubbles
And the gods are absent and the men are still –
    Noli me tangere, my soul is forfeit.
Some now are happy in the hive of home,
    Thigh over thigh and a light in the night nursery,
And some are hungry under the starry dome
    And some sit turning handles.
Glory to God in the Lowest, peace beneath the earth,

Dumb and deaf at the nadir;
I wonder now whether anything is worth
The eyelid opening and the mind recalling.
And I think of Persephone gone down to dark,
No more a virgin, gone the garish meadow,
But why must she come back, why must the snowdrop mark
That life goes on for ever? (*CP* 103)

The full rhyme of 'hill' and 'still', along with the feminine rhyme 'bubbles', loads pressure upon the fourth end-word, as does the subject matter, which has risen from the first Section into a high symbolic tone: MacNeice's response is 'my soul is forfeit', which, in terms of tone, sound, meaning, register, perspective, is extraordinarily isolated and isolating. The continuation squeezes it tighter, the enumeration of 'Some … some … some' strongly defining the speaking voice as *not among those*, as does the remarkable concision with which the lives of 'some' are implicitly both waved away ('the hive of home') and longed for ('Thigh over thigh and a light in the night nursery') – mind, those four long 'i's don't make it sweet or easy to think of. A thought isolated either by sound or meaning will echo longer, because it has no line to answer it, heal it, hush it by addressing it. The words 'my soul is forfeit' simply hang there untended, one more sharp edge keeping the poet awake.

The next of the unrhymed fourths 'And some sit turning handles' is equally isolating, only this time the sense is political rather than personal. The labour of the 'Lowest' is not ameliorated in the ear by rhyme or rhythm: it is dogged, unnoticed, dull. It has no chime with 'thigh' or 'light' or 'nursery' or 'starry'. Its only vestige of fellow-feeling is a whisper of alliteration that aligns 'handles' with 'hungry'. It trails off into blankness, 'turning handles …'

MacNeice now takes this shadowy panorama, with its echoes of the Nativity, and lifts it wryly, scornfully, into the light: 'Glory to God in the Lowest, peace beneath the earth' – that is to say, he plays the vast chord of a hymn, the most four-square form of all, thus daring the fourth to *nevertheless* unrhyme, turn its back, be otherwise, and it duly does, it has to, it cannot sleep, it rolls away with a dizzying downward movement into the personal, the private, the unconsoled: 'I wonder now whether anything is worth / The eyelid opening and the mind recalling…' This is the nocturnal creature shutting his eyes on Creation.

Or on the Christian version, for he strikes out now into the more fondly known classical, and the tone is, in contrast, personal, emotionally close and heated: 'And I think of Persephone ... Why must she come back?' Yet once again the unrhymed word shakes off associations, Christian or classical, tending to isolate the human voice from the chorus: 'why must the snowdrop mark / That life goes on for ever?'

So the Open Form, with its unrhymed fourth, can point up isolation, disenchantment, loss of faith, religious or political: it tends towards memory, regret, the corporeal, the night-time. Hearing the close of Section II (Open Form) coupled with the beginning of Section III (Closed Form) one can hear the sound of an anxious insomniac awake the next day in the crush of oblivious passing people, private to public, *il penseroso* jump-cutting to *l'allegro*:

> Spider, spider, spin
>   Your register and let me sleep a little,
> Not now in order to end but to begin
>   The task begun so often.

III

> August is nearly over, the people
>   Back from holidays are tanned
> With blistered thumbs and a wallet of snaps and a little
>   *Joie de vivre* which is contraband ... (*CP* 104–5)

Once again the public are subject to a tolling yet quickening 'fourth'. For these odd-numbered 'Closed' sections are generally set *today*, refer to the newspapers, feature the poet elbowing his way through the sunlit citizenry, with scarcely time to ponder or philosophise. Section III ends with MacNeice at his most optimistic, almost engaging with the creeping despair of 'Spider, spider' point-by-point. But because we have heard him in the darkness, sensing the opposite in the dead of night, turning his 'face to the wall', the sentiment here seems forced: not because it is not true and MacNeice is faking it, but because it is only true *sometimes*, in the light of day, and he knows it and has shown us it already:

None of our hearts are pure, we always have mixed motives,
　　Are self deceivers, but the worst of all
Deceits is to murmur 'Lord, I am not worthy'
　　And lying easy, turn your face to the wall.
But may I cure that habit, look up and outwards
　　And may my feet follow my wider glance
First no doubt to stumble, then to walk with the others
　　And in the end – with time and luck – to dance. (*CP* 107–8)

For, in a system of alternating strophes and antistrophes, a rhymed
fourth like this, in the Closed Form, can end on the high note, can
hope all it likes, can pound its major chord for all it's worth – but
there will come a *turn against*.

　　Section IV, an Open stanza, starts with a cheery, generous (possibly
over-generous) outward-looking gaze, but the unrhymed 'fourth' is
taking it away from the public, is moving it inwards, where it really
wants to go. The ninth line will show you where:

IV

September has come and I wake
　　And I think with joy how whatever, now or in future, the
　　　　　　　　　　　　　　　　　　　　　　　system
Nothing whatever can take
　　The people away, there will always be people
For friends or for lovers though perhaps
　　The conditions of love will be changed and its vices
　　　　　　　　　　　　　　　　　　　　diminished
And affection not lapse
　　To narrow possessiveness, jealousy founded on vanity.
September has come, it is *hers* … (*CP* 107)

Italics *his*. The rest of the Section (64 lines) is a painful, generous
(truly generous), unstinting stare at a lost love, a heart-sore passage
never salved by a healing 'fourth':

I shall remember you in bed with bright
　　Eyes or in a cafe stirring coffee
Abstractedly and on your plate the white
　　Smoking stub your lips had touched with crimson. (*CP* 108)

The poet stumbles, then limps, then proceeds, with a slightly forced dignity – given the sensuality and longing of what has passed before – to this conclusion:

> And though I have suffered from your special strength
> > Who never flatter for points nor fake responses,
> I should be proud if I could evolve at length
> > An equal thrust and pattern. (*CP* 109)

Then watch how the next Section (Closed again) is bright, sunlit, public, and inescapably, terribly of the moment:

> V

> To-day was a beautiful day, the sky was a brilliant
> > Blue for the first time for weeks and weeks
> But posters flapping on the railings tell the fluttered
> > World that Hitler speaks, that Hitler speaks ... (*CP* 109)

I turn against, I turn: the continual alternation from Open to Closed and back again suggests that both the public and the private realms – the diurnal and nocturnal – become in their separate ways intolerable after time, like, say, a rhyme-scheme. Put crudely, to remember a monster can, at times, be preferable to remembering a lover. But not for long: Section V ends with the Present unbearable, and with the next section MacNeice does not turn his face from the dreadful politics of the age, but from the light of day:

> And a train begins to chug and I wonder what the morning
> > Paper will say,
> And decide to go quickly to sleep for the morning already
> > Is with us, the day is to-day.

> VI

> And I remember Spain
> > At Easter ripe as an egg for revolt and ruin
> Though for a tripper the rain
> > Was worse than the surly or the worried or the haunted faces
> With writings on the walls –

Hammer and sickle, Boicot, Viva, Muerra;
With café-au-lait brimming the waterfalls,
    With sherry, shellfish, omelettes;
With fretted stone the Moor
    Had chiselled for effects of sun and shadow;
With shadows of the poor,
    The begging cripples and the children begging. (*CP* 111–12)

The Open Form hurries him on, tumbling through memories, at first of the politics, but in short order of the food, the decay, and on into the booze and the bullfights. If the Closed Form tends to foreground the Poet, the Open Form tends to foreground the Person, because the flourish of its fourth line is always *away* from form, from music, from connection.

It is interesting to contrast this anatomisation of a society with one of Auden's, the first two stanzas of 'The Fall of Rome':

The piers are pummelled by the waves;
In a lonely field the rain
Lashes an abandoned train;
Outlaws fill the mountain caves.

Fantastic grow the evening gowns:
Agents of the Fisc pursue
Absconding tax-defaulters through
The sewers of provincial towns.[2]

As a vertical dissection of decadent society – social, spatial, economic, first coast-to-mountain, then palace-to-sewer – this can hardly be bettered. And it could scarcely be more different. The eye that roams 'The Fall of Rome' has an objective omniscience, does not see like a person *then* but like a poet *now*, from afar, while MacNeice's travels through his memories of Spain are the very sounds of a single human: hungry, hopeful, thrilled, disabused. Auden's ABBA form seals each vision, tolls the knell of what is coming, lets the chill wind of stanza-breaks blow around the monuments; MacNeice's ABAC, never pausing for breath, topples him from scene to scene through an over-ripe, spilling chaos.

The break between Sections VI and VII exemplifies another use for the 'turn and turn against'. MacNeice observes how the 'grief', 'aspirations', and 'blunt ideals' of his cadre 'would find their whet-stone' and 'that our spirit / Would find its frontier on the Spanish front, / Its body in a rag-tag army.' The unrhyme – 'army' – escapes, goes beyond what is foreseen, outstrips the theory, comes in the frightening shape of the Present – which, to speak Houyhnhm for a moment, might adequately be described as *what's not quite foreseen*. Or, to quote Les Murray, in 'The Future': 'all our projections / fail to curve where it curves'.[3]

Then of course the *turn* comes, London again, daylight again, the drumbeat of the Closed Form, but preceded by an explicit scorn – both historical and prescient – of those who try to form or forge the Present by talking and hoping:

VII

Conferences, adjournments, ultimatums,
    Flights in the air, castles in the air,
The autopsy of treaties, dynamite under the bridges,
    The end of *laissez-faire*.
After the warm days the rain comes pimpling
    The paving stones with white
And with the rain the national conscience, creeping,
    Seeping through the night.
And in the sodden park on Sunday protest
    Meetings assemble not, as so often, now
Merely to advertise some patent panacea
    But simply to avow
The need to hold the ditch … (*CP* 114–15)

The 'sodden park', 'trees on Primrose Hill', 'St John's Wood station', the poet drifts around the capital, his personal hope and anguish, his perspective, visible between iron bars of *what's going on*, his flesh the flesh on a spine of rhyme:

The wood is white like the roast flesh of chicken,
    Each tree falls like a closing fan;
No more looking at the view from seats beneath the branches,
    Everything is going to plan.
They want the crest of this hill for anti-aircraft,
    The guns will take the view

And searchlights probe the heavens for bacilli
  With narrow wands of blue. (*CP* 115)

Form is how poetry expresses time. The rhyming force of an uncontrollable Present — 'Each tree falls' — mutates so easily into an
inexorable Future — 'The guns will' — that it seems to be happening
already. The searchlights are seen *now*, the sense of MacNeice *fore-
seeing* them is vestigial. It is his form that gives him this sense of the
Past and Future bearing down on the beleaguered Present between
them, a giddying fear and enthralment which was perhaps the stuff
of which the very atmosphere of London — on the brink of God
knows what — was composed.
  Section VIII duly turns against, towards the Open, but at first
seems just as daylit and urban (albeit Birmingham not London) and
present as the preceding Closed section. It starts out as a song, but by
definition — having no fourth rhyme — ragged and wry like one of
Brecht's:

Sun shines easy, sun shines gay
  On bug-house, warehouse brewery, market,
On the chocolate factory and the B.S.A.,
  On the Greek town hall and Josiah Mason;
On the Mitchells and Butlers Tudor pubs
  On the white police and the one-way traffic
And glances off the chromium hubs
  And the metal studs in the sleek macadam. (*CP* 117)

The Open Form suggests here a reality too manifold and cluttered
for song to smoothly accommodate, just as Birmingham's jumbled
centuries and memories ('Greek town hall', 'Josiah Mason', 'Tudor
pubs' 'sleek macadam') are too much for the eye to quite absorb.
MacNeice is driven into the jumble of his own past:

Eight years back about this time
  I came to live in this hazy city
To work in a building caked with grime
  Teaching the classics to Midland students ...

The recurring *unrhyme* is, once again, a manifold individuating
force, foregrounding the human creature against backdrops of past

and present. Here it expresses *what happened instead of what was meant to*:

> Just as in Nineteen Thirty-One
>   Sun shines easy but I no longer
> Docket a place in the sun –
>   No wife, no ivory tower, no funk-hole. (*CP* 118–19)

Here it enacts the shadow of the looming future falling on a present which, though tense and martial, has typically soon become routine for the English:

> Black-out practice and A.R.P.,
>   Newsboys driving a roaring business,
> The flapping paper snatched to see
>   If anything has, or has not, happened.

And here it articulates hope at its most hopeless, a single weak proper noun, a buzzword, made to bear a load most obviously too much for it:

> And negotiation wins,
>   If you can call it winning,
> And here we are – just as before – safe in our skins;
>   Glory to God for Munich. (*CP* 119)

(Those who nowadays find the semi-colon simply too much for the cerebrum to cope with should perhaps witness the above – a poet making it crawl with sarcastic life.)

Back comes the Closed Form, back explicitly comes daylight, and we become aware of the terrible paradox MacNeice finds in the hour and bodies forth in the rhyme-scheme: that the Past feels richer with possibilities and pathways than the Present. Perhaps that is what's in the air when planes and bombs are.

> Now we are back to normal, now the mind is
>   Back to the even tenor of the usual day
> Skidding no longer across the uneasy camber
>   Of the nightmare way. (*CP* 120)

This is of course the Section that turns to a meditation on the classical world, culminating in the poet's ironic disavowal of it all – 'And how one can imagine oneself among them / I do not know; / It was all so unimaginably different / And all so long ago' – the full, long-vowelled rhymes that close the Section are closing off a way of thinking and living, as passing time passes judgment, but of course the unrhymed lines speak for the individual, for enthusiasm, for chaos and joy in the past, and as such they colour, complicate, humanise the effect.

Section X begins four-square in the here and now ('And so return to work') but the Open Form with its habitually want-away fourth *unrhyme* quickly takes us back into that paradoxically more open past, with its heart full of options, its portholes on the Ideal:

> And I think of the beginnings of other terms
> > Coming across the sea to unknown England
> And memory reaffirms
> > That alarm and exhilaration of arrival...
> [...]
> And reading romances we longed to be grown up,
> > To shoot from the hip and marry lovely ladies
> And smoke cigars and live on claret cup
> > And lie in bed in the morning ... (*CP* 122–3)

The Section ends with this rude awakening: 'And now, in Nineteen-Thirty-Eight A.D., / Term is again beginning.' Term, term against, so to speak.

The holding, tightening grasp of the Closed Form and its a-coming rhyme here takes on a darker role: the unrhymes as both the struggle to be free of sexual memory and to reach the refuge of dream; the rhymes, as they cannot help doing, forbidding such forgetting:

> For suddenly I hate her and would murder
> > Her memory if I could
> And then of a sudden I see her sleeping gently
> > Inaccessible in a sleeping wood
> But thorns and thorns around her
> > And the cries of night
> And I have no knife or axe to hack my passage
> > Back to the lost delight. (*CP* 126)

As mentioned above, this two-step of Open and Closed evolves into
something more complex from here on in the poem, but the development seems natural, even organic. Whatever uses MacNeice makes
of Open Form and Closed Form in the first half of *Autumn Journal* –
day and night, Past and Present, private and public – what he is really
deploying is either light or thought, light being what passes by, what
strikes him, what he sees and hears and recalls, thought being what
he makes of those external lights within – what is *formed* by light.

These eight lines from Section XXIII seem to grasp together
almost every strand of the poem, and the hushed complexity of the
scheme – ABBCDEFD – articulates the sound of the human not *only*
seeing, or *only* thinking, or *only* remembering, but helplessly, hope-
fully, doing all of these at once:

> I admit that for myself I cannot straiten
>   My broken rambling track
> Which reaches so irregularly back
>   To burning cities and rifled rose-bushes
> And cairns and lonely farms
>   Where no one lives, makes love or begets children,
> All my heredity and my upbringing
>   Having brought me only to the Present's arms … (*CP* 160)

An equally complex 'DNA' – ABACDEFD, with which *Autumn
Journal* ends – is the sound of the mind, overwhelmed by day, trying
to surrender to night. Rhymes lull, unrhymes nag. Poetry is always
trying and failing to sleep, trying to be the blank page again, as poets
wish for that dream-world wherein the blank page asks nothing of
them:

> Sleep, my body, sleep, my ghost,
>   Sleep, my parents and grand-parents,
> And all those I have loved most:
>   One man's coffin is another's cradle.
> Sleep, my past and all my sins,
>   In distant snow or dried roses
> Under the moon for night's cocoon will open
>   When day begins. (*CP* 161)

Now, I feel more than the poet's traditional sense of critical entitle-

ment in making the following judgment, simply by dint of being one
of the only other people in the twentieth century (in 1999, so only
just) to have attempted a very long poem in *terza rima* …

Autumn Sequel (1954) fails because it is in *terza rima*. Perhaps it fails
for various reasons, to do with the poet, to do with his psychology,
to do with a more exhausted and less compelling historical moment,
and perhaps it is too early to say it fails at all – but I do say it fails, and
because of the *terza rima*. This does not require much explanation,
only illustration.

> August. Render to Caesar. Speak parrot: a gimmick for Poll.
> Castle your king in sand; as the dog days die,
> I hate the grey void that crams the guts of the doll
>
> And deplore each megrim and moan I scrawled on the sky
> In my hand of unformed smoke those fifteen years
> A-going, a-going, ago. I to I
>
> Is not for that self and me; the long surge nears
> The crumbling drawbridge and the tears of things
> Will drown out his and mine and all such partial tears,
>
> While the cracked voice calls Check, the sandfly stings,
> The cage is ungilded, the Parrot is loose on the world
> Clapping his trap with gay but meaningless wings.
>
> Fifteen years – and enough. Plain or pearled,
> Chequered or lacquered, I do not want them again;
> Though golden curls in lockets come uncurled,
>
> Put back no clock; clocks were made for men.
> It is not time I resent, it is that the hand should stick
> On a lie which the heart repeats again and again. (*CP* 373)

The formal infelicities are almost too numerous to mention. The
comparatively inflexible pentameter, a fairly loose one but far from
being the multi-talented swinging line of the *Journal* – distorts
MacNeice's natural, 'creaturely' style, elongates thoughts that sound
ridiculous dwelt upon ('the Parrot is loose on the world / Clapping
his trap with gay but meaningless wings') or bloats asides into showy

banality ('A-going, a-going, ago'), while the introduction of stanza-breaks burns unwelcome light upon some of the metaphorical – or in this case nonsensical – flourishes ('I hate the grey void that crams the guts of the doll'). But above all there is the overbearing, unfulfillable demand of the Great Creditor – the full-rhymed *terza rima*. You cannot write full-rhymed *terza rima* in English in the twentieth century. You – or rather I – could at least attempt it (as I did in *Time's Fool*) with half-rhymes, even 'trace'-rhymes, with the third of the rhymed trio sometimes bearing only the faintest echo of the first. You – or rather Shelley – could write it in the nineteenth, on a poetic ear more attuned to the lyrical full rhyme, and in any case only for seventy lines and grouped into five sonnets.

Casting a giant shadow is of course *The Divine Comedy*, and this advice from Mandelstam's great 'Conversation about Dante' makes the point precisely: 'Take the entire Italian dictionary and leaf through as you please. Here everything rhymes. Every word cries out to enter into *concordanza*.'[4] What works in Italian does not work in English. One can find the words 'furled' or 'unfurled' in just about every poet in Palgrave, as the great and the good try to sneak the word 'world' into their poems, but here MacNeice is saddled with having to find the word *two* dancing partners, which leads him stumbling first into the indignity of 'Plain and pearled, / Chequered or lacquered' (what are – the years? the tears? the wings?) and then a line mutilated into archaism and inferior to every single line in the *Journal*: 'Though golden curls in lockets come uncurled'.

Therefore I would surmise that *Autumn Sequel* failed before it even began, at the moment MacNeice chose to give it the form he gave it. That these first lines of the unreadable *Sequel* so frankly disavow the unforgettable *Journal* as 'each megrim and moan I scrawled on the sky / In my hand of unformed smoke those fifteen years / A-going, a-going, ago' makes it remarkable that he ever returned to form, by which I mean the *right form for the right matter,* but he did, three years later, which I shall prove in the right way for a poet to prove it, by showing it, pausing only to note the endless, restless, turn and turn-against of this most feeling, most creaturely of poets:

House on a Cliff

Indoors the tang of a tiny oil lamp. Outdoors
The winking signal on the waste of sea.

Indoors the sound of the wind. Outdoors the wind.
Indoors the locked heart and the lost key.

Outdoors the chill, the void, the siren. Indoors
The strong man pained to find his red blood cools,
While the blind clock grows louder, faster. Outdoors
The silent moon, the garrulous tides she rules.

Indoors ancestral curse-cum-blessing. Outdoors
The empty bowl of heaven, the empty deep.
Indoors a purposeful man who talks at cross
Purposes, to himself, in a broken sleep. (*CP* 516)

'THE PARROT'S LIE':
AUTUMN SEQUEL AND THE BBC

Clair Wills

Louis MacNeice's poetry of the early 1950s has gained few enthusiastic admirers. The tone may have been set by contemporary reviews such as A. Alvarez's swingeing attack on *Autumn Sequel* in the *New Statesman*: 'weary, knowing and bored', 'the voice no longer comes fresh from the page'.[1] From that moment to this, volumes such as *Ten Burnt Offerings* and *Autumn Sequel* have been considered a problem, to the extent that they have been considered at all. Criticism has focused on the poetry's flatness, its over-explicitness, its self-indulgent length. Samuel Hynes describes the poems as 'dull and garrulous, like the conversation of someone you might meet in a pub'; Edna Longley puts them down to 'an attack of wordiness', 'the thirties verbal mill goes on loosely grinding without its grist. MacNeice flounders between travelogue and metaphysics and efforts to unite the two.' The best that can be said, for example by Peter McDonald, is that these poems of the middle stretch are valuable experiments without which the later lyrics would not have been possible.[2]

These complaints express a regret for the shift away from thinking through metaphor and image, the loss of the intensity and compression of the lyrics of the 1930s and early 1940s in an excess of 'volubility'. There are certainly longueurs in the poetry of the early 1950s, and *Autumn Sequel* in particular suffers from 'wordiness', yet that very volubility sits oddly with MacNeice's claim for the poem as 'A Rhetorical Poem in XXVI Cantos'. As McDonald has argued, the form of *Autumn Sequel* should be understood as an attempt on MacNeice's part to contrive a structure through which the 'false documentaries' of journalism, as Canto I puts it, might be set aside.[3] In the 'Prefatory Note' of 1954 MacNeice clearly announces that the poem is to constitute a new autobiography, with a similar relationship to the autumn of 1953 as *Autumn Journal* had to the autumn of 1938. But in *Autumn Sequel* he rejects the principle that a poem can offer 'a slice of life', rejects reportage in favour of system and architecture – thus the poem 'by its nature occasional, is less so, I think,

than its predecessor' (*CP* 806). The poem is rhetorical because it
argues a case, or at the very least sets up a debate, but also because it
was written with radio, and with the spoken word, in mind:

> August. Render to Caesar. Speak Parrot: a gimmick for Poll.
> Castle your king in sand; as the dog days die,
> I hate the grey void that crams the guts of the doll
>
> And deplore each megrim and moan I scrawled on the sky
> In my hand of unformed smoke those fifteen years
> A-going, a-going, ago. I to I
>
> Is not for that self and me; the long surge nears
> The crumbling drawbridge and the tears of things
> Will drown out his and mine and all such partial tears,
>
> While the cracked voice calls Check, the sandfly stings,
> The cage is ungilded, the Parrot is loose on the world
> Clapping his trap with gay but meaningless wings. (*CP* 373)

These first lines, as they insist on the differences from *Autumn Journal*,
fifteen years previously, also direct us straight back to John Skelton,
by way of Yeats's anarchy loosed upon the world. Part of the point
of Skelton here is to alert us to the structure of extended analogy
which underlies the poem, an experiment with medieval system also
signalled by the use of Dante as model (an experiment which will
bear fruit in the later 'parable' poems). But Skelton's satirical purpose
in 'Speke Parrott' is probably more germane to a reading of the poem.
Throughout *Autumn Sequel* the enemy is claptrap, the boring and
meaningless repetition of empty phrases and received opinions, the
'uniform sterility' which seems to MacNeice the mark of this 'brash
new age' (*CP* 460). MacNeice himself is not immune to this sterility,
of course. For while it is the task of the inspired poet – such as Dylan
Thomas – to 'throw the Parrot's lie, back in its beak', 'on the other
hand' (and the poem keeps shifting from 'one the one hand', to 'on
the other'), poet and parrot are one. This twinning between poet and
parrot – we should call him a porret, perhaps – is particularly true of
the radio poet. What is he after all but a voice talking from a box in
the corner of the room, not so far from Skelton's description of his
cage in 'Speke Parrott':

A cage curyowsly carven, with sylver pynne,
Properly paynted to be my coverture;
A myrrour of glasse, that I may tote therin;
These maydens full meryly with many a dyvers flowur
Fresshely the dresse and make swete my bowur,
With, 'Speke, Parott, I pray yow,' full curteslye they sey,
'Parott ys a goodlye byrde and a pratye popagay.'

Wythe my beke bent, and my lytell wanton iye,
My feathyrs fresshe as ys the emerawde grene,
Abowte my necke a cerculett lyke the ryche rubye,
My lytell legges, my fete bothe fete and clene,
I am a mynyon to wayte apon a quene;
'My propyr Parott, my lytell pratye fole.'
With ladies I lerne and goe with them to scole.[4]

While Skelton's parrot stands in MacNeice's poem as a symbol of empty and meaningless repetition, it also functions as a way of thinking through the artist's relationship with his audience. Skelton's parrot-cum-'court poet' is typical of the kind of tension between incompatible authorising figures or belief systems which occurs in his poetry: the struggle to reconcile belief in the poet's inspiration (he's a bird of paradise) with the need to find and claim a position in courtly society. As inspired poet he believes himself the natural spokesperson for the king as god's representative on earth, and the figure who holds the entire memory of a society in his keeping. So in 'Speke Parrott' Skelton lines up the muses as proof of his divine inspiration, and at the same time parades his ostentatious loyalty to the king to show how he is putting his insights to good social and hierarchical use. But he is driven to fury by the court's failure to recognise his divine credentials. He starts by portraying himself as an insider, in that very intimate relation with the ladies around his cage, trying for collaboration or even conspiracy with his audience (the ladies/ the readers), but ends up as a didactic outsider, telling people over and over again what they have refused to deduce for themselves (on the principle that 'what I tell you three times is true', or, as it appears in *Autumn Sequel*: 'I told you so, I told you so', *CP* 422).[5]

I want to come back to how this may help us read *Autumn Sequel* by way of the system of mirrors in 'Speke Parrott', beginning with the mirror that hangs in the parrot's cage, 'that I may tote therin'.

The basic function of this mirror is to remind us of the poem itself as 'dark mirror' or allegory – the 'mirrour that i tote in quam diaphonum, vel quam speculum, in enigmate'. But 'Speke Parrott' also plays with the idea that the Parrot-poet is a kind of mirror himself: a bird who can only quite literally 'parrot' back what he hears. Potentially all the parrot's phrases have their origin in the expressions of those ladies who surround him. At the same time, however, because Parrot's parrotings do create a kind of synthesis, he becomes the controlling intelligence in the poem. Thus the 'ladies' (the court: both source and audience for the satire) can only under-stand what they have said when they hear their words digested and regurgitated by Parrot.

How does this bear on the parrotings of *Autumn Sequel*? We can think of the BBC as a modern-day court, the poet as propagandist of the welfare state, but at the same time inspired 'maker', and enter-tainer all at once. In part MacNeice is satirising his own endeavour in *Autumn Sequel*, and even his 'parrot-like' use of Dante's form and midlife paralysis. (Those references to his 'thrusting paunch' make this a poem quite literally about the middle stretch.) By extension he mocks his greater confidence in *Autumn Journal* that it is possible to speak representatively, and his myth-making tendencies more gener-ally. Yet at the same time he wants to give his work some credence, and to suggest that these public service, welfare state compromised parrotings can and do make a new synthesis. MacNeice keeps shifting between contempt for his mass audience and what he has to produce for them, and a sense that his poetic output for the BBC involves him in a big nation-making project of which he approves, and which is mirrored through the various journeys punctuating the poem – to Oxford, to Norwich, to Glastonbury – taken together making up a kind of pageant of Englishness for the new Elizabethan age.

It is worth remembering that the idea of Skelton as a precursor for thinking through the role of the poet in society was current at the time. A wartime analysis of Skelton Laureate had drawn connections between T.S. Eliot's sense of cultural values under threat, and Skelton's warnings of cultural crisis and the threats to his city and civilisation from another 'brash new age'.[6] There is a connection here with the figure of Thucydides, who is used throughout the poem as a kind of touchstone for thinking through the relationship between art, civic values, and Demos, or the common man, in the context of a city-state about to collapse. The epigraph to 'Speke Parrott',

Lectoribus auctor recipit opusculy huius auxesim (by his readers the author achieves completion of his little work), signals both the importance of audience, and the difficulty for any artist whose work is dependent on his audience, and its willingness to follow him. MacNeice's poem worries about the poet's capacity to function as the voice of a society, and the extent to which his ability to do so depends upon his readers' willingness to grant him that role – a relationship made all the more difficult by the fact that he has little respect for his readers, or listeners, anyway.

Autumn Sequel offers different models of the poet's relationship to his audience – the poet as one of a group of friends; as the orchestrator of a national pageant for the new Elizabethan age, one decked out in the modern media language of radio and TV; as public spokesperson and propagandist; as entertainer. It was written to be aired, and bears all the marks not only of MacNeice's ambivalence about his role, but also of the contradictory role of the BBC as 'on the one hand', a patron of the arts, but on the other, a vehicle for raising cultural standards through the medium for entertainment. On the one hand, as Harrap (the real life Archie Harding) points out in Canto IV, the job is mainly mess and compromise; on the other, you get paid.

One of MacNeice's chief complaints focuses on the routine and bureaucratic nature of his work. The parrot, in fact, is surrounded by woodpeckers, or typists; he is harangued by the two black telephones which sit on his desk, at the mercy of subcommittees, a conscript worker 'in a hive which holds no dance or magic', an automaton moving up and down the moving stairs to the tube, caught on a 'conveyer belt' which 'moves on for ever till we die'. In places the poem reads like a kind of tragic version of Chaplin's *Modern Times*, but one subject not to the excesses of capitalism but the bureaucratic dictates of the welfare state. Just occasionally, to MacNeice's relief, 'our work tastes like the work not of machines but men', and the poet can acknowledge the ambition which lay behind the ideal of national entertainment during the war:

What was in print
Must take on breath and what was thought be said.
In the end there was the Word, at first a glint,

Then an illumination overheard

Where the high towers are lit. Such was our aim
But aims too often languish and instead

We hack and hack. (*CP* 387)

The repetition is telling here – the high towers are undercut by
'copy'. There are numerous examples of parroting and repetition in
the poem: 'a typewriter taps and taps', 'miles on miles of carbon
copies', 'copy and yet more copy' (*CP* 387–90). Then there is the
thumping use of cliché and colloquialism, the hackneyed phrases, as
MacNeice recycles the language he hears. In narrative terms too the
poem is powered by repetition – perhaps not surprising in a poem
about work – 'Purgatory – routine, routine, routine … waiting and
working one's way not even to Heaven but a bit further up the spiral.'
Then there are the repeated sequences, for example, the train journeys out of and back into London, where the poet seems to make no
effort not to sound bored as he runs through the urban–suburban
cycle again. Or the recurring weather reports focused on Regent's
Park, which seem to have little point except to prove, again, that he
has nothing to say: 'The rose garden / In Regent's Park continues
full of roses' (*CP* 475). Most of all, perhaps, the recurrent repairing
to the pub – now to the Lamb and Flag, or now to the Woolpack,
Adam and Eve, the Evening Gun – emphasises the emptiness of the
routines of work and leisure. MacNeice's reflection on the drunkenness of things being the same is mirrored in the sameness of things
being drunk.

It was not always so. In 1947 MacNeice argued that radio could
end the 'alienation of the artist', dispense 'a cure for those lonely poet-
blues'. And even in 1953 he was still able to argue that radio 'has
something to offer the poet', in that it allows space for the listeners'
visual imagination and does not force him to find visual images to
represent abstract ideas.[7] The period of *The Dark Tower* was probably
the height of MacNeice's faith in the medium of radio as an art form,
as a way of communicating, as Harrap puts it, with millions and at
the same time with one at a time. The possibilities of radio were being
everywhere proclaimed in the late 1940s. For example, here is
George Orwell, in his article 'Poetry and the Microphone': 'By being
set down at a microphone, especially if this happens at all regularly,
the poet is brought into a new relationship with his work, not otherwise attainable in our time and country.'[8] Cecil Day Lewis, writing

in 1950, agreed. By being pitched towards his audience the poet is encouraged to 'extend his technique upon less purely subjective material',[9] a creative process resulting in self-consciously 'radio-phonic' poems, such as David Gascoyne's 'Night Thoughts', commissioned for the Third Programme.

But if rut and routine are the enemy of art, the injunction to entertain may be more corrupting. Beyond the danger of becoming a hack parrot, there is the danger of becoming a merely pretty one. The squawk of the parrot lurks behind V.S. Pritchett's 1947 warning of what happens when the writer gives up the silence of the page to become a 'talking writer'. Once culture is to be consumed it is debased to mere entertainment (the basic conundrum of the BBC's high cultural programming). Let out of its cage and loosed upon the world, how is poetry to maintain its distance from mass cultural entertainment? The fact that by the 1950s there was a radio-parrot in nearly every sitting room in the country made for a great many ladies to please. In his preface to 'Christopher Columbus', MacNeice had acknowledged the problem, admitting that in order to overcome the difficulty of making contact with an audience 'so attuned to bad art' and 'so easily bored' the poet must concentrate above all on sound.[10]

This emphasis on form and structure is embodied in *Autumn Sequel* as 'rhetoric', and the practice, which MacNeice seems to approve of in the first canto, of 'contriving the truth'. 'On the other hand' it is precisely this contrivance that gets the poet down, for example in Canto III, as he attempts to fit sound to image for the film about the conquest of Everest:

> What price
> Should we demand for turning what was rare
> Into a cheap couvade or proxy paradise,
>
> Just one more travelogue to make the groundlings stare? (*CP* 384)

In the Everest film, in the Christmas broadcast with which he (nearly) ends the poem MacNeice describes himself formulating events as national story and as entertainment. The joint purpose of educating and pleasing his audience brings these features close to the propaganda that MacNeice had been producing during the war. At the time he had argued that propaganda features were 'necessary', and that he did them well. According to MacNeice's boss, Laurence

Gilliam, by sitting somewhere between drama and documentary, features managed to be at once the pinnacle of realism and the democratic expression of the people and at the same time to allow and even encourage the individual expression of the writer/producer. This balance between social documentary and individual creativity may have been strained but it was given purpose by the war. As MacNeice describes it, postwar that balance has been upset. In the preface to *Visitations* he describes *Autumn Sequel* as 'an attempt to marry myth and actuality'. But what happens in the TV studio in Beaconsfield is that the mythic, transcendent, element in the quest for the summit of Everest is undermined by suburban actuality, and the caution it brings out in the programmers: 'our aim / Is popularity, not palinode' (*CP* 385).

MacNeice's discomfort needs to be understood within the context of the growing fear in the early 1950s of state control of the arts, but also to be distinguished from it. One way of reading *Autumn Sequel* is as an example of postwar disillusionment in which the crisis of national identity (the retreat from Empire, the bureaucratic march of the welfare state) is twinned with a crisis of confidence in the craft of letters. There is an unmistakeable post-imperial atmosphere to the poem, as MacNeice sets events in Korea and India in the balance against his personal friendships, not to mention the standoff between Moscow and Washington, which he aligns with the battles between ancient empires:

Much talk throughout the world of action and reaction
And explanation centres and isotopes
And interzonal permits; for distraction

Much talk of football pools and Britain's hopes
On the greens of Virginia Water. (*CP* 416)

MacNeice seems to make the link between post-imperial decline and the decline of letters explicit, particularly in Canto V. While once his group of friends felt able to take the measure of the totalitarian state, now 'we no longer speak so confidently'. He laments 'The maker I might have been'; 'the Muse has defaulted' (*CP* 392). The figures he prizes are those who have retained their individual voice in the face of uniformity. In the second Oxford canto he presents E.R. Dodds as an example of 'humaner letters' against the 'fetters forged in the name of freedom' (*CP* 429). Dylan Thomas or 'Gwilym' is praised because he wrote 'regardless' of society. Arguing with Thucydides that the Demos in 1953 is no longer that of the city-state but the welfare state, he maintains that poets 'born all fire' can have no truck with 'this huge and lukewarm monster' (*CP* 457). Or as Kathleen Raine put it dramatically in the *New Statesman*, Thomas was a bard, dealing in 'those feelings which spring from nature and which modern civilization is calculated to deaden and kill'.[11]

Even amongst those who did not share this view of Thomas, the sense of cultural crisis was widespread. It was rife amongst the post-Bloomsbury set to which MacNeice was vaguely attached in the postwar years. (Much of *Autumn Sequel* was written in the Regent's Park house which had been Elizabeth Bowen's – with the MacNeice-Anderson literary salon taking the place of Bowen-Cameron). In a late issue of *Horizon* Cyril Connolly described a numbed and 'uniformly sterile' British population: 'Here the ego is at half-pressure; most of us are not men or women but members of a vast, seedy, overworked, over-legislated neuter class, with our drab clothes, our ration books and murder stories, our envious, strict, old-world apathies and resentments – a care-worn people.'[12]

In addition to the belle-lettristic dislike of planning, regimentation, and the bureaucracy of postwar society, the arts were one of the victims of postwar austerity measures – lack of paper, for example, led to a contraction in publishing and the failure of numerous little magazines and journals. The lucky few had sinecures in the British Council or the BBC (MacNeice had both), but censorship, and the injunction to reflect respectable orthodox opinion, at the same time as seeking audience ratings, meant that the writer was not far from being a 'minor official' as Orwell put it: 'Any writer or journalist who wants to retain his integrity finds himself thwarted by the general drift of society rather than by active persecution.' In *New Soundings*, a 1952 broadcast version of the then defunct *Penguin New Writing*, John Lehmann lamented: 'The poets of today have as their inheritance a peace that has never succeeded in becoming real, a ruined economy, and a thick atomic fog of insecurity over the future of Europe, of the world.'[13] The fourth programme in the series was devoted to the relationship between poet and a hostile public. Should the poet try to represent the 'spirit of the age' or accept his isolation from society?

As Robert Hewison has pointed out, what new cultural ventures there were in the early 1950s, such as Lehmann's *London Magazine*, tended to act as a showcase for the literary reminiscence of an earlier generation of writers. In 1956 the editor of the *TLS*, Alan Pryce-Jones, gave a description of the lacklustre stock in trade of current writers which sounds uncomfortably like a description of *Autumn Sequel*. With war over and political commitment tainted, there was nothing for it but autobiography – the writer could keep going by writing about the loss of faith in his art.[14]

But despite MacNeice's disenchantment with BBC hackery, his take on the role of the poet in society was not entirely pessimistic. *Autumn Sequel* does showcase the problem of the writer disillusioned with the possibilities for art and turning in on himself, and thus reinforces one stereotype of the post-war cultural malaise. A typical example might be Doris Lessing's description, in *The Four-Gated City*, of the atmosphere of the early 1950s, as a retreat to the Ivory Tower in the face of Cold War antagonisms. But although MacNeice refuses the 'journalism' and reportage of the 1930s, and the language of political commitment, he also refuses the tower. We can think of the autobiographical thrust of the poem as a way of looking for something worth believing in and writing for, as much a response to middle age as to a postwar, and – almost – post-austerity context. For all the language of decline and lack of confidence, MacNeice thinks about the loss of Empire less as a retreat than a process of coming to terms with new realities, matched by a need to come to terms with his thinning hair. He continually tries to find ways of overcoming his lack of conviction, of forging a sense of connection. Take, for example, his habit of reading a news story for any possible personal connections he can find. At the same time he wants to give primacy to literary structures (the mythic journey, the metaphysical quest) as a way of bringing all this 'occasional' material together into a larger architectonic whole – primacy to literary structures rather than the political or social narratives which may have done the work in the past.

Between one hand and the other MacNeice keeps trying to hold open a space in which 'truthful' connections between art and society can be formed. In Canto XIX the figure of Thucydides describes the choice for the postwar writer:

Even today it seems there are two schools

Of thought upon this subject; one reviles

The notion that any artist could fulfil
A conscious social role; the other files

Art in the civil service. (*CP* 458)

Neither allows for the possibility of art in the service of civility, and
both should be rejected. Despite his frustration with the state of
letters, MacNeice is still committed to finding an accommodation
between modern parrot speak and literary culture.

For if the poem is a metaphysical, and personal, quest, it is also a
national story, a poem very deliberately about the 'condition of
England', or rather of England and Wales.[15] It tells an island story,
and one built around the national institution of the BBC. There are
several aspects to this story of England – a tramp through architec-
tural styles – the move from Oxford to Bath, to Wells to Glastonbury,
for example, from classical back through gothic and celtic styles – or
the round-up of literary tradition from mumming and miracle play
to renaissance drama to modern mass-cultural entertainment. There
is even a survey of local crafts and trades (a 'badger' is a huckster):
'The saddler, dowser, badger, thatcher and wheelwright / And all the
others for whom the curfew tolls / Their banishment to inorganic
night' (*CP* 410); and of course there are the journeys around England
and Wales which bring these elements together.

This is a celebration of tradition, rather than an argument about
history, constructed in the manner of a pageant, and it is related, I
think, to the revival of national pageant in the early 1950s.[16] I am
thinking first and foremost of the Festival of Britain, which had been
subtitled 'The Autobiography of a Nation' – the various exhibits
given the status of chapters of the 'island story'. The Humphrey
Jennings film commissioned for the opening of the Festival, and entitled *Family Portrait*, celebrated deep England, tradition, and the
nation's past through a similar kind of regional round-up of the
national family. MacNeice was out of Britain for much of Festival
mania, and wrote to T.S. Eliot of his relief at being able to avoid it
(*L* 575), but pageantry only gathered pace under what became known
as the new Elizabethanism. Royal pageants, copied in miniature in
towns and villages across the country during coronation year, were a
mishmash of medieval, Tudor, Jacobean, Georgian, and modern
elements, with the stress above all on continuity and conciliation.
Even the more explicitly experimental forms of artistic endeavour,

such as the documentaries associated with the Free Cinema movement, were not immune from celebrations of traditional Englishness.[17] In the same way the juxtapositions in *Autumn Sequel* of celticism, medieval grail legend, renaissance and augustan England are less ironic counterpoint than hoped for continuity and synthesis.

In his 2003 study, *A Shrinking Island*, Jed Esty examines the turn towards insular communal traditions in late modernist works by Forster, Woolf, and Eliot, arguing that the contraction of Empire encourages these writers to focus on national culture as a source of renewal. He instances the pageant of *Between the Acts*, and the pageant plays of Eliot and Forster, as works which find consolation in the loss of Empire insofar as the shrinking of the island enables a return to a bounded and knowable community.[18]

Esty attempts to draw a sharp distinction between this late modernist generation, seeking to build within English tradition, and looking to a broader definition of English culture as a source of renewal, and the writers of what he calls the Auden-Orwell generation, those who came to prominence in the era of 1930s political commitment. For these writers art rather than national culture is the source of redemption or meaning – they have no faith in the national community.

While this perspective may illuminate aspects of Auden's later work and even Orwell's it does not fit easily with MacNeice's poetry of the late 1940s and early 1950s. Certainly the atmosphere of postwar stagnation is hard to miss, especially when combined with his self-parody as ageing hack. The trips to India, Greece, and Egypt offer opportunities to explore England's broader geographical connections, though MacNeice's increasing disillusionment with institutions such as the British Council suggests his strong sense of the limitations of that cultural reach. But at the same time the poems offer clear evidence of a retrenchment into Englishness and an attempt to find a way of speaking adequate to the new, bounded, nation. For example, he suggests that that list of old English crafts and craftsmen proves 'that England is still with us'.

It may be difficult, from a twenty-first-century perspective, to see this often cosy, nostalgic celebration of old England as a 'positive' aspect of *Autumn Sequel*. It is at its most relentless in the earlier, wartime poem 'The Kingdom', though even here I think there is something to be said for the attempt to write a poem like a Powell and Pressburger film – the tone, but also the structure are reminiscent of the panoramic English village scenes in *A Matter of Life and Death*, but also of Jennings's wartime films.

The tone in which this story of England is told may be elegiac, but *Autumn Sequel* itself attests to the desire to draw these materials together and connect them with the present – and particularly with contemporary suburban and urban London. It is this desire which gives rise to the main formal problem of the poem, however: the attempt to create continuity and synthesis through juxtaposition. Juxtaposition is a trait throughout MacNeice's poetry, but here it becomes the primary principle of composition. Early on he draws an analogy between *terza rima* and knitting – purl and plain, the weaving of the rhymes draws all the different elements into relation with one another. 'Senseless beaks / May iterate what they will' (*CP* 374) but, he seems to be saying, knit it all into a whole and you will create a synthesis that goes beyond parrot repetition. This method of overlaying and combining (rather like that of the features producer, perhaps) is not enough and MacNeice is uncomfortably aware of that. Hence the final canto in which he piles everyone onto the train with him, including the refugees and victims of modernity and total war, carrying them all towards but never quite arriving at the promised fulfilment of the holy family. In the end the compromised parrot gives way to the homing pigeon, the dowser's hand, as MacNeice reaches for nature and instinct as a way of resolving the poem's contradictions.

MacNeice was to return once more to his compromised bird of paradise in the late poem 'Budgie', which offers a far bleaker picture of the impact of mass entertainment on the figure of the artist. *Autumn Sequel* attempts to hold on to the possibility that the parroting 'copy' and hackery of routine work at the BBC may yet enable 'illumination' in the midst of 'much work / Of a purely ephemeral kind'. Parrot and poet, though they mirror one another, are yet distinct. In 'Budgie' that distinction has blurred; the bird sees only itself in the mirror and its repetitions are limited to self-delusions: 'So *Let me attitudinize, / Let me attitudinize, let me attitudinize, /* For all the world is a stage is a cage...' (*CP* 602). In an article in *Encounter*, offering memories of Dylan Thomas in 1954, MacNeice had suggested that while Thomas had been an actor, 'he was not an attitudiniser', implying that it was Thomas's lack of self-consciousness which enabled him to do battle with the parrotings of the arts institutions

(*SLC* 185). It is tempting to interpret the bleaker vision of 'Budgie', in which actor and atttiduniser have merged, as a consequence of the turn to vision itself. The shift to television and away from radio had increasingly sidelined the work of MacNeice and other writers in Laurence Gilliam's Features Department, and MacNeice himself spent much of his last full year at the BBC, in 1960, attached to television.[19] But the fear was that the requirements of television might also increase the tendency of the BBC to move towards more simple entertainment. If there was something to be salvaged from the welfare-statism of the British Council and the BBC of the 1950s, the isolation and self-regard of the artist in the brasher, more commercial, new age of the 1960s had nothing to recommend it.

'BULBOUS TALIESIN':
MACNEICE AND DYLAN THOMAS

John Goodby

1

At first glance, Louis MacNeice and Dylan Thomas might seem to be rather improbable candidates for poetic friendship; the Marlborough and Oxford-educated MacNeice, a university lecturer in classics and sometime employee of the BBC and the British Council, a friend of W.H. Auden, Cecil Day Lewis, and Stephen Spender, would seem to have little in common with Thomas, a schoolmaster's son, who left the local grammar school at the age of fifteen (having come bottom of the class in all subjects except English, in which he was first), after which he worked for a few months as a journalist, thereafter living precariously on his writing and his wits. Yet both MacNeice and Thomas were outsiders in upper-middle-class England, as MacNeice's memoir *The Strings are False* makes clear, with several shared passions outside of their writing – watching cricket and hard drinking among them – who, after a certain initial distrust, came to form a warm friendship during the war years. Indeed, Thomas would play a significant role in MacNeice's conception of poetry, one which enabled MacNeice, alone among those associated with the *New Country* poets, to absorb the lessons of the stylistic shifts in English poetry during the 1940s, and use them to revivify his poetry after Thomas's death in 1953.[1]

The two first met in Manchester on 18 October 1938, as contributors to a BBC radio broadcast entitled 'The Modern Muse'. Presented by Michael Roberts, it also involved Auden, Spender, Lewis, Kathleen Raine, and Charles Madge, with Thomas presumably representing the latest wave of poetic talents which Roberts had identified in his *Faber Book of Modern Verse* of 1936. Earlier contact between Thomas and MacNeice had certainly been considered; in a letter of 10 March 1938, Thomas had told Keidrich Rhys, the editor of the journal *Wales*, that he was about to write to MacNeice, possibly to ask him for a contribution.[2] However, no letters between the two survive, and it is unlikely that any were exchanged at this point. Thomas's attitude towards the *New Country* poets was hardly uncritical in any case. In his contribution to the *New Verse* double issue, published to mark Auden's thirtieth birthday in November 1937, he observed:

> I sometimes think of Mr. Auden's poetry as a hygiene, a knowledge and practice, based on a brilliantly prejudiced analysis of contemporary disorders, relating to the preservation and promotion of health, a sanitary science and a flusher of melancholies. I sometimes think of his poetry as a great war, admire intensely the mature, religious, and logical fighter, and deprecate the boy bushranger. I think he is a wide and deep poet ... and as potentially productive of greatness as any poet writing in English. He makes Mr. Yeats's isolation guilty as a trance.

He then added as a P.S.: 'Congratulations on Auden's seventieth birthday'.[3]

The too-feted, 'boy bushranger' Auden is, to Thomas, a kind of bloodless poetic 'head prefect' who leads a 'gang' of lesser poets who 'haven't the strength to stand and fight as individuals', and who 'even as "gangsters", [have] machine-guns ... full, not of bullets, but of dried peas'.[4] A few months later, he was discounting the *New Country* poets individually, to Henry Treece, claiming 'MacNeice is thin and conventionally-minded, lacking imagination and not sound in the ear', while in a later letter to Treece, in July 1939, he fantasised gloomily about having to exchange his happiness for 'something entirely useless like an old bird-bath or a book of MacNeice's poems'.[5]

MacNeice himself did not even remember the Manchester meeting, believing that he and Thomas had first encountered each other in 1941. Of that occasion, he recalled in his article 'I Remember Dylan Thomas', written a year after his friend's death, that it

> was not a great success, partly because from the start he was somewhat suspicious of me ... and partly because I unwittingly confirmed this suspicion by telling him that in his last book there were five – or maybe it was six – poems which I thought were really good. Dylan obviously considered that such a specification of good poems was patronizing. (*SLC* 195)

Thomas probably also remembered, if MacNeice did not, MacNeice's review of *18 Poems* (published in 1934), in which he had described the poems as 'a series of nonsense images, the cumulative effect of which is usually vital and sometimes even seems to have a message', like 'wild and drunken speech, but with the saving grace of rhythm'.[6]

Given this inauspicious start, it seems all the more remarkable that, if Auden was the contemporary who dominated MacNeice's criticism of contemporary poetry in the thirties, this role (in lesser, differently defined form) was taken by Thomas between 1942 and his death in 1953. How did such a reversal come about? In what follows I shall argue that while MacNeice and Thomas seem as different as it was possible to be for two poets in mid-century Britain, there are similarities between them, and these have been neglected, not only because some of the differences are real enough, but also because criticism has more generally neglected the 1940s, the decade in which the rapprochement between Thomas and MacNeice took place. Indeed, the fact that it did occur – to the extent that Thomas steals the show in MacNeice's *Autumn Sequel*, and seems to act as one of the models for MacNeice's late lyric flowering – flies in the face of the received wisdom (a still-lingering legacy of the Movement) that the 1940s were, poetically, a dire decade.

One reason for this is likely to be the half-century of mainstream English critical antipathy to modernist-influenced poetry (as much of Thomas's is). It is hard to think how otherwise the decade which saw the writing of David Jones's *The Anathemata*, Lynette Roberts's *Gods with Stainless Ears*, H.D.'s *The Towers Fall*, T.S. Eliot's *Four Quartets*, Dylan Thomas's *Deaths and Entrances*, and W.S. Graham's *The Night-fishing* could be deemed inferior to the decade which succeeded it.[7] Another is the way Auden's death in 1973 triggered the elevation and canonisation of an 'English Auden', not in the radical spirit of Auden himself, but by way of a nostalgic and little-England reaction to post-imperial decline, which required Auden's elevation as a great poet to set against the Americans Pound, Eliot, Williams, and Stevens, and for the 1930s to be rendered even more exclusively 'the Auden Decade'. The bombinating Celtic fly in the ointment of this 'sinking island' syndrome, as Hugh Kenner called it, was Dylan Thomas.[8] Neither Samuel Hynes's *The Auden Generation* (1976) nor Valentine Cunningham's *British Writers of the Thirties* (1988) discuss Thomas much, and flagrantly misrepresent him when they do. Misplaced, misread, Thomas has been seen as peripheral to accounts of English twentieth-century poetry ever since the mid-1970s.

Something similar happened in reverse to MacNeice of course; he was, for at least two decades after his death, read as Auden's clever, but less memorable epigone, the specificity of his Irish and Ulster heritage submerged. But MacNeice has been rescued from this species of metropolitan condescension, partly because the excellence of post-1960s Northern Irish poetry retrospectively established a tradition which could reclaim and make the case for him from the 1980s onwards. No such renaissance of Welsh poetry, or criticism, has enabled a similar service to be performed for Thomas yet; indeed, .Welsh criticism remains ambivalent about his status to this day.

2

Looking back with the benefit of even limited hindsight, it is possible to see how Thomas and MacNeice resembled each other rather than the *New Country* poets, with the most significant resemblance being MacNeice's acute sense of flux and fragility. Thomas's early poetry, in lyrics such as 'The force that through the green fuse drives the flower', is based on what has been called the 'process poetic', a sense of the inextricability and simultaneity of growth and decay, dark and light, birth and death, as well as the interconnectedness of inner and outer 'weathers', or, as MacNeice himself puts it, 'the tides in the human body mingle with the tides of the macrocosm' (*SLC* 223). The metamorphic moments and states on which these poems focus – embryonic, neonatal, adolescent, orgasmic, and dying – are those of maximum change in the human life-cycle, and are often presented so as to be indistinguishable from each other. The one constant, in this post-Darwinian, post-Einsteinian universe, is change. Yet this is not a detached, stoic knowledge; life is a tragic yet exuberant spending which makes nonsense of the commonsense self's attempt to hoard experience. At a time when most poets embraced a positivist belief in the efficacy of systems, Thomas's work insisted on the limits of ratiocination, the embodied nature of consciousness, and the materiality of language. Yet MacNeice, too, dissented from 1930s orthodoxy in making the great theme of the poetry Heraclitean flux and metamorphosis, and there is an affinity between his 'green grave' and Thomas's 'green fuse' (*CP* 593; *TCP* 13). Both MacNeice's 'A Cataract Conceived as the March of Corpses' (*CP* 623) and Thomas's

'clocking tides' (*TCP* 14) display a more exacerbated sense of mutability than was allowed by the three modes of *New Country* poetry,
the topical, the gnomic, and the heroic. Thus, if Thomas works
through a knotting of sexual compulsion and the inseparability of
Thanatos from Eros in a way which is specific to his Welsh origins, a
similar womb-tomb equation appears in MacNeice as early as 'Mayfly'
(1929), although it is more literary and less visceral, invoking the *carpe
diem* tradition: 'Let us too make our time elastic and / Inconsequently
dance above the dazzling wave' (*CP* 32). Yet if MacNeice's scepticism of systems is ironic rather than gothic, he nevertheless registers
more of the 'febrile grotesqueness' of the slide towards war than the
Olympian Auden and his followers.[9] By *Autumn Journal* (1939), like
Thomas in *The Map of Love* (also 1939), he was reflecting the 'subjective, self-critical turn' associated with the New Apocalypse and
Neo-Romantic poetic movements of the late 1930s and early 1940s.[10]

The credentials of these movements, so despised for so long, have
been redeemed in recent years by James Keery in a series of brilliant
articles in *PN Review*. Coming to terms with them is essential to
understanding Thomas and his influence on MacNeice.[11] Terence
Brown's term for Thomas's version of what Keery calls this poetry,
'in the mode of visionary modernism and in particular on the theme
of (im)mortality', is 'existential humanism'.[12] This sells its vatic
credentials a bit short in Thomas's case, but will do for MacNeice's
response, which is clear enough, despite his habitually clipped tones.
'The Death-Wish' (1940), in which a suicide 'jump[ing] the rails' is
likened to the action of those 'mad to possess the unpossessable sea /
As a man in spring desires to die in woman', is in the sex-and-death
spirit, if not style, of Thomas (*CP* 200). Indeed, the very title of the
collection in which it appears, *Plant and Phantom* (1941), sounds like
one of Thomas's, kin to his 'intricate image' which 'stride[s] on two
levels': 'Image of images, my metal phantom / Forcing forth through
the harebell, / My man of leaves and the bronze root, mortal,
unmortal …' (*TCP* 33). Occasional MacNeicean intimations of
mortality and suicide – the 1930s Thomas is obsessed with suicide,
usually out of Hamlet's soliloquies – are reminders that Thomas's
work is informed by the knowledge that the biological urge to
procreate is a compulsion to self-undoing. In creating new life, the
body's spasm is always already a shudder of self-extinction, or what
might be called a biological reduction of Yeatsian gaiety. As
MacNeice would put it in 1954, 'Many of his poems are concerned

with death or the darker forces, yet they all have the joy of life in them', and this is a reminder that writing his pioneering study of Yeats was surely one of the things which sharpened MacNeice's alertness to the new temper of the times (*SLC* 183). At the same time, as MacNeice would later note, the distinction between 1930s and 1940s styles has been exaggerated too:

> This game of pigeonholing literary generations has gone too far … the Augustan-Romantic antithesis [is irritating] … Posterity may find our generations closer than we care to think. Such a line as 'Beginning with doom in the bulb, the spring unravels' could well have been written by Auden or Day-Lewis. And
>
> > Some life, yet unspent, might explode
> > Out of the old lie burning on the ground
>
> could well have been written by Spender. (*SLC* 207–8)

Both examples, tellingly, are taken from Thomas, and MacNeice's argument anticipates that of Gabriel Pearson, who argued in 1971 that the 1940s styles emerged from the same intellectual contexts (Freud, Lawrence, Eliot) and the same historical crisis (the Depression and the success of Fascism in Germany in 1933) as those of the *New Country* poets, with Thomas representing not a reaction against *New Country*, but rather the anti-positivist, intuitive, existential-religious response to that crisis by the same 'spiritually orphaned generation'.[13] And yet, of course, the differences are profound too. Although, as Terence Brown avers, when MacNeice came to reassess Thomas's craftsmanship in the 1940s, he was pleased to find that he was 'par excellence a shaper', MacNeice's own attitude to form was far less rigorous than Thomas's (*SLC* 140). Indeed, Thomas's treatment of traditional metrics and stanza-form was always ambivalent, and its hyper-elaborateness was not quite the same as what MacNeice was talking about when he claimed, in 'The Traditional Aspect of Modern English Poetry', that 'Most of the younger generation have returned to more regular forms [than Eliot] while trying to be their masters, not their slaves' (*SLC* 141). In MacNeice's work, the poet *can* be the slave of a form to the degree that his forms often seem not much more than handy receptacles in which to pour content. In 'The Traditional Aspect', MacNeice rebuts the arguments of those who object to modern poetry's 'flatness', 'cerebration', 'intellectual expression[s] of love', 'cynicism about sex', startling images, 'obscurity' and 'unworthy' simplicity, by simply citing examples of these things in Shakespeare (*SLC* 136–7). It is brilliantly done, but ultimately it is a reviewer's trick which does not address the fact that all the examples are actually in the same metre, whatever their content. Thomas's metres and stanza-forms are, to the contrary, almost invariably bespoke, more organic, gothic even, in their willingness to be awkward if that is what is required; they parodically exaggerate the exigencies of regular forms to show that, although he is indeed one of the 'younger generation', he is sending up as well as exploiting 'more regular forms'.

Thomas and MacNeice have fundamentally different attitudes to poetic language too. Of course MacNeice, like Thomas, allows wordplay to flourish in his work. There is a Sitwellian zinginess to several of the earliest pieces – 'The Creditor' and 'Elephant Trunk', for example – and several poems celebrate the autonomy of language, as shown by the internal rhymes of 'A Cataract ...', or the taste for refrain and repetition displayed in 'Invocation' or 'Nature Notes' (which could be retitled 'Variations beginning with the word "incorrigible"') (*CP* 527, 548). On one or two occasions, the later MacNeice even sounds like a Thomas impersonator, as in 'Visitations I': 'Never so lithe in the green dingle, / Never so ripe in the green hay' (*CP* 517). However, as with the other *New Country* poets, MacNeice's wordplay is on the surface of his work – which does not mean that he is not attuned to some of its possibilities, but rather the language just is not accorded enough materiality and opacity for wordplay to be used as generatively as it is in Thomas.

Thomas's only consistently repeated poetic dictum was that poetry should work 'from words' rather than 'towards words', and this was one of the main distinctions he drew between the work of the Audenesque poets and his own; whereas the poems of Cameron and Madge, as he put it, moved concentrically round a single image, his own allowed an initial image (or phrase, or word-cluster) to 'breed' a 'host' of others, all pitted against each other in a controlled destabilisation, according to what he called, in a famous letter to Henry Treece of 1938, 'my dialectical method': 'The life in any poem of mine cannot move concentrically round a central image; the life must come out of the centre; an image must be born and die in another; and any sequence of my images must be a sequence of creations, recreations, destructions, contradictions.'[14] MacNeice, like Cameron and Madge, might be an example of a poet who begins with a central idea or subject, and then works towards the words which would describe or express it best. Despite his interest in wordplay, MacNeice always delimits 'the colour of saying', flagging it up as childlike synaesthesia, for example, in 'When we were children': 'When we were children words were coloured / (Harlot and murder were dark purple) / And language was a prism ...' (*CP* 250).

For Thomas, by contrast, a poetic based totally on process requires that process be embodied genetically in language itself. Language is not only an abstract system for representing the world but a material object in that world, and therefore subject to process at the level of syntax and the individual word. This is why his poems accumulate long chains of appositive clauses, delay and disguise main verbs, sabotage the usual hierarchy of grammatical subordination, and create effects of simultaneous eventhood across their parts – although it should be noted that grammatical norms are never quite ruptured, the collage disjunctiveness of *The Waste Land* or *Cantos* never quite reached. Words are ceaselessly manipulated, enacting the paradoxical nature of change in linguistic terms; signifiers seem both mysteriously mimetic and motivated, items from a personal lexicon or mythology, and at the same time so polysemous as to be wholly arbitrary. This is not poetry which begins with a concept which it then tries to verbally 'clothe'.

3

When Dylan Thomas and Louis MacNeice met for a third time, in 1942, it was under different circumstances than hitherto. Thomas had begun, in September 1941, to write film scripts for Strand Films, a company whose entire output was bought up by the Ministry of Information. MacNeice, too, was producing propaganda, for the BBC. Although writers resented being conscripted in this way, the Blitz and shared wartime suffering had had the effect of creating a common cause, breaking down some of the barriers between the intelligentsia and the general population. The influx of continental intellectuals and artists had also created what was, perhaps, the only true Bohemia in twentieth-century Britain, in London's Fitzrovia, where it was centred on pubs such as the Stag's Head, the Wheatsheaf and the George, frequented by Thomas and MacNeice.

Thomas began broadcasting, and then writing features for the BBC during the war years, and it was in this new role that he met MacNeice again. It is also important to note that there had been a shift of public taste, under wartime conditions, towards acceptance of what had previously been considered too-'difficult' modernist art; conversely, modernist-influenced artists had moved towards styles of greater intelligibility by way of expressing solidarity with the nation at war. It applies chiefly to visual art – think of Henry Moore's drawings of shelterers in the Tube, or the wartime paintings of Graham Sutherland, John Piper, and Paul Nash – but awareness of a public sphere larger than his earlier, more or less avant-garde, coterie clearly affected a poet like Dylan Thomas. His work became less dense after 1944, as *Deaths and Entrances* (1946), the collection MacNeice thought his best, demonstrated.

Another factor making for friendship between Thomas and MacNeice was that both experienced the Blitz in terms of Freudian-surreal apocalypse, or what Stuart Sillars calls 'the Blitz sublime', by which the raids appeared as a manifestation of repressed psychic energies. Material from the Mass Observation project (a spin-off from surrealism's valorisation of the uncanniness of the everyday) shows that 'an element of exhilaration [was] very common' among those witnessing the Blitz bombing, with 'initial fear giving way to an awareness of the beauty of the night sky lanced through by searchlight beams'.[15] This had a political aspect; many on the Left viewed the bombing with a sense of *schadenfreude*, capitalist Babylon-London burning in the flames of a belated revolutionary justice, imagining that disaster would provoke a revolt against the ruling class who had brought war about (it is no coincidence that one Apocalypse journal was called *Arson*). MacNeice's 'Brother Fire' neatly captures (without endorsing) this aspect of the response:

O delicate walker, babbler, dialectician Fire,
O enemy and image of ourselves,
Did we not on those mornings after the All Clear,
When you were looting shops in elemental joy
And singing as you swarmed up city block and spire,
Echo your thoughts in ours? Destroy! Destroy!' (*CP* 217)

Like Thomas's 'Among those Killed in the Dawn Raid was a Man Aged a Hundred', or MacNeice's own 'The Trolls' and 'Troll's

Courtship', this poem is aware that the destruction, and its bitter-sweet impact, was taken as proof of Freud's theory of the human subject; as the breaking-out of its destructive, often surreal desires and fantasies, from obscurity, or what David Gascoyne in 'Inferno' calls the 'Bottomless depths of roaring emptiness'.[16] Indeed, figuring this outbreak as an escape of passional, animal energy, became a cliché in writing, art, and film, revealing a collective fantasy according to which the burning city matched its inhabitants' engulfment in conflicted desire and rage for liberation from psychic and sexual impasse. The knowledge of the possibility of impending extinction made the sexual impulse stronger, and wartime poetry charts how unmarried couples disregarded pre-war codes of conduct before they were separated, often for ever, by the war. And, in the most basic, practical sense, the Blitzed city was unavoidably a place, a state of mind, which – due to the disruption of daily routines, to chance encounters, and the cover afforded by blackout – facilitated sexual liaisons, spying, and the activities of spivs. As Lyndsey Stonebridge notes: 'Surreally particular to the British Home Front was the uncanny way in which the anxious space of a nation under siege, ghosted by phantoms half-glimpsed in the black-out, exteriorised the unconscious, made fantasy look like reality', and so fuelled an 'erotically-charged public sphere.'[17] Revolutionary and regressive, psychic and sexual energies ran together, inextricably bound up with death in a dynamic, radical equilibrium, according to which exultant release co-existed with loss and grief.

Swayed by such novel and uncanny energies, 'with [his] verse admitting mystical, even religious dimensions that had never been absent in their various ways from Yeats's and Thomas's writings', MacNeice's poetry adopted existential themes in the 1940s, and these would return, transmuted as parable, in his last three collections.[18] Or, as MacNeice himself put it in *The Poetry of W.B. Yeats* (1941), 'To both the question of pleasure and to the question of value the utili-tarian has no answer. The faith in the *value* of living is a mystical faith' (*PY* xviii). Of course, both poets were subject to common influences; the Metaphysical poets, always a Thomas favourite, are clearly in evidence in 'Prayer before Birth' and 'Vision and Prayer', reflecting the influence of George Herbert's 'shape' poems 'Easter Wings' and 'Sighs and Grones' in the waxing and waning stanza forms they use to depict embryonic growth.

It was during the middle years of the war, as already noted, that

Thomas began to work at the BBC and came to know MacNeice. In MacNeice's words, 'I gradually got to know Dylan through my work for the BBC, where as a producer I realized that he was a godsend to radio ... I cast him (and was never disappointed) in a variety of dramatic parts, including that of a funereal but benevolent raven in a dramatized fairy story' (*SLC* 196). (This was MacNeice's own best radio play, *The Dark Tower*, 1949.) Other parts included the brilliant casting of Thomas as Aristophanes in another MacNeice piece, 'Enemy of Cant' (1946).[19] Throughout the 1940s, their friendship extended itself from between-recording pints to lengthier furloughs; in 'I Remember Dylan Thomas' MacNeice gives an account of an enviable day-long spree in 1948, involving a cricket match at the Oval, 'much curious lore about cricketers' private lives', champagne in 'a very good underground wine bar', and Portuguese oysters at the London Casino. 'After that', as MacNeice noted, 'we were always, I think, at ease with each other' (*SLC* 196–7). If MacNeice understandably praised Thomas's professionalism after his death, during his lifetime he also used him as an example to encourage other writers, among whom there was a certain snobbery about writing for radio; it was not just out of friendship that, in 'Scripts Wanted!', an article for the *BBC Year Book for 1947*, he cited among those who had 'descended' to this work, 'two of the best writers of our times, V.S. Pritchett and Dylan Thomas' (*JS* 352). It is important to add that the personal and the professional aspects of their friendship went hand in hand, for Thomas and MacNeice drove up standards at the BBC; thus, according to Terence Tiller in 1948, 'Thomas and MacNeice, almost alone and in their different ways, have maintained a high minimum and a sharply rising maximum of excellence [in BBC radio productions]' (*JS* 369). Such details make more comprehensible the fact that, when MacNeice was appointed Director of the British Institute in Athens in 1949, he proposed to his employers that Thomas should be given his job while he was away. That proposal, of course, 'did not find favour with his superiors in the Corporation' (*JS* 376).

4

Thomas's death hit MacNeice hard, and his response to it was eloquent. It was at the MacNeices' home at 2, Clarence Terrace, that Thomas's London friends assembled for a kind of wake on learning of his death in New York on 11 November 1953. One of MacNeice's friends, Margaret Gardiner, later recalled how, as she was putting on her coat to leave, after midnight, MacNeice touched her arm: "'Don't go yet, you" he pleaded. "Please stay a little longer. Please." Seeing the look of desperation in his eyes, "Of course I will", I said' (*JS* 403). Gardiner sat up talking with MacNeice until dawn. MacNeice happened, at the time, to be writing *Autumn Sequel*; and, in addition to the two critical appreciations-cum-memoirs of Thomas, and reviews of *Under Milk Wood* and *Quite Early One Morning*, he decided to memorialise his friend in his poem.

There is, it seems to me, a difference between the way Thomas is treated in the articles and reviews, and in *Autumn Sequel*. All of the accounts are warm, and concerned to defend Thomas's reputation against the gathering backlash. In 1954 MacNeice observed that 'the near-apotheosis of Dylan Thomas has already provoked certain spiteful reactions in England' (*SLC* 200). However, the critical prose is alert to the danger of the Thomas legend in a way that the poem is not. MacNeice the critic on Thomas the poet is shrewd, if not entirely reliable. This is a passage from the first memoir, 'Dylan Thomas: Memories and Appreciations', which appeared in *Encounter* in January 1954:

He was not just a poet among poets; he was, as has often been remarked, a bard, with the three great bardic virtues of faith, joy, and craftsmanship ... [M]any of his poems are obscure, but it is never the obscurity of carelessness; though I, for one, assumed it might be when I first read his early work ...

The next few years will obviously see a spate of writing about Thomas – his vision, imagery, technique, etc. – and the writers will be beset by two distinct and opposite dangers – the danger of trying to equip him too exactly with a literary pedigree and the danger of isolating him as a sport, a Villon figure, a wild man who threw up works of genius ... the 'wild man' conception, immediately after Thomas's death ... was exploited in its most disgusting and imbecile form by certain of our daily papers. Of course Thomas liked pints of beer (so what? He also like watching cricket) but he did not write poems 'with a pint in one hand'; no writer of our time approached his art in a more reverent spirit or gave it more devoted attention. One glance at a Thomas manuscript will show the almost incredible trouble he took over those elaborate arabesques that could yet emerge as fresh as any of the 'woodnotes

wild' expected from a born lyric poet. In fact he was a born lyric
poet, but it was a birthright he worked and worked to secure. (*SLC*
183–4)

This is a perceptive assessment of Thomas, and its insistence on the
'incredible trouble' he took over his poetry would be confirmed three
years later with the publication of Vernon Watkins's correspondence
with Thomas.

The same can be said of MacNeice's review of *Under Milk Wood*,
published in *London Magazine* in April 1954:

> Thomas in some respects possibly had not fully grown up but he
> had a mature common sense; he also, together with his lions and
> fires, had a fine amount of good rich earth in him. This earthy side
> showed itself in his conversation ... It is this side of him which
> found expression in [his] prose works [and] ... *Under Milk Wood*.
> Compared with his best poems these may be minor works but they
> are excellent work of their kind and quite unlike anything I know
> of by a contemporary. Where else can you find such a natural lack
> of both bitterness and self-pity, such a natural blend of slapstick
> and reverence, of fantasy and flesh-and-blood? ...
>   As for his reading, he was saturated in the Bible and in folk tales,
> revelled in *Mayhew's London* and used to relax with space fiction.
> (*SLC* 186–7)

Here MacNeice rightly sees that *Under Milk Wood* is a minor work,
compared with the best of the poems, but unique and 'excellent ...
of [its] kind'; he answers the question 'had not fully grown up' might
raise by noting later on that 'It is all about love (in Thomas one can't
call it sex)', which is a fair enough comment on the erotic but asexual
pastoral of Llareggub and the later poems; and he is also one of the
few to understand (and condone) the hybrid and heterogeneous
nature of Thomas's talent, in his writing as in his reading (I take 'space
fiction' to be Sci-Fi).

In the last piece he wrote on Thomas, a review of *Quite Early One
Morning* for the *New York Times Book Review* in December 1954,
MacNeice added the important point that 'Just as Thomas was not
afraid in his poetry to be fastidiously, even archaically, "poetic", so
in his prose he was never afraid to be hail-fellow. Too many writers
nowadays are terrified of appearing either sentimental or vulgar' (*SLC*

200). The sentimentality and vulgarity were part of Thomas's hybrid, hyphenated Anglo-Welshness, of course, and MacNeice was far closer to understanding what made his friend tick than the many later critics who have rather snobbishly pounced on Thomas's archaism and kitschiness (but often missed their own in the process).

On the other hand, Thomas's calculated naivety seems to be taken too literally by MacNeice at times. This, I think, is largely because that is the function MacNeice wants Thomas to perform for him; and Thomas, born entertainer that he was, performed that role happily enough. When, in his review of *Under Milk Wood*, MacNeice adds that 'Though he [Thomas] read a great deal of English poetry I find him nearer to the folk world than to the bookish world', one senses the danger of simplification, however much praise is intended, and the 'folk' Thomas is one aspect of his depiction in *Autumn Sequel* which does not ring true. Yet MacNeice was in good company when he wrote of Thomas being not of the modern world – 'it was late / For his strange kind of poet', as he puts it in *Autumn Sequel* – and claiming elsewhere that 'Dylan in his poetry avoided all mention of the urbanized, industrialized, commercialized, politically conscious and embittered modern world' (*SLC* 195). Leslie Fiedler, for example, complained, in 1947, that Thomas's poetry was devoid of 'all manufactured things more recently invented than ships'.[20] This remains a common misperception, but is no less wrong for all that. What we find is that contemporary properties feature – 'macadam', 'celluloid', arc-lamps, drills, gears (in engines and cars), 'carbolic', 'cistern', poison gas, barbed wire, fuses, allotments, oil wells, ships' propellers, photographic 'stills', 'cyanide', solder, 'hangar', glands, hormones, unemployment, 'currencies', 'radium', and so on – but in a disguised form, often in combination with an organic term, to give a submerged, surreal effect. Thus, Thomas corrected Treece in 1938, arguing 'it is evasive to say my poetry has no social awareness ... quite a good number of my images come from the cinema & the gramophone and the newspaper, while I use contemporary slang, cliché, and pun'.[21] Indeed, cinema is crucial to an understanding of Thomas's early poetry; it is the technology most often referred to, used to represent the simultaneity of process and because it can dramatise the relationship between surface and depth. MacNeice, too, makes much of cinema in his 1930s poetry, although he is more concerned with its ability to symbolise a culture of surface than is Thomas.

The same could be said about the political content of Thomas's work. Its political essence, in a deeper sense than MacNeice saw, lies in the way it resists the 'subversion of depth' by attempting to reinstate 'genuine paradox' in the form of the process poetic. 'Self and world' were to be altered, not externally by realism and irony, but internally by absorbing dialectic and paradox. Deep 'irrationalist' modes of writing, such as the gothic and grotesque, rather than irony, became the mode of critique, as already noted. So, several of Thomas's early poems follow the Hegelian-Marxist triadic movement from thesis to antithesis to synthesis. MacNeice is Marxist too in a (albeit rather vague) sense; his insistence on intersubjectivity as definitive of the human condition in the Plato vs Aristotle section of Canto XVII of *Autumn Journal* echoes the humanism and alienation-*kritik* of Marx's *Economic and Philosophical Manuscripts* (first published in 1932):

> ... other people are always
> Organic to the self, ... a monologue
> Is the death of language ...
> [...]
> the current
> Jumps the gaps, the ego cannot live
> Without becoming other for the Other
> Has got yourself to give. (*CP* 42)

Perhaps, then, MacNeice did find in Thomas just this kind of 'Alter Ego' 'organic to the self' in his own work. Thomas (as 'Gwilym') is one of *Autumn Sequel*'s twenty-five 'personal friends' most opposed to the mechanistic drabness of postwar administered society, and its empty, unoriginal repetitive culture, represented by Parrot. Gwilym features as *the* figure of poetry, although from his first appearance, in Canto II, he is an example of the legend:

> For Gwilym is a poet: analogues
> And double meanings crawl behind his ears
> And his brown eyes were scooped out of the bogs,
>
> A jester and a bard. (*CP* 380)

Gwilym is contrasted with the kind of poet the narrator is; a performer, he is less a prisoner of systems than the narrator, more

starkly opposed to modernity, alert to the wiles of the 'spider who
offers time, money, and status and would like / The poet hamstrung
and his art trepanned' (*CP* 380). Gwilym alone

> ... stands alert to strike
> All eight legs off and drown that spider's bag
> In wells of glass or pewter, where blind pike
>
> In the dark dregs may gulp it. Let money brag,
> The poet will not be bought, he has powerful friends
> Who are his own inventions – the one-eyed hag
>
> Whose one is an evil eye, the maiden goddess who sends
> Her silver javelin straight, the Knave of Fools
> Who cocks his snook and blows his dividends,
>
> The soldier with the nosebag who breaks the rules
> Wide open ... (*CP* 380–81)

and 'we need [him] ... late and soon / To fight our false friends for
us'. The trouble is that these 'inventions' have nothing of the gothic-
grotesque power of Thomas's imaginings; the silver javelin, Knave of
Fools, one-eyed hag and the rest sound more like Hans Andersen,
classical legend or Graves's *The White Goddess* than the burning
babies, incestuous preachers, and wandering madmen of Thomas's
Jarvis Hills stories. In other words, these are more like the 'friends'
the 'bookish' MacNeice would ascribe to a 'folk' Thomas, and
unconvincing as a result. Moreover, while MacNeice's description
of the rotund Gwilym as 'Like Saturn swathed in ring on ring of
smoke' is a nice touch, adding that he will talk until 'a dwarvish folk'
and 'their pagan lore' emerge and 'dolmens r[i]se about us' has the
poem lurching towards Arnoldian stereotypes of the Celt. 'Dolmens'
is a reminder that those stereotypes are Irish as well as Welsh (the
'bogs' of Gwilym's eyes are hardly Welsh either). The short-lived
F.R. Higgins (as 'Reilly') makes a 'Celtic cousin' of Thomas, as
Terence Brown notes, and W.R. Rodgers ('Gorman') is Thomas's
living Irish analogue.[22]

Canto XVIII, the point at which Thomas dies, is both an elegy for
Thomas and, like Dunbar's 'Lament for the Makers', for the spirit of
poetry itself. Arguably, this is where MacNeice manages to get past

the previous stereotypes – or, more accurately, engage with them creatively – and produce one of the poem's high points. The energy of genuine lament manages to overcome the logorrhoea; there are even touches of humour: 'And did we once see Gwilym plain? We did. // And heard him even plainer' (*CP* 454–5). Still, the attempt to represent Thomas presents MacNeice with a difficulty, and it teeters on the brink of absurdity in a passage which brings together Thomas and the ascent of Everest, another theme of the poem. This mountaineering / poetry analogy is extended:

> On high ice
> An ice-axe falls and flounders down a slope,
> The last step has been cut, the last device
>
> Devised, and we below must give up hope
> Of seeing Gwilym again, he stays above
> Somewhere upon the mountains while we grope
>
> Our own way back. (*CP* 454)

Although this is sporadically magnificent, even moving, there is a jarring incongruity between its heroism, and the Thomas envisaged as 'bulbous Taliesin' who appeared six lines before; it is as if we are getting an image of him, a cigarette dangling from his mouth, clutching a pint in one hand and with the other hacking his way up an Everest cliff-face with his ice-axe. MacNeice is more consistently successful, it seems to me, when he deals with Thomas's *absence*; the account of travelling to Wales for the funeral, in Canto XX. This section of the poem is bleak, but energisingly so:

> One could think
>
> That all these shots of whisky, pints of beer,
> Make one Pactolus, turning words to gold
> In honour of one golden mouth, in sheer
>
> Rebuttal of the silence and the cold
> Attached to death. (*CP* 462)

There is no compensatory flourish, and something like the negative theology of MacNeice's last poetry emerges from the 'uncanny quiet' of Laugharne, and the dissolution of Thomas into the elements:

> My fingers close
>
> On what green thoughts this acre still can yield
> Before we leave that deep, that not green, grave,
> That letter to be superscribed and sealed
>
> Now that it has no contents; wind and wave
> Retain far more of Gwilym. (*CP* 463)

Here Thomas does not signify, for once, a fine Celtic excess. In the end it is his *lack* which 'shames' cherished MacNeicean 'illusions' concerning 'the grace / Of some afterlife'. In what feels like a genuinely speculative moment in a too-mechanical poem, MacNeice ruminates:

> If a birth
> Extends a family circle and glasses fill
>
> Confirming its uniqueness and the worth
> Of life, I think a death too does the same,
> Confirming and extending. Earth to earth,
>
> But to the whole of it. (*CP* 463–4)

In this communal linkage of birth and death, and acceptance that Thomas 'will ... keep us waiting' forever, we forget the metropolitan–Celtic antithesis that dominates the other sections of the poem. True, MacNeice has turned Gwilym into the 'wind and wave' of the natural world, as if to confirm his position outside culture; but ultimately that is everyone's fate.

5

Thomas's later work, in poetry and prose, is based on a subtle manipulation of stereotype and cliché, largely pastoral, and it is no coincidence that MacNeice should have reflected this – albeit in a way which sometimes succumbs to clichés in a negative sense – in

constructing Thomas as an alter ego, one route forward for his own
poetry. The reverse was never true, since Thomas was a completely
self-sufficient sort of poet, but one would like to think that he learnt
something from MacNeice about the way a lyric might remain a
personal utterance and yet have popular appeal. Whatever the consistency of the representation of Thomas/Gwilym, MacNeice worked
hard for a just appreciation of his friend's work by others. On 25
January 1954, MacNeice was one of the organisers of a gala for a
Dylan Thomas memorial fund held at the Globe Theatre in London,
at which he read Canto XVIII from *Autumn Sequel* (when asked what
Dylan would have thought of the evening, which raised £1,169 5s.,
Caitlin Thomas replied, 'He would have liked the cheque').[23] Nor
should MacNeice's point about too many writers being afraid of
sentimentality be forgotten; his defence of Thomas applies to his own
representations of his friend, to some extent. Even more, I think it
applies to Hedli MacNeice's moving tribute, 'The Story of the House
that Louis Built', which compares her former husband to a house
structured as a succession of inner sanctums, the receding depths of
MacNeice's complex self:

> It was a handsome house with thick walls. The windows on the
> west side looked towards Connemara, Mayo and the Sea. Those
> to the south scanned Dorset, the Downs and Marlborough – the
> windows to the north overlooked Iceland and those to the east,
> India.
>   The front door was wide and always open.
>   The Antechamber was full of people coming and going, admin-
> istrators … critics, power men … who if asked would say that
> Louis was shy, arrogant, cold, polite, unapproachable, they didn't
> really know him they would say … (*JS* 481)

But beyond this there was a 'second chamber … with a Bar against
which Louis would lean watching the door for the unexpected and
exciting', a room entered by poets, actors, 'journalists with travellers'
tales of distant wars', people with 'something to offer'. Further still,
through a 'door locked to all but a few' was a room with shabby furni-
ture, an open fire, and 'books everywhere', a room for those few
friends with whom he felt at ease and to whom he gave 'all his affection and loyalty'. Beyond this room there was, she says, 'a very small
one, just space for two: himself and a Welsh poet Dylan Thomas or

an Irish W.R. Rodgers. With them, he would, manuscripts in hand, discuss the making of poetry, but only with them' (*JS* 482).

This extraordinary piece of writing is above all a poignant elegy for Louis MacNeice. But its generosity to Thomas is extraordinary too. It is also a reminder of how much has been lost with the fragmentation of literary culture since the mid-twentieth century. Before the war, there existed numerous journals – and an audience for them – which carried work by avant-garde writers and Georgians, modernists, and *New Country* Marxists. Naturally, readers had their preferences, there were cliques and savage literary wars; but it was really the academicisation of poetry, and rigidly enforced cartels of taste and publishing, which created a situation, from the 1950s on, in which it became possible for so-called 'mainstream' and 'alternative' poetries to ignore each other. For all their differences, Thomas and MacNeice shared an older, more inclusive poetic culture; and both of them (and Thomas to this day) problematise the rigidities of what succeeded it. Certainly, in a purely literary sense, it was posthumously, in their final poetry – Thomas's *In Country Sleep* project, and MacNeice's *Solstices* and *The Burning Perch* – that they came closest to each other, and challenged the new orthodoxy that was asserting itself. Written under the shadow of the Bomb, like the fiction of William Golding and Samuel Beckett's drama, this poetry makes sustained use of the allegory and parable MacNeice so ably analysed in *Varieties of Parable* (1965). I like to think that, had Thomas lived, he would, for once, have been able to give his heartfelt praise to MacNeice's work; and that he and his friend would have had more than ever to talk about, together in that 'inner room'.

WHEN I THINK OF MACNEICE

Thomas McCarthy

Coming from the South of Ireland, as far South as you can get on the Waterford coast, and coming from a culture that must seem completely alien to anybody from MacNeice's background, why do I adore Louis MacNeice? Let me tell you.

First of all I admire his reticence. As Michael Longley has said 'Ireland had inoculated him against political certainties'. That's very important. Reticence, I think, is a highly educated stance in a poet. It takes learning and a certain amount of artistic good-breeding.

I admire him because he was not afraid of the ambiguities of the Irish situation. He also knew that politics alone could not save the individual from himself or herself: no political issue can prevent personal memory or the nightmares of childhood. These are addressed head-on in MacNeice's poetry.

Because he had a distinct sensibility. Yet he knew sensibility was not enough: an insight that Stephen Spender could not proclaim until he was in his seventies. MacNeice knew this from the beginning. His own sensibility is more than a Protestant thing; it is an angle or a tilt towards belief and patria. One finds this in Elizabeth Bowen – at least I do – in the character of Lois in *The Last September*. This sensibility is also in the travel writing of a Cork writer, Robert Gibbings. His journals of Tonga, his understanding of the work that goes into cutting stone: MacNeice has that. MacNeice was just too illuminated to allow chauvinism or nationalism to take hold of processes that were much deeper than anything political. I admire him for that, having been steeped in politics from childhood myself.

I admire him and adore him for his times, I mean the times he lived in. We cannot really praise a poet for his own era, but we can actually praise his responses. The thirties were a frantic and frenzied era. The evil of the era was astonishing and very early on MacNeice, because of his world view, so to speak, which was quite different from the Irish world view in the 1930s, was already engaged with that evil emotionally. In fact, he was so engaged with the struggle against Fascism and the evil that was Hitler, that it is difficult to see how he could have maintained any kind of imaginative intensity in the bleakness of the 1940s or the 1950s. One could say, looking at him, that he was the first of the 'Less Deceived' in this world. It was not so much Larkin as the critical conditions that granted a poetic license to Larkin to be the poet he became; and a lot of that license had been worked on already by MacNeice. Looking at this from the point of view of a public librarian, it is no accident, really, that Larkin was a professional librarian in Belfast – and was celebrated as a poet while he was a librarian.

I love MacNeice because he's not Daniel Corkery. He did not presume to speak for Ulster and he certainly had no intention of speaking for the crowd that assembled at the Munster Hurling Final in Thurles, County Tipperary in the Introduction to Daniel Corkery's *Synge and Anglo-Irish Literature*. Politically and culturally the Second World War gave Eire to itself and it heightened, also, Ulster's moral sense of itself. It is interesting to look at the publications, those documents, and that frenzy of publishing, in the immediate aftermath of the victory of Eamon de Valera in the General Election of 1932 and the Eucharistic Congress that was equal in influence, culturally, upon the South. The events that are linked in the minds of the Irish, events that completed a vision of Ireland that first arose in the era of Daniel O'Connell and the Repeal Movement of the 1830s, seemed to complete some sense of National Being by the time of the centenary of Catholic Emancipation. Ireland was complete but Ulster was elsewhere. Louis MacNeice knew that and he lived with it. So did Elizabeth Bowen, I think.

I adore his work, also, because he discovered that poets don't live in a country. They live in a 'Bohemian air pocket' – a lovely expression that Peter McDonald used in a recent poem in the *TLS* when writing about the Lyric Theatre and its Belfast milieu. That 'Bohemian air pocket' is where we all survive while writing, typing, sending away, publishing, assessing the response. MacNeice knew that the poem could be a long form like the novel, without ever becoming a novel. *Autumn Journal* is one of the great masterpieces. It has never been equalled, not even in Yeats. 'Nineteen Hundred and Nineteen' is probably more ambitious at one level, but to me *Autumn Journal* was already vulnerable to aerial bombing, if you like. This work is more like The *Anabase* of St Jean Perse or the *Axion Esti* of Elytis. Like all great work *Autumn Journal* carries a series of dialogues before itself and beyond itself in time. MacNeice knew that a great poem could be a prodigious search of appearances, as Wallace Stevens wrote. The MacNeice poem survives every kind of assault.

Recently in Cork City Library I was working my way through the old Stores, thousands and thousands of books and journals on the Gaelic world and on Irish history: more than a thousand printed in 1938 alone. That was a kind of post facto establishment of who we were, now that we had made ourselves whole, a twenty-six-county Republic. At that moment there was an overwhelming coherence in Irish life, a mass moral frenzy. Remember, the main battle in Irish life in the 1930s was not against Fascism, but against Jazz dancing. It animated more editorials, sermons, public admonishments, and pamphlets than anything else. Flann O'Brien estimated from the granting of Public Dance licenses in 1937, 1938, and 1939, that there were on average 10,000 Jazz dances in Ireland every year of those years. So it was not really the mass mobilisations of Fascism and their Nazi salutes that outraged opinion but foxtrots and other occasions of sin. Whenever a boy or a girl met in a story by Sean O'Faolain or William Trevor there was the certain end of one kind of Ireland-whole.

So, I love Louis MacNeice for his reticence, his authority as a poet, his belief in the hermetic air pocket where poets survive – a kind of layer either beneath or above our country.

And then there's his shyness. A composed shyness, perhaps a Protestant gentility: one finds it in Beckett, too, or in Hubert Butler. With MacNeice it is certainly a characteristically Ulster reticence, sometimes hidden. Here, let me quote from the journal of the Greek poet, George Seferis, then a Greek diplomat in Ankara. It is Seferis's entry for Monday, 11 December 1950:

> I met Louis MacNeice; he read poems from Yeats down to his own generation, in a small packed room at the University; except for a few men, all young girls. I was impressed with the way his recitation changed, when at the end he read three of his own poems: another tone, warmer, at times carried away with himself. I wouldn't say, as one might think, that he didn't care for the other poets; I suspect that, since he's such a shy man, he had to gather more momentum to present his own self.

How brilliantly perceptive that is about MacNeice. And here, now, as I write, I have other documents of the age before me: *Horizon*; and the *Kenyon Review* with a very interesting essay on the Nazi purge of philosophy in Germany (the Summer 1941 edition); and a copy for Winter, 1941, with poems by – who do you think? – Louis MacNeice. All of these things merely serve to remind us, as we celebrate MacNeice, that what we are is conditioned by circumstances where evil and good are relative to ourselves; ourselves, you must understand, who are creatures of our era. What MacNeice taught us was that sense of duty: that all who write carry an obligation to gather enough momentum to present, however briefly, a report of the true self.

'HIS INTURNED EYES':
MACNEICE IN THE WOODS

Paul Farley

Star-gazer (from *The Burning Perch*, 1963)

Forty-two years ago (to me if to no one else
The number is of some interest) it was a brilliant starry night
And the westward train was empty and had no corridors
So darting from side to side I could catch the unwonted sight
Of those almost intolerably bright
Holes, punched in the sky, which excited me partly because
Of their Latin names and partly because I had read in the textbooks
How very far off they were, it seemed their light
Had left them (some at least) long years before I was.

And this remembering now I mark that what
Light was leaving some of them at least then,
Forty-two years ago, will never arrive
In time for me to catch it, which light when
It does get here may find that there is not
Anyone left alive
To run from side to side in a late night train
Admiring it and adding noughts in vain. (*CP* 607–8)

In the autumn of 2008, I took a train from London Waterloo to Sherborne in Dorset, and felt the full scale of the MacNeician planetarium. I had a copy of *The Strings are False*, his unfinished autobiography that was passed on for safekeeping in 1941 and published after his death in 1963. There, I read a description of an incident that must have also been stored safely away:

In January 1921 I found myself wonderfully alone in an empty carriage in a rocking train in the night between Waterloo and Sherborne. Stars on each side of me; I ran from side to side of the

carriage checking the constellations as the train changed its direction. Bagfuls and bucketfuls of stars; I could open my mouth to
the night and drink them. (*SF* 78)

There was something pleasing about the nested-ness of all these dates,
of the light taking so long to arrive, so to speak, while at the same
time something frustrating. I was on the same length of track, and yet
the current South West Trains rolling stock don't make it easy to rush
from side to side (and you'd be caught on CCTV if you did). What
seemed most appealing was a sense of absolute modernity, the idea
of the mobile gaze, and a sense also of sight drawing on the other
senses. It reminded me of how, when I first read MacNeice, it often
felt like entering both a thicket and an echo chamber.

   In an essay of 1936, 'Subject in Modern Poetry,' MacNeice alights
on the matter of 'subject anxiety', one of the major literary issues of
his day:

   It is sometimes objected against these younger poets that their
   'modern' stage-properties are a little obvious; that they introduce
   pylons and gasometers as automatically as older poets introduced
   roses and nightingales. This is often true, but it should be remembered that pylons and gasometers are not merely décor. (*SLC* 72)

Apart from the inturned smile this might provoke when any
youngish poet reads it – it seems there are always young poets criticised for reaching too readily for the newfangled and the immediate,
and it is always intriguing looking back at the perpetually awful state
of contemporary poetry – it also suggests important questions about
the writer and his or her context; about the world the writer inhabits
and moves through as always being a place of value and interest,
regardless of age and epoch.

   There was of course an anxiety concerning the journalistic and the
documentary operating at this time (the 1930s). And by the end of
his life, MacNeice had grown circumspect about the journalistic. But
I have often wondered how much he could have imagined or foreseen a contemporary context so completely disengaged from the
enormous past, either as an archive and resource, or an available
panoply, as the one we find ourselves in now, where everything can
seem to be happening all at once and time really is 'away and somewhere else'.

For poets of my generation, the year of MacNeice's death, 1963, represents something of a Year Zero, Larkin's *annus mirabilis*, though in the book he did not quite live to see published that year, *The Burning Perch*, MacNeice is more interested in the *Magnus Annus*, Pythagoras's idea of the whole of history happening in a great year, and everything having to go round again. The poet Peter Porter once said 'we are living in the Permanent Museum, whether we like it or not', perhaps corrupted by another poet, Michael Donaghy, who described our culture as 'a vast, posh shop with the security cameras switched off'.[1]

From early on, MacNeice seems able to look in two directions at once: on the one hand, the enormous past is available to him, to be recalled and re-imagined: 'It was all so unimaginably different, and all so long ago' he says, opening a tunnel that leads us all the way back to the classical world. At the same time, his poems are also very alive to the world he inhabited, right down to the consumerist brand names and shiny surfaces that had mobilised between the wars, and whose furnishings and ethos we are still – just about – inhabiting and enduring. So we find Hamlet in the shadow of the gasworks. We get sarcophagi and celluloid. We get roses and cigarettes.

But beyond MacNeice's willingness and ability to fuse the classical and the immediate, the vernacular, to bring the past and present into unexpected proximities in his poems, there lies a more interesting impulse, which concerns the question of selfhood and identity moving through the same imperfect space we all have to share, and – most interestingly, I think – what it means to see the world over and again as both a mediated thing and as a thing in itself.

Writing about Malory's *Morte d'Arthur* in 1961, MacNeice describes the book as 'a wood which one can get lost in – but then what are woods for?' (*SLC* 233). In that spirit, I should like to look at MacNeice's poem 'Woods', which first appeared in his collection *Holes in the Sky* in 1948:

> My father who found the English landscape tame
> Had hardly in his life walked in a wood,
> Too old when first he met one; Malory's knights,
> Keats's nymphs or the Midsummer Night's Dream
> Could never arras the room, where he spelled out True and Good
> With their interleaving of half-truths and not-quites.
>
> While for me from the age of ten the socketed wooden gate

Into a Dorset planting, into a dark
But gentle ambush, was an alluring eye;
Within was a kingdom free from time and sky,
Caterpillar webs on the forehead, danger under the feet,
And the mind adrift in a floating and rustling ark

Packed with birds and ghosts, two of every race,
Trills of love from the picture-book – Oh might I never land
But here, grown six foot tall, find me also a love
Also out of the picture-book; whose hand
Would be soft as the webs of the wood and on her face
The wood-pigeon's voice would shaft a chrism from above.

So in a grassy ride a rain-filled hoof-mark coined
By a finger of sun from the mint of Long Ago
Was the last of Lancelot's glitter. Make-believe dies hard;
That the rider passed here lately and is a man we know
Is still untrue, the gate to Legend remains unbarred,
The grown-up hates to divorce what the child joined.

Thus from a city when my father would frame
Escape, he thought, as I do, of bog or rock
But I have also this other, this English, choice
Into what yet is foreign; whatever its name
Each wood is the mystery and the recurring shock
Of its dark coolness is a foreign voice.

Yet in using the word tame my father was maybe right,
These woods are not the Forest; each is moored
To a village somewhere near. If not of to-day
They are not like the wilds of Mayo, they are assured
Of their place by men; reprieved from the neolithic night
By gamekeepers or by Herrick's girls at play.

And always we walk out again. The patch
Of sky at the end of the path grows and discloses
An ordered open air long ruled by dyke and fence,
With geese whose form and gait proclaim their consequence,
Pargetted outposts, windows browed with thatch,
And cow pats – and inconsequent wild roses. (*CP* 271–2)

MacNeice's father – who, we discover from another poem in *Holes in the Sky*, 'The Strand,' 'Kept something in him solitary and wild' – is a conduit towards a 'true wild', the West. And yet, there is also this 'English choice'. For MacNeice, it has become almost a critical axiom to recount his betwixt and between-ness: his 'foreigner' status with an Irish readership, and his sense of 'Irish-ness' to people over the water. This sense of apartness was even broader, and not only founded along lines of nationality. As a discernible quality, it cuts right through his life on many levels, and MacNeice must have been partly complicit in presenting himself as a detached observer. At Oxford in the late 1920s, he remembered: 'the air was full of the pansy phrase "my dear". I discovered that in Oxford homosexuality and "intelligence", heterosexuality and brawn were almost inexorably paired. This left me out in the cold and I took to drink' (*SF* 103). His own imaginative sense of being 'out in the cold' can be examined through his poems, and it is interesting that by the time he wrote 'Woods', the mid-1940s, he is able not only to manage a sufficient distance from his childhoods, but to hold his plural pasts in a kind of creative opposition, balancing landscape, family, myth, and reading. MacNeice takes us on a walk through the woods, recalling his schooling at Sherborne by leading us into 'a Dorset planting, into a dark / But gentle ambush', but as we enter the woods' enclosed space the poem suspends time, opens out, and explores the different versions of landscape available to the poet; literary, picture-book, mythical memories nested within actual memory.

The Strings are False provides a comprehensive key to so much of this: there we can find his master at Sherborne, Littleton Powys, reading him Herrick, we can find Malory's *Morte d'Arthur* and what we would now call 'role playing', and the little shocks of geology and topography that registered as the difference between Ireland and England. We also know that MacNeice was brought up with stories of the far West of Ireland in his ear. In 'Landscapes of Childhood and Youth', he talks about his childhood construction of dream worlds. Unlike those of his friend W.H Auden, who at the same time was constructing a depopulated private world made of limestone, abandoned lead mines, slag heaps, and machinery (and even at a tender age had the textbooks to valorise 'his ideal scenery'), MacNeice's consisted of places he thought were really on the map, the first of which was 'The West of Ireland': 'a phrase which still stirs me, if not like a trumpet, like a fiddle half heard through a cattle fair. My parents came from that West or, more precisely, from Connemara, and it was obvious that both of them vastly preferred it to Ulster ... So for many years I lived on a nostalgia for somewhere I had never been.' (*SF* 220)

'A nostalgia for somewhere I had never been' really hit home with me (if you'll pardon the atrocious pun). Growing up in Liverpool in the early 1970s, I did not believe a place called 'England' really existed. Cricket on the village green, sunken lanes, bridleways, and chalk downs formed the visual fabric of picture books, but nothing I read about connected with the bin sheds and unremitting concrete and greyness outside. Later on in the same piece, MacNeice describes being sent to school in England aged ten, and we hear of another strangely dislocating episode:

> Transported across the Irish Sea and seated in an English train ... I kept saying to myself 'This is England' but I did not really believe it and, as it was night, could not see those differences which stamp a thing as real. But, though full of disbelief, I was vastly excited, and when daylight came I perceived that England was not just an imitation of Ireland; the fields and hedges and houses were different, and as for London when we got there ... it was not Belfast, it was foreign. And foreign it has remained to me. (*SF* 220–1)

We get this sense, then, of MacNeice being twice removed from his familial source, and of also being both afloat and acutely aware of the shortfall between expectation and actuality, of being able to lever open and examine his perceptions. In 'Woods' we see a parsing of personal iconography and a way with myth that looks ahead to the poems of the late fifties and early sixties. But it strikes me mostly as a poem concerned with the difficulty of getting any access to 'the real', whatever that means. The poem's resolution – if we can call it that – leads us back into daylight ('And always we walk out again ...') and into an ordered world where even the sky is framed ('An ordered open air long ruled by dyke and fence') and lands on 'inconsequent wild roses'.

Mention of roses is likely to prick up the ears of any MacNeice-watcher, but again these flowers are looking ahead to later blooms. They are wildness framed, wildness neutered within a vast field of order, husbandry, and tameness. They prefigure the blooms in a much later poem, 'Flower Show', published in *The Burning Perch* in

1963, where 'massed brass bands of flowers' keep a man trapped in a flower show tent in their sights; these are flowers which 'have long since forgotten, if they ever knew, the sky', and the only way out of this locked groove nightmare is a reconnection with flowers and their living context:

> [...] and now there is no way out
> Except that his inturned eyes before he falls may show him
> Some nettled orchard, tousled hedge, some garden even
> Where flowers, whether they boast or insinuate, whisper or shout,
> Still speak a living language. (*CP* 582)

'Flower Show', in *The Burning Perch*, is flanked by 'Pet Shop', and its animals taken out of a living context: 'Once there was the wild, now tanks and cages' (*CP* 582), and 'In Lieu', and its 'Roses with the scent bred out' (*CP* 583). If MacNeice's early poetry, from *Poems* (1935) to *Autumn Journal* (1939), accommodates the world of consumer goods, factory hooters, and glossy surfaces, the later work can be said to move back into the same frames but with a renewed sense of purpose concerning authenticity and artificiality, the vitality of living variety and the deadening, distancing effects of the manufactured and the repetitive. In a way, all our perceptions of the natural world are mediated to some degree, but to get a sense of how nightmarish and enclosed the 'canvas cathedral' of 'Flower Show' really is, it should be read alongside Patrick Kavanagh's 'On Reading a Book of Common Wild Flowers', published just a few years earlier: 'I knew them all by eyesight long before I knew their names. / We were in love before we were introduced.'[2] Like John Clare before him, Kavanagh is able to suggest an unmediated, unconditional wildness in the world; Clare famously 'found the poems in the field, / And only wrote them down'.[3] MacNeice's 'inconsequent wild roses' are deadheaded, their wildness cancelled out by a thing called *England*.

If we really believe that MacNeice's poetry contains forces disruptive enough to work against the organising tendencies of the canon, then it might be useful to cast the net wider and think about his work in hitherto unexamined relationships with some unusual suspects, and with such a blood-chilling caveat, I wanted to think about MacNeice in the light of a poet working a century earlier: John Clare. On the face of it, the two have next to nothing in common: Clare the 'Northamptonshire peasant poet', the son of a flail thresher who was only intermittently educated, a worker in the fields around his birth home of Helpston, whose London publishers took advantage of a metropolitan vogue for rural verse that had persisted since Robert Burns; alongside Clare, MacNeice seems impossibly urban, urbane, and worldly, and on the face of it the comparison would seem to suffer immediately simply because of the conflicting historical time-frames the two writers occupy, the context Clare was working in – in every sense – being so utterly removed from the one MacNeice inhabited. But, without wanting to force connections, the two writers do share something quite fundamental and important, and that is their apartness, their homelessness.

We know that Clare and John Keats came close to meeting: they shared the same London publisher – Taylor & Hessey of Fleet Street – and at their offices, Keats actually scribbled a note on the nearest paper to hand, which was the back of a letter from Clare. And the two knew each other's work: when Keats was shown Clare's poem 'Solitude', he though 'the Description prevailed too much over the Sentiment'. And when faced with Keats's nightingale, this is what Clare had to say: 'he often described nature as she appeared to his fancies and not as he would have described her had he witnessed the things he described'.[4]

Clare is suspicious of Keats's allusiveness, the availability of an enormous past, and this vast life-support system of classical mythology (what Philip Larkin would witheringly refer to as 'the myth kitty' a century and a half later). He values firsthand experience, accurate description, the thing being described rendered faithfully from what is seen in the field, with no qualifying, intermediary apparatus. But Clare himself is only able to write following the dispersal of print culture. In fact, the discovery of books, the availability of books, precipitated a kind of crisis for Clare, albeit a crisis that generated some of his best work. Immersed in a vernacular culture of folk song and verse, Clare's exposure to the dissemination of printed poetry – already widespread by the beginning of the nineteenth century – provokes an engagement that will isolate and alienate him within his native culture and community. Taken to London to promote his first collection – *Poems, Descriptive of Rural Life and Scenery*, in 1820 – Clare finds himself in the fashionable drawing rooms of the metropolitan literati, and realises he can never be a part of this. He is caught in an appalling double bind. He is 'out in the cold'.

A common theme is flux, and rate of change. For Clare, we might think of each microcosm going about its interconnected business, but there is an excitement and dread associated with the storms and floods that assail his landscapes, and from reading his letters as well as the poems, it is easy to imagine how contingent his situation was, especially by the 1830s. A poem such as 'The Flood' shows a part of Clare's world – the River Welland at Lolham Brigs – moving so quickly it seems to be coming apart as the river in spate dismantles and takes things away in its current:

> Trays – uptorn bushes – fence demolished rails,
> Loaded with weeds in sluggish motions, stray
> Like water monsters lost: each winds and trails
> Till near the arches – then as in affright
> It plunges – reels – and shudders out of sight.
> [...]
> The chill air comes around me ocean blea.
> From bank to bank the waterstrife is spread.
> Strange birds like snow spots o'e the huzzing sea
> Hang where the wild duck hurried past and fled.
> On roars the flood, all restless to be free
> Like trouble wandering to eternity.[5]

From the outset, MacNeice is interested in Heraclitean flow: a very early poem, 'A Cataract Conceived as the March of Corpses' from 1927, shows us a river in spate:

> The river falls and over the walls the coffins of cold funerals
> Slide deep and sleep there in the close tomb of the pool,
> And yellow waters lave the grave and pebbles pave its mortuary
> And the river horses vault and plunge with their assault and
> > battery ... (CP 623)

Thirty years later, the same concern intensifies and culminates in poems such as 'Reflections' and 'Variation on Heraclitus'.

Even though Clare and MacNeice can be said to share a kind of access-all-areas homelessness, we would be wrong to pigeonhole the two writers as otherwise moving in entirely separate spheres of interest. You could make a case for the symmetry of their respective writing careers: after early success and critical reception, Clare's work fell out of favour and slowly slipped from view into the late 1820s and beyond, even though the poet was very much active and indeed producing some of his strongest writing; MacNeice did not quite fall off the radar, but nevertheless the 'early promise – later neglect' pattern does broadly obtain. The 'unsophisticated' Clare, labelled and marketed as the 'Northamptonshire peasant poet,' was capable of seeing his world through the lens of art, and producing complex, ekphrastic lyrics, for example on the work of the painter Peter de Wint. And the 'sophisticated', metropolitan, London-loving MacNeice was perfectly willing to rent a place in the sticks in order to get some writing done. The point is also worth making, lest any gasometers or pylons obscure our view, that MacNeice seems to have been preoccupied to a degree with the relationship between urban and rural in several early poems such as 'An Eclogue for Christmas' and 'Turf-stacks'.

In March 1946, the MacNeices had rented a house in the village of Tilty in Essex, which is where 'Woods' was probably written. It is only a few miles up the road from High Beech and the asylum where John Clare was first treated as a voluntary patient (and from where Clare walked home on foot to Northamptonshire: the famous 'flight from Essex' prose description). Here is a poem that Clare wrote shortly before he fled this Essex asylum:

London Versus Epping Forest

The brakes, like young stag's horns, come up in Spring,
And hide the rabbit holes and fox's den;
They crowd about the forest everywhere;
The ling and holly-bush, and woods of beach,
With room enough to walk and search for flowers;
Then look away and see the Kentish heights.
Nature is lofty in her better mood,
She leaves the world and greatness all behind;
Thus London, like a shrub among the hills,
Lies hid and lower than the bushes here.
I could not bear to see the tearing plough
Root up and steal the Forest from the poor,
But leave to freedom all she loves, untamed,
The Forest walk enjoyed and loved by all![6]

Clare's walk through the woods, like MacNeice's, is also concerned with what is 'untamed', and on first thinking about this poem I was thrilled at the thought of having maybe come across an all-too-neat analogy; especially in the way that Clare, like MacNeice, is self-consciously pulling different kinds of environments into broad contrast, even using an atypically adversarial title to signal the poem's project of comparison and estimation, a weighing up. But the more I thought on it, the more the differences overcame any tidy parallel. It is not just that one poet uses literary allusion, or invokes a familial relationship between what is 'wild' and what is 'tame' in his idea of woods; it is not just that the other poet looks outward more, seeing a continuum from these woods and their plant and animal inhabitants to the human world and 'the poor'. It is more to do with Clare's locating of 'freedom' here, in the woods, because his woods begin and end in themselves, and exist in their own self-contained right. They heal themselves, conceal or shelter their inhabitants, and are openly available to all. Can we really say the same of MacNeice's woods?

It might be easy to dismiss this as a criticism of a poem not doing something its maker was not interested in it doing in the first place, and MacNeice's poem has other strengths anyway; and yet, I was intrigued by MacNeice's description, in 'Landscapes of Childhood and Youth', of forging a real connection between himself and his environment. At Marlborough, forced to take compulsory runs called 'sweats' against the clock through the north Wiltshire downlands and forest, he describes how:

> I loathed the conveyor belt of trees which I had to force behind me through my own leg power, and the ever-receding grey brow of the downs with their aristocratic indifference to our rainsoaked wasplike jerseys. But after a year or two of this lungs and legs became free and in pounding over the elastic earth one felt attuned to this country ... Physical discomfort, it dawned on me, my hair one river of sweat, could be a bond between myself and my context. Or rather could help me to make a context ... (*SF* 224)

This chimes with Clare's own sense of significant places – the woods and fields and heaths of pre-enclosed Northamptonshire – as being able to support the work *and* the play of the people who lived there, the last of the pre-industrial English contexts supporting all manner of human and natural activity, seen and felt and experienced physi-

cally through an intimacy with landscape. Even though we acknowledge the world of difference between a public school cross-country
run and a life spent working on the land.

And a world of difference, finally, between Clare's much-anthol-
ogised poem 'I Am' and MacNeice's 'I twitter Am' from the cage of
his 'Budgie.' Entering MacNeice's 'alluring eye' reminds me of
entering the dark of a cinema, and since I first read 'Woods' I have
been particularly reminded of a film that was released in the same year
it was written. (I hope this is not blasphemous or tendentious, if only
because MacNeice seems so obviously open to the idea that what we
have read, and what we have seen framed, materially alters the way
we view and reconstruct the world — and that increasingly includes
the hourly assault of images.) This film is *A Matter of Life and Death*,
Powell and Pressburger's 1946 wartime love story starring David
Niven and Kim Hunter, and screwing the focus even tighter, particularly that scene in which Niven and Hunter are relaxing in a
Technicolor grove when there is a visitation from a heavenly emis-
sary (played by Marius Goring), who comes down to earth and enters
these woods in order to stop time and speak with Niven. In the deep,
rich foliage of a sound stage, our celestial messenger takes a long sniff
of the rose in his buttonhole, and laments the way 'One is starved for
Technicolor up there', pointing towards what I think of as a very
MacNeicean concern: that shortfall between seeing things firsthand
and through books and the various distorting lenses of the twentieth
century. It should also be acknowledged that this film is deeply
indebted to radio, and particularly the period of experimentation that
MacNeice, working for the BBC, was such a part of during the war
years, especially his version of Eisenstein's *Alexander Nevsky* in 1941,
which heralded a series of radiophonic verse epics.

Filters and intervening media, whether they be print, photographs,
picture books or film, are only one way in which MacNeice is
distanced: we have to also consider ideas of childhood's unalloyed
perception. Is the American poet Louise Glück correct when she
writes, in her poem 'Nostos', that 'we look at the world once, in
childhood. / The rest is memory'?[7] Is the first blossom always the best
blossom? 'The grown-up hates to divorce what the child joined',
MacNeice tells us in 'Woods,' and the poem poses its post-
Wordsworthian questions about how our engagement with the real
is injured, compromised or diminished through time and ageing, and
how our pasts might always be malleable, unresolved. But MacNeice

never ran out of childhood. Even in the poems from *Visitations* to *The Burning Perch*, he is still able to mobilise memory not simply for its own sake, or sentimentally to record a loss, but to examine its securities and test its boundaries with the world.

In MacNeice's hands, there is an urgency where matters of perception are concerned; it is this dimension of his work – first encountered through 'Woods', though soon evident at all stages of his writing life – that I continue to be most excited by. What does it mean to grow up, to enter into time and consciousness, with our formative years full of broadcast music and images? How do we remember, having intimately known the microcosms of our rooms and houses and streets, but *also* the phantoms and chimeras of cinema and radio and television, while we were young, to a greater degree 'out of time' and 'living in the moment'? I have often wondered if this kind of introduction to the world is inauthentic in some way. I should like to end by reproducing, in its entirety, a beautiful but sad short lyric from 1957's *Visitations*; terrifying actually in the way it manages to suggest to me a point in time – not so unimaginable now – when the synapses are finally connected directly via Wi-Fi to streaming (or, in spate) broadband:

To Posterity

When books have all seized up like the books in graveyards
And reading and even speaking have been replaced
By other, less difficult, media, we wonder if you
Will find in flowers and fruit the same colour and taste
They held for us for whom they were framed in words,
And will your grass be green, your sky be blue,
Or will your birds be always wingless birds? (*CP* 495)

'COMING UP ENGLAND BY A DIFFERENT LINE': LOUIS MACNEICE AND PHILIP LARKIN

Stephen Regan

For admirers and detractors alike, Philip Larkin is a quintessentially English poet. If his poems openly acknowledge the 'mortgaged half-built edges' and the 'bleak high-risers' of the changing postwar landscape, they never entirely relinquish their vision of a more appealing English pastoralism (*LCP* 136, 189). In their tonal qualities, too, the poems are often harsh and demotic, but they never completely abandon the elegant ease of a more traditional English lyricism. The critical construction of English Larkin came, in part, from his involvement with the Movement and its perceived anti-foreign, anti-modernist tendencies, but it was also the product of Larkin's own seemingly insular and narrowly nationalist viewpoints expressed in interviews, letters, and essays. The Englishness of Larkin's verse was given a sudden, complicating twist in brilliant critical essays by Barbara Everett and Edna Longley in the 1980s, both of them pointing to the undeniable influence of nineteenth-century French decadent and symbolist poets, including Charles Baudelaire and Stéphane Mallarmé, an influence all the more impressive for its unlikely appearance in the work of a poet who had registered no interest whatsoever in 'foreign' poetry.[1] Around the same time, Seamus Heaney and Andrew Motion began to wonder if Larkin had shaken off the influence of W.B. Yeats quite as easily and as completely as he claimed, though it was generally accepted that it was the very English Thomas Hardy who had dominated Larkin's writing procedures and literary ideals from the mid 1940s onwards.[2]

In his introduction to the 1966 reissue of *The North Ship* (1945), Larkin claims that Yeats had been the most potent influence in his work from 1943 to 1946, when he rediscovered the poems of Thomas Hardy. As an illustration of the transformation in his work, he points to 'Waiting for breakfast, while she brushed her hair', a poem written in December 1947 and added to *The North Ship* nearly twenty years later. Larkin memorably writes of that poem, now strategically situated as the closing piece in the new issue of *The North Ship*, that it 'shows the Celtic fever abated and the patient sleeping soundly'.[3] The Celtic influence is strangely pathologised here, as if caught and internalised in some intense and uncontrollable way before a return to healthy normality. Stranger still is the compelling suggestion in the poem itself that if the Celtic fever is abated, it is not altogether eliminated. The tense 'waiting' of the opening line, the subtle eroticism of the brushing of hair, and the speaker's looking down in abject pathetic fallacy at the 'empty hotel yard' and wet 'cobblestones' are all evocative of Hardy's wistful love poems, but the sharp insistent questions at the end of the poem carry the unmistakeable imprint of Yeats: 'How would you have me? ... Are you jealous of her?' (*LCP* 20). The overblown conception of the poet as 'Part invalid, part baby, and part saint' is deeply Yeatsian, as is the starkly dramatised choice at the end of the poem between the perfection of the life or the perfection of the work of art, recalling one of the most haunting and troubling questions in 'The Tower': 'Does the imagination dwell the most / Upon a woman won or woman lost?'[4]

The Yeatsian presence is more powerful and persistent in this early poem than Larkin admits, and one of its effects is to override a more subtle Irish influence emanating from the work of another writer who was to assume a critically significant role in Larkin's development as a poet. Despite its unpromising opening, the poem turns on a momentary rediscovery of tenderness and love, opening into one of those rare epiphanies in Larkin's work: 'Turning, I kissed her, / Easily for sheer joy tipping the balance to love' (*LCP* 20). This turning, with its deftly placed adverbial auxiliary – 'Easily' – is also a turning to Louis MacNeice, and it provides a striking instance of 'the sophisticated sentimentality' that Larkin was later to admire in the work of his near contemporary.[5] The poem lacks a title, other than its opening line, but it functions as an aubade or dawn song, a form that Larkin found appealing in his reading of MacNeice. At a crucial mid-point in the poem, the speaker looks through glass, establishing a demarcation between exterior and interior spaces, between the realm of stubborn actuality and the realm of imaginative desire: 'beyond the glass / The colourless vial of day painlessly spilled / My world back after a year, my lost lost world'. This attempted framing of the complex transaction between mind and world is derived from MacNeice's 'Snow', in which 'There is more than glass between the snow and the huge roses' (*CP* 24). Looking through glass was to become a habitual way of seeing the world for Larkin, and it provides the means of poetic vision in the title poems of his two major volumes of poetry: *The Whitsun Weddings* and *High Windows*.

Larkin's diagnosis of the Celtic fever in his work disguises the complex interplay of voices and allusions in poems written as early as the 1940s. The alleged casting out of Yeats allows the smuggling in of a complementary but more up-to-date Irish influence. However, for a poet whose early instinct is to situate himself rather tentatively within an undemonstrative English tradition of writing that included A.E. Housman, Thomas Hardy, and Edward Thomas, even the Northern Irish MacNeice is initially held at bay, hence the myth of Hardy as the presiding influence. There is clearly more going on here than repression, in the sense in which Harold Bloom uses the term, and any easy psychologising of strong poetic fathers and their aspiring offspring is complicated by the manifold ways – sometimes pronounced and sometimes covert – in which MacNeice's presence makes itself felt. What prompts the eventual legitimation of MacNeice is Larkin's own brief domicile in Belfast in the 1950s. It is MacNeice, more than any other poet, who provides for Larkin a way of writing a modern urban lyricism, ironically detached in its scrupulous observation of people and places, but also given to an occasional unsettling of its own calm demeanour with unforeseen moments of tenderness and compassion.

MacNeice's 'Snow' drifts gently into one of Larkin's most intimate and personal poems in the 1940s, a poem so painfully candid that it was never printed in any of Larkin's individual volumes of poetry and eventually reached a general readership only with the publication of Anthony Thwaite's edition of the *Collected Poems* in 1988. 'An April Sunday brings the snow' was written just a week after Larkin's father died on Good Friday, 26 March 1948. The Eastertide imagery seems propitious, but its function is to surprise us out of our habitual perceptions and draw attention to the delicate ways of nature rather than guarantee any resurrection of the dead: 'An April Sunday brings the snow / Making the blossoms on the plum trees green, / Not white. An hour or two and it will go' (*LCP* 21). In that short white interlude, the speaker goes about the work of mourning, shifting jars of jam his father made from the same plum trees. The novelty of blossom looking green against white snow is supplemented by the image of the father as jam maker. Although there is no explicit reference to the biographical circumstances of the poem, this touching detail serves to present the father as 'someone gently and surprisingly feminine'.[6] The philosophical reflections prompted by MacNeice's glass take on a new ontological severity as Larkin's poem reflects on the surplus produce that exceeds the dead man's days: 'Behind the glass, under the cellophane, / Remains your final summer – sweet / And meaningless, and not to come again.' If these lines have more than a touch of English lyric plenitude flowing from Shakespeare ('summer's lease hath all too short a date') and Housman ('Now, of my threescore years and ten, / Twenty will not come again'), they also suggest how close to Samuel Beckett's unrelenting vision of final things Larkin sometimes came.[7] Initially, the glass invokes a quaint museum-like sense of preservation, but it carries into the final lines a beautifully enigmatic quality that anticipates the existentialist vistas of 'the sun-comprehending glass' in 'High Windows' (*LCP* 165). The swelling thought of death in these closing lines is rhythmically and empirically checked by the mundane 'cellophane' – just the kind of diction that MacNeice made possible in poetry, amidst the 'buyable beauty' ('celluloid, painted ware … parchment lampshades') in 'Belfast' and 'Birmingham' (*CP* 22, 25). The verbal 'remains', conjuring up its associated deathly noun, is also typical of MacNeice's felicitous wordplay, as is the laconic but devastating enjambement that takes us from 'sweet' to 'meaningless', preparing us for the skilfully placed caesura and the final, monosyllabic rebuff of redemptive theology.

Although *The North Ship* is commonly regarded (with Larkin's own endorsement) as a volume pervasively influenced by Yeats, it takes its bearings from the various literary endeavours of MacNeice and Auden in their *Letters from Iceland* (1936), which Larkin read at King Henry VIII School in Coventry. In his final year at school, Larkin and his friend Noel Hughes composed a light-hearted 'Last Will and Testament' modelled on the 'Last Will and Testament' with which MacNeice and Auden concluded their *Letters from Iceland*. The poem was published in the school magazine, *The Coventrian*, in September 1940. MacNeice's mordant comedy shows up later in poems such as 'Dockery and Son' and 'Naturally the Foundation will Bear Your Expenses', but what also emerges from this early exposure to MacNeice and Auden is a poetry of departures and returns, a poetry of journeying that sometimes depends on ships and cars, but increasingly comes to rely on trains. If these modes of transportation

open up for Larkin new ways of looking at the world, they also introduce, as they do for MacNeice, a whole new technological
vocabulary associated with transport and traffic.

The experience of travelling by train and the sensitive recording
of the changing visual perspectives that are opened up by movement
through a variegated landscape are as familiar to MacNeice as they
are to Larkin. In MacNeice's *Poems* (1935), to focus on just one early
volume, the preponderance of trains and train journeys is striking (as
discussed in the contributions in this volume by Terence Brown,
Leontia Flynn, and Hugh Haughton). As late as 1963, the exhilarating
'Star-gazer' recalls an empty 'westward train' that allows the traveller
to look out on 'a brilliant starry night'. The effort of remembering
an event 'Forty-two years ago' prompts thoughts about the speed of
light and lifts the poem into a startling existential meditation, as the
speaker wonders if, when the light arrives, there will be 'Anyone left
alive / To run from side to side in a late night train / Admiring it and
adding noughts in vain' (*CP* 607–8). MacNeice, not just a 'thirties
poet', but a fellow-traveller of Larkin in 1963, might seem at this
point to have achieved a cosmic sublimity far removed from Larkin's
'cut-price crowd', but Larkin has his moments of sublimity, too, most
powerfully rendered in what is probably the final instance of
MacNeice's dark metaphysical influence on his work: 'The sure
extinction that we travel to / And shall be lost in always' (*LCP* 208).

'I Remember, I Remember', one of Larkin's earliest train poems
(written in January 1954), is an affectionate parody of Thomas
Hood's Victorian childhood idyll of the same title, and it sets up an
ironic distance between itself and the fabulous literary childhoods of
such writers as Dylan Thomas and D.H. Lawrence. Once again,
however, it is MacNeice who proves to be the most enabling influence, not just in making it possible for Larkin to write in a seemingly
effortless way about the experience of travelling by rail, but in
prompting a poetry of deracination and uncertain belonging. Larkin's
reflections on his place of birth are strongly reminiscent of
MacNeice's ambivalent attitudes to place: 'I leant far out, and squin-
nied for a sign / That this was still the town that had been "mine"'
(*LCP* 81). In effect, Larkin signals a new way of writing about
England in the postwar years precisely by avoiding any overt or stri-
dent sense of national belonging. Far from endorsing a poetry of
secure attachment to England and English literary traditions, Larkin
offers a comic, deflationary view of his own midland birthplace, an

aberrant viewpoint that culminates in the solving emptiness of the poem's final, isolated line: 'Nothing, like something, happens anywhere.' What MacNeice bequeaths to Larkin most crucially is perspective, a way of looking on life from the vantage point of elsewhere, a way of 'Coming up England by a different line'.

It comes as no surprise, then, to discover that 'I Remember, I Remember' was written in Belfast during Larkin's four-and-a-half-year stint as librarian at Queen's University. He lived and worked in Belfast from September 1950 to March 1955, one of the most intensely productive periods of his entire career. 'The best writing conditions I ever had were in Belfast,' Larkin told an interviewer for the *Paris Review*.[8] According to Edna Longley, 'Larkin completed all his creative apprenticeships in his Belfast years', and for John Goodby those years were decisive in establishing Larkin's distinctive voice: 'There can be little doubt that the relatively strange surroundings in Belfast either precipitated the change in Larkin's poetry or, what is more likely, confirmed the tentative steps he had made and speeded the process immeasurably.'[9] There can be no doubt, either, that it was the influence of MacNeice, and not just Belfast, that speeded the process and prompted the impressively prolific writing of a poetry of arrivals and departures. There is a new freshness of vision, a new alert sensitivity to sights and sounds in the urban pastoral poetry that Larkin begins to write in Belfast: 'This town has docks where channel boats come sidling; / Tame water lanes, tall sheds, the traveller sees... / And hears'. 'Arrivals, Departures' acknowledges a poetic rebirth for the journeying poet, however inauspiciously announced: 'His advent blurted to the morning shore' (*LCP* 65). What he comes to share with MacNeice is an immensely creative disengagement from any stable sense of identity or attachment, a profoundly liberating sense of disavowal, as in 'Places, Loved Ones':

No, I have never found
The place where I could say
This is my proper ground,
Here I shall stay. (*LCP* 99)

One of the first poems to be written by Larkin after arriving in Belfast was 'The March Past' (dated 25 May 1951 but not included in *The Less Deceived*). Tom Paulin sees this poem 'about a military band' as an intensely Yeatsian performance in its exploration of feelings of 'remorse',[10] but it is surely MacNeice who prompts the images of stationary cars, the delicate interplay of sunlight and 'street-shadow', the Neoplatonic 'Pure marchings and pure apparitions', and the alliterative hyphenated adjectives in 'credulous, prettily-coloured crowd' (*LCP* 55). The strangely muted close of the poem, however, derives from another poem inspired by military music, Edward Thomas's 'Tears', in which music similarly prompts deep feelings ambivalently connected with national pride. The presence of Thomas is also strongly marked at the end of 'Arrivals, Departures', with its melancholy echo of the night-time cry of 'The Owl': 'never knowing … if, this night, happiness too is going' (*LCP* 65). Despite the attractions of Thomas's low-keyed English lyricism, the influence of MacNeice persists, and it is there unmistakeably in one of the first poems to be written by Larkin after his move from Belfast to Hull.

'The Importance of Elsewhere', written in June 1955 and included in *The Whitsun Weddings* (1964), is explicit about the experience of living in Ireland and the benefits that paradoxically arise from sepa-ration and difference: 'Lonely in Ireland, since it was not home, / Strangeness made sense. The salt rebuff of speech, / Insisting so on difference, made me welcome' (*LCP* 104). For Edna Longley, 'The Importance of Elsewhere' is Larkin's *ars poetica*, 'a poem about the enabling effects of distance', but it is also a poem about 'the disabling effects of closeness'.[11] In a manner that recalls MacNeice in his most exhilarating shifts of register, the poem transforms itself from a gritty denotation of Belfast sights and sounds ('draughty streets, end-on to hills, the faint / Archaic smell of dockland, like a stable, / The herring-hawker's cry') into an elevated existentialist meditation on the predicament of living in England: 'Here no elsewhere under-writes my existence' (*LCP* 104). The cunning, proto-Derridean pun on 'underwrites' both acknowledges the extent to which belonging is a matter of written guarantees, of 'customs and establishments', and simultaneously throws open to speculation the very idea of trying to substantiate one's presence in writing.

Larkin's admiration for MacNeice wavered slightly when he came into personal contact with him in the 1950s, but his respect for him as a poet never diminished. A clear indication of Larkin's high regard for MacNeice is evident in a letter written to his friend Jim Sutton in May 1950. Reporting that a copy of *The North Ship* has found its way to MacNeice, he tells Sutton, 'I am moving among the gods now'.[12] That elation was renewed a few years later in 1957, when

Larkin was asked to edit an anthology of new poems (*New Poems 1958*) for PEN, with MacNeice and Bonamy Dobrée, but it quickly vanished when MacNeice proved elusive and difficult to work with. Larkin complained to PEN at one point: 'Why should MacNeice do less for his money than we?'[13] Larkin gave a positive review to MacNeice's *Visitations* in the *Guardian* in June 1957, and in 1962 he wrote an appreciative account of the Argo 'Masters' Voices' recording of MacNeice reading his work, in which the poet is nicely caricatured as 'a sophisticated, almost dressing-gowned figure, dropping epithets into place effortlessly and exactly'.[14] Larkin's most candid and illuminating account of MacNeice's influence on his own generation of poets, however, can be found in the brief obituary (just two paragraphs) which appeared in the *New Statesman* on 6 September 1963, three days after MacNeice's death:

> When we were young, the poems of Louis MacNeice were not recommended to us in the same breath as those of Eliot and Auden. Perhaps for this reason, the secret taste we formed for them was all the stronger. He was, as his photograph in Grigson's *New Verse* showed, a town observer: his poetry was the poetry of our everyday life, of shop-windows, traffic policemen, ice-cream soda, lawn-mowers, and an uneasy awareness of what the news-boys were shouting. In addition he displayed a sophisticated sentimentality about falling leaves and lipsticked cigarette stubs: he could have written the words of 'These Foolish Things'. We were grateful to him for having found a place in poetry for these properties, for intruding them in 'the drunkenness of things being various'.[15]

The 'sophisticated sentimentality' that Larkin notes here was a quality that he began to cultivate in his own work from the late 1940s onwards, and it can be seen in a number of poems that carry other signs of MacNeice's influence. 'Lines on a Young Lady's Photograph Album', the opening poem of *The Less Deceived*, has an Augustan elegance and formality befitting its title, but this only barely controls 'the drunkenness of things being various', with the speaker simultaneously devouring and feeling overwhelmed by the many delectable photographs of the young woman in question: 'Too much confectionery, too rich: / I choke on such nutritious images' (*LCP* 71). Like MacNeice, Larkin is able to indulge in the glut of sensation while maintaining distance and propriety through a careful manipulation of perspective. The beautifully poised ending of 'Lines on a Young Lady's Photograph Album' edges towards sentimentality, but dispels the illusion of eternal loveliness with cunning, allusive diction, delicately balancing the pathos of diminishment with a clear-sighted knowledge of inevitable change and loss: 'It holds you like a heaven, and you lie / Unvariably lovely there, / Smaller and clearer as the years go by.'

Entirely at ease with a poetry of photographs, news-reels, radio broadcasts, and other new media, MacNeice enables Larkin to write a poetry equally at home with the popular technology of communication. The landlady in 'Mr Bleaney' listens to 'the jabbering set he egged her on to buy', even after her lodger has departed, and radio provides the inspiration for the sublimely uplifting love poem, 'Broadcast', written for Maeve Brennan in November 1961 (*LCP* 102, 140). The poem depicts two people listening to the same music, one in a concert hall and the other by a radio set, with that imagined intimacy momentarily and precariously held in place by 'glowing wavebands'. The debt to MacNeice is most evident in the skilful contrivance with which Larkin is able to suggest the loss of imaginative vision that accompanies the loss of transmitted sound: 'Here it goes quickly dark. I lose / All but the outline of the still and withering // Leaves on half-emptied trees.' Larkin appears to be writing his own version of 'These Foolish Things', finding an objective correlative for feelings of separation in poignant images of clothing: 'One of your gloves unnoticed on the floor / Beside those new, slightly-outmoded shoes'. The gloves have a strange proleptic presence in the poem, preparing us for the final image of hands, a memorable instance of sophisticated sentimentality neatly held in place by the verbal adroitness and perspectival ingenuity of the closing line: 'Your hands, tiny in all that air, applauding' (*LCP* 140).

Larkin, like MacNeice, becomes a town observer in his poems, most obviously in *The Whitsun Weddings*, published in 1964, just a year after MacNeice's death. The *New Statesman* obituary reveals his familiarity with a number of MacNeice's urban lyrics, including 'Birmingham', with its memorable image of the pivoting traffic policeman halting cars in the city centre: 'Behind him the streets run away between the proud glass of shops, / Cubical scent-bottles artificial legs arctic foxes and electric mops' (*CP* 22). This is a particular way of seeing the city, capturing objects and events with rapid simultaneity, but it is also the cultivation of a particular style appropriate to modern city life. Larkin emulates this way of seeing and writing about urban experience in his depiction of Hull in 'Here', the opening poem of *The Whitsun Weddings*, in which 'residents from raw estates' arrive on trolley buses and 'Push through plate-glass swing doors to their desires – / Cheap suits, red kitchen-ware, sharp shoes, iced lollies, / Electric mixers, toasters, washers, driers – ' (*LCP* 136). MacNeice can be seen and heard here in the abundance of compound nouns and adjectives and in the tumbling catalogues of objects. What we see is not just an acute apprehension of the changing urban and suburban landscape, but also a skilful fusing of lyric and dramatic modes of writing to forge a style appropriate to the energies of the city and the surfeit of consumerist goods on display.

This is a complex way of seeing and with both poets it often edges towards an attitude that might be read too easily as comic satire, as with the shopgirls' empty faces in 'Birmingham' or the eager 'cut-price crowd' in 'Here' (*CP* 22; *LCP* 136). In both cases, the dramatic impulse and the occasional tendency towards exaggeration and caricature produce an apparent condescension. Hugh Underhill has argued that although the work of both poets is informed by 'the intellectual's consciousness of the mediocre and venal', both Larkin and MacNeice succeed in producing a poetry of democratic urban sensibility. What Underhill draws attention to very effectively is a shared ironic recognition of how 'the Platonic Form has fallen and how it has become a tool of commercial interest for consumer manipulation'. For both poets, he argues, 'essential beauty' is 'a dream which eludes us all, poet and intellectual as much as cut-price crowd'. Although MacNeice's work is more obviously distinguished by its show of classical learning, Larkin's poetry similarly exposes the ironic distance between desire and fulfilment, between seductive dreams and sordid actualities. Both poets, according to Underhill, are 'aware of the banality of this world and how much is missing from it', but simultaneously 'relish its humanised non-ideality'.[16] Larkin's version of the pursuit of Platonic Forms is amply evident in 'Essential Beauty', 'The Large Cool Store', and 'Sunny Prestatyn'. Like MacNeice, Larkin exploits the distance between modern commerce and the traditional concerns of aesthetic philosophy, turning the advertisement hoardings in 'Essential Beauty' into urban pastoral images ('these sharply-pictured groves / Of how life should be') and giving

them a playfully Platonic role within a debased contemporary existence:

> they rise
> Serenely to proclaim pure crust, pure foam,
> Pure coldness to our live imperfect eyes
> That stare beyond this world. (*LCP* 144)

If MacNeice provides for Larkin an appealing lyric and dramatic
style, and a way of manipulating voice and mood, he also provides a
startling new repertoire of images and a technique that encourages
the compression and collision of those images. MacNeice's 1949
essay, 'Experiences with Images', offers valuable insights into the kind
of lyric poetry that both he and Larkin came to stand for. 'All lyric
poems, though in varying degrees, are *dramatic*', according to
MacNeice. 'The voice and mood, though they may pretend to be
spontaneous, are yet ... a *chosen* voice and mood' (*SLC* 44). The felicitous coincidence of style and seeing that creates the impression of
spontaneity in the early MacNeice is a persistent feature, and it can
be found in poems written as late as 1960. Not surprisingly, 'Flower
Show' (1961) gives full vent to the dramatic, exhibitionist tendency
in MacNeice's style, foregrounding images of artificial 'blooms'
through a dense and bewilderingly adjectival syntax: 'Squidlike,
phallic or vulvar, hypnotic, idiotic, oleaginous, / Fanged or whale-
boned, wattled or balding, brimstone or cold / As trout or seaweed'
(*CP* 582). 'Flower Show' provides a model for Larkin's 'Show
Saturday' (1973), with its 'lambing-sticks, rugs, // Needlework,
knitted caps, baskets ...' The alliterative, hyphenated assortment of
people in 'Show Saturday' – the 'dog-breeding wool-defined
women' and 'car-tuning curt-haired sons' – step straight out of
MacNeice's poems, but any hint of condescension is this time
compensated for by an enlarged generosity of spirit and a shrewd
appreciation of what the show signifies 'below / Sale-bills and swin-
dling' (*LCP* 201). MacNeice's flower show takes place in a 'canvas
cathedral', while Larkin's agricultural festivity, with its sacramental
vision of 'blanch leeks like church candles', is a show Saturday that
might as well be Sunday: 'Let it always be there' (*CP* 582; *LCP* 201).
As MacNeice goes on to say in 'Experiences with Images', the lyric
poem is not only potentially dramatic and ironic, it is also symbolic.
Both poets avail themselves of this symbolic potential, frequently

presenting it as a sudden play of light. MacNeice's 'Morning Sun' (1935), in which 'Everything is kissed and reticulated with sun' (*CP* 15), has its counterpart in Larkin's brilliantly imaginative 'Solar' (1964), in which the sun is not only elaborately figured as a 'petalled head of flames / Continuously exploding', but is reinstated as a deity: 'Unclosing like a hand, / You give for ever' (*LCP* 159).

While working on many of the poems that were to appear in his final volume, *High Windows* (1974), Larkin was also editing *The Oxford Book of Twentieth-Century English Verse* (1973). In 1966 he had been invited by Oxford University Press to update *The Oxford Book of Modern Verse* that Yeats had edited in 1936, but as Jon Stallworthy points out, the delegates' first choice of editor had, in fact, been Louis MacNeice (*JS* 470). MacNeice was approached in 1962, but died the following year. Larkin is often taken to task for having manufactured and promoted an anti-modernist and stridently English line of poetry in *The Oxford Book of Twentieth-Century English Verse*, but far from being narrowly English, the book pays homage to lines of descent that MacNeice would surely have endorsed. As well as including poems by Yeats, Joyce, and Synge, Larkin has selections from Oliver St John Gogarty, Padraic Colum, James Stephens, F.R. Higgins, Austin Clarke, Patrick Kavanagh, John Hewitt, Donagh MacDonagh, and W.S. Graham. There is, in addition, a judicious selection of poems from the work of MacNeice himself, exemplifying both his abundant technical inventiveness and his acute political awareness. The chosen poems are 'Wolves', 'Snow', 'The Sunlight on the Garden', 'Bagpipe Music', Section VII of *Autumn Journal*, 'Dublin', 'The Taxis', and 'Tree Party'.

It would seem that Larkin was at pains in his editing of the Oxford anthology to play down any obvious English line of descent in his account of modern poetry. In his own poems written around this time, he is equally eclectic and imaginatively wide-ranging, producing what was to be his most allusive, esoteric, and adventurous collection of work in *High Windows* (1974). Grevel Lindop has shown how Larkin in the 1970s was intent on writing poems that would make him sound 'different from himself'.[17] One of these experiments in voice was 'Dublinesque', a gentle elegiac evocation of Dublin that seems to recall the moral dichotomies of James Joyce's *Dubliners* in its juxtaposition of a funeral procession with a 'troop of streetwalkers' (*LCP* 178). The name Kitty is sometimes read as an allusion to Katharine O'Shea and the death of Charles Stewart Parnell, but there is no clear indication that this is *fin de siècle* Dublin or that Joyce is the primary influence. The 'stucco sidestreets' and the shops with their 'race-guides and rosaries' more obviously derive from the Dublin of MacNeice in 'The Closing Album', a city similarly evoked in terms of 'seedy elegance' and fading memories: 'And all her ghosts that walk / And all that hide behind / Her Georgian façades' (*CP* 179).

High Windows achieves for Larkin the maturing and darkening of vision that he had perceptively and appreciatively noted in the late poems of MacNeice. The closing paragraph of his obituary for MacNeice acknowledges the startling qualities of the early work – the acute attentiveness of the town observer, the sophisticated sentimentality, 'the drunkenness of things being various' – but it moves beyond these qualities to a recognition of MacNeice as a poet acutely concerned with human suffering and the ameliorative role of art:

> Now we are older, some of these qualities have faded, some seem more durable. Against the sombre debits of maturity that his later poetry so frequently explores – the neurosis, the crucifying memory, the chance irrevocably lost – he set an increased understanding of human suffering, just as against the darkening political skies of the late Thirties he had set the brilliantly quotidian reportage of *Autumn Journal*. In what will now be his last collection, *The Burning Perch*, the human condition is shown as full of distress. If it is described not too solemnly, the chances are, he seems to be saying, it will become easier to bear.[18]

The 'sombre debits of maturity' are all too apparent in *High Windows*. The opening poem, 'To the Sea', draws vitality from MacNeice in its denotative rendering of the poetry of everyday life – 'Steep beach, blue water, towels, red bathing caps' – and its optic simile also suggests the durable influence of MacNeice: 'Like breathed-on glass / The sunlight has turned milky'. 'To the Sea', like 'Show Saturday', affirms the importance of annual rituals and festivities, but its final emphasis is not just on teaching children but on 'helping the old' (*LCP* 173). For Larkin, 'the neurosis, the crucifying memory, the chance irrevocably lost' reach a terrifying crescendo in 'The Old Fools': 'Why aren't they screaming?' (*LCP* 196). 'The Building' ends with one of his most powerful existentialist meditations: 'nothing contravenes / The coming dark, though crowds each evening try // With wasteful, weak, propitiatory flowers'. As if restating his own verdict on the later poetry of MacNeice and its capacity for enduring human suffering, Larkin contemplates the extent to which poetry itself becomes 'a struggle to transcend / The thought of dying' (*LCP* 192–3).

It is through high windows rather than great bay windows that Larkin looks on an imagined paradise that 'Everyone old has dreamed of all their lives', but there is clearly more than glass between mind and world in the title poem of Larkin's final volume. Thoughts of sexual freedom give way in the final stanza of the poem to a sublime apprehension of infinitude in the 'deep blue air' that is at once immensely alluring and ultimately unattainable (*LCP* 165). For Liam Harte, this latent Romantic sublimity is a characteristic which MacNeice and Larkin share in their tentative exploration of a world seemingly devoid of meaning: 'In a number of poems they evince a remarkably similar variety of responses to desacralised existence, ranging from nihilistic despair at life's apparent meaninglessness, to humanistic endorsement of the potential value of community, to quasi-mystical affirmation of the intrinsic value of being.'[19] 'High Windows' is a resilient restatement of the underlying philosophical conviction in MacNeice's much earlier poem, 'The Window' (October 1948): 'Even at the heart of lust and conflict / We can find form, our lives transcended / While and because we live' (*CP* 312).

The enigmatic blue sky in 'High Windows' has its source in MacNeice's 'Aubade', written in November 1934. Larkin's recollection of 'newsboys crying war' in his obituary of MacNeice derives from the same poem:

Having felt with fingers that the sky is blue,
What have we after that to look forward to?

Not the twilight of the gods but a precise dawn
Of sallow and grey bricks, and newsboys crying war. (*CP* 28)

MacNeice's later 'Aubade for Infants' (July 1945) is similarly intent on subverting the romantic associations of the traditional dawn song, welcoming the breaking light of day and dispensing with the window blind: 'Snap the blind; I am not blind, / I must spy what stalks behind / Wall and window' (*CP* 270). Both poems bleed into Larkin's own imposing 'Aubade', published in the *Times Literary Supplement* just before Christmas 1977. Larkin is not as explicitly Nietzschean as

MacNeice in equating dawn with the twilight of the gods, but his conception of what we have to look forward to is every bit as disconcerting: 'total emptiness for ever, / The sure extinction that we travel to / And shall be lost in always' (*LCP* 208). The speaker's disturbingly candid contemplation of 'how / And where and when I shall myself die' echoes Edward Thomas's sombre meditation in 'Rain' ('Remembering again that I shall die'), and the deathly depiction of the sky, no longer blue but 'white as clay, with no sun' recalls Thomas Hardy's 'Neutral Tones'.[20] The overall conception, however, bears the strong imprint of MacNeice. The poem takes us from the brightening curtain-edges of a single room to the 'uncaring / Intricate rented world' in which 'telephones crouch, getting ready to ring / In locked-up offices' (*LCP* 209). The dutiful postmen who 'like doctors go from house to house' offer little more comfort and assurance than the workmen in MacNeice's 'Windowscape' (1961), in which 'Window-cleaner and postman call just once a year / And never a priest' (*CP* 554).

For over thirty years, MacNeice was a powerful and compelling influence in Larkin's poetry, never fully acknowledged in the way that Thomas Hardy and Edward Thomas were, and rarely mentioned by critics of his work. A secret taste to begin with, MacNeice became the poet against whom Larkin habitually measured his own achievements. The quelling of the Celtic fever in *The North Ship* was intended to chasten and subdue the overblown Yeatsian tendencies in Larkin's early work, but MacNeice was to prove a more potent and more enabling Celtic presence than Yeats. What MacNeice provides is perspective: a way of registering the sights and sounds of modern urban existence, of looking at the variousness of things from unexpected and unusual vantage points, but above all it is MacNeice's deep ambivalence about place and belonging that suggests to Larkin an appropriate way of thinking about identity and nationality. MacNeice's restless imaginative journeying prompts a poetry of arrivals and departures, and encourages in Larkin's writing a sense of place that is always sensitively alert to its own provisional status and its own imaginative construction. That journeying was to take on an increasingly dark, metaphysical dimension in the work of both poets, along with a sceptical but compassionate look at the desperate human endeavour 'To bring to bloom the million-petalled flower / Of being here' (*LCP* 196). It is deeply ironic, then, that Larkin's preoccupation with displacement and his troubled existentialist meditations should have been repeatedly characterised as English gentility and English empiricism. MacNeice destabilised any easy, straightforward sense of poetic tradition and showed to Larkin a way of 'Coming up England by a different line' (*LCP* 81).

THE SAME AGAIN?
MACNEICE'S REPETITIONS

Neil Corcoran

1

The enlarged edition of the excellent *Princeton Encyclopedia of Poetry and Poetics* published in 1974 makes Louis MacNeice prominent in its entry for repetition. One of the many kinds of repetition it catalogues is when the verses of a poem are linked by the repetition in the opening line of each new one of the final word of the previous one, and the example given is 'Leaving Barra'. That exquisite poem, written in 1937, was published in MacNeice's unclassifiable potboiler would-be travel book *I Crossed the Minch* in 1938, where he tells us that he did in fact write it on board the boat *Lochearn* as he left the Hebrides. The poem does what the *Encyclopedia* says it does, as the word 'island' is picked up from the first quatrain by the second, 'garbage' from the second by the third, and so on through the poem's thirteen verses, in a way musically mimetic, it seems, of the mind in progress – self-scrutinising, self-corrective, advancing hesitantly but keeping moving – while also sustaining an ear-delighting system of aural patterning.

In fact, MacNeice's systems of repetition in this poem are more varied than the encyclopedia tells us, since the poem features other kinds of repetition too: when the phrase 'phantom hunger', for instance, at the end of the fifth verse, is separated out into its parts, so that both 'hunger' and 'phantom' form end-words of lines in the next; when words are echoed within lines – 'The belief that is disbelieving' in the seventh verse, and 'Loving the rain and the rainbow' in the eighth; and when the mode of repetition that is alliteration operates in 'Wake with the knack of knowledge' in the tenth, with its sudden knock of Anglo-Saxon metre. All of the end-words of the poem's lines – 'darling', 'channel', 'taking', and 'island' in the opening verse, for instance – constitute a form of repetition too, since all fifty-two of them have trochaic feminine endings – stressed followed by unstressed syllables – a cadence presumably picked up from both words of the poem's title, 'Leaving Barra': so, you might say, a cadence inhering in the action being evoked – 'leaving' – and in the very name of the place being left, 'Barra'. And – one final repetition – the last line of all, the final ending, includes the first line of all, as the poem ends by closing its circle or eating its tail:

> The dazzle on the sea, my darling,
> Leads from the western channel,
> A carpet of brilliance taking
> My leave forever of the island.
> [...]
>
> For few are able to keep moving,
> They drag and flag in the traffic;
> While you are alive beyond question
> Like the dazzle on the sea, my darling. (*CP* 88–9)

The effect of the repeated feminine endings may be usefully glossed by what Christopher Ricks in his book *Dylan's Visions of Sin* says about comparable endings, also picked up from the proper name in the title, in Bob Dylan's great song 'The Lonesome Death of Hattie Carroll'. 'The feminine ending', Ricks says, 'naturally evokes a dying fall or courage in the face either of death or of loss, something falling poignantly away.'[1] In 'Leaving Barra' the island is falling poignantly away, as the speaker seems to realise he will never revisit it and compares its imagined ideal of existence to the reality he returns to; not, in fact, that MacNeice had much wish to revisit it since the two visits to the Hebrides which are the subject of *I Crossed the Minch* were not, according to the book's account, particularly happy ones. This was despite the fact that MacNeice was accompanied there by the painter Nancy Sharp (Coldstream) who contributed some drawings to the book. She must be the addressee of 'Leaving the Island', even though she is never included in the book's prose narrative, presumably because this was an adulterous relationship – albeit, Jon Stallworthy tells us in his biography, one conducted with her husband's agreement.

Something else, however, is also falling poignantly away, as it does in many of MacNeice's poems: that thing imagined in this poem as a 'hankering after Atlantis'. This may be a general metaphysical longing from this son of the episcopal palace, and the persistent desirability of such a mythical place is envisaged in the poem as something which might prove a quasi-Petrine betrayal of a secular humanism committed, in a now collusively ironic alliterative repetition, to 'Loving the beast and the bubble'. But this fictional, unobtainable Atlantis may also be that idea or ideal of the West which ghosts much of the sense of longing in MacNeice, since *I Crossed the Minch* makes it plain that he comes to understand in the Hebrides the depth of his alienation from the inhabitants of the Western Isles, given his inability to speak Gaelic. By implication, he must have also been realising on Barra how such incapacity cut him off too from the lives of those who continued to speak Irish in the West of Ireland.

'Leaving Barra' resolves the urgency of its longings finally into a set of 'inklings' of what might offer and sustain a scale of value distinct from the materialist one dominant in the culture of metropolitan London to which the poet is returning (and where he is just about to write probably the most notably inclusive and analytical poem of his time and its values, *Autumn Journal*). These inklings are: 'The beauty of the moon and music, / The routine courage of the worker, / The gay endurance of women.' The aestheticism of the first is unexceptionable if a little sentimental; the implicitly socialist politics – or at least leftish obeisance – of the second seems, in context, a bit *voulu* and itself negatively rather than affirmatively 'routine' in this poem of the 1930s; but the third line's celebration of women is heartfelt, genuine, and strongly declarative, possibly in large part because the poem's formal play with enduring feminine endings has prepared our ears for precisely such a declaration. In addition, the word 'gay' is striking, partly since the phrase 'gay endurance' is almost an oxymoron. The word now has specific connotations which it would almost certainly not have had for MacNeice; but it has never in fact been an easy word, as Yeats knows when he activates various connotations of it in 'Lapis Lazuli', moving from the women of his opening lines who are 'sick ... / Of poets that are always gay' to the famously ringing, if problematic, assertion that 'Hamlet and Lear are gay'. MacNeice's appreciative near-oxymoron in 'Leaving Barra' surely picks the word up from Yeats who in 'Lapis Lazuli' transfuses its initial connotations of airiness and self-indulgence – this being what the women object to in poets – with the immense stiffening of its association with the endurance of tragedy in his paradoxical line. Not long after writing 'Leaving Barra' MacNeice was to write the first

critical book on Yeats, *The Poetry of W.B. Yeats* (1941), which is still
a matchless introductory study.

If the feminine endings of 'Leaving Barra' evoke courage in the
face of loss, something falling poignantly away, they also provoke
here an image of delighted appreciation, something set determinedly
against loss, 'alive beyond question'. And both inhere in that remarkable trope which is sudden, surprising, unforgettable, and pretty
impatient of explication, as MacNeice sometimes is, when the
woman is celebrated in the poem's penultimate quatrain for 'the
example / Of living like a fugue'. What does MacNeice have in mind
here? Assuming that he means the musical form of fugue, we might
conceive of someone living like counterpointed music, I suppose, by
living with a kind of regulated, always charming variety of interest
and affect; and this might be exactly the kind of thing the celebrant
in 'Snow' of 'the drunkenness of things being various' would find
desirable in a woman – or, indeed, in anyone. And the verse repetitions of 'Leaving Barra' may themselves be thought to form an
appropriate fugal counterpoint to this theme, or even to constitute a
linguistic fugue of their own, as words are repeated with a difference:
the difference made by their new contexts, in which they sometimes
match, sometimes modify their preceding connotations.

There is also at least the possibility, though, in this instance of what
'Donegal Triptych' calls 'the glad sad poetry of departure' (*CP* 498),
this poem entitled with a 'leaving', that the word 'fugue' is ghosted
here by its use in Freudian psychoanalytic theory: the fugue as a flight
from identity which may involve travel to some unconsciously
desired locality. The poet Louis MacNeice may well find such a
thing, together with its associated repetition compulsion, almost
perversely exemplary, given that one thing you can certainly sense
being repeated in various forms in his work is that melancholy-
depressive thing conjured in the poem 'Autobiography' (written in
1940) – 'When I was five the black dreams came; / Nothing after
was quite the same' – with its dejected, even abject refrain which
itself contains a repetition, circling on itself, '*Come back early or never
come*' (*CP* 200). The MacNeicean autobiography of which this is, as
it were, the poetically distilled essence prominently includes the death
of the mother and the ensuing catastrophe of the child's forever
inconsolable distress.

In fact, 'Autobiography' can be read in terrible tandem with that
essay in which Freud analyses repetition compulsion, 'Beyond the

Pleasure Principle', where the (temporary) disappearance of the mother is assuaged by the control or revenge of the *fort / da* game in which the child's inevitable passivity in the face of loss is combated by the game's repetitions. All poetry may be read as compensatory repetition of this kind, of course, retrieving with the toy of verse what has inexorably disappeared from experience, and all poetry involves repetition, since rhythm and rhyme are themselves repetitions, and even free verse is disciplined and recognisable by the necessity that one line stop and another begin, again and again and again. Nevertheless, the chilly, minatory repetitions of the eight rhyming tetrameter couplets and the eight repeats of the tetrameter refrain in 'Autobiography' make the poem readable almost as an allegory of Freudian repetition. The couplets and refrain turn into the game of poetry the suffering before which the child was of necessity cowedly passive in life. And who is commanded by the refrain's imperative, who is being ordered to come back early or never come? Is it the mother who, by never coming, is ordered vengefully away for ever? Or is it the son himself who, by endlessly repeating the traumatic event in the repetitive game of poetry, is ordering himself never to re-enter the primal scene of his distress?

2

Both 'Leaving Barra' and 'Autobiography', then, illustrate some of the ways in which repetition at the formal or technical level is thematically, emotionally or psychologically functional in MacNeice. Many other poems underwrite the point. Some examples. There is the cascade of 'I give you's that forms a long toast in the last five stanzas of 'Train to Dublin', where the repetition is a generously cumulative expansiveness, 'turning a sentence', but also, in negative form, an explicit political refusal: 'But I will not give you any idol or idea, creed or king, / I give you the incidental things which pass / Outward through space exactly as each was' (*CP* 17). There is the woven intricacy of 'The Sunlight on the Garden', where the rhymes repeated at line-beginnings as well as line-endings, and then repeated across opening and closing verses, create a gorgeously memorable verbal music. Irony becomes virtually a principle of form here, since the attractively harmonious musicality is so threateningly apocalyptic too in the period immediately preceding the Second World War; and the poem actually envisages the time about to come as the time when music must end: 'And soon, my friend, / We shall have no time for dances' (*CP* 57). There is the phrase 'On those islands' in 'The Hebrides', also first published in *I Crossed the Minch* (where it is actually entitled 'On those islands'), which has an almost Homerically insistent reiterativeness as it opens each syntactically sinuous section of this lengthy poem, situating a topography and a culture both analytically and tenderly. There is 'It's no go' in 'Bagpipe Music', whose almost demented repetitiveness propels the poem's hurdy-gurdy rhythmic relentlessness, as if the repeated phrase has taken over the poem, the lunatic has taken over the asylum. There is the repeated opening and closing line of each stanza of 'Meeting Point', that almost archetypal MacNeicean love poem of enraptured mutuality, beginning 'Time was away and somewhere else', and closing 'Time was away and she was here' (*CP* 183–4). The device, working almost like a series of variant refrains, poignantly but also proudly establishes the separate togetherness of lovers, isolated in a crowd, and the distinction between the time they spend together and ordinary, quotidian time. In verse after verse of 'Meeting Point' the repeated lines meet pointedly, enclosing an ecstasy.

'What will you have, my dear? The same again?' asks the drinker, repeatedly, in 'Homage to Clichés', that very artful poem in which MacNeice writes virtually a knowing meta-poem on this aspect of his work. The poem celebrates 'the automatic, the reflex, the cliché of velvet' as the source of erotic allure but also of panic at what it calls 'finality'. It rings the changes through its eighty-two lines on a tiny cluster of images associated with fish, cat, and bell until finality encroaches inexorably on temporality, reminding us too how the inexorable is also, always, necessarily, an aspect of refrain:

> Somewhere behind us stands a man, a counter
> A timekeeper with a watch and a pistol
> Ready to shoot and with his shot destroy
> This whole delightful world of cliché and refrain –
> What will you have, my dear? The same again? (*CP* 68)

In the delightful world of cliché and refrain, having the same again seems both an avoidance of the knowledge of death, and an inevitable confrontation with it: both at once, the same again. Woven into the very fabric of cliché and refrain is the knowledge of termination; and poems employing metre, 'numbers', and rhyme are always 'counters' too as they count their stresses or construct their rhyme schemes. In this sense all poems are about time and its passing. It seems wholly characteristic of MacNeice that his figure for this should be the invitation to have another drink; you have to get one in of course before time is called. That often only artificially intimate bonhomie may hide an abyss; and it is a figure inspired, probably, by the seasoned drinker's (alcoholic's?) knowledge that, where drinking is concerned, repetition may lead all too literally to death.

3

That repetition is the same again but the same again with a difference is the ambiguous knowledge plotted into MacNeice's extensive use of the 'delightful' device of refrain. A few examples. In his obituary for MacNeice Philip Larkin says, approvingly, that his lyricism and musicality as a poet were sometimes akin to those of popular song-writers.[2] He could, Larkin thinks, have written 'These Foolish Things'; and in fact games with assonance and internal rhyme, often very witty ones indeed, are probably more characteristic of writers of the classic American songbook such as Cole Porter and Ira Gershwin than they are of conventional poets. MacNeice does write a kind of would-be popular song in 'Swing-song', a poem written in the character of what it calls 'a wartime working girl' in a deafening machine shop. The poem's refrain is her figuring to herself of the way her bomber pilot 'young man' talks on his intercom:

> So there's no one in the world, I sometimes think,
> Such a wallflower as I
> For I must talk to myself on the ground
> While he is talking to his friends in the sky:
>   K for Kitty calling P for Prue ...
>   Bomb Doors Open ...
>   Over to You. (*CP* 223)

The three-line refrain here takes the sharpness of its edge from the fact that her bereft loneliness must cope with the way the code-names of his 'friends' – his fellow bomber pilots, or their aircraft – are gendered as female and, of course, from the way the innocently girlish diminutives Kitty and Prue disguise and contrast with the murderous nature of the bombing raids being undertaken in which, no doubt, other working girls talking to themselves on the ground will be horribly killed and mutilated. In an introduction to his radio plays in 1947 MacNeice says of the writer lucky enough to be involved in a radio production of his own work that he cannot get 'more closely in touch with his work-in-performance than he can be anywhere else unless he is Mr Noel Coward'.[3] This seems both admiring and a little envious of a popular singer-songwriter. If MacNeice could have written 'These Foolish Things', however, maybe Coward could have written 'Swing-song', and it would have been excellent to have had a musical setting and accompaniment for MacNeice's words.

Then there is 'Babel' in *Springboard* (1944) which could be said to have, in a way appropriate to its title, three refrains; or – an alternative way of regarding it – it is, most unusually, a poem which has more refrain than verse. The three repeated lines – 'There was a tower that went before a fall', 'Can't we ever, my love, speak in the same language?' and 'Have we no aims in common?' – are all bent around the remaining seven lines in four rhyming quatrains (*CP* 227). The poem therefore seems a lot like a villanelle, in a structure which is not at all that of a villanelle. The result is a kind of stuck-in-the-groove monotony, an inability either to communicate or to advance an argument. This is the point of a poem which, as far as the relationship between its lovers is concerned, might be regarded as an out-of-love poem, the repetitive refrains as functional as a gagging in the throat. Yet the ramifying repetitions also insist that the personal babel the lovers manage to create by their linguistic confusions, evasions, and misunderstandings becomes quickly a public and political linguistic hell too, as 'Patriots, dreamers, die-hards, theoreticians, all, / … go, still quarrelling over words, to the wall' (*CP* 228), where the cliché is disturbingly electrified so that going to the wall while still quarrelling is not just registering a willingness to go to the ultimate point of an argument but facing a firing squad for one's contrarian beliefs. Repetition is itself hell here, and the poem hideously makes a kind of satanic reversal of Christ's consolatory insistence that where two or three are gathered together there he will be also. In MacNeice's 'Babel', on the contrary, 'The more there are together, Togetherness recedes'. Formal repetition in 'Babel' is therefore an instruction in the alienatingly recessive ability of human beings to be together at all, ever, in any state of harmony; and the MacNeice of such poems is no distance at all from the Larkin for whom, in 'Wants', 'Beneath it all, desire of oblivion runs' (*LCP* 42).

Then there is the just-posthumous book *The Burning Perch* (1963), a volume much given to thematic repetitions and returns of various kinds: to MacNeice's own childhood, certainly, but also, as Peter McDonald has demonstrated in *Louis MacNeice: The Poet in his Contexts*, to the ghosts of 'the poet MacNeice once was'. Among so much returning and repeating, refrain in this volume becomes destabilised, self-deconstructing, and altogether anxiety-inducing. 'The Taxis', written in 1961, is paradigmatic:

> In the first taxi he was alone tra-la,
> No extras on the clock. He tipped ninepence
> But the cabby, while he thanked him, looked askance
> As though to suggest someone had bummed a ride.
>
> In the second taxi he was alone tra-la
> But the clock showed sixpence extra; he tipped according
> And the cabby from out his muffler said: 'Make sure
> You have left nothing behind tra-la between you.'
>
> In the third taxi he was alone tra-la
> But the tip-up seats were down and there was an extra
> Charge of one-and-sixpence and an odd
> Scent that reminded him of a trip to Cannes.
>
> As for the fourth taxi, he was alone
> Tra-la when he hailed it but the cabby looked
> Through him and said: 'I can't tra-la well take
> So many people, not to speak of the dog.' (*CP* 583)

Strictly, 'tra-la' in that poem, occurring once or twice in each of four quatrains which all figure a taxi ride of vertiginous, even uncanny eeriness, is not really a refrain. It is a 'repetend', a term defined by the *Princeton Encyclopedia* as 'a recurring word, phrase or line. As distinguished from refrain, repetend usually refers to a repetition occurring irregularly rather than regularly in a poem, or to a partial rather than a complete repetition.' But 'tra-la' is not really a word or a phrase or a line: it is a sort of interrupted or fragmentary musical phrase. The phrase is usually taken to be 'tra-la-la', although it does in fact feature famously in Nanki Poo's solo, 'The flowers that bloom in the spring tra-la', in *The Mikado*, and MacNeice the admirer of popular song may even have had Gilbert's lyric and Sullivan's music in mind when he wrote the poem. The fact that it seems inter-rupted, however, or fragmentary, and is spoken, not sung, makes for a dead weight, a dead hand, and a dead echo in the poem, as the repe-tend moves from the end of the opening lines of the first three stanzas, where we might at least expect to find it (and do find it of course in Gilbert and Sullivan), to the disconcerting mid-final line of the second stanza and the opening of the second line of the final stanza ('As for the fourth taxi, he was alone / Tra-la when he hailed it ...'). These repetitions include its final appearance in the taxi driver's quoted speech – '"I can't tra-la well take / So many people, not to speak of the dog."' – where it may be intended, it seems to me, as a print euphemism for the now outraged 'I can't fucking well take ...' That the repeated 'tra-la' – spondaic, unsung, and in print – is actu-ally hard to voice is apparent when we remember the opening of *A Portrait of the Artist as a Young Man*. The linguistic hornpipe danced there has its rhythm completed:

> Tralalala lala
> Tralala tralaladdy
> Tralala lala
> Tralala lala

But 'tra-la'? Its musical inertia is a function of the wryly skewed black comedy being enacted in the poem: skewed, maybe, in the way a taxi driver's neck is skewed to look back at you, or through you. It is also more black, probably, than comic, even though a large part of the poem's memorability has to do with its spooky unresolvedness of tone, and the concluding dog is a joke, certainly, self-reflexively suggesting that the poem is something of a shaggy dog story bathet-ically lacking a punchline.

'The Taxis' may, however, owe something to the taxi rides which conclude Elizabeth Bowen's *The Death of the Heart* and 'The Demon Lover'. At the end of *The Death of the Heart* the much put-upon servant Matchett is put into a taxi without knowing its destination and has to endure the vaguely threatening hostility of its driver; and at the end of the truly terrifying wartime story 'The Demon Lover', which is much taken up with repetitions of a sadistic and masochistic kind, the terrified Mrs Drover is driven off by a taxi driver who appears to be the ghost of her lover long since killed in the First World

War: he may be driving her to a loathsome shared eternity. Certainly, the more they are compelled to be together, as this taxi recedes, the more Togetherness will recede too. Not only the uncanny element of 'The Taxis' but also its hallucinatory cinematic quality is shared with Bowen's story, one of her greatest.[4]

The deconstructed refrain 'tra-la' in 'The Taxis' seems to do the opposite of what the *OED* tells us the musical phrase 'tra-la-la' should do: be expressive of gaiety or joy. It trivialises the taxi occupant's predicament while also sinisterly emphasising it. He is of no consequence, tra-la, but being of no consequence is his predicament, he who seems to have several selves but is still looked through as if, transparently, he has none. This crisis of identity and high pitch of anxiety can be read under the rubric of various kinds of existential predicament; and the taxi driver's presumptuous authoritativeness is forbiddingly judgmental and discountenancing. MacNeice certainly picks up here, as Bowen does too, on what can sometimes be the all too real anxiety of taking a taxi alone, especially in a strange place. It is, after all, one of the very few situations in which you voluntarily place yourself under the total control of someone completely unknown.[5]

Given the parabolic nature of some of MacNeice's late poems, however, it is also feasible, I think, to read 'The Taxis' as a representation of what a poet might become in his or her poems, dissolved – sometimes, it must seem, unnervingly and discountenancingly, even uncannily – into language, and then into the opinions and interpretations of reviewers and critics. 'The Taxis' may even be glossed by what MacNeice wittily but almost tauntingly says about himself as poet in *The Poetry of W.B. Yeats*, discussing the Crazy Jane poems, those poems which also prominently employ refrain and seem in some oblique ways related to these parable poems of MacNeice's. MacNeice evidences there what might seem almost a postmodern conception of identity, were it not that so much that has been classified as 'postmodern' is actually a feature of the 'modern' too: 'If you know what my whole self and my only self is, you know a lot more than I do. As far as I can make out, I not only have many different selves but I am often, as they say, not myself at all' (*PY* 146). Not myself at all; or, the same again?

With appropriate finality, MacNeice's last published poem, 'Coda', written in 1962 and published as the final poem in *The Burning Perch*, is a perfectly pitched exercise in the repetitive:

Maybe we knew each other better
When the night was young and unrepeated
And the moon stood still over Jericho.

So much for the past; in the present
There are moments caught between heart-beats
When maybe we know each other better.

But what is that clinking in the darkness?
Maybe we shall know each other better
When the tunnels meet beneath the mountain. (*CP* 610)

The repeat here is very much a repetition with variation – 'Maybe we knew each other better', 'When maybe we know each other better', 'Maybe we shall know each other better'. Past, present, and future are all rendered uncertain and unstable by that slippery, repeated, Janus-faced adverb of contingency, expressive of both possibility and regret, 'maybe'. And there is variation too in the positioning of the repeat across the poem's three tercets – opening line in the first, closing line in the second, middle line in the third. This is a wavering of positioning – maybe – to reflect the wavering uncertainty of the thought. And the poem's title is also waveringly uncertain. Is this poem a coda to the volume *The Burning Perch*, or is it a coda to the relationship being represented in its ruminative address? (It can certainly be read as a coda to 'Babel'.) The relationship is not exactly over, clearly, despite the title, but it has never been engaged wholly successfully either, it appears, since mutual knowledge is speculative even at the point of apparent origin when, significantly, things were 'unrepeated'. The mysterious suggestiveness of the poem's final lines – 'Maybe we shall know each other better / When the tunnels meet beneath the mountain' – is apparently inspired by the building of the Mont Blanc tunnel which was still uncompleted at the time of the poem's writing. The image conjures therefore an indefinitely postponed insecurity about another 'meeting point'. This poem of repetitions, by including in the second line of its first tercet the word 'unrepeated', seems held in tension by the consideration that repetition itself may be the coda to relationship, that repetition may be a living death.

4

And indeed the quick poetic liveliness of repetition, refrain, and repetend in MacNeice – even when, as in 'The Taxis', the repetend is being more emotionally (but not poetically) deadly than lively – may be one way in which this poet defies what his work frequently finds wearyingly repetitive: that is, the actual, unavoidable routines of ordinary living. Louis MacNeice's poetry sometimes conveys a strong sense of staving off boredom. One of his major figures for this is that of the parrot; who, of course, can only copy and repeat what he hears. *Autumn Sequel* opens with such a bird, in a perhaps mimetically garrulous hypermetric line: 'August. Render to Caesar. Speak parrot: a gimmick for Poll'; and several lines further on, the bird appears again, dignified, or mock-dignified, with an initial capital: 'the Parrot is loose on the world / Clapping his trap with gay but meaningless wings' (*CP* 373). Clapping his trap, the Parrot must be beating with his wings a device once known as a 'claptrap' and now usually known simply as a clapper, in order to applaud himself narcissistically: but he is also speaking claptrap, whose meaning has varied from 'cheap, showy sentiment' to its current almost exclusive use for nonsense or rubbish. This claptrapping Parrot appears also to trick out the parrot of John Skelton's scathing fifteenth-century satirical poem 'Speke Parrot' – a poem much admired by poets of the 1930s – with the modern plumage of Yeats's 'The Second Coming'. The Parrot 'loose on the world' evokes but also renders bathetic the 'rough beast' apocalyptically 'loosed upon the world' in that poem, offering a preposterous bird in a state of purposeless unrestraint ('loose') in place of a terrifyingly indeterminate animal all too determined in its malevolence ('loosed').

It has always seemed to me that, at the beginning of *Autumn Sequel*, a very long poem with a Dantean shape, this figure of MacNeice's which aligns fifteenth-century Skeltonic satirical invective with quasi-Yeatsian apocalyptic modernity had at least the potential to become one of the great modern poetic figurations, one of the great modernist intertexts. So it is a distressing irony that the poetic repetitions of *Autumn Sequel* are so jejune compared with some of those I have been discussing, seeming as they do so often mechanical or flaccid rather than thematically, emotionally or symbolically functional or telling. Notably, the brilliant repetitiveness of the rhetoric of *Autumn Journal* with its hammering polysyndeton – the word 'And' repeated propulsively again and again and again – is replaced by the inert, inexpertly managed derivativeness of the repetitions of *terza rima* in *Autumn Sequel*; and the poem is, as a consequence, no true sequel at all but hypertrophic succession. MacNeice in fact appears to make his own damningly accurate self-assessment of this in Canto V: that 'the Muse has defaulted // And left me an apparatus, rivet and link, / With nothing to link or rivet' (*CP* 392). After such self-knowledge, the reader might well ask, what forgiveness for allowing the poetic enterprise to extend for a further twenty-one cantos? MacNeice had undoubtedly mistaken himself and is, at least over this distance, neither a satirical nor mythological poet.

Still, the richly accoutred parrot of *Autumn Sequel* returns, maybe, even if a little the worse for wear, in 'Budgie', the poem from which the title of *The Burning Perch* derives. Given that the Yeats of 'The Second Coming' is part of the Parrot's generation, this bird figures in the appropriately apocalyptic context of what appear to be intimations of nuclear catastrophe. The caged budgie once again narcissistically stares into its mirror in the poem, repeating '*Let me attitudinize, / Let me attitudinize, let me attitudinize*', 'Its voice a small I Am', 'peep[ing] like a television / Actor admiring himself in the monitor' while his perch burns as 'the human / Race recedes and dwindles, the giant / Reptiles cackle in their graves, the mountain / Gorillas exchange their final messages' (*CP* 602). MacNeice's poetic repetitions may be regarded as engaged in a tacit battle with this kind of parroting narcissism – with *psittacism* indeed, from the Greek for parrot, *psittakos*: 'the mechanical repetition of previously received ideas or images that reflects neither true reasoning nor feeling', as the *OED* puts it, with an almost Leavisian disdain.[6] MacNeice also realises that poetry itself may be psittacism, an inertly parroting kind of repetition of various masters' voices; and Derek Mahon has provocatively suggested that we read 'Budgie' as 'perhaps … a satire on the poetic vocation'.[7] A satire on the poetic vocation, maybe; but possibly also a self-lacerating satire on one potential of MacNeice's own work: its tendency to prolixity, the tendency which, as we have seen, he himself castigates *Autumn Sequel* for indulging, even while he is in the very act of continuing to write it, and its propensity to indulge a merely journalistic image or impulse, or to purvey what Tom Paulin once memorably called a 'throwaway lyricism'.[8] Although these are temptations which MacNeice's most memorable and enduring work seems almost self-chastisingly to cast itself clear of, with disciplined resourcefulness, both parrot and budgie are self-inclusive too in the inclusivity of their figurations.

5

Louis MacNeice is manifestly aware, then, of what is at issue, and also of what he risks, in repetition; but he spells it out in *The Poetry of W.B. Yeats* when he discusses refrain in the Crazy Jane poems (*PY* 145–8). In the twentieth century, he says, refrain has been in many circles for a long time under taboo, considered merely decorative or sentimental, regarded as nothing but 'a rhetorical seductiveness'. The epithet 'rhetorical' here picks up what Yeats famously opposes to the argument with oneself which constitutes poetry: the argument with others which constitutes rhetoric. This prejudiced taboo, MacNeice insists, with a tacit allusion now to Eliot, 'is based on the assumption that a complex, unmusical world demands – in all cases – a complex, unmusical poetry – an assumption which Yeats never makes'. It is an assumption which MacNeice never makes either. Even so, it is worth saying that MacNeice's refrains never sound at all like Yeats's. Those of other poets of the 1930s sometimes do. This, for instance, from a poem of 1935: 'Cried the cripples to the silent statue, / The six beggared cripples'. Not the later W.B. Yeats, not even the W.B. Yeats of the Crazy Jane poems published in 1932, but the earlier W.H. Auden, in 'Song of the Beggars' from the 'Twelve Songs' of 1936.[9]

When MacNeice says that Yeats had 'a quite child-like liking for the simple poetry of the folk type', particularly Irish folk song and street ballad (and, we might add, nursery rhyme), he is also talking about himself, I think, and in his critical writing elsewhere he makes it plain that for him sentimentality is a danger the poet ought to risk. He also defends his use of the word 'vulgarity' as a term of approbation: poetry should be of the *vulgus*, of the crowd. MacNeice believes this despite his very firm objections to the view of Irish poetry expounded by F.R. Higgins in the 1939 BBC radio dialogue published as 'Tendencies in Modern Poetry' and made prominent more recently by Paul Muldoon as the 'prologue' to his *Faber Book of Contemporary Irish Poetry* in 1986. Lurking in Higgins's conception of the 'magic' of Irish poetry MacNeice finds a reprehensible, dangerously sentimental form of nationalistic 'race-consciousness'.[10] There is a principled, democratising, anti-authoritarian impulse in this discrimination of MacNeice's in favour of a form of vulgarity which never courts opportunistic populism. His modernism, for all that it opposes a preening psittacism of modernity, is equally untempted by modernist hauteur of the Eliotic or Poundian varieties, however indebted MacNeice's practice is, in some of its forms, to an Eliotic model. This is a further reason why his satirical, mythological Parrot never gets very far off the ground in *Autumn Sequel*. Successful modernist myth in poetry (as opposed to prose, where *Ulysses* is always the counter-example) seems to demand hauteur of the patrician and varyingly reactionary variety. Scandalously, perhaps, such hauteur is rich with poetic possibility: but there is very little in MacNeice that can rise, or stoop, to such occasions. In *Autumn Sequel*, to his credit but unfortunately not greatly to the credit of the poetry, he is all too easily distracted from detraction.

In his critical essays MacNeice sometimes admires the ways in which repetition and refrain can bring to what would otherwise be mere flux the structure of an architectonic; and we should read MacNeice's own practice in the light of this. Indeed, if we substitute for the notion of flux something of what inheres in MacNeice's conception of psittacism – the parrot's mechanical, repetitive, vain, narcissistic preenings as a function and outstanding feature of modernity – then the repetitions of his own poems, which acknowledge old cultural continuities, affiliations, and attachments, become a mode of critique. In his prose MacNeice also understands poetry as developing from the desire to combine accessible communication and some kind of ritual. Poetry as communication, not solipsism, is a form of hostility to some of the kinds of modernism which developed from symbolism: but the concept of ritual returns the element of symbolist or modernist magic or metaphysic to the communicative act, slyly retrieving with the left hand what the right has appeared to give away.

Communication made very strange to itself by surface ritual is one way of regarding two late poems of MacNeice's which actually take repetition as preoccupation and theme, 'Reflections' in his penultimate volume *Solstices* (1961) and 'Soap Suds' in *The Burning Perch*.

In the former, in a kind of apotheosis of the imagery of mirror and window which figures so significantly elsewhere too in MacNeice and, as we have seen, in 'Budgie', the mirror repeats the image of the self already mirrored in the window of the room (*CP* 561). In this dizzyingly multiple reflectivity the self becomes uncannily self-estranged: to the point, indeed, of being able to recognise itself only in its self-estrangement. It becomes even surrealistically self-estranged, since the poem's image of 'standing back to my back' recalls and may remember Magritte's painting *La réproduction interdite* (1937) and its representation of the terrifying depersonalisation involved in looking into a mirror and seeing there the back of your own head and shoulders: turning away from yourself, giving yourself the cold shoulder. The repeated reflections of this extraordinarily, even syntactically, reflexive and self-reflexive poem bring the idea of the self to a point of comparably radical destabilisation. They also bring the writer at his desk to an impossible and unsustainable position; since, in the poem's final lines, his reflection reverses his writing right hand to make him left-handed and he is unable to write at all. He becomes therefore a writer unable to 'reflect' any further, at least in writing; and the poem's reflections culminate in a form of writerly self-deconstruction.

'Soap Suds' (*CP* 577) repeats through the agency of smell the child's experience in the adult's, a 'return' in memory effected by a very delicately managed quasi-cinematic dissolve and then by a brilliantly speedy linguistic fast-forward. Self-reflexively too, the poem actually uses the word 'dissolves' as it evokes a long since completed game of croquet. The far-off moment of childhood returns to the adult by way of the recollected smell of soap while he is washing his hands. Washing his hands of what, though? The poem catalogues the 'joys' of the big house he visited when he was eight, where he played the recalled croquet game: but it fixes on, or is fixated on, an adult voice crying 'Play!' The first time the voice does so, in the third verse, it does so neutrally, with no qualifying adjective: but when it does so again in the next verse and once again in the final one the voice is 'angry' and it cries from the grass of a croquet lawn now grown impossibly 'head-high'. It is anger that survives in the ageing memory, then, not joy, and an anger all the more disconcerting for the lack of specification of its origin or motive. 'But the ball is lost and the mallet slipped long since from the hands / Under the running tap that are not the hands of the child': the loss, the slippage, the repetition, and the return may recall once more the game or the 'play' of 'Beyond the Pleasure Principle'. The poem retrieves the moment but still says to the moment, '*Come back early or never come*'; and some of MacNeice's most powerful poems are those in which the past returns to shadow or even dominate the present, without mercy and without release.

THE SEAL AND THE CAT

Nick Laird

Introducing his own reading of MacNeice's poems, Alan Bennett recounts an anecdote from Stephen Spender about him; how, when Russia entered the war in 1941, the ambassador to Russia, Sir Archibald Clark Kerr, thought he should give a party for British poets to put them into contact with their Soviet counterparts. Throughout this party MacNeice, dark, sleek, and expressionless, leant against the chimneypiece, glass in hand, looking infinitely removed from his colleagues. At the end of the party, Clark Kerr went up to him and said, 'Is it true that you were brought up in Carrickfergus?' 'Yes, it is,' MacNeice replied. 'Ah,' said Clark Kerr, 'then that confirms a legend I have long heard, that centuries ago a race of seals invaded that coast and interbred with the population. Good night.'

Bennett tells the story as a slight takedown of MacNeice, as if the Irishman gets his pedigree and comeuppance from the English diplomat. The tale is meant to illustrate MacNeice's lack of clubba-bility – if that's the right word to use in connection with seals – but the point I take from it is that MacNeice, like the seal, moved in many worlds but was wholly at home in none of them. The seal, though a mammal, is in a sense amphibious, and can survive on land and in water, if not completely adapted for either. MacNeice's child-hood in Ireland, 'born to the Anglican order', and his subsequent education and adulthood in England, created a persona who was from somewhere but not *of* it, and he lived everywhere as a foreigner, a few degrees removed. His aloofness is the consequence of never quite fitting in.

Every adolescent feels that, of course, and when I first read MacNeice I responded to that implicit detachment and drift in him. Didn't Eliot somewhere describe him as a solitary cat out for a walk? (And note MacNeice's over-identification with that animal. In the minor epic 'The Death of a Cat' what is effectively eulogised is the 'self-contained life', *CP* 361.)

But, to re-begin: I grew up in Cookstown and from early on, I knew that poetry was something I was interested in. The town had no bookshop and once a month or so my family would head up to Belfast to go shopping: I would get dropped off in the morning at the Waterstones bookshop near Castlecourt and then picked up there in the afternoon. I'd sit in the poetry section and work my way through the books. I discovered lots of writers like that – and one of the most important to me was MacNeice.

He gets you at first with that conversational immediate tone: 'I do not want to be reflective anymore, / Envying and despising unreflective things ...' ('Wolves', CP 26). His language has a surface loveliness, and after the grey shadows and dour demeanours of the rectory in Carrickfergus, the work revels in shimmer and gloss. There are scores of examples but I think immediately of the sea like 'a carpet of brilliance' in 'Leaving Barra', or the exoticised colours in 'Flowers in the Interval', 'onyx and cantaloupe, / Wet seaweed, lizard, lilac, tiger-moth ...' (CP 88, 368).

MacNeice also represented an engagement with the wider world, with Spain, and America, and politics and war. It was exciting to realise that poetry could do these things, could be a living commentary. And for me also, the complex relationship with Ireland that MacNeice had was crucial. It certainly did not mirror my own relationship with home in any way, but it complicated the picture, and seemed to allow varieties of Irishness beyond, say, W.F. Marshall or Padraic Fiacc or Yeats. And I identified with his frustration with Ireland. Growing up in Mid-Ulster in the eighties and early nineties, you were subject to certain received narratives, from your school or the church or the news, and MacNeice challenged those. I felt his disenfranchisement: lines like, of Dublin, 'This was never my town ...' and all the *Odi atque amo* stuff directed towards Ireland in *Autumn Journal*. MacNeice made it okay to be yourself, and he made it okay to be immensely angry. I think I read his Irish poems as almost like contemporary commentary on what we were then living through.

He is also, sometimes, funny, and he's always a great love poet. I remember being both shocked and delighted by that line in his early poem 'Mayfly', 'I want always to be near your breasts' (CP 32). He has a seductive voice, he charms: 'Were it not that scratching your elbow you are too lovely by half' ('Déjà Vu', CP 578). But it is his refusal to be taken in by big ideas that marks him out for me as one of the most significant voices in the century. He resisted nationalism and communism, even when the majority of his friends and contemporaries were signing up as fellow-travellers. I liked most his intolerance to intolerance, his anger at sloganeering, at the 'mass production of neat thoughts'. He understood the complexity of existence and, to go back to the anecdote of the seal, he celebrates that necessarily amphibious state of life – to be apart and be a part, to be both an individual and also a component of the world.

And MacNeice had an ability to live in contradictory states, and write out of them. One thinks of the ambiguities in that line from the celebrated 'Snow', 'There is more than glass between the snow and the huge roses' (*CP* 24). The word 'between' takes on the work of both joining (there is something – a connection – between them) and dividing (there is something – a barrier – between them).

So what do these things add up to for a young person who is interested in poetry? They enable you, and they provoke you, and they provide touchstones of phrases and new slants on the world. For me, MacNeice expanded the possibilities of language, and therefore of thought.

NOTES

PREFACE

1   Peter McDonald, *Serious Poetry* (Oxford: Oxford University Press, 2002), 186.

2   Alan Gillis, interviewed by Aaron Kelly, *Edinburgh Review* 131 (March 2011), 8–9.

3   Philip Larkin, *Further Requirements*, ed. Anthony Thwaite (London: Faber, 2001), 18.

THE PITY OF IT ALL

1   Wilfred Owen, *The Complete Poems and Fragments, II: The Manuscripts and Fragments*, ed. Jon Stallworthy (London: Chatto & Windus, Hogarth Press, and Oxford University Press, 1983), 535.

2   W.B. Yeats, Introduction to *The Oxford Book of Modern Verse 1892–1935* (Oxford: Clarendon Press, 1936), xxxiv.

3   Peter Allt and Russell K. Alspach, eds, *The Variorum Edition of the Poems of W.B. Yeats* (Basingstoke: Macmillan, 1957), 119.

4   W.H. Auden, *The English Auden: Poems, Essays, and Dramatic Writings 1927–1939*, ed. Edward Mendelson (London: Faber, 1977), 207.

5   'Later I visited my mother in hospital and she offered me a box of chocolates. Something evil came up in me – I knew it to be evil, although it was quite different from the wrong-doings for which I was going to Hell – and I refused to take the box. I wanted the chocolates very much and also I wanted to be gracious to my mother, but some-thing or other made me spite myself and her and stand there surly and refuse. When I got home the box was there (someone had brought it back furtively) and I was filled with remorse ...', *The Strings are False* (London: Faber, 1965), 42–3.

6   Thomas Ken, 'All Praise to Thee, my God, this Night', *A Morning, Evening and Midnight Hymn* (London, [1703]), 4–5.

7   T.S. Eliot, 'Shakespeare and the Stoicism of Seneca', *Selected Essays* (London: Faber, 1951), 130.

8   *The Faerie Queene*, ed. A.C. Hamilton (Harlow: Longman, 1977), 394.

MEMOIRS

1   Dan MacNeice, who spent his later life in New Jersey, wrote 'That Was Then, This Is Now' in November 1987. Subtitled 'Autobiography of Daniel J. MacNeice', this memoir was sparked by the requirement of an adoption agency, to which he and his second wife Charlotte were

applying (successfully, as it proved), that prospective adoptive parents should supply personal data relevant to how they would approach parenting. For Dan, this became more than an official exercise. Shortly before he died (in January 2009), he revised the piece and wrote two further brief memoirs. One of these, 'A Grandson's Memories of Bishop's House', appears as the second section of 'Memoir'. A few details from the second, a biographical sketch of 'Mary (Ezra) MacNeice (1908–1991)', have been inserted in 'That Was Then', which has been edited and abridged by Edna Longley.

PURE FORM, IMPURE POETRY, AND LOUIS MACNEICE'S LETTERS
1 Bolingbroke, 9 April 1730. Quoted in Frank and Anita Kermode, eds, *Oxford Book of Letters* (Oxford: Oxford University Press, 1995), xvii.
2 Peter McDonald, *Louis MacNeice: The Poet in his Contexts* (Oxford: Clarendon Press, 1991), 40.
3 MacNeice to Eleanor Clark, 6 December 1940. Unpublished letter, *Clark Papers*, Beinecke Rare Book and Manuscript Library, Yale University.
4 W.B. Yeats, 'A General Introduction for My Work', *Essays and Introductions* (London: Macmillan, 1961), 509.
5 *The Variorum Edition of the Poems of W.B.Yeats*, ed. P. Allt and Russell K. Alspach (New York: Macmillan, 1957), 576.
6 See *Time Was Away: The World of Louis MacNeice*, ed. Terence Brown and Alec Reid (Dublin: Dolmen Press, 1974), 35.
7 Blunt, 'Some Aspects of Modern Art', *Heretick* 1 (March 1924), 11; quoted in McDonald, *Louis MacNeice*, 41.
8 MacNeice to Clark, 19 November 1939, unpublished, *Yale*.
9 MacNeice to Clark, 17 April 1940, second letter, unpublished, *Yale*.
10 MacNeice to Clark, 25 May 1939, unpublished, *Yale*.

'I WILL ACQUIRE AN ATTITUDE NOT YOURS': WAS FREDERICK MACNEICE A HOME RULER AND WHY DOES THIS MATTER?
1 I have chosen the forename Frederick rather than John since the latter name seems almost never to have been used in his signature until his elevation to the bench of bishops in 1931 (though John alone appears on the birth certificate). His lifelong alternation between the initials 'F.J.' and 'J.F.' is notorious, exhibiting a family disposition to live uncomfortably with any particular name: see Jon Stallworthy, *Louis MacNeice* (London: Faber, 1995), 5. In the notes that follow, father and son are referred to respectively as 'FM' and 'LM'.
2 See, for example, Terence Brown, 'MacNeice: Father and Son', in Terence Brown and Alec Reid, eds, *Time Was Away: The World of Louis MacNeice* (Dublin: Dolmen Press, 1974), 21–34 (23); Brown, *Louis MacNeice: Sceptical Vision* (Dublin: Gill & Macmillan, 1975), 8–10; Adolphe Haberer, *Louis MacNeice, 1907–1963: L'homme et la poésie* (Talence: Presses Universitaires de Bordeaux, 1986), 15; Edna Longley,

Louis MacNeice: A Study (London: Faber, 1988), 19, 22; Longley, '"Defending Ireland's Soul": Protestant Writers and Irish Nationalism after Independence', in Longley, *The Living Stream: Literature and Revisionism in Ireland* (Newcastle upon Tyne: Bloodaxe, 1994), 130–49 (131); William T. McKinnon, *Apollo's Blended Dream: A Study of the Poetry of Louis MacNeice* (Oxford: Oxford University Press, 1971), 9–10; Seán McMahon, 'A Heart that Leaps to a Fife Band: The Irish Poems of Louis MacNeice', *Éire–Ireland* 11.4 (1967), 126–39 (129–31); Robin Marsack, *The Cave of Making: The Poetry of Louis MacNeice* (Oxford: Clarendon Press, 1982), 1; Stallworthy, *MacNeice*, 34. Among the few critics who have examined Frederick MacNeice's influence on Louis *without* the explicit attribution of nationalist sentiments are Peter McDonald, *Louis MacNeice: The Poet in his Contexts* (Oxford: Clarendon Press, 1991) and McKinnon, in his enigmatic but suggestive reappraisal of 'The Rector's Son' in *The Honest Ulsterman* 73 (1983), 34–54.

3   By a family account summarised in Stallworthy, *MacNeice*, 5, a fracas in Claddaghduff on 23 March 1879 led immediately to the 'flight from Omey': 'The following night, friends of the MacNeices brought a coach to the mainland side of Omey strand, and William, Alice, and their eight children were driven the sixty miles to Galway and put onto the Dublin train.' In reality, William Lindsay MacNeice appears to have departed alone, leaving his family in a state of siege on the island for several months. For full documentation, see David Fitzpatrick, *Solitary and Wild: Frederick MacNeice and the Salvation of Ireland* (Dublin: Lilliput Press, 2011).

4   Louis MacNeice, *Zoo* (London: Michael Joseph, 1938), 80.

5   Elizabeth Nicholson, 'Trees were Green', in Brown and Reid, eds, *Time Was Away*, 11–20 (15). In *The Strings are False* (London: Faber, 1965), however, LM claims that 'remembering my father and Home Rule, I said I thought Carson was a pity', when challenged for his views by a 'tipsy American soldier' on a train in spring 1919 (71). He also recalls having 'heard political arguments' before the Great War, which 'were all about Orangemen and Home Rulers' (53). Elizabeth's sensitive and detailed recollections of her parents and brother stop short of attributing nationalism to Frederick, while stating that 'his political opinions differed widely' from those of 'the Northern people whom he served' (14).

6   Christopher Fauske, *'Side by side in a small country': Bishop John Frederick MacNeice and Ireland* (Newtownabbey: Church of Ireland Historical Society, 2004), 4.

7   FM, *Carrickfergus and Its Contacts: Some Chapters in the History of Ulster* (Belfast: Mayne, 1928), 70, 75. Publication was preceded by full weekly serialisation (in a prominent position and an unusually large font) in the *Carrickfergus Advertiser*, 27 January to 29 June 1928.

8   See, for example, George Rutherford, 'John Frederick MacNeice', in *Carrickfergus and District Historical Journal* 7 (1993), 38–46; Stallworthy, *MacNeice*, especially 34–7, 172–4; Fauske, *'Side by side'*.

9   *Carrickfergus Advertiser*, 6, 20 September 1912.

10 *Carrickfergus Advertiser*, 4 October 1912; quoted in Stallworthy, *MacNeice*, 35, and in many other studies.

11 FM, *Carrickfergus*, 72. The Covenant was, however, signed by Frederick's curate, Robert Newett Morrison, and by the two Presbyterian Ministers at nearby Woodburn: Ulster Covenant, signature sheets (online), PRONI (Public Record Office of Northern Ireland).

12 Nicholson, 'Trees were Green', 15.

13 *Carrickfergus Advertiser*, 4 October 1912.

14 Letter from Lady Elizabeth Nicholson, quoted in McKinnon, 'Rector's Son', 53.

15 *The Ulster Guardian: Organ of the Liberal Party in Ireland* (Belfast), 5 October 1912 (second leader).

16 *Carrickfergus Advertiser*, 3 October 1913.

17 *Carrickfergus Advertiser*, 29 May 1914.

18 FM, *For Peace with Honour between North and South: An Address to Orangemen … on Sunday, 9th July, 1922* (Carrickfergus: Bell, 1922).

19 Revd George McKay to Very Revd Patrick Convery, published in *Carrickfergus Advertiser*, 10 December 1920 (from *Irish News*).

20 *Belfast News-Letter*, 22 July 1935.

21 FM to LM and Mary, 16 September 1935; LM Papers, Box 7, Bodleian Library (uncatalogued).

22 FM, *Reunion: The Open Door: A Call from Ireland* (Belfast: Mayne, 1929), especially sermon delivered in Trinity College, Dublin, 10 March 1929.

23 Carrickfergus RFC, Minute Book, 13 September 1909; in private hands ((I am grateful to Jane Leonard for alerting me to this fact).

24 *Northern Whig*, 22 February 1936. These rolls of honour, though ascribed to the 36th (Ulster) Division in the Board's statement, were presumably the eight volumes of *Ireland's Memorial Records, 1914–1918* (Dublin, Irish National War Memorial Committee, 1923). For letters to MacNeice from the deans of eleven English cathedrals, in response to his inquiry about precedents (not in file), see FM Papers, Bodleian Library, dep. c. 759.

25 FM to LM, 24 February 1936; LM Papers, Box 7, Bodleian Library (uncatalogued).

26 Francis J. McKenna to FM, 28 October 1935; FM Papers, Bodleian Library, dep. c. 759.

27 Extract from 'Parish Notes' by Canon Marable Williams (incumbent of St Luke's and precentor of Connor), in *Lower Falls Magazine*, December 1935; *Irish News*, 5 December 1935, 6 January 1936.

28 *Belfast News-Letter*, 23 October 1935, echoing his tribute to the living statesman in *Carrickfergus*, 71: 'He had great qualities of head and heart; he had courage, enthusiasm, quickness, eloquence.'

29 *In Memoriam: Last Honours to Ulster's Leader, Lord Carson of Duncairn* (Belfast: Baird, 1935), 5, 24–5, 29; from *Belfast Telegraph*, 26 October 1935; *Belfast News-Letter*, 28 October 1935.

30 Nicholson, 'Trees were Green', 16.

31 Society for Irish Church Missions to the Roman Catholics (ICM), annual MSS Agency Books, 1856–1905; ICM Office, Dublin.

32 *Belfast News-Letter*, 9, 12 February 1935.

33 FM was elected as a Deputy Grand Chaplain for Belfast for the years 1903–9 (except 1905) and as a District Chaplain for Belfast Districts Nos. 6, 10, 3, and 1 for various years (successively as a member of Lodges 410, 631, and 938). See annual officer lists in Grand Orange Lodge of Ireland, *Report of the Half-Yearly Meeting*, and in annual reports of the Belfast County Grand Lodge; Schomberg House, Belfast.

34 *Carrickfergus Advertiser*, 6 August 1909.

35 *Carrickfergus Advertiser*, 21 April 1911; L.O.L. 1537, Minute Books and Roll Books; in private hands.

36 *Carrickfergus Advertiser*, 12 July 1912. Five men were eventually imprisoned following attacks on thirty-three houses, only four of which belonged to Protestants; *Carrickfergus Advertiser*, 27 December 1912.

37 *Carrickfergus Advertiser*, 2 February, 1 March 1912.

38 *Carrickfergus Advertiser*, 15 January 1915.

39 *Carrickfergus Advertiser*, 26 March 1920. Mrs Greer was a leading figure in the Ulster Women's Unionist Council and (by 1927) in the Carrickfergus Women's Loyal Orange Lodge No. 7. She was perhaps the 'Belfast aunt, lately engaged in gun-running', with whom Louis and John Hilton dined in September 1928; see MacNeice, *Strings*, 269.

40 *Belfast News-Letter*, 14 July 1902.

41 *Carrickfergus Advertiser*, 16 July 1920.

42 *Carrickfergus Advertiser*, 16 July 1909.

43 *Belfast News-Letter*, 1 July 1935; Rutherford, 'John Frederick MacNeice', 41–2.

44 Letter from FM, 8 July 1935, in *Belfast News-Letter*, 9 July 1935.

45 *Belfast News-Letter*, 22 July 1935, reprinted in FM, *Our First Loyalty* (Belfast: Mayne, 1937), 61–8. In 1938, however, he watched 'a very large procession', from the front of St Thomas's rectory and then from the junction of the Lisburn and Malone roads, exclaiming 'But what does it all mean, and why are Clergymen in it?' See FM, Diary, 12 July 1938; FM Papers, Bodleian Library, dep. c. 758.

46 Louis MacNeice, 'Northern Ireland and Her People', in Alan Heuser, ed., *Selected Prose of Louis MacNeice* (Oxford: Clarendon Press, 1990), 143–53 (148–9).

47 'The Gardener', in MacNeice, *Collected Poems*, ed. Peter McDonald (London: Faber, 2007), 188–90; MacNeice, *Strings*, 47–8; 'Childhood Memories' (recorded for BBC, Belfast, 2 July 1963), in MacNeice, *Selected Prose*, 267–73 (269). Archie White's mark appears among the Carrickfergus signatures to the Ulster Covenant: PRONI.

48 Consider also LM's jeer that 'the potboy priests and the birds of prey were still the dominant caste' in the Dublin of September 1939; MacNeice, *Strings*, 213.

'WHAT AM I DOING HERE?' TRAVEL AND MACNEICE

1   See Hart Crane, 'Modern Poetry', in *The Complete Poems of Hart Crane* (New York: Liveright Publishing, 1933, 1958), 181–2.

2   *Complete Poems of Hart Crane*, 37, 41.

3   Simon Workman has recently completed an interesting doctoral thesis at Trinity College Dublin in which he explores the aural aspects of MacNeice's poetry as well as his radio drama.

4   See Terence Brown, 'MacNeice's Ireland, MacNeice's Islands', in *Literature and Nationalism*, ed. Vincent Newey and Ann Thompson (Liverpool: Liverpool University Press, 1991) and John Kerrigan, 'Louis MacNeice among the Islands', in Peter Mackay, Edna Longley and Fran Brearton, eds, *Modern Irish and Scottish Poetry* (Cambridge: Cambridge University Press, 2011).

5   Valentine Cunningham, *British Writers of the Thirties* (Oxford: Oxford University Press, 1988), 351.

6   Louis MacNeice, *Out of the Picture* (London: Faber, 1937), 49.

7   His companion was Anthony Blunt: the canto involves irony at the expense of Blunt's Communism, although MacNeice (it seems) never knew of his role as a Soviet agent.

MACNEICE AND THIRTIES (CLASSICAL) PASTORALISM

1   See Valentine Cunningham, *British Writers of the Thirties* (Oxford: Oxford University Press, 1988), 37–40.

2   *Hamlet*, 3.2.113.

3   George Orwell, *Manchester Evening News*, 20 April 1944; *Collected Essays, Journalism and Letters*, III: *As I Please, 1943–1945*, ed. Sonia Orwell and Ian Angus (Harmondsworth: Penguin, 1970), 66–8.

4   *Earth Stopped: or, Mr Marx's Sporting Tour* (London: Collins, 1934), 176.

5   *England Have My Bones* (London: Collins, 1936), 194ff.

6   See Andy Croft, *Comrade Heart: A Life of Randall Swingler* (Manchester and New York: Manchester University Press, 2003).

7   William Empson, *Some Versions of Pastoral* (1935; London: Hogarth Press, 1986), 6.

8   C. Day Lewis, Stanza 5 of 'Dedicatory Stanzas, To Stephen Spender', *The Georgics of Virgil*, trans. C. Day Lewis (London: Jonathan Cape, 1940), 10.

9   'The Elusive Classics', review of R.C. Trevelyan, trans., Virgil, *Eclogues and Georgics*, *New Statesman* (5 May 1945), 293 [the left-wing *New Statesman*, of course], in *Selected Literary Criticism of Louis MacNeice*, ed. Alan Heuser (Oxford: Clarendon Press, 1987), 124–7.

10 Introduction to William Adlington, trans., *The Golden Ass* (London: John Lehmann, 1946); Heuser, ed., *Selected Literary Criticism*, 127–32. John Lehmann was, of course, the leftist garden-loving editor of the famous 1930s *New Writing* collections. His own first volume was *A Garden Revisited*, 1931. Though a product of the Eton classical mill – a contemporary, there, of Orwell's – he read History and Modern Languages at Trinity College, Cambridge. So not one of the leftist clas-

sicists himself, though an aider and abettor of such.

11   MacNeice's just-graduated translation from Merton College, Oxford, to assistant lecturer at Birmingham is lovingly recalled by Dodds, in 'Louis MacNeice at Birmingham', in *Time Was Away: The World of Louis MacNeice,* ed. Terence Brown and Alec Reid (Dublin: Dolmen Press, 1974), 35–8.

12   V.V. Radlov: great Russian expert on the language and *Volksliteratur* of Turkey, Siberia, the Mongols of the eastern steppes.

13   Thomson, *Studies in Ancient Greek Society: The Prehistoric Aegean* (London: Lawrence & Wishart, 1949), 540.

14   In 'The Tower that Once', *Folios of New Writing* 3 (Spring 1941), 37–41: reply to Virginia Woolf, 'The Leaning Tower', *Folios of New Writing* 2 (Autumn 1940), 11–33, in Heuser, ed., *Selected Literary Criticism*, 123.

15   Louis MacNeice, *Out of the Picture* (London: Faber, 1937), 81–2.

16   E.R. Dodds, ed., *Journal and Letters of Stephen MacKenna*, with Memoir (London: Constable, 1936), and, for example, Dodds, trans. and ed., *Select Passages Illustrating Neoplatonism* (London: SPCK/Macmillan, 1923).

17   The poem whose lines gave its containing volume *The Earth Compels* (1938) its title, was originally titled merely 'Song' in *The Listener* (22 January 1937), 151.

18   Robin Skelton, 'Celt as Classicist: The Versecraft of Louis MacNeice', in Reid and Brown, eds, *Time Was Away*, 43–53.

ECLOGUES BETWEEN THE TRUCULENT

1   First published in *Castles on the Air* (Belfast: BBC Northern Ireland, 2007).

MACNEICE'S VEHICLES

1   Richard Aldington, 'The Poet and his Age', *Literary Studies and Reviews* (London: Allen & Unwin, 1924), 215.

2   Elizabeth Bowen, *Pictures and Conversations* (London: Allen Lane, 1975), 42.

3   Ezra Pound, 'Provincialism the Enemy' (1917), *Selected Prose 1901– 1965*, ed. William Cookson (London: Faber, 1973), 169.

4   See John Urry, *Mobilities* (Cambridge: Polity, 2007).

5   Urry, *Mobilities*, 129.

'WHO WOULD BE LOVED BY A GODDESS?' GRAVES, MACNEICE, AND THE LYRIC OF CLASSICAL MYTH

1   Robert Graves, *Collected Writings on Poetry*, ed. Paul O'Prey (Manchester: Carcanet, 1995), 296.

2   See Fran Brearton, 'Beyond Graves: Collaborations with the Dead', in Dunstan Ward, ed., *The Art of Collaboration: Essays on Robert Graves and His Contemporaries* (Palma: University of the Balearic Isles Press, 2008), 215–37.

3   Robert Graves and Alan Hodge, *The Long Weekend: A Social History of Great Britain, 1918–1939* (1940; Harmondsworth: Penguin, 1971), 335.
4   'A Brilliant Puritan', review of Robert Graves, *Collected Poems*, *Listener* 20, 517 (8 December 1938), Supplement, viii.
5   Robert Graves and Laura Riding, *A Survey of Modernist Poetry* (London: Heinemann, 1927), 117.
6   Graves, *Writings on Poetry*, 230, 117–18.
7   Graves, *Writings on Poetry*, 261, 271.
8   Louis MacNeice, undated notes, quoted in Peter McDonald's valuable essay, '"With Eyes Turned Down on the Past": MacNeice's Classicism', in Kathleen Devine and Alan J. Peacock, eds, *Louis MacNeice and His Influence* (Gerrards Cross: Colin Smythe, 1998), 39.
9   Graves, *Writings on Poetry*, 320, 13; Robert Graves, *The Greek Myths*, I (Harmondsworth: Penguin, 1955, 1960), 19.
10   Graves, *Greek Myths*, I, 12.
11   Graves, *Greek Myths*, I, 20.
12   Robert Graves, *Poetic Unreason and Other Studies* (London: Cecil Palmer, 1925), 2.
13   Robert Graves, *The White Goddess: A Historical Grammar of Poetic Myth* (London: Faber, 1961), 486.
14   D.N.G. Carter, *Robert Graves: The Lasting Poetic Achievement* (Houndmills: Macmillan, 1989), 83.
15   Graves, *Greek Myths*, I, 20, 13.
16   John Gould, 'On Making Sense of Greek Religion', in Gould, *Myth, Ritual, Memory and Exchange: Essays in Greek Literature and Culture* (Oxford: Oxford University Press, 2001), 209–11.
17   *Between Moon and Moon: Selected Letters of Robert Graves 1946–1972*, ed. Paul O'Prey (London: Hutchinson, 1984), 104.
18   Robert Graves, *The Anger of Achilles* (London: Cassell, 1960), xxxiii–iv.
19   Graves, *The Anger of Achilles*, xxxii, xxxiv.
20   Graves, *The Anger of Achilles*, xxxiv.
21   Quoted in Miranda Seymour, *Robert Graves* (London: Doubleday, 1995), 308.
22   Graves, *Writings on Poetry*, 3.
23   S.J. Harrison, ed., *Living Classics* (Oxford: Oxford University Press, 2009), 15.

THE PERNING BIRCH: YEATS, FROST, MACNEICE

1   *The Variorum Edition of the Poems of W.B. Yeats*, ed. Peter Allt and Russell K. Alspach (New York: Macmillan, 1957), 441.
2   *Selected Letters of Robert Frost*, ed. Lawrance Thompson (New York: Holt, Rinehart & Winston, 1964; London: Jonathan Cape, 1965), 98.
3   See 'Tendencies in Modern Poetry', *Listener* (27 July 1939), 185–6.
4   W.H. Auden, *The Dyer's Hand and Other Essays* (London: Faber, 1975), 346.

5   *Selected Letters of Robert Frost*, 70.

6   W.B. Yeats, *A Vision* (1937; London: Macmillan, 1962), 268.

7   *Variorum Yeats Poems*, 439.

8   *The Variorum Edition of the Plays of W.B. Yeats*, ed. Russell K. Alspach (London: Macmilllan, 1966), 1084.

9   *Variorum Yeats Poems*, 439.

10 *Variorum Yeats Poems*, 442.

11 *Variorum Yeats Poems*, 442.

12 *Variorum Yeats Poems*, 149.

13 Louis MacNeice, *Astrology* (London: Aldus Books, 1964), 132.

14 Ted Hughes, *Listener* (2 October 1964).

15 'Tendencies in Modern Poetry', 185–6.

16 Auden, *Dyer's Hand*, 348.

17 Auden, *Dyer's Hand*, 346.

'THE LADIES WOULD SAY THAT HE LOOKED LIKE A POET': TOM AND THE SELLING OF LOUIS

1   T.S. Eliot to Willard Thorp. Princeton University Library, Manuscripts Division, Willard Thorp Papers CO 292, Correspondence Box 4, Folder 3 (Thomas Stearns Eliot), 2 March 1939.

2   Ron Schuchard has written with elegance and humour of Eliot's music-hall, vaudeville interests in *Eliot's Dark Angel: Intersections of Life and Art* (Oxford: Oxford University Press, 2001).

3   W.H. Auden, 'Letter to Lord Byron', *The English Auden* (London: Faber, 1977), 195.

4   MacNeice, quoted in T.S. Eliot's obituary, *Newsweek*, Thorp Papers, Box 4, undated [1965].

5   MacNeice to Willard Thorp. Thorp Papers, Correspondence Box 6, Folder 10 (MacN–Martin, Bob), 25 March 1939.

6   *Daily Princetonian*, 14 March 1939.

7   *Daily Princetonian*, 21 March 1939.

8   *Daily Princetonian*, 14 April 1939.

9   *Daily Princetonian*, 14 April 1939.

10 *Daily Princetonian*, 15 April 1939.

11 Eliot to Thorp, Thorp Papers, Correspondence Box 4, Folder 3 (TSE), 9 May 1939.

12 Eliot to Allen Tate, Princeton University Library, Manuscripts Division, Allen Tate Collection 1931–1979 CO648, Correspondence Box 19, Folder 53 (Eliot), 6 May 1927.

13 Eliot to Tate, Tate Papers, Correspondence Box 19, Folder 53 (Eliot), 26 May 1933.

14 MacNeice to Tate, Tate Papers, Correspondence Box 29 (Mackensie–Maynard), 28 October 1952.

15 Caroline Gordon (Tate) to Margaret Thorp, Thorp Papers/Papers of Margaret Thorp, Subseries 2B/Correspondence, Box 22, Folder 19

(Allen and Caroline Tate), undated [1952].

16 MacNeice to Tate, Tate Papers, Box 29 (Mackensie-Maynard), 2 August 1963.

17 Eliot to Tate, Tate Papers, Box 19, Folder 53 (Eliot), 7 March 1956.

18 Valerie Eliot to Tate, Tate Papers, Box 19, Folder 53 (Eliot), 2 February 1963.

19 Eliot in *The Times* (London), Tate Papers, Box 29 (Mackensie-Maynard), undated [1963]; MacNeice clippings.

20 Tate, BBC broadcast typescript, Tate Papers, Box 29 (Mackensie-Maynard), 6 December 1963.

THE LIVES WE LIVE

1 Antonia Fraser, ed., *The Pleasure of Reading* (London: Bloomsbury, 1992), 52.

TURN AND TURN AGAINST: THE CASE OF *AUTUMN JOURNAL*

1 *Edward Thomas: The Annotated Collected Poems*, ed. Edna Longley (Tarset, Northumberland: Bloodaxe, 2008), 123.

2 W.H. Auden, *Collected Poems*, ed. Edward Mendelson (London: Faber, 1976), 257.

3 Les Murray, 'The Future', *Collected Poems* (1991; London: Minerva, 1992), 158.

4 Osip Mandelstam, 'Conversation about Dante', trans. Clarence Brown and Robert Hughes, in *Selected Essays*, trans. Sidney Monas (Austin: University of Texas Press, 1977), 5.

'THE PARROT'S LIE': *AUTUMN SEQUEL* AND THE BBC

1 A. Alvarez, *New Statesman and Nation* (11 December 1954), 794; quoted in Jon Stallworthy, *Louis MacNeice* (London: Faber, 1995), 411.

2 Samuel Hynes, *London Review of Books* 11.5 (2 March 1989), 6–7; Edna Longley, *Louis MacNeice: A Study* (London: Faber, 1988), 114; Peter McDonald, *Louis MacNeice: The Poet in his Contexts* (Oxford: Clarendon Press, 1991), 153.

3 McDonald, *Louis MacNeice*, 148.

4 John Skelton, *The Complete English Poems*, ed. John Scattergood (Harmondsworth: Penguin, 1983), 231.

5 See Chapter 4 of Jane Griffiths, *John Skelton and Poetic Authority: Defining the Liberty to Speak* (Oxford: Oxford University Press, 2006), 79–101.

6 See Ian Gordon, *John Skelton, Poet Laureate* (Melbourne and London: Melbourne University Press, 1943), 158, 161. For examples of Skelton's popularity during the 1930s see W.H. Auden, 'John Skelton', in Katherine Garvin, ed., *The Great Tudors* (London: Ivor Nicholson & Watson, 1935), 55–67; Ralph Vaughan Williams, *Five Tudor Portraits: A Choral Suite in Five Movements Founded on Poems by John Skelton* (London: Oxford University Press, 1935).

7 MacNeice, 'Introduction to Scripts', in Rayner Heppenstall, ed.,

Imaginary Conversations (London: Secker & Warburg, 1948), 17; MacNeice, 'A Plea for Sound', *BBC Quarterly* (Autumn 1953), 131, quoted in Kate Whitehead, *The Third Programme: A Literary History* (Oxford: Clarendon Press, 1989), 71.

8   George Orwell, 'Poetry and the Microphone', in Sonia Orwell and Ian Angus, eds, *Collected Essays, Journalism and Letters of George Orwell*, II (London: Secker & Warburg, 1968), 331, quoted in Whitehead, *Third Programme*, 159.

9   Cecil Day Lewis, 'Broadcasting and Poetry', *BBC Quarterly* (Spring 1950), 3.

10 V.S. Pritchett, 'Broadcasting about Literature', *BBC Quarterly* (Summer 1947), 82; Louis MacNeice, *Christopher Columbus* (London: Faber, 1944), 9.

11 Kathleen Raine, *New Statesman* (14 November 1953), quoted in Robert Hewison, *In Anger: Culture in the Cold War 1945–60* (London: Weidenfeld & Nicholson, 1981), 89.

12 Quoted in Hewison, *In Anger*, 14.

13 Orwell, *Polemic* No. 2 (1946), quoted in Hewison, *In Anger*, 37–8; John Lehmann, *New Soundings*, 1, BBC Third Programme (9 January 1952), quoted in Whitehead, *Third Programme*, 182.

14 See Hewison, *In Anger*, 81–4.

15 In addition to Skelton and Dante, MacNeice was keen that readers should be aware that Spenser's *Faerie Queene* was an underlying model for the poem. See, for example, his letter to T.S. Eliot, 10 March 1954, in Jonathan Allison, ed., *Letters of Louis MacNeice* (London: Faber, 2010), 573. MacNeice had produced a reading of *The Faerie Queene* over twelve programmes on the Third Programme in the autumn of 1952.

16 It was the 'overwhelmingly British contemporary background' of the poem which made MacNeice's American publishers, Knopf, lukewarm about publication. See Allison, ed., *Letters*, 571, n.4.

17 See, for example, the 1954 documentary 'Wakefield Express'. MacNeice also describes Dylan Thomas's *Under Milk Wood* (1954) as a 'pageant', in 'Sometimes the Poet Spoke in Prose', *Selected Literary Criticism of Louis MacNeice*, ed. Alan Heuser (Oxford: Clarendon Press, 1987), 200.

18 Jed Esty, *A Shrinking Island: Modernism and National Culture in England* (Princeton: Princeton University Press, 2003).

19 Barbara Coulton, *Louis MacNeice at the BBC* (London: Faber, 1980), 175, 196.

'BULBOUS TALIESIN': MACNEICE AND DYLAN THOMAS

1   The *New Country* anthology, edited by Michael Roberts, was published in April 1933 and contained work by Christopher Isherwood, Stephen Spender, Cecil Day Lewis, W.H. Auden, and others. The anthology is taken to mark the decisive emergence of the politically Left, social realist style, which was to dominate the work of young English writers during the 1930s. I use the term in this essay as shorthand for the broad social

realist trend of the 1930s; however, it should be noted that while MacNeice had much in common with the core group of Auden, Day Lewis, and Spender, he was not included in *New Country*, and frequently drew attention to the weaknesses of their politically committed writing.

2   Dylan Thomas, *The Collected Letters*, ed. Paul Ferris (London: Dent, 2000), 320.

3   *Dylan Thomas: Early Prose Writings*, ed. Walford Davies (London: Dent, 1971), viii.

4   Thomas's comments were sent to Geoffrey Grigson, editor of *New Verse*, on 7 September 1937. See Stan Smith, '"The little arisen original monster": Dylan Thomas's sour grapes', in John Goodby and Chris Wigginton, eds, *Dylan Thomas: A New Casebook* (London: Palgrave, 2001), 20-21. Also Andrew Lycett, *Dylan Thomas: A New Life* (London: Weidenfeld & Nicolson, 2003), 109.

5   Thomas, *Collected Letters*, 328, 442.

6   Quoted in E.W. Tedlock, ed., *Dylan Thomas: The Legend and the Poet* (London: Heinemann, 1960), 248.

7   See, for a fuller discussion, my 'Dylan Thomas and the Poetry of the 1940s' in Michael O'Neill, ed., *The Cambridge History of English Poetry* (Cambridge: Cambridge University Press, 2010), 858–78.

8   Hugh Kenner, *A Sinking Island: The Modern English Writers* (New York: Knopf, 1988).

9   R. George Thomas, 'Dylan Thomas and Some Early Readers', *Poetry Wales*, Dylan Thomas Special Issue, 9.2 (Autumn 1973), 11–12.

10 The phrase is John L. Sweeney's, who also notes Thomas's influence on MacNeice's 'Prayer before Birth'. See *Dylan Thomas: Selected Writings*, ed. John L. Sweeney (New York: New Directions, 1946), ix–x.

11 See the series of articles '"The Burning Baby" and the Bathwater', by James Keery, published in *PN Review*, between 2003 and 2006.

12 Terence Brown, 'The Irish Dylan Thomas: Versions and Influences', *Irish Studies Review* 17.1 (February 2009).

13 See Gabriel Pearson, 'Gabriel Pearson on Dylan Thomas', *Spectator Review of Books* (20 November 1971), 731.

14 Thomas, *Collected Letters*, 328-9.

15 Stuart Sillars, *British Romantic Art and the Second World War* (New York: St Martin's Press, 1991), 96-7.

16 David Gascoyne, *Selected Poems* (London: Enitharmon, 1994), 82.

17 Cited in Neil Reeve, 'Surrealism, William Sansom and the London Blitz', in *Surrealismo y literatura en Europa*, ed. Angels Santa and Marta Giné (Edicions de la Universitat de Lleida, 2001), 193.

18 Brown, 'The Irish Dylan Thomas', 49.

19 MacNeice's tribute to Aristophanes, introduced as 'an author of infinite fantasy, a lover of slapstick and beauty, a good hater and a hard hitter, a live man, an Enemy of Cant', suggests, as Stallworthy notes, 'an epitaph for himself or ... Thomas.' Jon Stallworthy, *Louis MacNeice* (London: Faber, 1995), 347.

20 Leslie Fiedler, 'The Latest Thomas', *Western Review* (Winter 1947), 105.

21 Thomas, *Collected Letters*, 359. Among the slang items we find some taken from Hollywood film: 'lammed', 'dumb', 'gangster and his moll', for example.

22 Brown, 'The Irish DylanThomas', 47.

23 Andrew Lycett, *Dylan Thomas*, 377.

'HIS INTURNED EYES': MACNEICE IN THE WOODS

1   Peter Porter, Introduction to *The Faber Book of Modern Verse*, ed. Michael Roberts, rev. Peter Porter (London: Faber, 1982); Michael Donaghy, Interview with John Wall, *Verse* 14.1 (1997), repr. in Michael Donaghy, *The Shape of the Dance: Essays, Interviews and Digressions* (London: Picador, 2009).

2   Patrick Kavanagh, *Collected Poems*, ed. Antoinette Quinn (Harmondsworth: Penguin, 2004), 200.

3   John Clare, 'Sighing for Retirement', in *The Later Poems of John Clare*, I (Oxford: Oxford University Press, 1984), 19.

4   For Clare as a reader of Keats (and vice versa), see Jonathan Bate, *John Clare: A Biography* (London: Picador, 2003), 188–9.

5   'The Flood', *John Clare: Poems Selected by Paul Farley* (London: Faber, 2007), 76–7.

6   *The Later Poems of John Clare*, I, 28.

7   Louis Glück, *Meadowlands* (New York: Ecco Press, 1997).

'COMING UP ENGLAND BY A DIFFERENT LINE': LOUIS MACNEICE AND PHILIP LARKIN

1   Barbara Everett, 'Philip Larkin: After Symbolism', in Stephen Regan, ed., *Philip Larkin* (Basingstoke: Macmillan, 1997), 55–70; Edna Longley, 'Poète Maudit Manqué', in George Hartley, ed., *Philip Larkin 1922–1985: A Tribute* (London: Marvell Press, 1988), 213–19.

2   Seamus Heaney, 'The Main of Light', in Regan, ed., *Philip Larkin*, 23–31. Andrew Motion, *Philip Larkin: A Writer's Life* (London: Faber, 1993).

3   Philip Larkin, *Required Writing: Miscellaneous Pieces 1955–1982* (London: Faber, 1983), 30.

4   W.B. Yeats, *The Major Works*, ed. Edward Larrissy (Oxford: Oxford University Press, 2001), 98.

5   Philip Larkin, *Further Requirements: Interviews, Broadcasts, Statements and Book Reviews 1952–85* (London: Faber, 2001), 18.

6   Motion, *Philip Larkin*, 177.

7   *The Norton Shakespeare*, ed. Stephen Greenblatt et al. (New York: Norton, 1997), 1929; *The Collected Poems of A.E. Housman* (London: Jonathan Cape, 1977), 10.

8   Larkin, *Required Writing*, 58.

9   Edna Longley, 'Philip Larkin and Belfast Literary Culture', *The Yellow Nib* 1 (2005), 26; John Goodby, '"The importance of elsewhere", or "No man is an Ireland": Self, Selves and Social Consensus in the Poetry

of Philip Larkin', *Critical Survey* 1.2 (1989), 132.

10   Tom Paulin, 'Into the Heart of Englishness', in Regan, ed., *Philip Larkin*, 161.

11   Longley, 'Philip Larkin and Belfast Literary Culture', 27.

12   Philip Larkin, *Selected Letters of Philip Larkin 1940–85*, ed. Anthony Thwaite (London: Faber, 1992), 161.

13   Motion, *Philip Larkin*, 286.

14   Larkin, *Required Writing*, 140.

15   Larkin, *Further Requirements*, 18.

16   Hugh Underhill, 'Poetry of Departures: Larkin and the Power of Choosing', *Critical Survey* 1.2 (1989), 189–90.

17   Grevel Lindop, '"Being different from yourself": Philip Larkin in the 1970s', in Peter Jones and Michael Schmidt, eds, *British Poetry Since 1970* (Manchester: Carcanet, 1980), 46.

18   Larkin, *Further Requirements*, 18.

19   Liam Harte, 'Living Beyond the Severed Ends: Poetry of Louis MacNeice and Philip Larkin', *Studies* 89.353 (2000), 46.

20   *Edward Thomas: The Annotated Collected Poems*, ed. Edna Longley (Tarset, Northumberland: Bloodaxe, 2008), 105; *The Complete Poetical Works of Thomas Hardy, I*, ed. Samuel Hynes (Oxford: Oxford University Press, 1982), 13.

THE SAME AGAIN? MACNEICE'S REPETITIONS

An earlier, shorter version of this essay appeared in *Cambridge Quarterly* 38.3 (September 2009).

1   Christopher Ricks, *Dylan's Visions of Sin* (London: Viking, 2003), 222.

2   Philip Larkin, *Further Requirements: Interviews, Broadcasts, Statements and Book Reviews 1952–85* (London: Faber, 2001), 18.

3   Louis MacNeice, *The Dark Tower and Other Radio Scripts* (London: Faber, 1947), 15.

4   MacNeice knew Bowen and took over the magnificent Regent's Park house she had lived in when she gave it up. The house, 2 Clarence Terrace, is fictionalised in Bowen's *The Death of the Heart*.

5   An outstanding literary representation of this anxiety is the gondola journey taken by von Aschenbach to the Lido, initially entirely against his will, at the beginning of Thomas Mann's *Death in Venice*. The gondolier's palpable malevolence there finds a near-equivalent in both Bowen and MacNeice, who would almost certainly, of course, have known the story.

6   MacNeice himself ought to have used the word 'psittacism' in an undergraduate paper of his which he quotes, a little self-approvingly perhaps, in his book *Modern Poetry*, where he says that 'we must know how to be *new*, as contrasted with repetition – psittacosis – on the one hand and with escape from tradition – aphasia – on the other'. Psittacosis is actually a contagious disease of birds transmissible, especially from parrots, to human beings as a form of pneumonia. Desirable as it is to avoid it,

it cannot therefore be what the young, forgivably peacocking MacNeice actually meant. He meant 'psittacism'; and he gets it right when he repeats the statement, more or less, in the essay 'Poetry Today', of 1935. See Alan Heuser, ed., *Selected Literary Criticism of Louis MacNeice* (Oxford: Clarendon Press, 1987), 13.

7   Quoted in Peter McDonald, *Serious Poetry: Form and Authority from Yeats to Hill* (Oxford: Clarendon Press, 2002), 179.

8   Tom Paulin, 'The Man from No Part: Louis MacNeice', *Ireland and the English Crisis* (Newcastle upon Tyne: Bloodaxe, 1984), 76.

9   W.H. Auden, *Collected Poems*, ed. Edward Mendelson (London: Faber, 1976), 116.

10   See 'Tendencies in Modern Poetry', *Listener* (27 July 1939), 185–6.

GUIDE TO FURTHER READING

Richard Danson Brown, *Louis MacNeice and the Poetry of the 1930s* (Tavistock: Northcote/British Council, 2009).

Terence Brown, *Louis MacNeice: Sceptical Vision* (Dublin: Gill & Macmillan, 1975).

Terence Brown and Alec Reid, eds, *Time Was Away: The World of Louis MacNeice* (Dublin: Dolmen Press, 1974).

Castles on the Air: The Life and Work of Poet and Broadcaster Louis MacNeice (Belfast: BBC Northern Ireland, 2007).

Barbara Coulton, *Louis MacNeice in the BBC* (London: Faber, 1980).

Valentine Cunningham, *British Writers of the Thirties* (Oxford: Oxford University Press, 1988).

Kathleen Devine and Alan J. Peacock, eds, *Louis MacNeice and His Influence* (Gerrards Cross: Colin Smythe, 1998).

Alan Gillis, *Irish Poetry of the 1930s* (Oxford: Oxford University Press, 2005).

Samuel Hynes, *The Auden Generation: Literature and Politics in England in the 1930s* (London: Faber, 1976).

Edna Longley, *Louis MacNeice: A Critical Study* (London: Faber, 1988); *Poetry and Posterity* (Tarset, Northumberland: Bloodaxe, 2000).

Peter McDonald, *Louis MacNeice: The Poet in His Contexts* (Oxford: Clarendon Press, 1991); *Serious Poetry: Form and Authority from Yeats to Hill* (Oxford: Oxford University Press, 2002).

William T. McKinnon, *Apollo's Blended Dream: A Study of the Poetry of Louis MacNeice* (Oxford: Oxford University Press, 1971).

Robyn Marsack, *The Cave of Making: The Poetry of Louis MacNeice* (Oxford: Oxford University Press, 1982).

D.B. Moore, *The Poetry of Louis MacNeice* (Leicester: Leicester University Press, 1972).

Clair Wills, *That Neutral Island: A Cultural History of Ireland during the Second World War* (London: Faber, 2007).

NOTES ON CONTRIBUTORS

JONATHAN ALLISON is Associate Professor of English at the University of Kentucky and was formerly Director of the Yeats Summer School, Sligo. He is the editor of *Letters of Louis MacNeice* (Faber, 2010).

TERENCE BROWN is Fellow Emeritus at Trinity College, Dublin, where he formerly held a personal chair in Anglo-Irish literature. He is a member of the Royal Irish Academy and of Academia Europaea. He has lectured on Irish literature and culture in many parts of the world. Among his publications are (with Alec Reid) *Time Was Away: The World of Louis MacNeice* (Dolmen, 1974) and *Louis MacNeice: Sceptical Vision* (Gill & Macmillan, 1975).

NEIL CORCORAN has taught at the universities of Sheffield, Swansea, St Andrews and Liverpool, where he was King Alfred Professor of English Literature until 2010 and is now Emeritus Professor. His most recent book is *Shakespeare and the Modern Poet* (Cambridge University Press, 2010).

VALENTINE CUNNINGHAM is Professor of English and Fellow of Corpus Christi College, Oxford. His books include *British Writers of the Thirties* (Oxford University Press, 1988), *The Victorians: An Anthology of Poetry and Poetics* (Wiley-Blackwell, 2000) and *Reading after Theory* (Wiley-Blackwell, 2002).

ANNE MARGARET DANIEL is the author of many critical essays on writers from Oscar Wilde to Bob Dylan, and she is finishing a book about cultural and literary representations of redheads. She teaches Irish studies and literature at the New School University in New York City, and is currently the Associate Director of the Yeats International Summer School in Sligo, Ireland. Contact her online at www.annemargaretdaniel.com.

GERALD DAWE's poetry collections include *The Morning Train* (Gallery Press, 1999), *Lake Geneva* (Gallery Press, 2003) and *Points West* (Gallery Press, 2008). Other publications include *My Mother-City* (Lagan Press, 2008) and *The Proper Word: Collected Criticism* (Creighton University Press, 2007). *Conversations: Poets and Poetry* is forthcoming. A Fellow of Trinity College

Dublin, he is Director of the Oscar Wilde Centre and Senior Lecturer in English at Trinity.

PAUL FARLEY is a poet and broadcaster. He has received many awards for his writing, including the 2009 E.M. Forster Award from the American Academy of Arts and Letters. His most recent book (with Michael Symmons Roberts) is *Edgelands* (Jonathan Cape, 2011).

DAVID FITZPATRICK is Professor of Modern History at Trinity College, Dublin. His most recent book, *'Solitary and Wild': Frederick MacNeice and the Salvation of Ireland*, was published in 2011 by the Lilliput Press.

LEONTIA FLYNN's first book *These Days* (Jonathan Cape, 2004) won the Forward Prize for best first collection. Her second, *Drives* (Jonathan Cape, 2008) won the Rooney Prize for Irish Literature, and a major individual artist award from the Northern Irish Arts Council. Her third collection, *Profit and Loss* was published by Cape in 2011.

JOHN GOODBY is the author of *Irish Poetry since 1950* (Manchester University Press, 2000) and *Work of Words: Re-reading Dylan Thomas* (Liverpool University Press, forthcoming 2012). His latest poetry collection is *Illennium* (Shearsman, 2010). He is currently preparing the official centenary edition of the collected poems of Dylan Thomas.

HUGH HAUGHTON was born in Cork and is Professor in the Department of English at the University of York. His books include *The Poetry of Derek Mahon* (Oxford University Press, 2007), and as editor, Sigmund Freud, *The Uncanny* (Penguin, 2003), *Second World War Poems* (Faber, 2004), and (with Valerie Eliot) *The Letters of T.S. Eliot,* 1: *1898–1922* and *The Letters of T.S. Eliot,* 2: *1923–25* (Faber, 2009).

NICK LAIRD is a poet and novelist from County Tyrone. He is finishing a third collection of poetry, *Go Giants*.

THOMAS MCCARTHY was born in Cappoquin, Co.Waterford, in 1954 and educated at University College Cork. *First Convention* was published by Dolmen Press in 1978, followed by seven further collections, including *Merchant Prince* (2005) and *The Last Geraldine Officer* (2009). He attended the Iowa International Writing Programme in 1978–79 and taught at Macalester College, Minnesota. He lives in Cork.

PETER MCDONALD is a poet and critic. He edited Louis MacNeice's *Collected Poems* (Faber, 2007) and co-edited his *Selected Plays* (Oxford

University Press, 1993). He is Christopher Tower Student and Tutor in Poetry in the English Language at Christ Church, Oxford.

DEREK MAHON was born in Belfast in 1941, and educated at Trinity College Dublin and the Sorbonne. His *New Collected Poems* was published in 2011, and his most recent collection is *An Autumn Wind* (Gallery Press, 2010).

GLYN MAXWELL's *One Thousand Nights and Counting: Selected Poems* was published by Picador in February 2011. His last collection, *Hide Now* (Picador; Houghton–Mifflin, 2008) was shortlisted for both the Forward and T.S. Eliot Prizes. His most recent play *After Troy* premiered in March 2011.

PAUL MULDOON is Howard G.B. Clark 21 Professor in the Humanities at Princeton University. His books of criticism are *To Ireland, I* (Clarendon Press, 2000) and *The End of the Poem* (Faber, 2006). He is scheduled to give the Clark Lectures at Cambridge in 2013.

STEPHEN REGAN is Professor of English at the University of Durham. His publications include *Irish Writing 1789–1939: An Anthology of Irish Literature in English* (Oxford University Press, 2004), *The Nineteenth-Century Novel: A Critical Reader* (Routledge, 2001), *Philip Larkin: The New Casebook* (Macmillan, 1997), and *The Politics of Pleasure: Aesthetics and Cultural Theory* (Open University Press, 1992). His most recent book (co-edited with Richard Allen) is *Irelands of the Mind: Memory and Identity in Modern Irish Culture* (Cambridge Scholars, 2008).

CLAIR WILLS is Professor of Irish Literature at Queen Mary University of London. Her books include *Reading Paul Muldoon* (Bloodaxe, 1993), *That Neutral Island: A History of Ireland during the Second World War* (Faber, 2007), and *Dublin 1916: The Siege of the GPO* (Profile, 2009).

INDEX